"A terrific story of how one brave and adv
upside down for God. Firestone teaches us, through the joys and sorrows of
her life, how our ancient traditions are calling out to us for renewal, and how,
through faith, honesty, and struggle, we are learning to respond." —RODGER
KAMENETZ, AUTHOR OF *Stalking Elijah* AND *The Jew in the Lotus*

"Rabbi Tirzah Firestone has a compelling story, a singular voice, and an
unusually fertile mind. Her spiritual journey is riveting." —RABBI JOSEPH
TELUSHKIN, AUTHOR OF *Jewish Literacy*, *Jewish Wisdom*, AND *Biblical Literacy*

"Candid, intense, and compulsively readable, this is spiritual biography at its
very best." —LETTY COTTIN POGREBIN

"Rich and inspiring...a page-turner. A daring exploration of different spiritual
paths...filled with joy, story, community, and a celebration of ancient wisdom.
I absolutely loved this book." — JOAN BORYSENKO, PhD, AUTHOR OF *Minding
the Body, Mending the Mind* AND *A Woman's Book of Life*

"Firestone's autobiography has all the suspense and excitement of a good
novel as it details her complex journey from a meticulously observant
Orthodox Jewish background to her current faith. She takes readers from
the static faith she experienced growing up through the geography of her
spiritual search in many religious traditions to her marriage to a Christian
minister and rejection of her birth family (with whom she later recon-
ciled) and then to her rediscovery of her Jewish roots in a renewed form.
Her story is a wonderful example of the transformation of what was, to the
author, almost a dead faith into one that is vital and transformational yet
accepting of Jews who define their faith more narrowly. Recommended
reading for spiritual seekers and feminists in various religious traditions."
—LIBRARY JOURNAL

"Rabbi Tirzah Firestone's epic pilgrimage invites the reader into the arena of
her God-wrestling. As we accompany her in her openhearted urgency, we
meet our own soul. She emerges transformed, triumphant, and heroic as a
rabbi with a great contribution yet to make." —RABBI ZALMAN SCHACHTER-
SHALOMI, JEWISH RENEWAL ELDER

"Filled with profound teachings from spiritual leaders, advice on intermarriage issues, and other practical nuggets of learning, *With Roots in Heaven* is a work as important as it is controversial, providing courageous insight into the core of religious belief systems." —INGRAM

WITH
ROOTS
—— IN ——
HEAVEN

ONE WOMAN'S PASSIONATE JOURNEY
INTO THE HEART OF HER FAITH

RABBI TIRZAH FIRESTONE, PhD

Monkfish Book Publishing Company
Rhinebeck, New York

Paperback ISBN 978-1-958972-21-2
eBook ISBN 978-1-958972-22-9

Library of Congress Cataloging-in-Publication Data

Names: Firestone, Tirzah, author.
Title: With roots in heaven : one woman's passionate journey into the heart
  of her faith / Rabbi Tirzah Firestone, PhD.
Description: Rhinebeck, New York : Monkfish Book Publishing Company, [2024]
Identifiers: LCCN 2023024635 (print) | LCCN 2023024636 (ebook) | ISBN
  9781958972212 (paperback) | ISBN 9781958972229 (ebook)
Subjects: LCSH: Firestone, Tirzah. | Women rabbis--United
  States--Biography. | Jewish renewal--United States.
Classification: LCC BM755.F489 A3 2024 (print) | LCC BM755.F489 (ebook) |
  DDC 296.092 [B]--dc23/eng/20230807
LC record available at https://lccn.loc.gov/2023024635
LC ebook record available at https://lccn.loc.gov/2023024636

Tree of Life illustration by Mila Perry
Cover and book design by Colin Rolfe

Monkfish Book Publishing Company
22 East Market Street, Suite 304
Rhinebeck, New York 12572
(845) 876-4861
monkfishpublishing.com

For my daughter,
Emily Sophia,
guardian of a precious legacy

CONTENTS

ACKNOWLEDGMENTS

I FEEL DEEP GRATITUDE FOR THE MAGNANIMOUS HELP OF FRIENDS AND COLLEAGUES, colleagues that enabled me to transform *With Roots in Heaven* from a passionate dream into the living offering that it has become. May all these gardeners who nurtured and blessed my project along the way be blessed in turn to see *With Roots in Heaven* bear healing fruit in the world!

Specifically, I wish to thank Donna Zerner, my brilliant Boulder editor and dear friend, who has shared my vision and painstakingly stewarded the manuscript from its very inception, often at great personal expense. Donna's deep wisdom and unflagging sense of humor continuously called me back to my purpose. Arielle Eckstut at James Levine Communications has been far more than an agent, believing in and nurturing this book with loving and expert guidance throughout. I have also been extremely fortunate to work with Deb Brody, senior editor at Dutton, who skillfully directed and pruned my work and made me laugh at the most dismal of moments.

Many dear friends helped me to bring *With Roots in Heaven* to life, providing both encouragement and advice at all hours of the day and night: Rabbi Joseph and Devorah Telushkin, Evan Hodkins, Rabbi Zalman Schachter-Shalomi, Eve Ilsen, Father John Dally, whose ordination poem I have excerpted in chapter 13. Thanks also to Charles Steinberg, Jeffry Raff, Laya and Tom Seghi, Robert Gass, Rodger Kamenetz, Priya Huffman, Rabbi David Cooper, Dena Gitterman, Annemarie Doherty, Jan Scarbrough, Kate Scott, Sat Tara Singh, Kent Meagre for all kinds of help, and little Fozzey, who kept me company on many a lonely night at the computer.

I am deeply grateful to my very exceptional congregation, the Jewish Renewal Community of Boulder, a loving and deeply spirited community who have always urged me to speak my truth, to grow beyond myself and to engage with them in the process of living Torah. My thanks to Rabbi Shefa Gold for graciously leading the congregation during my writing sabbatical.

Finally, and perhaps most important, I wish to thank my beloved partner David Friedman, who has faithfully stood by my side, keeping my other set of roots planted on earth with all manner of nourishment and good humor. It was by means of David's loving encouragement that I was able to venture forth to that auspicious wedding in Miami in 1997, and onward toward the healing and re-visioning of family in my life.

—B'EZRAT HASHEM
FEBRUARY 5, 1998
9 SHEVAT 5758

A FULL QUARTER OF A CENTURY HAS PASSED SINCE THE ADVENT OF THIS BOOK. I write these words in a startlingly new era in which the world and my own lens on life have changed radically.

The impetus to write *With Roots in Heaven* was a call to find meaning in the odyssey I had taken in search of myself. It was a chronicle of the wisdom, truths, and people that had brought me into harmony with my deep inner knowing. It soon became a clarion call to others to take their own journey.

The response to *With Roots in Heaven* both surprised and gratified me. I received letters (in those days, actual paper missives) from people all over the world. Readers told me their own stories of shedding old belief systems, leaving unhealthy relationships, and breaking away from too-tight religious constraints. I heard from many Jews hungering for God, and new ways of living into their Jewish heritage. I also heard from a good number of Christians and Muslims, who told me their tales of finding autonomy. The book had given all of them strength to find their own path in life.

Alas, my passionate return to self and a meaningful spiritual life was not as well received by my own family. Nor was becoming a female rabbi interested in interfaith dialogue, or being a Jewish leader who was prominently reclaiming the meditative, mystical, and ecstatic sides of the Jewish tradition. But my own interfaith marriage had forever changed me. It had helped me return to my birth religion in a radical manner, and had opened me to an ever-shifting hybrid world in which cultures were blending and morphing, and people were shedding religious norms in favor of creating their own traditions.

Life has many cycles. If we are lucky, we live many lives within this one. Forever a rabbi, I no longer serve at the helm of a congregation. I went back to school to earn my doctorate in Jungian and trauma psychology. In the process, my view widened to encompass the intergenerational influences that have impacted me, and those that affect us all as individuals and members of ethnicities. I am grateful that my research on intergenerational trauma has ignited a larger conversation in the Jewish world. My work, published in 2019 as *Wounds into Wisdom*, became part of a global movement that aims to reclaim much needed ancestral wisdom and heal painful trauma legacies that have been transmitted epigenetically.

When I wrote *With Roots in Heaven*, I was not yet cognizant of the trauma residues inherent in my own family. I had not considered that my mother had been a refugee who narrowly escaped Germany in 1939, or that my father had been a US soldier present at the liberation of Bergen-Belsen in 1945. But their histories had everything to do with how my siblings and I were raised.

The unspeakable Holocaust traumas that my parents, Hebrew school teachers, and Jewish leaders carried into the post-war era played heavily upon those who came next. Their still unprocessed shock and grief impacted us with a worldview that was often more guilt-inducing than joyous, rigid than loving, and mis-attuned to a new generation. My brother Danny's escape into Zen Buddhism, my sister Shulamith's rabid feminism, as well as my own flight from the tradition and intermarriage to a Christian must all be seen in this context. So must our parents' unfortunate reactions to us. In the years since writing *With Roots in Heaven* I began to see more clearly, and my heart has broken open with new understanding and compassion.

My beloved Rebbe, Rabbi Zalman Schachter-Shalomi died in 2016. My mother passed in that same year. I am a grandmother now. People sometimes refer to me as an elder. My community, work, and focus now extend all over the world. But it all started here, in the book you are holding. I pray that *With Roots in Heaven* inspires you to become more of who you already are.

—RABBI DR. TIRZAH FIRESTONE

MAY 2023

Every journey has a secret destination
of which the traveller is unaware.
—MARTIN BUBER

A FEW YEARS AGO, I was asked to speak at a conference on the relationship between mothers and daughters in the light of the Judaic tradition. What
seemed on the surface to be a reasonable request caused me great anxiety.
What could I possibly say about the topic? My relationship with my own
mother had been severed over a decade earlier and was for me a source of what
seemed to be un-resolvable woe. I demurred, but the conference director was
not easily swayed.

"Excuse me for being so persistent, Rabbi Firestone," she said after several
rounds of being put off, "but I feel certain that it is you we want to speak to us
on this subject. Please reconsider."

Finally I surrendered. I reflected that even if one or two people in the audience received something of value from hearing how the ruination of my family
life had spurred me on to discover my work in the world, then coming out with
my story would be worth my vulnerability.

On the evening of the lecture I did not hold back. I shared my story
frankly, describing the total alienation from my mother caused by my interfaith marriage and the grievous effects that alienation had wrought on my
life. The response from the audience was overwhelming. Dozens of people
approached me after the lecture with tears of gratitude and relief on their faces.
Their outpouring of personal stories made it clear that I was not alone in the
pain and shame I had suffered at being an outcast, nor in the deep yearning for
connection that had ultimately moved me to repair my brokenness.

That night was a turning point. Telling the truth became an imperative for
me, not only for its personal curative effects but also for the healing it produced
in those who heard it. More distinctly than ever before, I heard a compelling
inner call, prodding me to tell my story and, further, to speak about related
issues that too often have been obscured from the public eye: the poverty of

spirit that occurs when our religions become rigid or empty; the dangers that arise from a too-desperate longing for transcendence; the trials and anguish of intermarriage; the fear that comes with speaking out as a woman leader in a traditionally male leadership role. This book is the product of my inner directive to tell the truth about all of these things, however painful they may be.

I begin my story in 1974 when, at the age of twenty, I was a thoughtful yet wild young woman, running hard from all forms of authority. Like so many others in my generation, I had become disenchanted with the conventional models for life that I inherited, which in my case were the middle-class values of an Orthodox Jewish family in St. Louis, Missouri.

There were six children in my family and our parents raised us with an iron hand, rigid not only in religious doctrine but in methodology. This meant that, quite aside from living ritually observant lives, any personal choices outside of my parents' prescribed menu were minimal. My siblings and I grew up with an ever-present tension, an almost fanatical injunction to live "correctly" as dictated by our parents and their dogmatic religious approach. In the end, the Jewish heritage we received was, sadly, not enriched by the intensity with which it was transmitted, but rather drained of its intrinsic joy and goodness.

I took flight from everything I knew in an effort to find spiritual nourishment. In the drama that ensued, I traveled as far away from Judaism and anything representing my parents' values as possible. In the process, both my physical life and my soul's very balance were severely threatened. But, as the philosopher Martin Buber says, all journeys have a secret destination, and the destination that awaited me required every step I took along the way, however mad or dangerous.

Fortunately, I acquired some tools on my journey, the most valuable of which was the understanding of the psyche as put forth by Dr. Carl Jung, the noted Swiss psychiatrist. Jung's principles, as well as the powerful influences of my non-Jewish husband, Evan, and my teacher, Rabbi Zalman Schachter-Shalomi, allowed me to reexamine Judaism in a fresh way.

Ultimately, I discovered that Judaism intrinsically supports the unfolding of one's unique self. The same God who inspired the Jewish prophets and sages throughout the centuries was no different, I realized, than the guiding power of the Self about which Jung taught. This divine force beckons each one of us throughout our life to discover the fullness of our being, to arrive at our own secret destiny.

I never suspected that my journey would one day bring me full circle, back to the heritage of my birth. I had no inkling that all of the disparate teachings I sought out along my journey were, in fact, preparation for this return. Each one in turn deepened me so that I could receive what I had not been able to receive, shattered me so that I could finally love what I had not been able to love. Perhaps the internal voice that guided me back to Judaism is the same voice that is guiding so many of us nowadays to excavate and bring to life the ancient spirit of our traditions, too long buried. When I came back, I was not alone.

God speaks to us in many voices. One of these voices comes in the form of dreams. Ever since I was a young girl, I have felt the power of my dreams and scribbled them into my journals when I woke up each morning. Over the years of my life, these dreams have proved to be like so many clues sprinkled on my life's trail, correcting and directing my journey. The Talmud, too, concurs with Jung when it tells us that dreams are like letters from God, which require opening. Because these messages served to lead me further and further in the unlikely direction of my work as a rabbi, and toward my own transformation, I have included several of them in the book. I hope you will feel welcome to use these dreams, as well as the psychological and spiritual teachings I have woven through the book, as a springboard to contemplate your own spiritual journey.

For although it is distinctive, my story is not mine alone. In it are the elements, symbols, and longings not of one individual but of an entire generation. Though my personal story is peculiar in some of its specifics (for example, many of us grew up Jewish and married Christians, but not many of us turned out to be rabbis married to ministers!), I believe it also exemplifies an approach utilized by more and more people in our time: living life by following one's inner calling.

But simply following what feels right is not enough. Like many of us who have made it their practice to follow the inner voice, I eventually felt the need for something more, to inform my inner wisdom with what was ancient and would link me to my ancestors. Yet as I hungrily sought out the rituals and prescriptive wisdom of my religious heritage, I was also wary of those voices in the tradition that would negate my inner sensibilities. *With Roots in Heaven* is about the dialogue between one's inner guidance and the outer tradition, between the powerful wisdom gleaned from our life experience and the venerable wisdom of an ancient religion. This dialogue is going on for many people nowadays, and it is as crucial to us as individuals as it is to the evolution of our religions.

Religions were created to serve the evolving human spirit, not the other way around. But many of us have forgotten this, falling into the mistaken thinking that our religions are immutable and must be served at the cost of our souls. Those who are returning to their religions to nourish themselves, as I did, must remember that our religions are also in need of nourishment. They need to be replenished with our joy, vigor, and the broad vision we have gained from our own spiritual journeys. The Jewish Renewal movement is fulfilling this task for many Jews, as you will discover in this book, just as other religions are also being rejuvenated. I firmly believe that as we replenish our religions, so will we as a society be replenished.

Certain names and details in this book have been omitted or changed to protect individuals. But insomuch as the experiences I have recounted in *With Roots in Heaven* are true, I am quite aware that they may bring pain to some people. I truly regret this. I did not write my story bearing malice toward any person or act, nor is it my intention to bring anyone harm by means of this book. My writing was inspired (as was my becoming a rabbi) by a deep inner calling, which, I trust, comes from a source beyond me. In both cases, my intention is to help mend what has been broken in myself and others by bearing compassionate witness to the truth.

The Jewish tradition has a saying: *Words that come from the heart will return to the heart*. If my story touches your heart, if it reinspires your dedication to your own life's calling, helps you build a mental bridge or reach out your hand to another human being, then its purpose has been fulfilled.

CHAPTER ONE

THE LONG ROAD TO FREEDOM

IT WAS THE WINTER OF 1997. A full thirty-five years had passed since my brothers and sisters and I had all been together in the same room, when we celebrated the bar mitzvah of my brother Ezra. Through the revolving glass door of the ornate Miami hotel, I could see the finely coiffed and clad guests file up the escalator to the wedding hall. My heart began to race. I had fantasized about this day for years. Now it was here.

I rode up the escalator, keeping a watchful eye out for my brothers and sisters. We had each been asked to come an hour before the wedding so that family photographs could be taken. I marveled at the idea that the five of us would stand together for a picture, posing as one family. But I was here to honor the request, and to see what would come of it.

From the corner of the hall I spotted my sister Laya, the mother of Elianna, the bride, in a white linen suit, bustling about gaily. Laya was seven years my senior, and her hair had turned from brown to gray in the seven years since I had seen her. She looked happy enough, greeting her guests warmly and directing them toward a hallway where the photographer had begun his work. It took me a moment to realize that the figure in black moving slowly behind her was our eldest sister, Shulamith. I paused to study her. Shulamith's eyes had narrowed these past years, and her long thick hair was now shot through with white, but she had the same wise and sardonic expression that I remembered, only it was now a bit wearier. At the other end of the room stood my brother Ezra in a black suit and hat, speaking with other men in similar garb. I could see him spot me and turn away quickly. An age-old ache rippled through my chest. Ezra was five years my senior, a rabbi who lived in Brooklyn's Borough Park. I had not seen him since his marriage over twenty years earlier. But I sensed that even tonight, after so much time had passed, he still would not deign to speak to me.

The room was now filling with people and growing noisy. As I gave the bartender my order, I spotted my youngest brother gesturing to me with a cock of his head to join him. I had not seen Isaiah for fourteen years, since my marriage to a non-Jew. His choice to sever our relationship had been a particularly painful one for me. Isaiah and I had once been allies, having been the last ones to grow up together in our parents' home after our older siblings had already left. It was a home that looked typically suburban from the outside but that was more like a middle-class Jewish ghetto, rigidly insulated from the midwestern Middle American culture surrounding it.

Like our four elder siblings, Isaiah and I had been sent to Jewish day schools and had been trained in the strict ritual observance of our parents' home: not a spoon was allowed out of its place, nor an opinion. Our parents brought nothing into their home—food, idea, nor person—that they did not deem to be perfectly kosher.

My brother and I had found release in satire, impersonating the rabbis who stalked the halls of our school, laughing at our parents' judgments and deadly stares. Our comedy had sustained us, as had the contraband we had smuggled in from the outside world: rock music, nonobservant friends, even recreational drugs.

Life was still funny, full of incongruities and irony. But who was laughing now? I was a rabbi, and my little brother was a balding, middle-aged man, a settler on Israel's West Bank and an Orthodox court official. As I made my way toward him that evening, I wondered whether my face revealed my shock at the changes I beheld. We smiled at each other, sad smiles. It was clear by looking at each other just how much time had passed. I too had started to sprout the wiry white hairs of middle age, and the skin around my eyes had begun to wear the lines of my own long journey.

My brother and I sat down together on an overstuffed loveseat, our icy soft drinks in hand. I felt myself perspiring into my silk blouse. I decided not to hold myself back, come what may.

Isaiah proceeded to chat easily about his life. He had lived in Israel for over twenty years and his tongue had turned thick with his Israeli accent. I listened to him responsively, asking him questions about his work, his family, chuckling over stories about his five children. For a time we were safe. Then there was an uncomfortable pause.

"So what about you?" he asked. It was the only thing left to be said.

"Do you really want to know?" I answered.

"I guess so," Isaiah answered weakly, with a shrug.

I began to tell him about my life: what it was like to be a rabbi of a thriving congregation in the Rocky Mountains, how my work as a psychotherapist naturally dovetailed with being a rabbi, the unusual position I found myself in to reach hundreds of people in need of spiritual guidance. He had known I was a rabbi, he mumbled. Our sister had sent him newspaper clippings about me. As I continued talking, I noticed my brother shaking his head and laughing quietly to himself. At last I stopped speaking.

"Isaiah, are you aware that you're laughing?" His eyes turned back to me.

"Was I? Well, maybe just smirking" came his jocular reply.

"What exactly is funny?" I persisted, not playing into his lightheartedness.

"Look," he replied defensively, "you don't expect me to take all this seriously, do you? I mean, this brand of Judaism of yours... what do you call it, Jewish Renewal? It's ridiculous. There's only one Judaism, you know that; the real Judaism, the one we were raised with."

I began to cough up my ginger ale and quickly brought my cocktail napkin to my mouth. It was not my brother's lack of endorsement of my work as a rabbi that caught me off guard. I had expected that. It was that he had so guilelessly put into words the belief that I had struggled with for years: *There's only one real Judaism*. Rabbinic Orthodoxy is what he meant, an exclusive Judaism that I too had been trained to believe was the only authentic tradition. It was this very belief that had sent me fleeing from Judaism altogether.

I collected myself and looked into my brother's eyes. I could honestly say that I no longer shared his beliefs, not for an instant. I had once, which perhaps explains why I had to run so far away. But after years of searching and studying, I had come to see firsthand how vast and compassionate our religion truly was.

This was its paradoxical nature, after all: Judaism had never been monolithic. Throughout history it had changed, by necessity adapting itself to every climate and culture it passed through. And yet, the very soul of Judaism was beyond change. I had reengaged this soul after all these years—fiery and inconsumable, a soul that remained utterly untouched by time or the human dimension.

I had come to the conclusion that Judaism's very essence—as proclaimed in its central prayer, the Shema Yisrael—was rooted in a unifying source that seemed to beg for divergent interpretations and approaches: "Shema Yisrael! Adonai Eloheynu, Adonai Echad!" There was a dynamic balance between Judaism's adaptability and its constancy, I realized, that had allowed for its survival throughout the ages. I was certain that at this critical stage of our history, getting entrenched in absolutist models not only was antithetical to our Jewish spirit but was a threat to our very future.

"Isaiah," I said in a gentle voice, "you are living in a tiny corner of the world, thinking that you have the only truth. But there are many ways of finding God, and hundreds of thousands of people—deep, intelligent souls—who are searching for meaning in their lives, starving to connect with their spiritual roots." I paused to check the rising tide of my emotion. "What you have to offer will never reach these people. It's food that will never nourish."

For a second our eyes locked on each other. I thought I saw his eyes flicker with acknowledgment. Then our sister's voice from across the room announced that the photographer was ready for us. Isaiah looked up as if to heaven, in a mock gesture of prayer. "How did this crazy, renegade sister of mine ever turn out to be a rabbi?" Laughing, we both rose from our chairs.

IT ALL BEGAN with a journey, and the journey began with running away. I had dropped out of college in 1973, in my sophomore year at Stony Brook in New York, where I had been studying eastern philosophy. I had hitchhiked through Europe for nearly a year, harvesting grapes, tending children, scouting out holy sites, entertaining friends and lovers. I was hell-bent for freedom, but even at twenty, I knew something was wrong with my plan. Having distanced myself from everything familiar, I ached with loneliness. Yet I never stayed long enough in any one place to allow myself really to be known.

Summer was approaching and I was staying with a group of friends in Alicante, in northern Spain. One particular morning was a turning point.

I was standing at a phone booth on the esplanade, my hair blowing in the breeze, calling my mother in the United States. This was something I did rarely and only on a whim. From the other end of the long-distance line, there was a noisy fumbling and then a very faint hello, my mother's voice. Something was wrong but I could not grasp what.

"Hello?" she repeated dryly. Suddenly I was planted at the foot of my mother's bed, hearing her clucking sigh, the bedsprings' groan.

"Hi, Mom, it's me, Miriam Tirzah. Is everything all right? I thought I'd catch you before the holiday. Isn't Shevuos soon?"

"Yes, I think so," her voice droned slowly. "Where are you, Tirzahla?"

"I'm standing outside on the plaza of this beautiful little city called Alicante. How are you, Mom? Are you having company for the holiday?"

"Laya and Ezra are both home. Shuley was here and left again. Tell me, are you still in France?"

This was strange. It was a rare event when any of my older siblings showed up at my parents' home. The eldest, Danny, had cut himself off years earlier, and the others kept in only marginal contact. Only Isaiah, who was fifteen years old, lived with Mom and Dad at this point. I began to feel alarmed. There was a deadness in my mother's voice; she almost sounded drugged. And I had told her I had left France over a month earlier.

"I'm in Spain, Mom. I told you that. I'm staying with friends. Hey, is everything okay?"

"I'm in bed. I have an awful headache. Have a *gut Yom Tov*. Call again."

With that, she hung up. I grabbed the rest of my nut-milk li-quado and went to sit on a bench overlooking the ocean. Why on earth were the other kids visiting home now? Was there something I did not know? And my mother's behavior was so strange; could she be ill? Even so, to be in bed before a holiday—unthinkable! After all, it was late May and Shevuos was coming up, one of the most important holy days of the year, when everything ordinary in my parents' home ceased in order for them to prepare and celebrate. The house would normally be bustling with last-minute cooking and preparation for guests, deliveries of challah bread and starched linens for the table, telephone calls to and fro with holiday wishes from friends and family. It was not difficult to conjure up the holiday smells: silver polish and fresh mums, hot cherry pie and brisket in the oven, the white kid gloves my mother took out of storage for the occasion. It was supposed to be a joyous holiday, as it marked the day that the Jewish people had received the Torah. I had left all of that behind at age seventeen. My Jewish training had been so strictly regimented that by then I felt I had endured enough Torah study and holidays to last a lifetime. Growing up in my parents' home and studying in private Jewish schools all my life, I had never had a non-Jewish friend. Now I was determined to discover the world beyond Jewish walls, and to become part of it.

It was the first day of vacation for the Spanish schoolchildren and I watched them spill onto the shoreline with shrieks of delight. Often I would sit outside on a park bench like this, watching life from a distance, contemplating my existence, jotting notes and dreams in my notebook. Where was I going? Was there any meaning to my life? Beleaguered by my internal questions and the despair that rang out in response, I often thought of suicide. It would be easy enough; I had nowhere to report, no job or school awaiting me. My friends were scattered about in universities working toward degrees, or in Israel, studying holy texts or starting families. As for my parents, for all their worrying about my not following the prescribed Jewish path, they had given up on me, resigning themselves to having lost me to what they called wanderlust.

I had had another difficult night. The violence and fragmentation of my dreams had broken my sleep. I pulled my journal out of my bag and jotted down last night's harsh dream: *Some sort of ordeal. I jump out of a moving car and land sprawled on my belly. I barely live to tell of it. It was my only way to get home. When I arrive at Mom and Dad's there is some celebration, or is it mourning? Our old house is filled to capacity with people of all generations, people I haven't seen*

in years. It is also filled with flowers and cards wishing me and the family well,
tribute cards. It is Friday evening and getting late. We must hurry to light candles.
Suddenly, the friends are gone and my sisters are there, covering up all of the mir-
rors in the house.

I slid my pen inside the spiral of the notebook and felt my exhaustion—
partly the effect of awakening before dawn with a strange dream, but deeper
still, exhaustion born of rootlessness and the endless searching for my place in
life.

Although I knew I was lost, I could not bear to hear it from anyone else.
Earlier in the year, my Italian lover from La Spezia had gotten too close to
the point. "You are running from your life with all your travels, you know
this?" he had snapped at me over dinner one night. He saw my eyes narrow,
my breath quicken, yet he continued. "Such beauty. Such bravado," he said
with a snicker, obviously enjoying himself. "And underneath it, you are such
a baby, a stupid, lost child." In a flash of indignation, I flung my red wine into
his face and stormed out of the café. I had enjoyed the drama of the moment,
but as I walked home that night, I realized that a truth had been spoken that I
was not ready to hear.

Seized by restlessness, I knew I had to move on. Pretty as it was, I was
only languishing away in this little town. There was nothing more for me here.
I've got to get back, I thought. I can easily get myself to Barcelona and then
catch a boat back. A small trickster-ish voice laughed: *Get back to where? Where
is back?* I did not like this voice. I did not know the answer. I did not want to
admit how utterly lost I was. I threw my empty paper cup and notebook into
my wicker satchel and rushed off to pack my things.

As I look back on this time, I ask myself: Was this agony necessary? Did
I have to rip down all the structures I had been given in order to build a life
for myself? Although on the surface this period looked like wasted years, I do
believe that perhaps the only way for me to discover that having no boundaries does not equal freedom was to eliminate all structure. The loneliness that
resulted from having no limits, and the lack of form and authority that I called
freedom but that eventually sickened me, were requisite ingredients for my
later appreciation of spiritual discipline, ritual, and community. Ironically,
only when I allowed these elements back into my life did I eventually find my
freedom.

FROM A BLEARY sixth-story window I could see out over Istanbul: the bustling
bay, a slender yet forcefully erect minaret, and the large, curvaceous mosque

next to it. How blatantly erotic the architecture was, I mused to myself, while the streets themselves felt utterly cloistered.

I had decided to make my way slowly back to Israel, not even sure why. For a pittance, the freighter from Barcelona to Istanbul had carried about two dozen of us, bedraggled world travelers who would consent to sleep on deck in our own bedding. For five days I was mindlessly happy, talking and trading stories and books with the other backpackers, most of whom were a bit older and wearier than I.

As we cruised up the Bosporus I teamed up with Ron, someone I deemed to be a most remarkable character, a kindred spirit, a world traveler. Ron had spent the last four years in Peru, working in the fields around Cuzco, drawing and reading, chewing coca leaves with the peasants and reading mystical texts. Now he and his buddies were on their way to India. The temptation to join them overpowered me.

My attraction to Ron was not physical. His shoulder-length blond hair was scraggly, and beneath his thick glasses, his intense blue eyes squinted in a not altogether friendly manner. Rather, what was compelling about him was that he was on a spiritual journey. He seemed to know where he was going. He was on the road to enlightenment, and I wanted what he had to teach me.

We had found a room together in the Sultan Ahmet section of Istanbul just around the corner from the Pudding Shop, a bawdy, smoke-filled café where counterculture travelers, freaks from around the world, united. Ron called himself a freak, and proudly so. It was an appellation that bespoke his defiant exodus from the United States culture. He had dropped out of his California life after working as an assistant professor of psychology in the state university system. This was his fourth year abroad, years spent mostly in Third World countries, peering at world events through a lens of spiritual-minded disdain.

Possessions were light and were traded freely. Books were the most precious commodity for us both. Our tables and beds were littered with worn paperbacks. *The Morning of the Magicians*, *At the Edge of History*, *Autobiography of a Yogi*, and the *International Herald Tribune* were our daily diet. We would read and eat and walk and chat with other world travelers. Several times a day Ron would characteristically need privacy or take off and meet me later. These were his sacred hashish breaks, I finally figured out after two or three days of losing him. In all my travels, I had assiduously avoided drugs of any kind. I felt alarmed at Ron's need and his secrecy about it. Under his enamouring spell, I had taken far too long to realize that he had a serious addiction. When I spoke of it openly, Ron flew into a rage.

"Listen, Miriam, you hopelessly Jewish princess," he said with an acid sneer, "I can see you are trying hard to uproot your bourgeois tendencies, but you don't have a chance in hell unless you can leave off judging others, all right?"

I showed no reaction to his attack but took in his words deeply. More than anything I wanted to be a free spirit, free of judgment, free of my middle-class trappings. But emulating Ron stopped here. I could not accept his dependence on drugs.

I never said another word about it. That night when he was down the hall in the bathroom, I thumbed through his pocket diary. I quickly read the day's entry: *July 3, 1974. Miriam Tirzah: Dark and pretty Jewish lady I hooked up with on the boat over. Young and demure, well, not so demure. Leave for Afgh. this week. Alone or in her company?*

Later that week, after a slow morning of drinking strong chai, (tea) in the filtered city sunshine, I said good-bye to Ron and his buddies as they boarded a bus for Kabul. He would be in Afghanistan until August. I was to fly to Israel, gather my gear from my Aunt Ruth's apartment, and join him in Kabul within the month. Then we would make our way to India together.

I was convinced that if I could coast into Jerusalem as if it were any other city I had wandered in and out of, without succumbing to the pressure to blend into the prevailing Jewish consciousness, then I would have vanquished a huge part of my tribal nature. I was determined to stay aloof and non-identified with my Jewish roots. If I didn't, I told myself, I would be swallowed up. Through my young eyes, there were only two options regarding Judaism: all or nothing. There was the "right" way to do things, which meant total identification with being a Jew, which left me without any autonomy, or there was nothing at all. It was an easy choice. I chose nothing. That was the only way I could be assured of my freedom.

I returned to the Pudding Shop to write in my journal. But now, sitting quietly by the window was no longer an option. Suddenly I noticed there were men loitering at my table, looking over my shoulder, asking me questions, grabbing at my books, watching me. I realized that Istanbul would be a very different place without a man by my side. And I had this bruised feeling in my chest; my loneliness was back and I did not want to feel it. I packed up my things and rushed through the covered market. The July heat was sweltering, and the sounds of the city—honking cars, yelling voices, wailing sirens—all felt unbearable to me. I ran to the inauspicious-looking building that housed the Turkish bath. I had heard that this particular bathhouse dated back to 1640. It looked as though it had not changed much since then.

The great metal doors closed behind me. I stood on the inside of a round, marble vault, all cool and gray and quiet. There was not a hint of the twentieth century in here, except for a half-empty Pepsi bottle in the corner. The sounds of female giggles echoed from the fountain room. Dust and traffic fumes clung to my brightly colored freak clothes. I peeled them off and packed them away in a cubby hole. The bathing room was farther inside and was shaped in a great octagon. At each corner was a chiseled marble mouth spewing warm water onto the stone and down into a round canal below. Eight or nine young women were sitting around by these spigots, their fleshy female bodies shiny and pink from the steamy room. Several of them scooped up water and splashed it on themselves and their friends as they chatted aimlessly. Behind the echoing voices and laughter, a recording of Turkish chants played in the distance, accompanied by the endlessly trickling water.

A huge woman with wet gray hair moved toward me, her pendulous breasts and belly swinging as she walked. Her face, peppered with moles and chin hairs, was jovial, and her gray eyes told me she belonged here and was coming forward to help me. I looked over at her shyly, my naked body shivering despite the room's warmth. She motioned to me to join her near one of the spigots.

I ambled toward the running water, trying not to slip. Meanwhile, the woman had sat down on her bare bottom and spread her legs in an unabashed V. She patted the wet floor in front of her crotch, smiling a big toothless smile. Come on, she seemed to be chanting to me in Turkish, I won't bite you—sit! I cringed and came closer, wedging myself between her voluminous legs. She reached into a bucket of soapy water with a large sea sponge and went to work on me, greasing me up with soap and scrubbing me down as if I were a dirty pot. She missed no joint, no crevice. The soap's lather flew about wildly as her huge hands worked me over. So this is what it must feel like to be a child tended by a loving mother. I felt hot tears welling up, not those I had swept away at the morning's farewells, but old tears waiting for comfort I suddenly realized that it was the caring touch of a mother that I had been craving on my lonely travels, not the touch of a lover after all.

After being scrubbed, I was ushered to a warm, wet marble slab for my massage. Now the bath mistress was going deeper into my muscles. I felt my body writhe in rhythm with her movements. Being touched like this, with such strength and tenderness, was awkward and unfamiliar. She tisked many times, sounds that seemed to echo with their pity and care. She took my hand firmly and pulled me back up to a sitting position. Then bucket upon bucket of warm, clear water was dumped over my head, and from behind the incessant fall of water, I was lulled into a warm, delicious oblivion I had rarely felt before.

But my tender experience of being mothered could not protect me beyond the bathhouse. As the great metal doors slammed shut behind me, I realized that I was once again alone on the streets of Istanbul. I felt utterly vulnerable now. It seemed that only men were on the street and all eyes were on me. I slipped through the streets and back to the room that Ron and I had rented. There I dined on some leftover figs and cheese and put myself to bed.

What a relief to leave Istanbul the next day—how glad I was to be lifted up and out of that sultry city on an airplane. But the flight was too brief. Within an hour we were making the descent into Israel. My belly tightened; I was not prepared to deal with the conflict I knew awaited me here. I had been to Israel numerous times, to spend my summers, to work on a kibbutz or as a volunteer working with the needy. And never had I visited Israel without feeling caught in a thicket of feelings: On the one hand, I was deeply moved at the sense of belonging that I felt in the Jewish state, of having, perchance, found my spiritual home. On the other, I was alarmed at how easy it would be to slide into the normative Jewish culture, to utterly lose myself in this place.

I was determined not to lose myself. This, after all, was the vow I had made while still with Ron: to remain above the world, the Jewish world in particular, that could so easily pull me out of the spiritual freedom I had committed myself to.

As usual, I was met by the sweaty, bustling impatience of Israelis at Lod Airport. But I had to admit: these people had something that I had missed in Europe, a character and spunk, an underlying sense of community that flew in the face of the tumult they were constantly creating. They were so rough on the outside and so full of spirit and devotion underneath. Waiting for a taxi to Jerusalem, tears welled up in me, the nostalgia of coming home. I had to battle myself to keep my soft feelings in check.

I had last left Israel almost a year before, on the cusp of the Yom Kippur War, the air thick with prewar tension, everyone tight and growling. I was enrolled at the Hebrew University in Jerusalem and waiting for classes to begin. But I was restless and arrogant; I did not want to take part in a culture that was so uptight, so adversarial. It was my parents' desire to see me here, their dream to live in Jerusalem, not mine. After choosing my classes and finding myself an apartment, I found my way to the airport. I told myself I was simply going on a week's excursion to Greece. But once I had my feet on free soil, I bolted like a steaming pony, wanting nothing but boundless time and freedom to explore the world. I wrote a postcard to my parents in St. Louis announcing my change of heart and plans, and to Aunt Ruth, my mother's sister, who lived in Jerusalem, telling her to put my things in storage till I got back.

Since then, while roaming through Europe, I had become a citizen of the world. No longer did I feel the pressure of others' expectations. And without this pressure I had discovered my inner spirituality. It would rise in me like a swollen river whenever I approached, a genuinely holy place of any religion. I particularly loved the cathedrals of Lourdes and Notre Dame, and the small country churches of Crete and Provence. I had sat for hours in silence inside the vacant synagogue of Toledo and in the fields around the standing stone circles of Avebury and Stonehenge. For me, the cobblestones of Assisi still rang out with the songs of St. Francis and Sister Claire, and I vowed to return to the exquisite Alhambra in Granada, for the prayer it evoked in me was perhaps the most pure I had ever experienced. Other religions had opened to me with possibility. It seemed that a little bit went a very long way, while my own religion chafed me.

It would take me years to realize that being a lover of all religions did little to sustain me, that in order to embrace what is universally true and beautiful in life, I would eventually need a particular path to follow, through which I could deepen my soul. But during these young years, the broad path suited me best. Opening myself up to all forms of spirituality and nibbling bits from everything that appealed to me gave me inspiration I could not find at home and afforded me distance and time in which to explore my interior spiritual terrain.

Now being driven upward into the foothills of Jerusalem, I could not resist my awe at this land's beauty. The rocky earth itself seemed to be alive, the grasses swayed in the breeze, and blood red poppies sprouted up indiscriminately among the green. My eyes followed the spiraling stone terraces that ringed the hills as the taxi driver shifted gears to accommodate the steep ascent. The air began to cool. We were approaching the ancient city now, with her buildings of white stone and streets crammed with the mosques, churches, and synagogues of believers from around the world. My heart began to race. I felt that I could see the entire world out of my taxi window, that my heart wanted to leap from one hill to the next, to dance upon the crest of the city's great wall, to shout out "Hodu L'Adonai Ki Tov! Give thanks to God for God is good," just as King David had. I loved it here. Why deny it? A great compassion flooded me, for this city, for all the people of this land.

I brought my focus back inside the *sherut*, a multi-passenger taxi. Next to the olive-skinned driver, his wrists decked with gold chains and bracelets, sat a young man of no more than twenty-two or so, already looking withered from concentration and study. He was a Chasid, sitting hunched and poring over a small book, mumbling. On his clean-shaven head sat a large fur hat, out of which dropped two red sidelocks that bounced as we drove. Despite his hat and long black coat, he looked utterly oblivious to the heat. His pale and not unattractive wife sat in the seat directly behind him, next to me, with their small baby on her lap. Both mother and child dozed wearily. On her head she wore a large stylized brunette wig. Like her husband, she was young—too young, I felt, to be saddled with such a dutiful life.

In back of us sat three swarthy men, snacking on nuts and seeds out of small paper bags, clicking and spitting the shells with great facility and haste. They did not know I was listening nor that I understood their language. To them I was just another passing young traveler, an outsider. My scruffy clothes and my backpack said as much. I listened as a lull fell over their blithe conversation after the mention of Bentzi, a brother of one of them, it seemed, who had fallen in the war. From the rear I could feel the grief like a thickness in the air. To lose one's brother, how dreadful, I thought. And there must have been hundreds more like him that were lost. I had happily forgotten about the latest war, which had broken out just last year. It dawned upon me at that moment that not only the men in the back of the car but everyone in this small country must still be grieving their losses from the October before. Meanwhile, I had been lost in my own separate world, disconnected from the pain of my people.

The taxi deposited me in front of the Jerusalem train station. Looking for the right bus into the quarter called Rechavia, I found that my spoken Hebrew had hopelessly entangled itself with French. I rode standing on the packed Egged bus number 9 and got off downtown to mull around before going any further. The shops and stores were still closed for the afternoon siesta, as I dug out the two phone tokens that I had carried with me all though Europe and found a public phone.

"Aunt Ruth, is this you? It's Miriam Tirzah." Without answering, Ruth covered the mouthpiece of her telephone and she called with a great deal of urgency to others in the house to be quiet. Then, seizing a breath, she spoke to me.

"Well, shalom aleichem! Where are you calling from?" I explained to her that I had just gotten into the country and would be here briefly.

"Look, I know this is a surprise. If you have a full house I'm happy to stay in the hostel or with a friend."

"Don't be absurd! Come right away. It's important that you come. When will you be here? Are you coming right now?"

I was not ready for this family intensity.

"No, I have a few things to take care of in town. How about in a couple of hours? Maybe by seven. How's that?"

"Seven it is. *Lehitra'ot.*" She had the same way of smashing down the receiver that my mother had when finished with a conversation.

Well, here we go, I thought to myself. However different I felt after my time away, I should never expect my family to change. I turned to face the street. The Jerusalem sun had begun to fall and a rosy golden hue seemed to hover over the summer rush hour. Around me, throngs of Israelis scurried to catch their buses home, to meet friends, to pick up a quick snack before going on. Hoisting my pack up onto my shoulders, I started down Ben Yehudah Street. Seductive odors pulled at me, skewered lamb dripping its juices next to the hot steam of fresh roasted nuts and seeds next to frying falafel balls next to pizza. I tried to breathe all of these in without stopping. There were too many choices. I decided I would choose nothing. No food for me. Not eating kept me aloof from the drama around me, gave me a sense of being in control. And in Israel, especially around my family, control was at a premium.

As I walked, I focused on a cord of light running through me and repeated a fervent prayer, *Thy will be my will,* in order to steady myself. I had picked up these and many other spiritual techniques from my readings and conversations along my travels. Whatever worked I would use, regardless of its religious source, in an attempt to fill the spiritual void I felt inside. In this way, practicing equilibrium in the midst of outer tumult, I passed the time until seven o'clock.

Ramban Street, apartment 19. The smell of children and frying foods hung thickly in the foyer. I rang the bell. I heard a commotion from behind the door, then my aunt's unusually big smile greeted me. Uncle Bill stood in the background with a pallid face, his body stooped.

"Here, Miriam, let me help," he said, fumbling badly with my pack.

"Hi, everybody!" I called out. For a moment, there was a dead silence. It felt like the moment between acts, the moment actors take to strike their new positions on stage. Why was coming here so unbearably awkward?

"Shalom, shalom!" Aunt Ruth's voice rang out on cue. "Let's look at you." Her eyes scanned my body. "Well, you've certainly slimmed down, haven't you? Are you hungry, Miriam? Your cousins just left. There are plenty of leftovers. Have you eaten?"

"Yes, yes, I have," I lied.

"Are you sure? There's chicken here, and fresh salad, I know you like that." There was something uncomfortable in the air.

"I'm really fine. Thank you."

"Well, all right then. If you are absolutely sure. Let's come into the sitting room, shall we? And have a little talk. Are you ready, Bill?"

"In a minute," Uncle Bill grunted. He was uncommonly quiet this evening. He had gained weight in the last year and his normally sparkling blue eyes looked sad. I watched him disappear into the bathroom wondering if he was well. Maybe his real estate business was floundering, I thought. Since their emigration from the United States four years earlier, life had not been easy. They had had to rely in large measure on Ruth's earnings as a professor at the university. There had been many sacrifices made to live in this holy city.

The sitting room had not changed. There was the thinning Turkish rug in the center and many easy chairs around it. The day's newspapers, in both Hebrew and English, lay scattered around the place. At the far side of the room the dining table still wore its polyester lace from the Sabbath three days earlier. The silver candelabra brought with them from St. Louis and before that from Germany stood empty and covered with dripped wax. On a side table were a chipped but pretty china teapot, three glass tea mugs, and a small plate of cakes.

"Maybe you will change your mind after all, and have at least a little mandelbrot and tea, hmm? I admit they are not home-baked, but not bad," my hostess said. I put up my hand and shook my head.

"Still so stubborn. All right then," she said, pouring her own tea and one for her husband. "Tell us about your travels, Miriam. I'm sure you've learned a lot," she continued rotely as she settled into her chair. She was peering at me over the tops of her eyeglasses while Uncle Bill took up his tea cup and found his place in a chair to her left.

"Well," I began dutifully, trying to draw a big breath, "I've learned more this last year traveling than I could ever have in university. And I'm not through yet. I'm here to make a little visit and pick up some things, some of the clothes I left before—"

"Oh, your things. Ach, I forgot to tell you. But how could I have? We didn't know how to find you. We had a flood last November when the rains came. We were storing your things with the kids'downstairs in the basement and it was all totally ruined. I had to throw it all out. I'm sorry."

I swallowed hard, fumbling with my disappointment. Ron's face flashed in my mind's eye, and then his voice: *It was all that bourgeois stuff from the States anyway*. Okay, I rallied. I can do without. I felt Aunt Ruth's eyes. She wanted to continue.

"Miriam. There are some things you should know." She swallowed her breath hard. "Actually there is some news we have for you. Both good and not good." I glanced at Uncle Bill sitting to her left in silence. He had taken off his glasses and was rubbing his eyes with a full hand.

"The good news is that your brother Ezra has found a wife. So a *mazel tov* is in order! And her name is Miriam, too. Isn't that something? They are getting married in October." Her face searched mine for a smile. She found none. I was bracing myself for what was still to come. My aunt suddenly leaned forward as if ready to lurch. My stomach tightened.

"Miriam, there's been a fatal accident. It was your brother, Danny. His car went over a cliff, he was found dead. He must have died immediately. It was in New Mexico. They found him on an Indian reservation." She was firing out the facts to my paralyzed open mouth. "It's been a little while now. It was the end of May. Yes, it was just before Shevuos. Your parents thought it would be better not to tell you. That way you wouldn't have to sit shiva in a foreign country all by yourself."

It had been six weeks. What kind of a family was this? Didn't I deserve to know? Yet this news was strangely familiar to me.

"Danny. Dead?" I stammered.

She closed her eyes and nodded.

"Are you sure? I mean, that it was an accident?"

"As far as we know," Ruth replied, turning to glance at Bill. My mind raced. No wonder Mom was so strange and silent on that call from Spain. She was in bed during the shiva. Now it was all starting to make sense. My dream: *some sort of ordeal... careening out of a car... landing sprawled on my belly... returning home to the strange celebration... the house filled with people and flowers and tribute cards... my sisters covering up the mirrors.* It had been a dream about the accident and the mourning. Danny's accident had become my accident. Only I had succeeded and survived the will to die that I had been experiencing for the last year. Danny had not.

I excused myself early that night. When I climbed into the cold guest bed, my bravado melted into torrents of grief.

It was not an accident. Of this I was certain. In the following days, as I prepared for my journey not to India but to St. Louis, it dawned on me that I had been unconsciously following Danny's leadership to determine where the path of breaking away would lead. I foraged through my collection of letters for his last aerogramme to me. I had received it in the midst of a January snowstorm, where I was working at the French children's home: *"I'll be clearing out of this place soon, probably next month or so. You can't stay at a monastery forever. There's nothing left for me to do here unless I become a monk. Time to do it for myself. I'll probably head west. So you're traipsing around Southern Europe? Not surprised. We all need to flee the tribe sometimes."*

Here was Danny in all his cocky complexity, sitting right here in my hands, utterly alive.

He was ten years older than I. Even as a little girl I perceived him as a troubled mystery. His face was drawn inward, his clear blue eyes growing increasingly cloudy as he moved through his teens, his brow more and more furrowed, his jaw set with resignation and anger. As a young man he confided to me how he hated his thinning hair, his short stature, his Jewish nose. Like me, Danny was trapped under the weight of a religious training that held no regard for personal choice. Only Danny was the firstborn, and in religious Jewish families (particularly our own) the firstborn son was saddled with grand expectations. Coming from a lineage of rabbis on my mother's side, he was in line to become a religious scholar. Nothing else would do.

Before I was in first grade, Danny had already left for a rabbinical boarding school called Telshe Yeshiva outside Cleveland, Ohio. It was said among rabbis that there was no institute like it for serious Talmudic study in the Midwest, certainly not in St. Louis. The choice had been made on the basis of the advice of our mother's brothers, both rabbis ordained in Germany. Our father, who had come to a rigidly Orthodox lifestyle on his own as a young adult, agreed that his son would be a Talmudic scholar. Danny, of course, was never consulted.

I saw him only on an occasional Jewish holiday, when my parents flew him back to our home in St. Louis. His visits became rarer as the years went by. It was more important to spend the holy days at the yeshiva, where Jewish law was inscrutably applied and all prayers were said in an absolutely correct manner.

Danny excelled in that very masculine environment of yeshiva, where holy book learning and Torah study were the only staff and measure. He was considered the prize student. He confessed to me once that he had seen otherworldly lights dance to and from the Hebrew and Aramaic letters of the Talmud as he studied late at night. But instinctively he must have known that he needed more in order to grow up whole. His mind had begun to question. He wanted out.

At eighteen, Danny had a private appointment with the head of the yeshiva and informed him of his decision to leave. Their conversation was reported in detail to my father. Years later, Danny gave me his own account. The meeting took place in Rabbi Isen's back office.

"So, what will you do?" the rabbi began, without looking up from the sacred text he was studying.

"I want to study at the university."

"And what is there to study at the university?"

"Philosophy, I am interested in philosophy." This word seemed to rile the rabbi.

"We Jews don't have philosophy? You have to go elsewhere to find philosophy? The Torah is full of philosophy, the only kind you need."

"But Rabbi Isen, wait. I want to study the philosophy of other thinkers, too. I didn't say we don't have our own. I'll continue learning Talmud on the side. But I want to know from the outside, too."

"The outside! The outside! We don't need from the outside!" At this point the rabbi grew quiet. He slumped over his desk, his forehead in his hands, as if peering into a holy book.

"Daniel: A boy like you could be a real lamdan, a scholar of importance! Do you know this? This is the greatest thing you can do with your life, don't you see? I'm warning you now, it's a chilul, a desecration, to waste a mind like yours... on the outside! You won't last, I'm telling you that. Go on in this direction and you won't live past thirty. Do you hear? You will not live past thirty!"

The incident was no secret. It was reported to all of the siblings in warning by our father, who used the rabbi's words again and again to rail at us of the demise that awaited us should we ever leave the Jewish path.

"The Jewish way is our lifeblood. I'm warning you: Leave the Torah and you leave life. Never forget that," my father would boom at us.

He had flailed this talk at Danny on the Sunday afternoon he came by to announce he was leaving for the Zen monastery in Rochester, New York. By that time, 1970, my brother was an untenured professor at the University of Missouri. He had in the end left the yeshiva to study philosophy. But, as if living out the rabbi's words, Danny had never flourished. He lived an isolated life, failing countless times with women and having few male friends. After years of a career teaching classics and biblical criticism, Danny was utterly disillusioned. Even drugs, he admitted to me privately, could no longer give him satisfaction. By the age of twenty-seven, Danny's once-clear face wore the nasty cynicism of a bitter man twice his age.

Then he came across a book, *Three Pillars of Zen*, by the Zen *roshi* Philip Kapleau, and it seemed to turn his ailing life around. Kapleau's book gripped Danny, stumping his too quick mind and forcing it to transcend itself. Zen Buddhism was clean. It cut through the gummy emotional plane, allowing one to leave the insurmountable difficulties of one's personality behind. In a meaningless world, his soul seemed to have found water, the first draft since he'd left the yeshivah.

After hearing a few refrains of our father's predictable lecture, he excused himself to say good-bye to Mom.

"It's over, Mom. I've given up my job at the university," he told her as he stood in the kitchen, playing nervously with his keys. Her face looked ashen with disbelief. She had been getting out stew meat from the freezer for dinner and she forgot to shut the freezer door. She began to fire questions at him.

"How on earth can you afford to do this? You have to work, my God. What will you live on? What about the Jewish community in Rochester? Have you made any contacts yet? Do you know people there?"

"Mom," he stopped her, at this point close to laughter. "You're not listening. I'm going to Rochester to a Zen monastery, not to join the Young Israel Synagogue. Okay?" She looked at him with horror. Her questions continued.

"No, I already gave up my lease... No, my books are gone, sold 'em. I don't have anything else to take... No, it is not such a great job; teaching classics gets old, too... Drugs? Sorry, Mom. Even drugs couldn't help me now. Believe me, I know... No, I'm not crazy. I'm through here! That's all!"

Later that year, before Yom Kippur, there was a mad flurry on the part of my parents to "save" Danny. It was spurred by my mother's rabbinic counsel, her brothers. There had been no effort to contact Danny at the monastery throughout the summer. But suddenly it dawned on them. Not that Danny was in peril, sitting in silent *zazen* meditation for fourteen hours a day in a strange place with barely any human contact or warmth. What disturbed them was rather that Danny was now so far afield that he was beyond their influence.

Privately I cheered for Danny. He was doing exactly as he pleased, pouring himself into something that mattered to him alone. And he had succeeded in eluding the family's grip and the grip of Judaism. But would he get away with it? I wondered. Could it be that easy?

I overheard my mother crying to my father one Friday night. It was the end of a torpid summer. The High Holidays were but a few weeks away. Behind their bedroom door, my mother wept like a child.

"I just can't manage this year. It's like a nightmare I can't wake up from, to think of him there. Our firstborn son, gone to this! A*vo-dah zara*!" She blew her nose hard. "What will I say in shul when I'm asked? What will we say, Sol? What will we say?" Now she grew hysterical. "That our Danny has gone to worship idols in a Buddhist temple? I simply can't do it. I can't face it. *Gott in Himmel!* It's too much to face!"

As the autumn holidays drew near, more efforts were made. My father called the monastery repeatedly but was not put through. Telegrams with urgent words were sent, appealing to Danny's better sensibilities. There was no response. Danny was sitting in silence.

After that there was no communication between them. He had shunned them and they had cut him off. Of the rest of us, I was the only one who wrote to Danny, and then only sporadically. It was as if we were all immobilized by our parents' politics and could not take action of our own.

Two and a half years later, just after Danny's thirtieth birthday, our parents received word from the sheriff's office of Grants County, New Mexico, that a body had been found with the presumed identity of Daniel B. Firestone. My parents sent their closest family friend, Harry Goldspan, to fly down to verify that it was indeed their son.

You won't live past thirty. You won't live past thirty. The words came ringing back into my ears. He had said that, hadn't he? Had Rabbi Isen been given prophecy to have spoken those words? Or was this what was known as a curse? I wondered. Whatever it was, it felt eerie and loveless and it had come true.

As I made my way back to the United States and my parents' home, I consoled myself with the thought that perhaps Danny's death would be the painfully sharp instrument that would finally cut through the spiritual morass of my family. Surely everyone would finally unite in the undeniable recognition that life itself was more important that any specific form or tradition, that our connection and love for one another had to outstrip our beliefs and practices. Even Orthodox Judaism would have to yield in the face of living and dying. I looked forward to seeing compassion reign.

I SPENT THE next four months in my parents' home. It did not take me that long, however, to realize how naïve I had been to hope that this tragedy could fuel a new spirit of openheartedness for my family. Remarkably, nothing had changed. Orthodoxy (and my parents' use of it to control the family) still took precedence over compassion for one another. As for me, it was as if all the months spent abroad discovering the world and becoming a free person had never occurred. Not a question was asked about my travels, and the spirit of freedom and equanimity that I had gained quickly became a mere memory. Even my little brother, Isaiah, could not be bothered to listen to what I had to say.

The fact that Danny's death had been a suicide was common knowledge to everyone in my family and was discussed openly among us. Only the outside world was given the story of Danny's car going over a cliff. News of a suicide would incur too much shame, my parents reasoned. Besides, in the Jewish tradition, suicides were customarily buried at the farthermost corner of a Jewish cemetery, without a eulogy or burial Kaddish. And it was imperative to my parents that Danny be given a full Jewish funeral.

I could see that my parents were straddling two sets of rules, one for public use and one for behind closed doors. And like most young people, I was on the lookout for hypocrisy, particularly among the older generation. Although as a rabbi and a parent myself I now have far more compassion for the kinds of choices my parents made, it is still remarkable to me to observe when people adhere strictly to the law, and when they allow themselves to bend it, out of self-interest. What a shame that my parents' flexibility showed itself so late— only after Danny's death—and then only for themselves rather than for their child, who needed it in the form of kindness and understanding.

By the time I arrived home, my father was already back on the road. He traveled forty states, mostly by car, selling paintings and art accessories to galleries. It was his custom to arrive home for the Sabbath by late Friday afternoon and be gone by Sunday, leaving behind him a whirlwind of paper and cigar smoke.

The Sunday morning after my return home, he called me downstairs.

"Come here, Miriam, I want you to hear this." He was standing over the large mahogany dining table covered with his mail and business papers. He had been packing up to get back on the road when his friend Lester Bernheim stopped in.

"Lester, tell her what you just told me," he said, a cold cigar stub hanging from his lips. Lester looked up at me kindly. He removed the yarmulke from his head for a moment to scratch underneath it.

"Well, I was just telling your dad that when I figured it up, your dad had lost his father, his younger brother and now his eldest son all in the course of four months. It was a little bit eerie, right? You weren't here for it, Miriam. You know your dad never complains or sheds a tear. But Harriet and I, well, all of us were worried." My dad had already turned back to his work, fingering and filing his papers as Lester continued.

"So I knew months ago I was going to be on business in New York City and I got an appointment with the rebbe. The Lubavitcher rebbe, right? So you don't get to see that man too often one on one anymore, you know what I mean? So when all of this tragedy happened, I figured I would also ask about your dad." Lester had my attention now.

"So what did you tell him?" I asked.

"Well, just that. I said there is a very pious St. Louis businessman who gives a lot in charity and leads a very kosher and upright life and these deaths keep on happening."

"So what did he say?" I asked impatiently.

"Well, he didn't answer right away. First he, well, he sat back and closed his eyes and didn't say anything. As if he was meditating. He asked me to repeat your dad's name. I almost couldn't remember it in Hebrew, Sol. Then a few seconds later the rebbe looks up and says: 'Tell Mr. Firestone to check the mezuzah on his front door.'"

I looked at my father.

"Well? Did you?"

"Of course I did, what do you think?"

"So? What was there?"

"He was right. The entire parchment was out."

"Out? What does that mean?"

"Somehow, if had fallen out. I had just had it checked last fall. You know you're supposed to have it checked regularly, and I do. Always have. But after Lester came back I saw that the parchment was mysteriously gone! So we had an empty mezuzah guarding our house. Or rather, not guarding it. No Shema Yisrael, nothing." He came behind Lester and slapped him on the back. "It had fallen completely out of its case. It's no wonder at all."

Listening to Lester's story produced a sort of awe in me. I had heard of the Lubavitcher rebbe and his far-reaching vision and wanted badly to think that our lives had a simple, secret order, existing just beyond our view. What my father saw as the cause of our family disaster was his unwitting failure to follow a Jewish ritual. This was his way of making sense of a situation far out of his control. But even as a young woman, I knew I could not believe that the reason behind our family problems was as simple as this. Now I look back at this mysterious episode and view the power of the missing scroll certainly not as the cause, but rather as a synchronistic omen of the tragic events that were befalling my family.

My father was the fortunate one here. He was neither a mystic nor a Chasid, but he had awe for the right things, like God's overarching power. After Lester had left, my father asked to speak with me again.

"Doesn't that story prove to you how mysterious God is? Who would be stupid enough to mess with that kind of power? Your brother Danny was stupid. There's no other word for it. With all of his so-called education, look how he's ended up. Do you see now that leaving the Torah life is like a fish leaving water? It's deadly. You know Danny was forewarned. You remember the story. That story goes for you, too, Miriam."

"Would you stop it, Dad? Danny was lost. Don't you have any compassion for that? People lose their way."

"But that's exactly why we were given the Torah. So that we won't lose our way! Danny was told, fair and square, before he left the yeshiva."

My mother, I found, was of the same general mind as my father, only she would express her personal woe alongside her ideological certainty. She was torn up, that was clear, and I had guessed correctly: she had been given medication to handle the shock. She had stayed in bed for the funeral and for days after. By the time I arrived home, she was up and about the house, crying throughout the day.

"There is no tragedy like this one. None. To lose your own child, it's against nature. It's like giving birth in reverse, only there is nothing on the other end of the process." She began to weep loudly. My heart hurt for her. I reached my hand across the table to touch hers. She pulled it away.

"I just cannot see how he could have done it. What was he thinking? It's so meanhearted, so cruel to do this to a mother."

"Look, Mom," I tried to reason with her, "he was hurting. He was totally cut off from any humanity in that Zen temple. And face it, he certainly hadn't heard from you after that barrage of telegrams. What did you expect?"

"What did I expect? What did I *expect*?" Her voice turned angry. "I expect a child of mine to think of his actions, to think of the pain they may cause his mother."

"Well, what about the pain *he* was in? Doesn't anybody around here think about that? You think there was nothing we could've been doing?"

"Don't lecture me, Miriam. It is all straight and simple. You cannot leave your roots and expect to get away with it. We had no say in the matter."

I was silenced, smitten by my mother's words. What had happened to all the rabbinic sayings I had been reared on? *Never judge another until you find yourself in his place... Until the day you die, do not trust your own motives... Put your hand out ever to include the estranged person, for you yourself were once estranged...* Were these statements meant for everyone else but us? Had they broken down in our time of crisis, or were they just forgotten?

The longer I stayed in my parents' home, the more information I was able to patch together about how Danny had actually died. My brother had planned his death in scrupulous detail. Along with his personal effects, their friend Harry had brought my parents Danny's diary. It read as follows: *February 16, 1974. Commenced Sesshin. Poor sitting. Distracted. Overeat. Burn $20 twice.* There were only a few entries during that three-week period, all in staccato style, little bullets of pain. Danny was now acting as his own Zen roshi, a regimented taskmaster bound for enlightenment or his finish. He was coping with his own frustration and self-loathing by burning money. The last words in the diary were *May 16: Final ceremony.* What was that final ceremony? Harry had brought back the report from the Grant County sheriff's office. Danny had apparently rolled his car over an embankment, but his body was not found inside it, as my parents had told their friends. It was found in the meadow above, gun wound to the chest, keeled over in front of a large bronze statue of the Buddha. Two knee prints indented the green blanket just in front of the statue. The gun lay at his side. As an act of kindness to my parents, Harry had disposed of Danny's Buddha before returning to St. Louis.

As the drama unfolded, I got snagged in the inertia of my parents' home. My drive to discover the world flagged. I settled into their house for the fall. I got temporary jobs with Kelly Girl Temps for the first few weeks and finally as an order processor for Stromberg Carlson, a communications division of General Dynamics. But I still wore my Turkish bazaar treasures: long, colorful scarves and bright cotton shifts with embroidery and tiny mirrors sewn into the chest. They reminded me of the quest that I had begun and was determined to continue.

For comfort I had Katmouse, a furry gray cat. He was a gift from my sister Laya and her boyfriend, Tom, to ease the pain of living at our parents' house. Laya was seven years my senior and the sibling to whom I felt closest. She lived with Tom eighty miles from St. Louis on a farm just above the Mississippi River. They understood me and the fact that, living at my parents' home, I would need someone to hug and sleep with and talk to. Because of my parents' fragility after Danny's death, I now felt obliged to be their daughter as I had been years earlier. Even my little brother, now in high school, had abandoned the role of dutiful son years earlier. But now I was on hand, almost zombielike, to accompany them to synagogue services, to escort them to Jewish community functions. Frequently I was cross-examined by old friends and community members. Their questions were filled with assumptions about who they thought I was.

"So where are you going to school now, Miriam?"

"When will you be going back to Israel?"

"How are you enjoying being back on the home turf?"

I did not try to explain that I had begun a very different journey. I answered rotely, always polite, telling them that I was working in the business world for a while before going back to school. This was as much as I could say with any honesty. But the fact that no one dared to ask me the questions I ached to be asked, about the death of my eldest brother, about my travels and what I was searching for, only increased my growing sense of isolation.

My tough exterior grew tougher. I gave up on people and returned to Katmouse, to my bed, to smoking stale Gauloise cigarettes by my open window and reading Alan Watts. I lost myself in daydreams about God and the afterlife, and the purpose of the suffering that seemed just beneath the surface in everyone I met.

I now smile at the pathos of this scene, so dark and self-absorbed. Yet I realize that retreating into myself allowed me the time to speculate on my own views of life, which were distinct from those of my parents, yet not quite those of my world-traveling peers. And it was in my isolation that I began to rally the self-reliance I needed for the journey that lay ahead.

I was in the first stage of my spiritual quest, one that is characterized for many people by confusion and loneliness. Like all seekers, I was embarking on my life journey carrying heaps of baggage passed on to me by my family: prescriptions for happiness and meaning, unexamined fears and longings, and the values and beliefs of generations.

As precious and powerful as this family legacy may be, it must be set aside long enough for us to unclutter our minds and find our own ideals. It is only with free hands and clear eyes that we have the possibility of investigating our own beliefs and the values that will emerge naturally from within. Although this separation process is grueling, if it does not occur, we are in danger: The infrastructure of beliefs that gives shape to our adult attitudes—from how we deal with money to how we deal with the infinite forces—will not be our own, but will be dictated by others.

Why is this process of individuation so important? My experience has taught me that only through the arduous process of discovering our own vision of the world will we one day have a contribution to make, one based on the gifts that are genuinely ours. I believe that this is what God most wants of us: to discover and offer our true selves. According to the teachings of our Chasidic masters, each of us has a portion of God implanted within us as our truest nature. But this *chelek Eloha mima'al*—our divine portion—requires nurturing and development. In a very real sense, we are duty-bound to become who we were meant to be in this world, so that we can offer our unique gifts back to the world.

As we start out, the most arduous road, the one that we must bushwack for ourselves, is the one most worth taking; it is this tortuous road that will lead us to freedom, self-discovery, and ultimately to our true work in the world, that which only we can do.

The necessarily chaotic stage that young seekers go through as they separate and reject their heritage is paralleled by an equally difficult one for their parents. This is the requisite stage of surrender. As members of a new generation temporarily throw off what has been painstakingly given them in order to search for what is truly theirs, their elders must do their best to let go. This takes enormous restraint, but know that what is valuable and life-giving in one's heritage will be returned to in time and with great appreciation.

For both seekers and those who love them, being patient rather than rushing in to fill the uncomfortable void of searching is critical to the spiritual process. This nonactive holding back is known in the Kabbalah as *tzimtzum*. It comes from Rabbi Isaac Luria's depiction of how God created the world: by holding back, creating an empty void in which the new creation would unfold. For humans to be in a state of tzimtzum is to silently proclaim that we can afford to trust in a spiritual process bigger than ourselves, that we can afford to surrender and follow the deep wisdom that comes from our souls. However difficult and lonely the chaotic voids of our lives seem, if we can surrender to them rather than rushing to fill the emptiness, our next level of clarity *will* eventually emerge.

IN MID-SEPTEMBER I had a dream about my brother: *I am walking through a bustling restaurant. All of a sudden, I see Danny across the room. He is beaming. I run to him and begin to cry, wondering if news of his death had been a mistake after all. Danny holds me. Sternly, but with much love, he explains: "It is true; I have died. I am only back for a brief time to complete some unfinished business."*

I pull myself together, noticing that Danny's cynicism and contempt for the world are gone, his face is open and happy as a child's. Together we walk arm in arm to a table. At this moment I know with absolute certainty that there is no shortage of plenty in the world. Danny even has an unlimited money supply with him, now that it means nothing to him.

Danny is quiet as I deliberate about what to order. Perhaps a specially brewed beer, a French goat cheese, black bread? There are so many choices. Finally, Danny looks at me squarely and speaks: "At a place like this, it is best to trust the owners. They know what they do best and they offer it as the chef's special." He points to a blackboard with the day's recommended special on it. "That is what is best. Trust it. In the long run, it will save you a tremendous amount of struggle."

I awakened in the middle of the night, crying from the ecstasy and power of this experience. I was utterly certain—as I am to this day—that this was more than a dream; it was a visit from Danny's soul. There was a numinous quality about it, as if from the world beyond, a holiness so real that it became the foundation of my faith in the reality of an afterlife and the eternal nature of the soul.

Danny never again appeared to me like that, but his final words to me still remain vivid. I knew even then what he meant by "trust the owners." He was talking about trusting the lineage that was assigned to me at birth and the spiritual path that went with it. Yet despite the holy quality of Danny's words and the purity with which they were spoken, I was not ready to follow even his advice.

As I went through years of searching for God in Benedictine monasteries and Hindu ashrams, traveling to northern Minnesota to prepare for the apocalypse, and into Universalist churches to cry my eyes out, I sent his words away. I felt impelled to reject my heritage until I had found my own self. I had to choose everything on the menu that I fancied first, even if the process took me years, even if my choices led to suffering. And if I endured relentless inner and outer struggles, at least I was free and had won my dignity. For many years, what I thought was freedom was my only choice. The chef's special would have to wait.

CHAPTER TWO

OSTRICH FEVER

DANNY HAD CEASED TO EXIST FOR MY PARENTS YEARS BEFORE HIS DEATH. When his lifestyle became so contrary to their religious norms as to bring them unbearable disgrace and it became clear that all their promptings and threats had lost power, no other option remained for them than to block him out of their field of vision. I called it their ostrich treatment. They would simply disconnect themselves from the conflict by burying their heads. It was much simpler than all the ugly confrontations that bore no fruit, and because it required little or no contact with the opponent, it left their position intact and mighty, free from the painful reality on the other side.

Danny was not the only family member living in the cut-off, private hell that resulted from the ostrich treatment. The year of his death brought other nightmares to the surface. There was my sister Laya, for one.

Green-eyed and delicately built, in her twenties Laya still had the look of a young girl. But her natural gifts were those of a wizened crone, allowing her to penetrate into the heart of a person, to listen deeply, to mediate peace. For these talents my mother adored her; her bond with Laya was admittedly the strongest of her bonds with all of her six children. But the course of Laya's life had led her into a painfully tight corner, and for her there was no help. She had fallen in love with Tom, a non-Jew, years earlier, and the two of them were inseparable. Marriage was the obvious next step, but they knew this would infringe upon my parents' most sacred commandment: Thou shalt not marry a *goy*. Intermarriage was what my father called the greatest anathema to the Jewish people, a veritable posthumous victory for Hitler. It was never to be tolerated.

Inasmuch as both of my parents were deeply affected by the Holocaust (my mother was German and had escaped to England at the age of seventeen, and my American-born father had taken part in the Allies' liberation of the Nazi concentration camps), I have often wondered if their fixation on Jewish continuity was a response to their having survived the war, while so many Jews

around them—family included—perished. But having an objective discussion
about the topic was impossible. The very mention of the words *assimilation*
and *intermarriage* in our household triggered the most emotional of tirades
from my parents. Any rational thinking on the subject—in fact, anything but
total agreement with them—was instantly silenced.

By the time of Danny's death, Laya and Tom had been living together for
almost five years. In the beginning, my parents played oblivious and Tom and
Laya played along. They lived and traveled freely in many other states, always
avoiding the St. Louis area. When Laya came to visit, it was by herself. When
she called, Tom's name was not mentioned. If my parents needed to call her
and Tom happened to answer the phone, they would hang up instantly. This
went on for two years.

Then one night, Laya worked up the courage to broach the subject with
my mother over the long-distance telephone. I was in high school at the time
and Laya was in her early twenties. I picked up the upstairs telephone receiver
in mid-conversation to listen in. I remember hearing my mother's voice rising,
the edges of her German accent sharpening.

"No, there is nothing more to discuss, Laya. The only relationship between
a man and woman is with *chuppah* and *kiddushin*, a Jewish marriage. And we
don't invite a goy under the *chuppah*, God forbid! That is the beginning and
the end of this conversation." My mother was attempting to hold down her
fevered pitch. Her comeback was rapid-fire, as if she had been waiting for this
encounter all of her adult life. I knew that Laya had prepared herself, too, but
by this time her words faltered.

"Wait a minute, I understand. I do. But isn't there any way... I mean,
couldn't we just come and talk?" Laya was swiftly cut off. My mother's voice
slapped her back with indignation.

"That is out of the question! Altogether, out! That man has no place in our
home. No, we are not prepared to meet him. Any man who truly loved you
would leave you to your own people. Either that or he can become one of us.
Until that time there is no discussion."

Becoming *one of us*, of course, meant conversion. But no perfunctory conversion would do. It would have to be an Orthodox conversion, and that meant
that Tom would need to study to become an Orthodox Jew. He and Laya
would be expected to create a kosher home and undertake all of the Jewish
commandments. It also meant that Tom would have to undergo a circumci-
sion, a requirement that would produce second thoughts for any man in his
mid-thirties.

I chuckled to think of Laya and Tom living an Orthodox lifestyle. They were far too free to even consider such a move. I was invested in Laya and Tom's staying right where they were, in farflung locations, always colorful, my allies in outrageously alternate lifestyles. Tom came from a warm Italian family, and he himself was twinkly-eyed and affectionate. He loved to laugh and tease, but his remarks were never cynical. Tom practiced no religion, although as a baby he had been baptized in the Roman Catholic Church. He was an artist, and it was there that his natural spirituality lay. He painted and took photographs, and his eye seemed to be ever appreciative of the shifting of light and color around him.

Tom's relationship to the material world was completely foreign to me. Jews are often timid, even afraid of the mechanical realm of life. I never saw my father, for instance, change a flat tire or roll up his sleeves to unclog the garbage disposal. Instead, he would call in a specialist. Perhaps the mechanical ineptness (in my case, learned helplessness) found in many Jews is the result of having for centuries been forced into certain professions and not others. On the whole, we were not laborers; we were scholars, money lenders and merchants, always standing slightly outside of the culture that hosted us rather than belonging to it with our hands on. We naturally became more facile with words, numbers, ideas, and music than with plungers and wrenches.

Because of this, Tom's fascination with the physical world fascinated me. Not only could he make anything work—I had seen him repair trucks, boats, toilets—he could also take any piece of junk and make it useful, or at least show you the beauty in it.

Laya was the poet, the feeler. When they were together there was joy. And wherever they lived became my refuge. Their apartments, cabins, and houses were always filled with fantastic collections of colorful street art, blues and jazzy music and zany friends. Around Laya and Tom, the guilt and obligations of my upbringing seemed to lift off my chest; I could breathe and laugh more freely. With them it was clear that life was not meant to be pondered philosophically from a distance, as my parents were wont to do, but to be entered into and enjoyed.

I badly wanted to be like Laya and Tom, beholden to no person nor institution. After all, their lives were, like mine, a big experiment. Only they were further along and better at it than I. I watched them carefully for my next moves.

Even before Laya left home, I had absorbed all the culture she could offer me, idolizing her taste in music, poetry, and books. As the American rock music craze built to a frenzy, I took Laya's lead and listened to Beethoven's string quartets and Bach's cello suites, studied the lyrics of Bob Dylan's songs and crooned to gospel music and blues. Dylan Thomas, Kabir, and Nikos Kazantzakis were favorite poets of hers, and together we would write our own poetry and read it aloud to each other.

Likewise, it was Laya who had taught me about feminism, a legacy that had been handed down to her by our older sister, Shulamith. Shulamith had been sent to the girls'counterpart of Danny's yeshiva in Ohio. After high school, she too had dropped out, studying fine arts in college and graduate school, and eventually becoming a front-runner in the burgeoning radical feminist movement. Her controversial book, *The Dialectics of Sex*, was published in 1970, just as I was entering high school. The book created an uproar around the country, forcefully challenging the validity of the nuclear family and denouncing society's pressure on women to bear and raise children.

Despite its content, which so flagrantly opposed her own choice of lifestyle, my mother took pride in the fact that her eldest daughter's book was being used in feminist curricula around the country and was being translated and sold in countries around the world. My father publicly howled in laughter at Shulamith's outrageous views, declaring her manifesto to be the joke book of the century. I don't think he ever realized just how much his own rigid, patriarchal style had served to shape his daughter's politics.

As for me, the vehemence with which Shulamith wrote her book and the red-hot anger against men in the feminist proclamations of her cohorts scared me. Laya, by contrast, could explain the feminist mission to me in a more reasonable context. She helped me understand that major changes were needed to equalize opportunities for women professionally and socially, but that these changes did not require the end of loving relationships with men. But more important than her words, through her actions Laya modeled to me the capacity for independence and self-expression within a long-term love relationship.

In the area of spirituality, it was Laya who introduced me to a lifelong friend, the *I Ching: The Book of Changes*, the ancient Chinese oracle, which she taught me could be called upon as an ally anytime I needed to steady myself and meditate upon an upcoming decision.

"Everything you could possibly be going through is spoken about in here," she had said patting the yellow book. "It's like the Taoist Torah." Then she showed me how to throw the three Chinese coins to form hexagrams that could be deciphered into a wise, often wry accounting of the problem at hand. The *I Ching* astounded me with its uncannily accurate readings, warnings and advice regarding just about any question I asked, no matter how mundane it was.

"If only the Torah were this clear and concise, Judaism would be a whole lot easier to follow," Laya said wistfully one day. "Judaism is so broad and yet so narrow."

"It doesn't seem broad to me."

"I mean, there are so many thousands of rabbinic texts and interpretations, from so many centuries. All men's, of course. And they all seem to boil down to the same old laws and observances. You would think that with all those great minds working on the meaning of life and how to live it, they would have come up with *some* variations in ideology. There isn't much room for freedom of thought in Judaism, unless you keep your head down."

That was what Laya was doing now, keeping her head down. Growing up Orthodox, we had been rigidly trained that there was only one right way to be Jewish and that way did not include intermarriage. Laya, like so many other Jews, had gone underground with her variance in lifestyle and thinking.

I was secure in my belief that the straitlaced religion of my parents was antithetical to everything Tom and Laya stood for. Of course, I realized the bind they were in, trying to work out a relationship with my parents and be themselves at the same time. But their choices seemed clear and simple. To have any relationship with our parents, Laya would have to continue to play being single and Tom would have to play nonexistent. However uncomfortable this felt, I figured that choosing the alternative would be unbearable. It would mean utterly abandoning who they were in order to adopt a stiff and alien religion and lifestyle. I had no idea at the time the degree of psychic tension that this bind generated for my sister. Nor did I realize what a life-or-death call this choice would create for her.

The year before Danny died, Laya and Tom traveled down from Vancouver in search of land to homestead. After traveling around the States for months, they decided on a fertile little farm overlooking the Mississippi River, just eighty miles south of St. Louis. I was mystified. Why would they even consider a piece of land so near to my parents? Eighty miles from home was creeping dangerously close to the middle-class world in which Laya had grown up. Couldn't they find something in North Carolina or California?

What I could not see as a teenager was that my sister ached to move on with her life, to put down roots, to start her own family. To move from the role of daughter to that of mother, she needed to win the sanction of my parents. Living closer to them would push the issues; there could be no more ostrich play. Our parents would be forced to confront the truth about Laya's life. I could feel the conflict building in the wings, waiting to burst out onto our family stage.

The adventure of buying twelve acres of Missouri farmland with a tiny log cabin on it failed to make any outward impression on my parents. Rarely was it mentioned, and then with smug condescension, a chortle on behalf of Laya's juvenile idealism. But it was fear that was the truer feeling, for the problem they had dismissed was now encroaching. They had, of course, surmised that the homesteading project was a team effort on the part of Laya and her consort (his name would still not be mentioned in the house). The psychic wall erected to keep this loathsome and illicit lifestyle out of sight would have to become thicker and less penetrable.

One Sunday afternoon, Laya and Tom ventured a visit to my parents' suburban home. No sooner had they parked their green Ford pickup in front of the house than my mother grabbed her handbag, my father his smoking cigar, and out the door they marched into Dad's Pontiac Starchief. They screeched out of the driveway and zoomed in the other direction, without greeting, explanation, or contact of an eye. They must have forgotten that I was in the house or they would have torn me away, too, away from Tom and Laya's evil influence.

Laya slunk down in an easy chair in the living room; Tom stood beside her silently, shaking his head. I could not tell from the wide-eyed expressions on their faces whether they were going to burst out laughing at the stoogelike comedy that had just rushed by them or cry at the hopelessness of the situation.

"Another futile attempt. What did we expect?" Laya finally mumbled. Her face was pale, her chest caved in. Tom tried to lift her mood.

"We'll make the trip worthwhile, don't worry. We have plenty of stuff to take care of in town. It's just not going to happen this way. Your mom and dad won't be bulldozed," Tom answered.

"Aren't you insulted?" I asked Tom, looking into his stalwart face.

"I'm used to it by now," he answered. "It's not about me, anyway. Your folks are just stuck on their beliefs. C'mon Laya," he stooped to kiss the top of her head, "we'll find another way. Hey, anyone for ice cream?"

After this event, months went by without contact between Laya and my parents. Her calls were not answered, nor were her letters. For this delicate birdlike woman, given to thoughtfulness and nuance, to caring and reconciliation, no sensitivity was available. There were neither conversations nor negotiations because my parents refused to dialogue, and the innumerable shades of gray that Laya was accustomed to examining in any given problem were irrelevant now in this starkly black and white situation.

During this time, I was away in Europe and Tom and Laya kept themselves busy on their farm. Tom raised the cabin roof, built a stable, drank black coffee with the neighbors, and chopped plenty of wood. In this way he sloughed off the noxious gloom that seemed to be silently weaving its way down from St. Louis toward them, as thick and as muddy as the Mississippi River. It was Laya he was worried about. She was the fragile one, the peacemaker for whom peace could not be found.

Laya took refuge too, in the earth. There were the dogwoods to walk through, ginseng roots to be dug, goats to feed, and an enormous vegetable garden to plant. But she could fend off the tight pain of rejection less adeptly than her mate.

In May, when the call came that Danny was dead, Laya sped home to help. She knew our mother would not receive the news well. After months of no contact, my mother's favored daughter was ushered into her bedroom by Erna, a friend from the synagogue sisterhood.

"Kate, look, she's here," Erna announced loudly in an attempt to penetrate my mother's stupor. "You can rest easy now, Katie. Laya's arrived."

"Finally," my mother sighed, and Laya proceeded to take over, caring for my mother in a way that only she knew how. No word of thanks was offered for her coming, nor of apology for keeping her away. There was an emergency at hand, after all, and there was much to be done. For six weeks, Laya dutifully nursed our mother, mediating the well-wishers who flurried around her and listening to her bemoan her fate. Tom, of course, was obliged to stay away.

By the time I arrived on the scene in July, Laya was back on the farm with Tom. It was now my turn to listen to my mother weep, my father lecture. I called the farm frequently to report to my allies the emotional temperature of the family, my little brother's inability to communicate his feelings, my mother's preoccupation with how this was all looking from the outside. We would laugh off our father's predictable judgments, and they would listen compassionately to my disdain and deep disappointment at coming home to a family unchanged by tragedy. I noticed that Laya's name was barely mentioned around the house now, nor was her relationship nor the fact that she was now practically our neighbor. The emergency had passed and with it, Laya had been released to the other side of our parents' unspeakably cold psychic wall.

Though I rarely saw Laya now, living as I did under my parents' roof, I rested comfortably on the assumption that at least she and I were on the same side. Born into a family touted for its upright religious principles but whose spirituality was more difficult to detect, I relished my relationship with a sister who could support my burgeoning views about life. I would excitedly share with her my latest discoveries: the wry philosophy of Alan Watts, the poetry of Gerard Manley Hopkins, the channeled material of Seth. And always there were dreams.

"So, listen to this!" I reported to Laya one night on the phone. "Mom had a big dream about Danny last night. You know, the kind that feels real. She said he looked absolutely marvelous and was laughing all the way through it, only not at her, but just about life."

"Well, did he say anything to her?" Laya asked.

"Yeah. He told her he isn't really dead after all. That it was all a bad story and that he is just fine and very much alive now. So then in the dream Mom goes around and tells all of her friends: 'What a ridiculous mistake, he's not dead at all!' And she's elated about this news."

"What a great dream. Did it lift her spirits?"

"Actually, no. I thought it would, but she's really bummed out today. She says that the dream was rubbish, a trick of her mind. That it probably came out of indigestion of a heavy dinner. I think she missed the point of it."

"That Danny is still alive and well? Happier than ever to be liberated out of his mess of a life?" Laya chuckled. "What's the point of the dream to you?"

"Yeah, that his soul is free again. And also that Danny hasn't stopped trying to get through to Mom what's really important in life," I surmised.

At twenty, the message that I distilled from my mother's dream and others like it was becoming the foundation for the spiritual beliefs that I still hold to this day. I was beginning to understand even then that the soul, the eternal essence within all of us, wants badly to inform and guide us along our way—as it was guiding my mother through her dream. It begs us to look beyond the outward appearance of things to our greater potential. And we—that is, our personalities or egos—must be open to the guidance, allowing it to stretch us further and further with the new possibilities it presents.

Years later I learned that Jung had called this godly potential within each one of us the Self. This unique individuality—which we call in Judaism the *neshama Elohit*, or godly soul—does indeed want to make contact with the ego, the particular expression of the Self that we are at this moment and which is identified with all the memories, beliefs, habits, and behaviors we have accumulated.

Throughout Judaism is found the idea that God requires humans in order to become manifest on earth and to complete the act of creation. In the same way, the Self, the individual godliness implanted within each of us, requires the ego to do its bidding. The relationship between the ego and the Self is reciprocal: Without the ego, the godly Self within us cannot manifest on earth. But without the Self to guide and inform our small ego selves, we lose our moorings in life, we feel hollow inside, and our zest for life disappears.

During a crisis, our ego identity is challenged. When one goes through a severe loss, for example the death of a loved one, it is common to find that the beliefs and ideas that have gotten us through life thus far no longer match our experience. In our state of devastation, our old map of reality simply doesn't work anymore. Then we are confronted with a choice. We can surrender our old beliefs, allowing our egos to fissure and die a temporary death while guidance from the Self reshapes us into a new, bigger form. This option, which ultimately allows for enormous growth, can feel terrifying in the short term, demanding of us nothing less than walking in sheer darkness. Or we can try to avoid the humiliation and pain of our ego's temporary disfiguration and fight the process of change. This requires a white-knuckle approach, a holding on for dear life to what has served as our raft in the vast ocean of life even though it is full of holes.

Many of us choose to reject the Self's message, as my mother did in rejecting the dream, opting instead for the comfort and security of old beliefs. In this case, the message—that the soul is far bigger than our purview—almost made it across the threshold of my mother's consciousness, before it was rejected upon waking by her entrenched set of beliefs. The Self will try again and again to reach out to us in the form of dreams or intuitive guidance. Ultimately, though, it needs us to be receptive, to be in relationship with it, to allow its voice to be heard through the armor of our ego's defenses.

After several months had passed, the shock of Danny's suicide subsided and Laya's painful situation was again hidden. My parents resumed their lives, now more tenacious than ever in their convictions. The opportunity that the tragedy had presented them had passed. Slowly the familiar contours of social normalcy reemerged. My mother got busy again with her upkeep of a big house, her friends, her community functions and doctor's appointments. My father went back on the road, and my younger brother, Isaiah, to high school. Even the footloose youngest daughter seemed acceptable to the family picture now, having returned home to be close to her parents, to save some money and go back to school.

On the inside, however, I was different, changed by my travels and the small tastes of spiritual freedom I had been granted along the way. And I was watching on the sidelines as the family drama continued to unfold, waiting for a signal that would guide my next move. Release, I hoped, would come soon, because under the surface, I knew things in this family were desperately wrong.

After midnight one night early in November the phone rang. I was in bed reading a book by Krishnamurti and stroking Katmouse. Not wanting my mother to be awakened, I dashed to the old hall phone just outside my bedroom, thinking it was one of my crazy boyfriends. It was Tom, his voice sounding broken and exhausted.

"Listen, Miriam. Laya isn't well and I thought you should know."

"What's wrong? What does she have?". I asked, alarmed.

"I've got to believe she's going to be okay. But she's falling apart, tired and weak. Not eating." Tom was rambling, uncharacteristically upset, even scared. "I guess it's an accumulation of a lot of things," he went on. "All the stress she's been under this year, you know, with Danny dying and how your folks have been to us and all. It's all been so heavy for her."

For a brief moment there was silence between us and I could hear Tom's heavy breathing through the phone. It sounded like someone about to burst out in sobs. Fear ran through me. Then he spoke.

"Sometimes it's hard to keep from cracking under the strain," he managed. When I started to question him, he grew evasive. "Look, I've got to go now. It'll all work itself out. I've been through stuff like this myself. We'll be okay." With that he hung up.

I called the farm many times over the next two weeks but never reached Tom or Laya. I wrote them letters, sent Laya inspirational quotes and comical clippings, prayed, for what I did not know. When I did not hear back from them, I told myself that they needed space from the family for a while (a sentiment I well understood) and that I would hear from them shortly.

During those weeks, as the sunlight waned more each day and the Missouri hardwoods took the shape of naked bones against the graying skies, my loneliness began to creep up on me in an ominous way. I was accustomed to coming home from my clerical job and flying up the stairs to strip off my work clothes and don my jeans. Then I would call for my friend, Katmouse, who would skid forth from his play to receive my cuddles and recharge me with his licks and purrs and open-bellied play. Katmouse was a free spirit; having been born and raised on Tom and Laya's farm, he was a reminder to me of the carefree life on their land. Now he was bonded to me, his new owner.

One evening I arrived home from my job to an empty house. I felt chilled by the yawning darkness around me and uneasy with the feelings that wanted to surface from behind the cheery mask I wore at work. Like unwanted news, the tightness crept its way into my chest and then emerged as intense fear. I was used to holding it at bay these days, the fear about my sister's well-being, and just beyond it, the gnawing questions about my own life's direction. As I went to turn on lights and set up the thermostat, I realized that my little friend had not greeted me. Damn, I thought, my parents must have let Katmouse slip out as they left the house. Who knows how long he's been waiting for me in the cold? I threw my trenchcoat back on and clenched my arms around me as I went out to call for him. It had been drizzling and now the moisture seemed to hang in midair like a sharp coat of glass. I whistled for Katmouse and instantly spotted the flash of his green eyes signaling to me from the oak tree across the street. He had heard my call and began making his way down the old tree to come to me. But Old Bonhomme Road was still frenetic with evening traffic, tires crashing through the newly forming ice, drivers tense to make it home. No sooner had I lost sight of Katmouse's lithe body jumping out of the tree than I heard a screech of tires. I screamed. Then the line of cars began to pass again. No one had stopped. But Katmouse's broken body somehow made its way into my arms. He had lunged away from the car's blow back to me, not bloody but severed in many pieces under his loose skin.

I could see he was dying and raced for my car. "Little friend, don't leave me," I wailed. I put him in my lap and drove one-handedly at a furious speed to the after-hours Humane Society hospital. My other arm hugged Katmouse's trembling body to my belly. "I need you. Don't leave me behind, please!" I blubbered as I drove recklessly through the darkness, not caring whether or not I, too, was hit and lost to this world.

"He couldn't be saved," the veterinarian informed me gently at the clinic after examining Katmouse. His spine had been too badly mangled by the impact of the car. I had to say good-bye to him that night and I came home alone, in deep anguish. My parents were unusually gentle with me that night when they heard what had happened to Katmouse. They had complained bitterly about having to bear an animal in their house, but now even they looked sad to lose this affectionate little creature. Their kindness, however, was lost on me; I had removed myself to an unreachable territory of despair.

The next days I experienced a grief denser than I had ever known. I dressed in grays and blacks and noticed that everything around me had likewise become ashen. I dragged myself through the day as if in a dream, responding flatly when spoken to, caring little about my performance at work. Without the soft constancy of my little friend as a buffer, the questions and raw loneliness of my life felt like knives on all sides, threatening to slice me. But I had neither answers nor a defense; I did not know what I was doing in my life, and now my mentors were falling away. Laya seemed to be hanging in suspense somewhere, I was not sure where, inaccessible and floundering for her own life.

On Sunday morning about a week later my father appeared at my bedside. I felt him standing over me nervously. The bare November trees rattled in the wind, occasionally scraping my second-story window. I was still half asleep when my father spoke to me.

"Get up, Miriam. It's almost ten. Besides, I have some news for you."

"I'm just finishing a dream, can you hold it for a minute?" I mumbled up at him fuzzily.

"No, this is better than a dream," he answered eagerly. From the darkness of my pillow, I registered in his voice a certain vivacity that I had not heard from him in years. Then he began pacing to and fro like a little goat in my narrow bedroom, raising the blinds and picking up items of clothes off the floor as he went. I turned on my side and squinted to take in the sight of him.

"What's going on?" I finally asked.

"We have a *mazel tov* in the family, Miriam. Your sister is getting married. Can you beat that?" He was grinning now, a huge satisfied grin.

"*What* are you talking about?" I asked, both shocked and defensive at once.

"I'm talking about your sister, Laya, that's what. She's getting married. It's all set for next week."

"What is?"

"The *chasnah*, the wedding, Miriam, aren't you listening? We've had a big turnaround here." Looking distant, he paused and shook his head as if to penetrate his own disbelief. Then he turned back toward me. "Now get up, will you?"

I sat up in bed. There was that feeling again, the creeping sense of alarm inside my chest. What had been going on without my knowing it this time?

"To whom?" I asked wincing.

"To Tom, who else?" he replied as if stunned by my stupidity. Tom. My father had spoken the unspeakable name, the name of the goy that had brought anguish into their lives, the heinous name, never the man, that had taken their daughter off course. Now he spoke this name as if Tom were the synagogue treasurer.

"Tom's converted. He's a *ger* now. He did it entirely on his own. We just spoke to Rabbi Klein. And to Uncle Shomshon from Israel. It's totally kosher. They both said so."

I sank back down in bed and pulled up my blankets, staring up at the pink ceiling. What was he talking about? I *knew* Tom; they didn't. His life was being an artist, a free spirit. For him to become a Jew in the nominal sense was one thing, I reasoned to myself, but that had never been given as a way out of the crazy-making deadlock. The only kind of Jew my parents would consider accepting as their son-in-law was one who practiced as they did: strict adherence to the laws of kashrut and Sabbath. Yet I knew that Orthodox conversions took months, even years to prepare for—unless perhaps, a life was at stake.

I wondered if Tom had been secretly studying all along. I tried to imagine him wearing a yarmulke and donning *tefillin* in the morning, and Laya observing the monthly laws of purity and ritual immersion. If any of this were true, the ambling, free and breezy atmosphere of their lives was done for. I stopped myself; this thinking was all fool's play. Tom would never willingly sign up for such a thing, and in her sanest hour, Laya would not have asked him to do this.

"Are you sure?" I asked weakly.

"Of course I am. Tom was circumcised and the works. So get up now. Your mother could use some help. There's a lot to do."

This was all moving too quickly for me. I no longer knew where the sides lined up or whose side I was on. Tom a Jew. How could this decision have been made without me? Once my father flurried out of my bedroom, I threw the aging chenille bedspread around me and dragged myself into the bathroom with the black rotary hall phone. I dialed the farm.

"Tom, it's me. What's going on? Daddy is being incredibly pompous—"

"It's true, Miriam. What he's saying is true. I converted. The only reason I didn't tell you is that it all happened so fast. I just spent my first Shabbos as a Jew, and Laya's doing much better, thank God."

"Hold on. I just don't get it. I mean, why?" I stammered.

"It felt like an emergency. For Laya's sake."

I could not speak for some while. Then I managed to say, "I'm happy if you are, but God... who am I going to run to if you're one of *them*?" My attempt at a chuckle fell flat. "I mean, you're not really going to be Orthodox now, are you?"

"Yeah, I am. We are."

I suddenly felt dizzy. Still holding the black receiver to my ear, I dropped my head.

"Look, Miriam. The important thing is that Laya is going to make it." His voice was hoarse with exhaustion. *Make it?* I repeated to myself. What was he trying to tell me? He cleared his throat and continued. "She's coming back to life. Since I told her my decision to convert on Thursday she's put on four pounds. Can you believe that?" There was a long pause, then he continued. "It was getting scary. She kept getting thinner and thinner, disappearing." I could hear him fighting back his tears. The strain he was under felt to me like a broken tree ready to fall. His words came fast now. "So I started to pray. And it worked. It really worked. It all got clear to me when I prayed. God answered me. It was like a voice answering me and I knew what to do. That I could become a Jew now. That I needed to become a Jew. That's when I called Rabbi Klein. That was Wednesday night. It feels like a year ago."

"Wow," I said, staggering for my place. What could I say? I tried empathy. "Did it hurt?"

"What?"

"I hear you got circumcised."

"What do you think?" he answered. "Don't worry, it wasn't so bad. I'm okay now. And Laya's getting stronger each day. You'd be proud of her."

I cut the conversation short, leaving the black telephone on the bathroom floor and dragging myself back to bed. I did not know what I was feeling. I fell back into a heavy sleep until my little brother came to get me up.

FROM A DISTANCE, it all looked like a beautiful, even magical resolution to a painful story. As the news spread, the whole community was abuzz, calling and dropping by gifts. Laya appeared with Tom at her side the following week. She was extremely thin and more frail than anyone in my family had ever been. Tom was his forthright and friendly self, looking my parents directly in the face and shaking hands with each one. They sat down together quite joyfully over coffee and cinnamon babka. My parents reviewed with them the arrangements they had hastily made for the wedding, which would occur in three days'time. I stood off to the side, watching with amazement as Tom and Laya chatted with my parents. They looked worn but genuinely happy to be sitting there. I wondered to myself what had really gone on behind the scenes of this decision to convert and marry.

The wedding, which was held at Rabbi Klein's home, was small and intimate, and for this I was grateful because Laya seemed so fragile. She broke down once with profuse weeping and trembling after the glass was broken, and for a second Tom and I exchanged worried looks. But she made it through.

When they emerged from their private room just after the wedding ceremony, Laya came directly to me, squeezing my hand first and then hugging me hard with her slender little arms. I thought she was going to whisper something to me like "This doesn't mean what it looks like. Tom and I are still the same." But she never did. And after the wedding, Tom and Laya were not the same, for me. After partaking of toasts to their happiness and some delicacies that my mother had prepared, the new couple left for a brief honeymoon, with a suitcase full of kosher foods packed by my parents.

For a long time, I was in awe of Tom and Laya's largesse, having come the whole distance to meet Mom and Dad without any compromise on my parents' part. Nevertheless, I could not help but harbor some discomfort about how Tom and Laya now allowed themselves to be pampered by the very people who so recently had been so cruel to them. Gifts abounded from my parents: new dishes, a set for meat and a set for milk, of course, and their Passover dishes to come in the spring; new linens; new luggage; and lots and lots of instruction and advice to Tom (when to pray, when to fast, when he can work and what cannot be done on Shabbos). Never would I have permitted myself the whim of imagining Tom in a yarmulke or sitting at our Shabbos dinner table eating chopped liver, or seeing Mom flutter about in this uninhibited, careless love for Laya as she did now. Now it became a regular event to see Tom in synagogue standing dutifully next to my father.

Baffled, I wondered at the nature of this strange drama: Was it a tragedy or a comedy? I figured that only time would determine that. For now, I knew nothing but the immediate blow of betrayal, unintended as it may have been. The pain of my mentors' "defection" rippled throughout my young psyche; I now stood shockingly alone.

This event was one of my first ego deaths. Although I tried to stay stalwart and look on the positive side, my world—built upon the fragile structure of my mentors—had collapsed. Now, after having endured several more such experiences myself, and witnessing the phenomenon in my clients and congregants, I am more familiar with the territory.

The wrenching that follows a disappointed relationship, whether it be a betrayal, abandonment, or a simple parting of the ways, is one of the many times our egos will die as we travel through our lives. Each death seems to shatter us anew. But buried in our ego's wreckage lie the seeds of our own next blossoming. If we can allow ourselves to be true to our pain, neither distracting ourselves from it nor ameliorating it with some new fancy, the pain can guide us back to ourselves and a higher voice of wisdom.

The act of returning to ourselves and to the voice of our own *neshama Elohit* is known in the Jewish tradition as *teshuvah*. The cycle of Jewish holidays, particularly the High Holidays in the autumn, are specifically designed to help us do the work of introspection and coming home to ourselves. But we do not have to wait for the holidays; life presents us with ample opportunities to return to the Self all the time.

The process of returning to this larger Self is something like trying to see in one's own blindspot: It is ever so close yet inscrutable. In trying to know that which is us but is just out of our range of vision, it is very common to project the Self onto the screen of others, as I had done with my older siblings, investing them with the wisdom and the answers that we have inside ourselves but cannot yet access on our own.

The process of projecting Self onto others is universal. It usually begins with our parents and continues with friends, lovers, and teachers throughout life. It is the ego's way of growing, modeling itself on those that reflect back its own dormant qualities. Problems occur only when we remain ignorant that the projection is going on and, more important, when we do not eventually *reclaim our projection*. This means realizing that the people upon whom we have projected our wisdom are mere mortals, making their own way through life in the best way possible for them.

The growth and empowerment that occurs for us after we have reclaimed our projection necessarily comes by way of loneliness. With our Self no longer projected outwardly, we are thrown back on our own resources—which are usually greater than we give ourselves credit for. Then we must realize that ultimately there is no map to follow but the one we ourselves compose.

So it was for me. Now four of my elders had ceased, in one way or another, to be guides upon the way: Danny was dead, Shulamith had gone into a territory too militant for me to follow, and the most beloved of all, Laya and Tom, had defected. The strength and clarity I had projected upon them had shattered, and it was upon me to find those qualities within.

But it was not only my elder siblings that ceased to provide me with guidance and safe refuge. Judaism itself (at least my parents' version of it) had sorely disappointed me, too. I had seen how their Judaism, in a crisis, had exhibited little capacity to accommodate the ideals I valued so preciously: the freedom to find one's own way in life, and the need to honor love above all else. In God's book, was it *ever* correct to hurt outsiders, as Tom had been hurt?

I began to ask myself questions about my own allegiance to this heritage of mine. What would I do if someday I stood face to face with a similar dilemma, having to choose between my tribe and family and the yearnings of my heart? My answer was hard-nosed. For now, I had no taste for belonging to the Jewish world if it meant an abdication of my dream, which was to find a spirituality that could coexist with my freedom. If the religion of my birth could not accommodate my searching, questioning, freedom-bound nature, then I would have to find spiritual sustenance elsewhere.

Slowly, silently, I felt the heat of a secret stagelight shift in my direction. Soon, it would be my turn to make choices, to decide who I was and where I stood on life's stage. I now felt myself to be on my own more deeply than ever before. For the next leg of my journey, only I could lead the way.

CHAPTER THREE

ALTARED STATES

AFTER THE WEDDING AND THE SEVEN NIGHTS OF CELEBRATION FOR THE NEW bride and groom were over, I cleared out the drawers and closet in my childhood bedroom and packed my things tightly into the heavy Greek army backpack I had used to hitchhike across Europe. As I packed, I entertained the possibility of simply dropping out again. How free it would feel to cut loose from my family, from the entire American culture, and buy a ticket to Cuzco or Bombay to hook up with Ron and his buddies, or any of the myriad of footloose spiritual seekers I knew I would find on the road.

I resisted these fantasies, although they gave me temporary gratification. A new chapter was dawning for me, I could feel it, and my wanderlust was beside the point now. Rather than traveling outwardly, I knew the time had come to study the *inner* terrain, to study and strengthen myself inwardly so that I would never fall prey to the forces that seemed to have brought down my brother and sister. I figured that if I could always be within easy access of the universal truths I had discovered, which were far beyond the small-minded goals of culture and religion, then I would be invulnerable to those destructive forces.

I was committed, for example, to keeping my equilibrium and inner stillness, no matter where I was. This meant sitting quietly in some fashion every day and listening in. Although I had studied in Hebrew school about God coming to Elijah the Prophet in a "still small voice," it was only through Christian texts and then my own meditations that I realized we each have access to this interior voice of God. I wanted to hear it, too, and follow the guidance that it would give me.

My picture of God was in flux. The Jewish God had always been portrayed to me as ruling from the outside, as being bigger than life. And while I still held to a God who was imaged and referred to in masculine form, I wanted badly to believe that this God lived inside me as well as in the outer universe. I was certain that He spoke to me through my dreams and moved me by means of my spiritual drives. I wanted to study and cultivate this personal relationship with God; I had little use for religion. The goal of my birth religion seemed to me to have narrowed to the sole objective of keeping its flocks safe from straying so that its numbers would remain intact. I had no interest in such a narrow vision. I was on a quest for consciousness; I wanted to discover and strengthen the boundaries of my own psyche, and I had a fire inside of me waiting to fuel the expedition.

For fifty dollars a month I rented the third floor of a huge house in downtown St. Louis from a group of university students. It was far enough from the suburbs where my parents lived to allow me the freedom I needed to explore, and close enough to my well-paying job to allow me to continue working and saving money.

My new home was a tumbledown rental that assaulted visitors with the smell of cat urine, marijuana smoke, and spaghetti dinners when they walked through the door. Windemere, as it was fondly called by the four students from whom I rented my room, was not without its charm. Filled with spider plants and colorful rotting rugs, it blared endlessly with the music of the Allman Brothers and New Riders of the Purple Sage. The students divided their time between studying and smoking pot and hashish. While high, they were wont to dissect the world, the very one that they would soon be joining, with the cool sardonic edge that is the tool of complacent twenty-year-olds. I kept mostly to myself at Windemere, feeling a bit like an outsider. Internally, my father's voice berated me for not being a student like them, attending classes and "amounting to something." I would try to remind myself that I was following a different path, one that would only come clear to me in time.

On the first rare occasion that I accepted their invitation to join them for dinner, I was amused to find that three of my four housemates were Jewish. They would lovingly kibitz about their midwestern Jewish backgrounds and their financially supportive parents who were determined that the family agenda be adhered to: academic excellence, marriage to a Jew (preferably from a prosperous family), and financial success. Rarely did I mention my own parents; I did not want to draw undue attention to the queer and cumbersome baggage I was trying to leave behind. Nor were questions asked when I told my roommates that my parents lived in town but would not be visiting me—ever. It was I who was expected to visit them each and every Sabbath, which I did grudgingly, silently bearing their lectures about my wayward, godless lifestyle, which would surely lead me, God forbid, to my brother Danny's end.

From my new home I began to track down various classes and events that I wanted to pursue. I scoured bulletin boards and newspapers for the occasional lecture or coffeehouse poetry reading; there was not much to choose from. But I remembered an intriguing picture in *Life* magazine of a man sitting outside with his arms spread, his thumbs pointing upward and a look of concentration on his face that stunned me. The caption read: *American-born yogi practices Kun-dalini yoga on a mountaintop*. I wanted to develop concentration like that. To my amazement, I found a Kundalini yoga ashram listed in the St. Louis telephone book and immediately made plans to enroll in a class there.

The ashram was in a part of St. Louis I had never seen, where huge stone and brick mansions sat recessed on their perfectly manicured lawns, and even the overarching trees seemed to decorate the yards in prearranged bouquets. The inner city of St. Louis was full of such estates, for sale or rent by owners who wished to flee the ever encroaching urban unrest. Like the others on the block, this mansion-turned-ashram was formidable in size. On the other side of the grand front door, the broad polished wood floors reflected the sparkling chandeliers above. But the fine furnishings one expected to see next were not to be found. All was empty except for the mats and cushions neatly piled on the edge of the large room, a huge gong that sat in front of an empty fireplace, and the altar just a few feet away. The altar, devotedly tended by the women residents, always displayed a freshly lit white candle, a flower or two in a simple vase, and invariably the smoking stick of incense. An ornate brass bell from India also sat on the pure white altar cloth, as well as several pictures of Yogi Bajhan and other holy men from India.

It was in this opulent yet austere setting that I made the anomalous find of the St. Louis Sikhs, six young Americans who lived in the mansion, practicing and teaching the dynamic yoga form that their guru, Yogi Bajhan, had brought over from India in 1968. All of Yogi Bajhan's devotees dressed in pure white garments and covered their hair, just as their religious counterparts in India do.

I was used to head coverings; my father always wore a hat or yarmulke as a remembrance of God above and a sign of humility. Likewise, my mother covered her hair with turbans, scarves, and hats as a sign of wifely modesty. But the Sikhs were even more distinctive in their dress habits than were my parents and most other Orthodox Jews. In their turbans and flowing whites, they were willing to stand out blatantly from any ordinary crowd, having separated themselves ideologically from the mainstream with a rigor and devotion that intrigued me. Hungry to learn more about their practices, I enrolled for the beginner's class.

I arrived at the ashram every frigid, still dark morning at five o'clock. Sliding through the doorway and removing my shoes, I was greeted with a stinging combination of garlic, cardamom, and sandalwood, reminding me that this was no ordinary home. There was no earthly comfort to be had here

at all; it was a place of utmost discipline. For two and a half hours each morning, I would chant and ply my body into various contortions. With eyeballs
stretched and lungs working ferociously, I focused and sweated, burning my
muscles open and pushing my body's limits further than the day before. Then
I would fall back into rest and silence, blood whirring, cleaned out and mindless. At seven-thirty, energized yet internally quiet, I would bow to my fellow
students, mostly resident Sikhs, and drive off to work in an industrial park.

One Monday early in January, I was called into my supervisor's office at
work to be informed that I and eighteen other employees in our division would
be laid off at the end of the month. As I drove home that evening, I pondered the
empty days ahead, void of structure and responsibility. Even losing a schedule
and routine as vacuous as that of an order processer for a business I did not care
about sent a fretful chill through me. It was a little like the rambling loft I had
rented on the third floor of Windemere: so much space in every direction and
impossible to fill. The first time I brought my lover, Allan, into that room, he
exclaimed, "This room is right out of Poe, a perfect place to hang oneself."

He regretted his utterance as soon as he saw me grimace, but it was a point
well taken: too much empty space was not a good thing. Yet I knew that I
would not run out and get another job to replace the one I was losing. Now that
I was not living with my parents, there was no facade to keep up. I did not need
to answer to their friends' questions, nor did I know if and when I would be
back in school. I would sign up for unemployment benefits, collect a monthly
check, and use the time to examine my possibilities.

The only person home the evening I got laid off was Doug, a lanky and
easy-going senior. Together we decided to cook up an economical dinner of
red beans and rice, clearing out all the uneaten carrots, onions, and mushrooms
from the neglected fridge. I told Doug my news, and he was sweetly supportive
of my loss. Cooking together and chatting comforted my uneasiness. We ate
our stew and then departed for our respective parts of the house.

An hour later in a hot bathtub, my world turned inside out. As steam
furled around me, I watched as my journal began to write itself. Prolific prose
exploded through my pen, rife with cynicism and yearning. Who was writing?
The words thrashed and stormed onto the pages of my journal, railing about
a life beyond all appearances, one that thrived despite the melodrama of our
existence, one that demanded to be seen and heard. "Beyond the black and far
from white, our masks are farces of our mawkish plight. High lady, poet, pau-
per and priest, behind all these faces, who's here for the feast? Inconquerable
riddler! Well-hidden you ride me. Go laugh with the gods, but you better well
guide me."

After unfurling pages of mindless and mad poetry, I began to watch myself from above the bath and laugh. Who was I and what was I doing scribbling away like this, pouring forth these uncalled-for tides and rushes of what felt like the absolute truth? Yet I continued; I could not stop. And from the purview of the steamy bathroom ceiling and beyond, I could see myself as a tender young woman standing at the edge of a wild river, not knowing how to cross over. Passions of all sorts streamed forth from my being, and like so many themes and passages of a symphony, they wove themselves together into a bridge made of all the longing, fear, and exhilaration that the far shore evoked in me.

The veils of my unconscious had been mysteriously parted and I could see my life's journey stretched plainly before me. Questions hung about me: Would passion be enough to get me across the river that transected my life? I had lost my guides; could I trust myself to go on alone? Would I be able to abandon the safe world that I had been trained to be content with and venture into totally strange territory without getting lost?

All this while, I noticed a strange sensation of being tugged upon, as if some force greater than myself was urging me forward over the river. Something was calling to me to experiment, to discover, to become the person I was meant to be and who was, quite mysteriously, watching me from behind the veils of time. If my thinking happened to get snagged for more than a few seconds on self-pity or hopelessness or even on missing my beloved Katmouse, I would immediately experience the tugging again, like being yanked along, forced to slide over all of the sticky little hands that reached out to impede my movement.

At some point I was impelled to raise myself up out of the now tepid bathwater and throw on my big robe. I steadied myself and opened the bathroom door, climbing down the stairs. On the landing I met Doug.

"Doug," I managed, looking into his gaunt face, "are you by any chance... feeling strange tonight?"

Doug nodded. He was holding onto the banister. Several seconds of silence passed—then his eyes and mouth opened at once. He stammered, "The mushrooms. Must have been those black mushrooms we cooked in—"

"Oh, my God," I gasped, finally realizing that what I had been experiencing for the past two hours was not a spontaneous poetic emission, but a psilocybin induced trip! Now the nausea I had been experiencing all along reached my consciousness. I held my belly for comfort. Doug and I moaned together for a while, then separated again to follow the journey to the end of its course. Until six the next morning, I wrote, painted and danced. Finally, my body mercifully shut down. When I awoke at eight to call in sick, I saw the four-foot buffalo I had painted on my bedroom wall earlier that morning running in the wind, a memento of my voyage into the unconscious.

Despite the sickness I felt the next day (which magically returned as a wave of nausea whenever I was tempted to experiment further with drugs), I was in awe of what had been revealed to me. I had not received answers but something better, another dimension of my self. Not only had I gotten a glimpse of the road ahead of me, but I had also experienced some new part of myself—a wise, humorous, and caring guide—that I had not known was there. I felt safer now. If I had opted out of the safe domain of my parents and tribe, now I saw that there was some other guidance available to me from within.

This was my first vivid experience of my *neshama Elohit* or Self. It had, of course, been at work behind the scenes of my life all along, but the guidance of the inner Self is usually visible to us only in retrospect. This was a rare occasion, to witness this omniscient force—my own being—in action! It became clear to me then that the Self was both far greater than anything I knew myself to be, and yet utterly identical to my own being. I have been meditating on this paradox ever since.

It took me several days after my journey to gather the strength I needed to return to the Kundalini ashram. I was happy to get out of the dusty clutter of Windemere to spend a few hours in the ashram's pristine emptiness and utter quiet. I had already advanced to a more rigorous class by this time, taught by the ashram director, Gurutej Singh, an austere-looking man with a long red beard and a ceremonial sword in his sash. He commenced each yoga session with chants in Gurbani, the Sikhs' language. I had a vague understanding that I was singing to an ancient guru and about various noble truths, but mostly the words made little sense to me. This was not unlike the Hebrew liturgy I had sung in synagogue, the literal meaning of which I understood but which had very little relevance to my worldview. In the ashram, however, unlike in the synagogue, I had permission to belt it out, to sing with passion at the top of my lungs. Nobody seemed to think that women needed to remain demure, or hold their voices down to a delicate pitch. Or if they did, they never mentioned it to me.

Gurutej Singh led the breathing practices with such ferocious concentration and vigor that I came to understand the symbol of the teacher's sword. These practices were a form of warriorship, nothing less, using the sharply concentrated mind to surpass the boundaries of one's physical and mental limitations. The yoga postures were accompanied by rigorous patterns of breathing. We were taught to hold an intention throughout, to raise the body's energy up the spine to the third eye chakra. This was done by drawing the breath in sharply and deeply, holding it, and turning one's focus just between and above the eyes.

The breath of fire was the exercise I found most thrilling. While holding a steady posture, we were commanded to breathe rapidly, exhaling in stacatto blasts from the belly out through the nose. After bellowing this breath of fire for what felt an interminably long period of time, the teacher's barking order came.

"Pull it up!" Somehow he could actually speak while in the midst of this practice, making him sound like he was in the midst of drowning. The students all sucked in powerful drafts of air through their noses.

"Keep it up!" Gurutej would manage another command. I held in my breath at the uppermost portion of my lungs, thinking upward, holding upward, looking upward. My body vibrated, shook. Sweat poured out.

"Longer!" Gurutej commanded. "Stay high above the world! You can do it! " I could do it. I held my breath and my intention for as long as was required. I had a fervent drive to discipline myself, to channel my energies, to halt my mind's constant criticism and chatter. It worked. With the command to release the breath came an exhilarating relaxation and a mind quiet and free of voices. My face tingled; purple waves of energy broke over my exhausted body. This was joy.

Cultivating awareness in the third eye center seemed to be, like the Sikhs' dress and turban, another way of keeping oneself collected and separate from the many energies that distracted and ensnared one in life. Over time my own gaze turned inward and my concentration steadied. But I had doubts about the wisdom of holding my mental focus so high up when I was outside of yoga practice, as my Sikh friends were wont to do; I was not sure that I wanted to separate myself that much from the world.

On the other hand, I was not interested in the mainstream world, certainly not the Jewish one. One Saturday night as I drove by the Jewish Community Center, I noticed that Rabbi Shlomo Carlebach was giving a concert that very evening. Shlomo and I were cousins by marriage. But unlike my wing of the family, his had lost many to the Holocaust, and Shlomo had dedicated himself to reviving the joy and depth of the Jewish tradition through his music. When Shlomo sang, accompanying himself on guitar, he would go into such an ecstatic state that he would literally jump up and down in place, sweat pouring down, inspiring even the most lethargic of Jewish audiences to break into dance and song around him.

My family thought Shlomo was a nut. It was not that he wasn't religious enough, it was that he was a wild man. Why did he have to go around like that, hugging and kissing everyone, calling people *holy brother*, or *holy sister*, always personal, always overflowing with love? They made fun of him and called him the black sheep of the family. But though they rolled their eyes about him, they could not deny that his music was superb. He had composed hundreds of songs based upon Jewish liturgy and Torah, which were used throughout the Jewish world.

I had been driving to a late night of chanting and pranayama at the ashram, but something compelled me to turn into the parking lot, and I snuck into a packed auditorium. The concert was already well under way and Shlomo was standing on a table at the center, his yarmulke pushed back on his balding head, sweat drenching his graying curls, his eyes turned up. He was singing a refrain, "*L'Khavod Shabbos, L'Khavod Shabbos,*" for the glory of Sabbath, alternating with a true story about a man whose devotion to the Sabbath had gotten him trapped in the Holocaust. The audience swayed around the emotional rabbi in rapt attention. After the story was done, Shlomo looked out into the audience, back from the trancelike state he had been in.

"Who is that?" he asked looking my way with his hand over his brow. "Could that be my holy cousin? Miriam Tirzah, is that you?" I felt like running but froze in place. It had been years since I had seen Shlomo and I was caught off guard. I managed a little wave in his direction. Sensing my embarrassment, he then announced a short intermission, laying down his instrument and heading in my direction. I stood there stiffly as my cousin proceeded to ply me with hugs and kisses.

"I wondered what happened to you! How are you? I died a thousand deaths to hear about your brother, Danny, may he rest in peace. I am so, so sorry. What a deep soul he was. So tell me about yourself, Miriam. What's your life like?"

"I don't know," I answered. "I'm into yoga and meditation. I'm staying away from my family for a while. Looking at schools. You know."

"Do you know how much I care about you?" I didn't know what he meant. Why should he care about me? Was he trying to get me back into being Jewish? "Listen, you can visit me anytime," he continued. "Are you ever in San Francisco? We have the holiest shul there, the House of Love and Prayer. Will you visit us? I promise you'll feel comfortable."

"Maybe," I said, still stiff. Others were standing around, anxious to greet the rabbi, and I slipped away and out of the building before the concert recommenced. I felt more comfortable to keep my distance from the Jewish world. Even a black sheep like Cousin Shlomo was too close.

During this time my social life was sparce, consisting almost exclusively of my old school buddies and former boyfriends. Richard, one of my sister Laya's classmates from high school, had come back to town to visit his sick dad. As a girl I had had a crush on Richard, who was prematurely gray and played the guitar with a cool Bob Dylan air. Now, both in our twenties, we were suddenly peers, attracted to each other. I took to visiting him at his parents' rambling home near the university.

It was Richard's father, Morrie, whom I grew to adore. Morrie was a retired family therapy professor and a man of great humor, despite the fact that he was dying of Hodgkin's disease. Morrie engaged me, asking me questions about my life experiences and beliefs and then listening to my answers with genuine respect. Because of his openness, I was able to speak to Morrie about many things—the ecstasy I experienced at the yoga ashram, the conflicts I had with my parents, my fears and aspirations. How deliciously novel it was to be treated as a thinking person responsible for her own ideas, actually to be listened to by a person of my parents' generation, without crashing headlong into their tightly held beliefs and assumptions about how the world worked and how I should be following suit. No parent, uncle, or rabbi had ever listened to me with such open-minded respect. With Morrie, I could actually let down and tell my truth without fear of judgment. It was in Morrie and Annette's home that I discovered how a healthy family life operated and had my first experiences of the quiet, abiding love of a mother and a father. I had begun to reconcile myself to the probability that this sort of love might never come from my own parents, wedded as they were to their picture of how their children had to behave. This saddened me; yet now I had a taste of unconditional love, and I wanted more of it.

Though they were Jewish, Morrie and Annette belonged to an Ethical Culture Society rather than to a synagogue. They were agnostic, and felt it to be inauthentic to pray as Jews, since God was no more than an abstraction to them. The idea that these spiritual people could not sanction God's existence grieved me. I, who also would not attend synagogue unless I was forced to do so, prayed in private every day for Morrie's failing health.

I had free access to Morrie's library and would cart home armloads of his books, devour them, and bring them back for more. As Annette prepared dishes that I had never before tasted, like shrimp cocktail and Thai chicken, Morrie, Richard, and I would sit at the kitchen table and the four of us would talk voraciously about topics ranging from psi phenomenon and psychic healing to drugs, the existence of God, and the power of prayer.

In June, my roommates graduated from the university. In the meantime, I was spending hours reading and researching schools of natural healing and alternative medicine around the United States. I knew that I wanted to be trained to be of service in the world, and my intuition and my tastes led me toward the field of healing. I toyed with the possibility of staying in town and studying to become a registered nurse as recommended by Laya and Tom, who were now living happily on their farm as observant Jews and expecting their first child. They wanted me to remain close to them and safe from the world of experimentation. But I had been gorging myself on the writings of Edgar Cayce, Carl Jung, and Carlos Castaneda, and I was convinced that we lived, as these authors described, in a world of unseen energies and energy fields, currents of emotion, and thought forms. It was clear to me that all of these had a great impact on one's physical health and well-being. My yoga practices had given me direct experience of my own electromagnetic field; I had witnessed how my breath, my voice, and the sound of the gong had vibrated it, purified and strengthened it. A conventional medical training, which would not recognize these invisible realities, was sure to leave me frustrated. Besides, I had no reason to stay in St. Louis; a new world was beckoning me.

A school of herbalism had just opened in Vancouver, British Columbia, and a college of naturopathy in Portland. But finally, Boulder, Colorado, won my attention. A smallish university town in the foothills of the Rocky Mountains sounded perfect to me. It was not the university that drew my interest, though, rather the number of healers, herbalists, and Oriental medicine practitioners that seemed to be gravitating to the area. I had heard that Boulder was becoming a hub for alternative medicine practices of all kinds. An osteopathic student I met at a party had just come from there and had reported on Boulder's "high vibrations." He had shown me his catalogue from the Boulder Community Free School and it made my head swim with possibilities. Offerings included reflexology, iridology, polarity healing, and massage therapies of Chinese, Japanese, and Western varieties. Instructors were local doctors and practitioners, and though courses were not free as the school's name implied, they were quite affordable. No certification was promised, but that was not among my requirements for the moment. I was after the sheer excitement of learning, nothing more.

At the same time, my interest was piqued by another school, the Arica Institute, which ultimately brought about a revolution in my thinking. Richard, whose appetite for personal growth had been whetted by the concept of an eclectic, nonreligious spirituality, had gone off to Maui after graduation from college to sign up for one of the first forty-day Arica trainings offered in the United States. He had returned to St. Louis reporting powerful internal changes in his attitudes and thinking. Even his physical well-being had visibly improved as a result of the training. Now he had connections with Arica followers all over the world; most important, he was happier than ever before.

Arica was a school of mysticism that took the form of multilevel trainings in higher consciousness based on the teachings of the Chilean philosopher Oscar Ichazo. Ichazo had spent his life studying the esoteric principles of many spiritual traditions: Egyptian, Hindu, Buddhist, Sufi, and the thinking of Gurdjieff. But he was not committed to the integral religion or beliefs of any of these paths, rather to gleaning from them the nuggets of psychological truth and the tools that would aid a secular Westerner to work with his mind, body, and emotions to evolve himself spiritually.

I was drawn to Ichazo's nonreligious approach to the development of consciousness. I studied the brochure. Trainings were being held in numerous locations around the world in the summer of 1975, but the one in New Mexico seemed to call my name. My brother had chosen to die in that state; maybe I could learn something from the land that could help me reach some understanding—or at least some peace—about his death. I enrolled in the Arica Institute's forty-day training held in Jemez Springs, New Mexico, mapping out my plan to visit Boulder for a weekend, then catch an overnight bus down to Albuquerque, where I would meet up with others en route to the Arica training.

When my parents heard that I was going to New Mexico, they were appalled. My mother would not speak to me; my father threatened her suicide for her.

"The last thing you need is more of this higher consciousness *me-shugas*, Miriam. And in New Mexico, yet! You couldn't choose any other place? Can't you see how you are killing your mother?" he demanded just before I left. "It will be on *your* head, Miriam, if your mother kills herself because of your stupidity, I'm warning you!"

I did not bother to answer. He was convinced that I was ruining my life, not to mention my mother's. I had tried to reason with him scores of times, but now I had no more energy to argue. I left for Colorado the next week, exasperated that my own parents still had no idea who I was or what I was after. Morrie, Annette, and Richard saw me off to my plane to Denver. With them I could celebrate the changes that awaited me.

FROM THE WINDOW of the airport shuttle, the descent into the Boulder valley by night looked as though we were sliding into a sea of stars. In the morning I was thrilled to behold the town, snuggled into the foothills of the Rocky

Mountains, with its three formidable Flatiron mountains rising vertically at its edge. Boulder's natural beauty had a powerful effect upon me. I walked for hours under azure blue skies, through and around the town, amazed by what I beheld.

Everywhere I went I saw people of the same age, my age or a bit older, mostly American, mostly white and extraordinarily convivial. People like myself, on bicycles or foot, made eye contact with me, greeting me cheerily, ready to engage me in conversation. Their faces and bodies seemed remarkably healthy and unfettered. Women strolled by in long dresses, bare feet, and handmade jewelry. Men wore long hair and yoga pants and were often shirtless. Like me, many I met that day had come to Boulder for some express reason, to study Rolfing or psychic healing or, most prevalent, to meditate and study with Trungpa Rinpoche, the Tibetan Buddhist leader who lived in Boulder and had just founded an institute there for Buddhist studies. As I sat by the creek that flowed down from the mountains and through the town, I spotted groups of Trungpa's followers walking erectly down the path carrying colorful meditation cushions on their way to classes, while others sat or lay basking in the sun, eating and playing the guitar.

Walking through downtown Boulder, I began to feel overwhelmed. Never had I seen bookstores so filled with books on topics such as Eastern religion, natural healing, and alternative lifestyles. Natural-food stores and cafés were also plentiful. Unprocessed and organic foods that were usually difficult to come by were sold in abundance in Boulder. Likewise, notices about scores of concerts and consciousness-raising events were plastered on kiosks throughout town. Programs that I normally would have had to travel great distances to attend in the past were happening every day and night in Boulder: visiting teachers and musicians, open drumming and dance sessions, meditation classes and herb walks.

Nobody that I spoke to there questioned my logic in considering a move to Boulder. They seemed to take for granted that it was a good idea.

"So, you're here to study healing arts," the man at the bookstore said amiably. "Go check out the back area. It has everything you could possibly want."

Everything I could want was indeed here, and more. Then why was I so uncomfortable? Maybe I was experiencing something similar to the agony that people supposedly suffer in paradise, where everything they have always wanted is finally available to them but with none of the earthly limitations they are used to. Boulder presented me with this sort of agony. After one day in this place redolent of the values, the colorful style, and the freedom of mind that I aspired to, I felt as though I was drowning.

How was I to fit in here? I was accustomed to being unique for my beliefs and tastes, which had always stood in contradiction to the mores of those around me. But in this place I was merely one of a multitude like me, neither different nor particularly unique. On the other hand, community would finally come easily in a place with so many like-minded people, and how quickly I would assimilate new information with so much of it at my fingertips!

Finding a Jewish community would, of course, have been my parents' first priority for me, and I was relieved to notice that there did not seem to be any organized Jewish community to speak of in Boulder. In none of my many conversations did the topic of Judaism even arise. This was a distinct selling point for me; I was happy for the time being to be free of my Jewish background.

With all of these thoughts churning away inside me, I boarded the bus for New Mexico the next evening. For hours I sat in sheer wonder at having found a place so utterly vexing and yet so perfectly agreeable at the same time.

The bus rolled into Albuquerque after dawn. The light was different here, it was red. So were the hills and mesas, I noticed. As I waited for other Arica trainees to congregate outside the bus terminal, I sat on my bedroll contemplating the open, expansive New Mexico landscapes I had witnessed out the bus window. I wondered how my brother might have seen them as he entered this state, looking for his enlightenment.

I did not have long to muse. People were arriving and it was time to get organized to drive down to Jemez. On the ride through the New Mexican pine forests, I closed my eyes, half dozing, half listening to the other trainees exchange their stories about how they had stumbled upon Arica. Now I was in for it, I thought to myself. That same sweet distress that I had experienced in Boulder was coming over me again. I could not fight off the sensation of being engulfed. I thought of ways I could bail out and go home, but where was home now? It was time to surrender and trust the force that had led me to my decision to be on this expedition into the unknown. I hoped it was the same guiding force that I had met on my journey in the bathtub. And I was not alone. I noticed that others were exhibiting nervousness as they talked and laughed as well. We were all in this together.

The training was set up in a former Boy Scout camp right in the middle of a fragrant ponderosa and pinyon pine forest. The group would meet for its training in the one large hall, called The Temple. Meals were made in the adjoining kitchen and eaten on the covered wooden deck. For those of us who had not brought tents, there were three-sided log structures for nighttime shelter. There were also outhouses and primitive showers, which, like the sleeping shelters, required a walk through the woods.

The first two and a half weeks I was in New Mexico, it rained without cease. I joked that maybe we were replaying the myth of the great flood, all huddled in a huge evergreen ark for forty days and forty nights. I was not far off: The power and rigor of the exercises we were engaged in enveloped all twenty-eight of us in a rather otherworldly embrace. At twenty-one, I was the youngest in the group, yet I knew enough to foresee that none of us would emerge from our ark without going through some kind of transformation.

The most marked changes took place as we learned the dynamic series of movements called psychocalisthenics, which the group did together in synchrony every morning to exhilarating, rhythmic music. Practiced mindfully, in harmony with the breath, these exercises were designed to tone the body and balance the nervous system, breaking down areas of personal armoring and so expanding one's capacity for breath and exuberance. Many of the trainees were pushed to their physical limits trying to master the headstand or the more rigorous belly exercises. Still, amid the complaints of sore muscles and dizziness, new bodies began to emerge, trim and strong and lithe.

Psychocalisthenics were followed each day by what was called *holy work*, a series of chanting and movement meditations, visualizations, and karma cleaning. Just as the psychocalisthenic exercises broke up areas of muscular holding produced by emotional responses to personal trauma, so the karma cleaning exercises were designed to help break up the calcified areas in the mental structures and deep beliefs harbored in our subconscious minds.

First we were asked to write (at great length) our free associations to hundreds of simple words, such as *fatherhood, tribe, work, independence, sex*. Then we were to speak about all aspects of our personal history in small groups, to elaborate in minute detail, to tell our stories as objectively as possible, and then to repeat them, until they were finally rendered void of emotion, just stories.

There was great resistance to these exercises in the group. Who wanted to admit that their most preciously held beliefs were simply mental constructs and not eternal truths? Likewise the dark areas that store themselves deep in the basement of the psyche—all manner of childhood terrors and shame, personal habits and fears, wounds born of encounters with violence and cruelty and rejection—all of these were invited out into the light of day for examination and sharing.

Through this exhaustive process, which forced me to express myself, listen to my own words, and hear back from my peers their reflections and challenges, I was forced to undress, layer by layer, the handsomely fabricated outer garments of my personal belief system. I was shocked to find that beneath the spacious liberalism that I myself believed I believed, lay the truth of how deeply I had bought and vehemently held to my parents' worldview. Through days of grueling disclosure, I was able to see that at the deepest fiber of my being, I had assented to an ideology that was childlike in its dualistic understanding of the world.

The world, I believed, was separated into holy and unholy, righteous and false, high and low. Male was fundamentally better than female and God Himself was holy, righteous, high, and male. What's more, God was invested in overseeing these demarcations. All wrong or wayward choices were seen at best as a waste of God's gift of life, and at worst as a flagrant insult to Him. This God yearned for His creatures to follow the high road and would punish those who did not.

But my realizations did not stop there. As days passed, I was able to uncover yet more of the beliefs underlying my worldview: that we Jews were radically different from other races, inherently more evolved and formed with a higher potential to do God's will and shed light in the world than any other people. If you were unlucky enough to be born a Gentile, then you had to make the best of it. But to be born a Jew was special, and there was one and only one way to be a Jew and that was to live by the Torah and the letter of its law as defined by the Orthodox rabbinate. Even though I had vociferously rejected my parents' religion, deep inside I still held that the rituals, prayers, and Orthodox norms I had been raised with were absolute and incontrovertible.

It took great courage to unearth these axioms of personal truth, and even more to speak them aloud. The views that I revealed in my group were first received with cynical titters of disapproval. Later, as it became apparent how these narrow beliefs were responsible for much of the pain and tragedy in my life, and how utterly wrenching it was to acknowledge them as the underlying foundation of my world, there was silent awe, support, hands and arms extended my way, even tears of resonance. I allowed myself to weep deeply in this group, and wondered if I would ever be able to change the mental patterns that seemed to be the legacy of generations.

I realized that, despite my best efforts, I saw myself much as my parents saw me: as a bad girl who had rebelled, flagrantly choosing the wrong path just as my brother had. In my family ruled not free will but some other force, powerful and vindictive, that would not let us stray far from the grip of our birth religion. Danny had left the fold under the rabbi's threatening prophecy, "You will not live past thirty," and had ended up by forfeiting his life. I feared that I, too, lived under the same threat and would ultimately get pulled back on a short leash.

What would it take to get *me* back on the straight and narrow road? I wondered. My sister Laya had shifted her wayward course in the knick of time, reversing her choices and saving her life. But although I could see that my inner Jewish dogma held me in a stranglehold, I believed that I had too much curiosity about the world and too much of a universal spirit to end up in a rigid, religious lifestyle. I realize now how naive I was.

All of the beliefs I had ingested whole from my family and culture were being stirred up at their core, and the identity I had slapped on over them—that of a liberated, open-minded, and egalitarian person—was falling away as the paper-thin facade it truly was. I was a fake. But not a deliberate one—rather, the kind of fake all of us are who have not deeply examined ourselves to differentiate between the beliefs that are truly ours and those we were raised with.

Until we do this soul-scouring work, we are living someone else's life, usually our parents', our culture's, or our tribe's, and who we think we are is made up of their dictates. Meanwhile, our authentic identity awaits our discovery. This is who we are in our very cells and in our deepest personal beliefs; it is guided and informed by the bigger Self and emerges slowly over time.

My beliefs lived so deeply in my cells that, as I unearthed them, my body began to show signs of severe stress. I began to break out in purple and pink mounds all over my thighs and torso. Every morning I would awaken with a ferocious itching to find that the rash had spread during the night. After several days of this, pus began to ooze, scabs formed, and the itching grew more extreme. It did not look like poison ivy or sumac, nor did it subside within a week or even two. Finally, beside myself with sleeplessness, I was taken to the hospital in Los Alamos. The doctors shrugged and prescribed cortisone. The symptoms subsided for all of twenty-four hours, and then a new rash, this time bright red, burst out all over my chest and neck. My body was screaming with a message that would not be subdued until it had its say. There was no fooling or ameliorating it; it wanted out.

A healing crisis such as the one I was experiencing, although scary, is actually a positive event. It is often an urgent signal from the more visceral identity forming within us that we need to be attending it. Our distressed physical condition lets us know that this new identity is making its way toward the light of consciousness and needs our conscious help to midwife the process.

One of the Arica trainers, Madeline, noticed my distress. She was somewhat older than the other trainers, with a quiet intelligence about her. One day, Madeline invited me to join her in the trainers' cabin after dark. I accepted.

When I arrived, candles were lit in all four corners of the small cabin. Two sitting cushions, zafus, were set out on the little rug in the center of the floor. Madeline motioned to me to be seated on one and then offered me a cup of mint tea. She sat opposite me on her zafu, and we chatted for a while. Madeline looked deeply into my face as we spoke. After a while, her tone changed.

"So, Tirzah," she began, slowly repeating the name by which I had asked to be addressed at the training. My first name, Miriam, was so full of my troubled past and the people I wanted to leave behind that shedding it was like taking off a cumbersome and ugly backpack that I had almost forgotten I was carrying around. Tirzah, my middle name, felt lighter and freer, like a new start. But even with a name change, I had to go through the hard work of letting go.

"Tirzah, let's say you could call anybody in here to join us tonight, alive or dead. Anybody you need to visit with, right now?"

No sooner had the words left her mouth than I saw Danny's face looming in the darkness. I told Madeline that I saw my dead brother. She set out a third zafu for him, had me face its direction and moved out of the way.

"Go ahead," she prompted, "talk to him as if he were right here. Don't hold anything back."

So I spoke to my brother just as if he were right there. At first I chatted glibly about the training and how much more fun it was than Zen, and how I wished I could talk to him about it. And then I felt a great crimson wave beginning to swell inside of me, hot and fast, building and rising to the surface. Seconds later, I was up on my feet, facing the flickering darkness of Danny's image and wailing loudly. The long chords of my cries pierced the night, higher and higher in pitch until I was on my knees, beating my fists down on Danny's pillow, his surrogate being, again and again.

"You bastard, you left me! You *left* me! You took the easy way out and left me. I can't do it myself! I can't do it alone! *I need you*, do you hear me? I need you!"

Now I was sobbing, bent over the pillow, over the body I had never said good-bye to, clutching it, clinging to it. "Don't leave me, Danny, please, I need you," I cried over and over again until I had exhausted myself.

Madeline sat closer now, a silent witness to an inner storm she had been watching build within me for days and which was finally being released. She offered me tissues and tea, stroking my back as I lay whimpering. Finally she spoke.

"Danny is on his own journey now, Tirzah. You know you need to let him go."

"I know," I answered bleakly. "I know, only tonight I needed to not be so grown up. I needed to be little and pissed off and afraid."

"And there may be more of those feelings in there still. But enough for tonight. Go take a hot shower and drink a lot of water before bed."

It was well past midnight by the time I got to my cabin. The next day, Madeline checked in with me. I was weak and my throat was raw from yelling, but I felt lighter and far more at peace. I had, of course, hoped to wake up the morning after my intense emotional outpouring washed clean of all bad feelings and healed of my skin disease. But it did not happen so simply. It took more work, daily ritual done on my own.

Madeline dictated to me the steps of a simple Arica ritual called the Memoriam Ritual. I was to do it once a day, she said, and it would help me to continue and deepen the work of releasing Danny that I had begun the previous night. First, I was to light a candle and chant om with a ritual bow. Then I was to bring my brother into mind, remembering his qualities and holding him in my mind in his most radiant, happy self. When I could see him clearly in this way, I would send a wave of compassion to him from my heart. The closing was blessing Danny with the highest possible evolution in his next incarnation, then a final om.

I thanked Madeline for this ritual and practiced it daily, despite the resistance and anger that often arose at having to let Danny go. I had a tiny photograph of him in my wallet and I placed it on my personal meditation altar just under my candle. I would slip away to do this ceremony whenever I felt depressed or lonely and every evening before sleep.

I had heard my mother tell a story of an old Jew who had lost his wife in the death camps. He could not make peace with her death, so a rabbi showed him how to use the Mourner's Kaddish as a daily encounter with her soul. Every day when he prayed he would close with the Kaddish, but he would talk to his wife first, from his heart, and tell her all the things he needed to say on that day. After months of this practice, he found his peace. I considered using the Kaddish, but I had been taught that it was a prayer that could be said only by Jewish men in a quorum of Jewish men. The Arica ritual was far more accessible to me. But I took the rabbi's idea and expanded upon it, talking to Danny as I had on that one night, telling him what I had learned that day, discussing his choice to leave and the effect it had on me, railing at him, joking with him, taking him off his pedestal and teaching him.

After a week of doing this ritual, I realized that I was falling into the most profound and untroubled sleep each night. It had been weeks since I had slept so soundly. The angry itching was passing, and every morning when I awoke, I noticed that my rash was less and less volatile, soon becoming merely a passing mark on my skin. My body was regaining its equilibrium, having harbored all of my unprocessed feelings—the hot rage of betrayal and the dark despair of abandonment—until I was ready to deal with them. I had learned that there is no good way to suppress true feelings. My body had forced me to let go, and for this I was thankul.

As for the layer of beliefs that, I had discovered, gripped me at my core, I had no resolution. I had not yet unseated my fear that deep down I shared my brother's fate, and that like him, I would not be allowed to abandon the absolutes that we were raised with. But I had gained insight into my psyche's inner workings, and my knowledge took me one step closer, at least, to being free.

As I entered the last days of the Arica training, I experienced the bittersweet grief of having to take leave of the people, the guidance, and the structure that had cradled me through so many changes. I was not alone in that grief. Several of us discharged our feelings by staying up late each night, drumming and dancing and talking about the impact that Arica had had on us, how our lives would continue to change, what practices we would take home with us and integrate into our daily routines.

As for me, I made up my mind to continue to live in all parts of myself, the spiritual and the animal sides alike, the high as well as the so-called lowly. I wanted to do away with the hierarchy that gave the spirit and mind elitist status over the body. For example, the breathy exhilaration that I got from the psychocalisthenic exercises showed me how much physical awareness and vitality were necessary for energizing the mind and spirit.

Chanting in the various body centers, or chakras, was another tool I would take with me to integrate my body and my psyche. I had learned to love chanting at the Kundalini ashram, but Arica's approach was different. We had been presented with seven simple *bijas*, or syllables, which, when resonated in the various centers of one's body, balanced the entire system.

Oscar Ichazo had taught that each one of the chakras was integral to one's psychophysical health. Rather than always drawing one's energy up into the third eye and crown centers, as I had been taught in my yoga training, it was preferable to open and activate all of one's centers equally. I was surprised to find that toning my voice in my *kath*, or belly center (an area not to be dwelled in if you were an aspiring ascetic), had the most beneficial effect on me of all, because it grounded me and helped me quiet my overly active, chattery mind.

Then there was the altar. At the beginning of the forty days, we had been given a directive to build our own little altars near our beds, as a set location at which to do our rituals and holy work. At first I felt reluctant to make mine. My bunkmate, Ellen, had watched me procrastinate. After erecting her own altar she asked me if I needed some help.

"No, thanks. I just can't get into it. It's so, well... so foreign," I thought out loud. "In someone else's ashram or temple I can tolerate it, but the idea of making my own altar feels really weird to me."

"Could it have to do with your Jewish upbringing? Jews don't pray in front of altars, right?" she asked. She herself was Jewish but did not know the first thing about Judaism.

"No, altars are definitely not Jewish." I replied. Now I was getting warmer. I felt a wave of fear and sadness sweep over me. "I think it may have something to do with my brother's last ritual." I had already explained to Ellen how Danny had shot himself sitting before his brass Buddha. That had been his altar. No wonder I hesitated to make one of my own.

Nevertheless, I did eventually make one, a cardboard box covered by a simple cloth. I had only a candle on it and a *yantra*, a colored geometric mandala tacked up above it to focus my attention. Over the next few weeks, this altar became my special little corner, as I displayed on it the beautiful stones and flowers I picked up on my walks in the woods. I went to it to do my work with Danny, to steady myself when I fell into negative thinking, or simply to get quiet and regain my objectivity. I was determined to make my own altar in my next home. And I was equally determined to use everything I had learned to help myself maintain what I had gained in the last forty days.

On the last day of the training, after a grand all-night party, the trainees and staff exchanged many tearful embraces and farewell blessings that would launch us each back to our respective homes, there to test out our new spiritual wares. I drove off in a '64 Chevy van with five other Aricans on their way to Memphis. The van broke down outside Little Rock and I elected to climb out there and hitchhike back to St. Louis by myself.

I arrived at my parents' door very late the following night, and slipped inside the quiet house. It was late August, and although the midnight air was thick and sultry, the house was chilly from being air-conditioned. Upstairs I put down my pack and pulled out my two souvenir treasures from New Mexico: a colorful shirt embroidered with Native American designs and a turquoise ring. I had found them on a group expedition to Taos one weekend during the training and they now seemed like priceless foreign objects.

Before falling into bed, I set up a little altar under my bedroom window, made of six shoe boxes and a silk scarf. It was my way of assuring myself that I would maintain some continuity of consciousness, even in my parents' home. Sitting before it, I placed a single Sabbath candle into a holder, lit the candle, and bowed, chanting om. I thanked God for helping me get home safely and for all the ways in which I had grown over the past weeks. Then I blew the candle out and went to sleep.

I woke up in the morning to Tom's and Laya's voices downstairs. They were having coffee with my mother; my father was on the road. I came down the stairs wearing my new shirt and ring, and stood just outside the breakfast room. During the moment it took for them to notice me standing there, I watched the family. Was I imagining it, or was there truly a look of deep contentment on their faces? Laya's small body was rotund, now in its ninth month of pregnancy, and Tom stroked her arm devotedly as he finished his coffee and got ready to leave for his new job at Lester Bernheim's insurance office. Tom and Laya were living in St. Louis now, for the time being.

I entered the room to my family's delighted surprise, happy to answer the few questions that came my way, but mostly talking about the forthcoming birth. Even my mother was chipper, clearly reveling in her imminent grandmotherhood. This was not the judgmental, hostile family I had been envisioning in my meditations these past weeks. Could I have seen them mistakenly, looking at them through a warped lens? Maybe it was time for me to let go of my own judgments.

I spent most of that first day back with Annette and Morrie, regaling them with all manner of wild tales and experiences from my Arica journey. Together we howled about my naïveté going into the experience and about how I never would have signed up for the training had I known what I would have to endure. They had known the depth of the work that awaited me and had concluded that I had made a dark descent after the first week, when they stopped hearing from me. Together we celebrated my emergence into greater wholeness. I felt as light as they said I looked.

Late in the afternoon I came home and detected a distinct difference in the air from that morning. My mother was huffing about, speaking to me only to answer my questions and then in cold monosyllables. I headed upstairs to lie down. When I opened the door to my room, I immediately noticed that my altar had been dismantled; it was gone. I raced downstairs.

"What went on in my room?" I demanded of my mother. "Can't I have some privacy in this house?"

My mother finally turned to face me. I commanded myself to look into her eyes, practicing the tools of open acceptance that I had been trained to use even in hostile situations, to silently hold the thought: *We are one.* But my mother's face scared me; her jaw jutted forward sharply and her breathing was rapid and hot. Her eyes met mine, ablaze with rage. No, we were not one, that was very clear.

"Don't you *ever* bring such filth into this house, do you hear me?" she roared.

"Filth?" I asked, confounded.

"There is no room here for your idol worship!" she yelled. "This is a Jewish house! You are a Jew! And may God never let you forget it!" Then she turned on her heel and stomped away from me, slamming the door behind her.

For a split second I stood there stunned, feeling as if I had been slapped in the face. Then I collected myself, shook myself like a cat just in from a rainstorm, and climbed the stairs to my room once again. Years of this sort of abrasive interaction had trained me to quickly discard my hurt feelings and simply move on.

How could I explain to my mother that my little shoebox altar was not meant for idolatry but for paying homage to the God within? It was meant only for my humble prayers to the One who was, at this very moment, guiding me through the chaos of my life toward my purpose. I realized that my parents would never be able to understand that my path had irrevocably diverged from theirs, that what they deemed to be dangerously far off the Jewish track was utterly necessary to my spiritual quest. The sound of the slamming door echoed in my head. I had no hope left of communicating to the people in this house; the distance between us had become unbridgeable.

The alienation that I felt in my parents' home was so profound that it sent me careening back out the door, determined to seek family elsewhere. I had naively come home wanting to share the enormous strides I had made in becoming my own person. It had not occurred to me that the process of examining my belief system, which had brought me such personal liberation, might not produce the same excitement in my family.

Coming home after the first inkling of self-discovery can be a dangerous venture. Families are usually primed to maintain their status quo, and the changes in consciousness that come through the front door can feel threatening, sometimes even triggering more than normal resistance to new ways of seeing life.

The polarization that occurred between me and my family was not the first cut between us, but one in a long series that ended in what seemed to be irreparable alienation. The antidote—respectful dialogue and the honoring of one another's differences—was tragically out of our reach.

The next week, on the Jewish New Year, my sister gave birth to a baby girl. She was named Elianna, which means God answered me. It was a time for new beginnings. I left shortly afterward for Colorado to find my new family.

CHAPTER FOUR

THIS ZAFU LIFE

D REAM, *November 1, 1975. I have decided to marry a young rabbi, and it is my wedding day. I eat a bowl of pure chicken soup and dress myself in synagogue clothes. The family is overjoyed because I will finally be safe and out of the way; my groom accepts me despite the fact that I am a new convert. In the middle of the ceremony, I ask to take a break, wondering how I will ever get out of this. I take off running. Once out of the wedding hall, I pass by my old house and stop to have a look in at my room, my altar, my candle, and my purple zafu. I announce, "This zafu life is now over."*

What a puzzling dream, I mused as I entered it into my journal. I had just begun to live "this zafu life" and it pleased me endlessly, so free and full of new ideas and comradeship. I certainly was not about to give this life up, especially to marry a rabbi!

I was now living in the Arica house, an elegant home near the governor's mansion in Denver, with three other Aricans. I had moved to Colorado one month earlier, expecting to plant myself in Boulder. I had enrolled in Free School classes, but I still could not shake my initial feelings of being overwhelmed by the spiritual marketplace there and all the New Age people who had come to shop. When I received an invitation from the Arica community in Denver to join them for an evening of holy work and a party, I jumped at the chance. An evening away from Boulder's overly spiritual air sounded like heaven to me. Boulder was too quixotic, and people there tended to take themselves with such dreadful seriousness. I missed the wry Arica perspective to which I had been exposed in New Mexico, the ability to laugh heartily at oneself even while being devoted to the spiritual path. And Denver's normalcy appealed to me. It was a real city and all sorts of real people lived there: black and white, fat and fit—not just the young, healthy, and privileged.

On my first visit to the Arica house, Herb, the owner of the house, flirted with me unabashedly. Herb was a divorced architect with triplet girls who lived with their mom a mile away. To me, he was a paunchy, older man, at least forty-two, and I was definitely not interested. However, my ears perked when he mentioned that there was a room in the house available for rent. It had belonged to an Arican named Madeline who had just left town.

"Madeline?" I asked. "Was she an Arica trainer with shiny black hair and a pointy nose? You mean she lived *here?*"

"Yup, that's her. She lived here for two years," he replied and showed me the room. It was a beautiful room, spacious and clean, with a window looking out onto the back garden. The fact that Madeline had lived in this room struck me as a sign. Even then I intuited that her skill and power as a female spiritual leader were qualities I wanted to emulate.

"I'm interested," I told Herb. "How much?"

"Two and a quarter," he answered, quickly adding, "but the money isn't as important as being willing to be part of the community here. We're looking for another Arican, someone who will really join the household in a big way. We do a lot together as a community here."

"Like what?" I asked, feeling a bit nervous.

"Well, every Sunday night we have a household meeting. We don't like stuff to build up between us. You know, money, chores, that kind of thing. So we do a weekly one-on-one karma cleaning to clear out all the unspoken stuff. We also cook and clean up together most nights. We do holy work together, too, but we're not rigid about it."

It sounded to me like heaven on earth. I went around the house that evening, peeking into all of the bedrooms. Each one was uniquely decorated to suit the personality of its occupant. David, the landscape architect, had a room crawling with plants, an aquarium, and a black light, while the room of Tracy, the garrulous medical student from Boston, was filled with Impressionist posters, mobiles, and hats. Herb, the new bachelor, had the third-floor garret, an architect's dream, replete with corners and gables and well-angled light for his drafting table and romantic boudoir. Going through the house, I noticed that each of the bedrooms had its own altar set up in one corner, with a meditation pillow, or zafu, in place for sitting meditations and rituals.

I moved in the very next week, hauling all my possessions in the rusted Volkswagen bug I had just bought with leftovers from my welfare checks. Boulder was only fifty minutes away, an easy drive on the highway. I could continue all of my classes by commuting three days a week. I was content.

I loved living in this house. It was a cross between Windemere and the Kundalini yoga ashram, a combination of the hedonism of the former and the distinct spirituality of the latter. Like the ashram, the Arica house was spacious and clean. The living room, for example, was an open and unfurnished space, with only a few conga drums, some healthy plants, and a pile of zafus around the edges of the carpeted room. Here my housemates and I would pass many hours, turning on the discreetly hidden stereo to dance, do psychocalisthenics, or just hang out on the floor and talk to one another.

Many other people came through this room, as well; here we hosted our parties, wild evenings of drumming and dancing, candlelight and meditation. These parties were not exclusively for Aricans, those engaged in Arica practices, but always the Arica atmosphere prevailed: lighthearted, classy, and attempting to hold some degree of consciousness about ourselves.

Next door was the dining room, another mostly empty room but for a low Japanese-style table with more zafus around it. The four of us sat here, legs folded beneath us, to eat our meals. We took turns cooking for one another, trying out extravagant yet healthy recipes, creating colorful feasts, hearty and aesthetic. We enjoyed our meals immensely, always taking time to do a brief Arica ceremony before digging in: stopping to observe, smell, and appreciate the food on our plates, chanting the *bija* syllable of the day three times, and then mentally offering the food to its highest purpose, to "help us reach our common evolution." What this common evolution was, I was never quite sure. But the ritual succeeded in fulfilling my two major dinner table needs, of which one had been inculcated in me as a child and the other I had developed on my own. The first was to make a blessing before partaking of food. It was unheard of in my home to put food into one's mouth before giving a blessing of appreciation to God, its provider. The second was the need for composure, peace, and awareness at the dinner table, which had been sorely absent in my home growing up.

It was not uncommon to have guests at our dinner table, Aricans traveling through or a character that one of us had brought home for entertainment. I was overjoyed finally to be part of a family that encouraged a variance of opinions and a free exchange of ideas, even those that were outlandish. Dinnertime at the Arica house was often the most mind-opening and entertaining part of the day.

During this period, even in the relative psychological safety of Denver, I was exposed to a plethora of new ideas and spiritual modalities that kept me in a state of continual agitation. Alongside of our Arica practices, the four of us in the household were going to prosperity consciousness seminars, where we were having our minds retrained about infinite intelligence, infinite wealth, our own self-worth, and the power of our thoughts to attract abundance. In addition, we were all immersed in various stages of the est training, learning how to stop making excuses for ourselves, take absolute responsibility for our lives, and start creating the reality that we believed we wanted. In addition, David,

Tracy, and I took tai chi lessons twice a week and were each being Rolfed once a month, to help incorporate all of these changes into our bodies. Along with Herb and his new girlfriend, Annie Silver, I had also joined the Heralds of Sirius, an occult astrological fellowship. Besides studying the principles and ramifications of astrology, we were taught to meditate to open up our connections to the astral and mental planes. I was also driving to Boulder to take classes in aura reading, foot reflexology, and the science of crystals and gems. For money, I waitressed at Denver's Bluebird Café.

Looking back, I am astonished by the energy and appetite I had to digest all of these new experiences. Although some of the courses turned out to be inane, the discipline they demanded of me as well as the discernment I developed in order to sort the meaningful from the faddish made this spiritual smorgasbord highly valuable.

Besides feeling enriched intellectually, this was the first time in my life when I felt that I truly fit into my living situation. My housemates and I functioned well together as a family. No one was able to get too carried away with a complaint or resentment because these would get regularly diffused at the weekly household meetings. Nor were we shy with one another in the interim. Each of us knew the others' "rackets," the unconscious schemes one resorts to, designed to manipulate any given situation so that one can avoid looking at oneself. For example, David had a melancholic streak that exhibited itself in a lounging-around lethargy; he had ingenious ways of getting others to do his work for him. Tracy, who small-talked endlessly to the point of hopelessly frittering away her study time, would go into angry panics and blame us all for not letting her get her work done. And Herb flirted excessively, constantly picking up women or scheming about doing so, to the point of being obsessive.

As for me, known exclusively as Tirzah now (the name Miriam had dropped away after my Arica training), I was exceedingly grateful to hear how I was perceived by others, despite my initial nervousness about receiving feedback at family meetings. My own racket, as expressed by David one evening as we did the dishes, had to do with all the "dogma" that I carried around with me and my belief that it was the objective truth, for myself and for everyone else as well.

I asked David to explain so I could take a better look at myself: "What exactly do you mean, dogma?"

"It's just that you have these beliefs and you hold on to them so seriously! You get really rigid, for instance, about the holy work, doing it at the same time every day or not doing it at all. And remember that embarrassing fuss you made last month at the est seminar? When you yelled back at Werner Erhard that we're not the only ones creating our reality, that it's God who's by far more powerful than we are? Jesus, were you intense!"

As he talked, I flashed back to my forty-day Arica training and the reflections I had received, which had sounded more like descriptions of my parents than myself.

"You look a little queasy," David remarked. "Is this too much for you?"

"No, go on. I can handle it. I think you're on to something."

"Well, then there are your food trips," he continued. "You know how you always scour the label on a can of beans or box of cookies for any ingredient that's the least bit unnatural? And there's your kosher trip; let's not even talk about last Sunday's bacon. I mean, to have to leave the house so you won't have to smell it? Isn't that going a bit too far, Tirzah? You looked at us like we were having human eyeballs for breakfast!" He was giggling now and I joined in. But something inside me was tense.

"They're only your beliefs, Tirzah. Whether it's about eating right or living right or getting enlightened right. You never say it directly, but my bet is that you think your dogma applies to everyone else, too. Lighten up—maybe we're just here to enjoy life and not worry so much about doing it the right way. Ever think about that?"

I tried to think about just enjoying life. I tried and tried. But how could I let go to simple enjoyment when everything in my life was suddenly bathed in such relativity? Choices were endless and there was no one but my own self to be morally accountable to. I was searching madly, despite myself, for an alternative morality to the clear-cut system of right and wrong that I'd been raised with. I scrutinized every new trick and tool of consciousness I happened upon, asking myself: Does this point to the ultimate truth? Could I live by this teaching without any reservations? Does it have meaning that will endure into the afterlife? I did not have the awareness then to see that each one of my undertakings held only a facet of the information that would serve the overall scheme of my growth. I was too busy looking for one infallible system.

I played with surrendering to the fun and pleasure of the experimentation game that we were all involved in, a game in which we tried out and traded everything available, from ideas to fashions to sexual partners and recreational drugs. And what was not available to us to check out and learn from? As long as we liked something, we did it. When we stopped liking it, we left it or threw it out.

David's words stuck with me; he had sniffed me out. He had noticed the streak of dualism that gripped me at my core, my checkerboard worldview of opposing values—high and low, worthy and not—which I could not shake, for all my willingness to do so. I was filled with contradictions. Despite my fervent commitment to freedom, despite all of my wild experimentations, I still adhered rigidly to several specific Jewish laws, such as *kashrut*.

What's more, David had caught me standing outside my life looking in. I was going through the motions, genuinely enthused to be learning so many new things, but always with a cocked eye and with skeptical questions that I held at bay. Was it acceptable to be gorging ourselves at this smorgasbord of consciousness without anyone to answer to? Was there no one on the outside, no God or standard of truth watching us, grading us, judging us, no one but our own selves? When my housemates referred to the higher power, there was no sense of moral authority associated with it. Where was the moral infrastructure that used to give everything its shape and meaning? Wasn't this all too easy?

Several months into my new life, I received a call from Richard. His dad had died peacefully in his sleep the night before. In the zeal and passion of beginning my new life, I had forgotten how fragile Morrie was, forgotten that he had been hanging on to life by Prednisone and a thin thread of will. When I hung up after talking to my grieving friend, I lay on my waterbed and mentally retraced the contours of my brief friendship with Morrie: slipping my hand into his as we walked, coming up behind him as he rested in his chair and massaging his shoulders and temples, his dubbing me "Fire'n'Brimstone," his nymphlike wink at me, always followed by "We love you very much."

It was Morrie who had once told me that he thought I was secretly searching for a rescue maneuver, a white knight who would answer all my questions, dispel all my doubts, and quench the anguish of my searching mind. I had denied his appraisal out of hand, my stalwart self-image flinching at the thought of needing anybody. But now that he was gone, I felt untethered, somehow more adrift in the world than before. Not that Morrie had ever given me the answers to my questions; he was too wise for prescriptions. But he had *listened* to my questions, and that simple, silent act had in itself validated my search and given me reassurance that the quest itself was a worthy one. Now I was at a loss. I did not know whether to pray for Morrie or talk to him. Was there a god waiting for those who did not subscribe to one? I hung Morrie's picture on the wall of my room and braced myself to continue the search without him.

The same week as Morrie's death, I got a special delivery package from my father. It was my brother Danny's *siddur*, the Hebrew and English prayer book, which had been found with his personal effects shipped back to my parents from his apartment in Rochester. The note in it said, "Miriam, we just had the unveiling of Danny's tombstone and it occurred to me that your prayers might raise his soul. Please use this. Dad." I felt tears welling up behind my nose, tears that I could not understand. Even if this was just another one of my father's sentimental ploys to get me back into the Jewish fold, it touched me deeply. I flipped through the book looking for some sign of my brother but found none. He had doubtless not opened it himself in many years. Yes, I would pray for Danny, and, more important, I would continue the search he had begun for a true spiritual path. But for now, I was so resistant to my Jewish background that I placed the book on a shelf and forgot it there.

Despite my desire to forget about Judaism, I found that during my meditations and even my dreams, Hebrew phrases and passages from the Torah and liturgy would frequently bleed through into my consciousness. Occasionally I would awaken in the morning with a lengthy passage from Psalms or Jeremiah fresh on my lips, tractates I had learned at school, or prayers that had committed themselves to my memory by force of repetition. I paid no attention to this strange trick of my unconscious mind. The words that surfaced meant as little to me as the passages of Philo's war accounts might to a scholar of the Greek classics. I dismissed them as little more than some meaningless burps from an overly stuffed unconscious.

Nor did I feel a need at this time for connection with the Jewish community. I was fully nourished in my spiritual community of choice, and I was sure that any contact with my Jewish roots would be devoid of meaning or prove to be shaming in some way. Nevertheless, since moving to Denver I had applied for a job as a substitute teacher at the Hebrew school of a Reform synagogue. I needed extra money and I thought teaching Hebrew to kids would be simple. After my interview with the school board, during which I told the committee that I had moved to Colorado to study alternative healing modalities, I was hired, but with reluctance.

"The board is concerned about you, Tirzah," the administrator confided later. "We enjoyed meeting you and would like to hire you, but... well, we felt that you may be reacting to your Orthodox upbringing with all these far-out cults you seem to be pursuing. We hope you will come around and leave those things behind."

By "far-out cults," they were referring to my healing-arts studies; I had never mentioned the more preposterous occult studies. My housemates David and Tracy, both from Reform Jewish backgrounds themselves, thought this was hilarious.

"If only they knew the half of what you're into!" they teased. "With all those scary and perverted classes you take, Tirzah, you are truly a danger and a menace to the Jewish children of the world!"

I laughed it off, too, and took the job. But my suspicions had come true: My contact with Jews in authority roles had led, once again, to feelings of humiliation. Why was being different so threatening to them? And why did Jews need to shame one another into conforming when they were different? My interaction with the Hebrew school board once more confirmed my negative belief: I could not be myself in the Jewish community and be acceptable. To be a Jew in a Jewish society, I had to hide my true self. This was why I had felt forced to leave.

The following February, I received notice that the growing interest of so many people in the healing arts had culminated in the opening of the Rocky Mountain Healing Arts Institute in Boulder. The school was dedicated to teaching natural healing modalities, including massage therapy, nutrition, and herbology. I enrolled in the first group of twenty students. My father refused to have anything to do with such seemingly useless studies and would not help support them financially, so I worked more shifts at the Bluebird, cut back on all my other expenditures, and began my first round of courses in anatomy, physiology, and massage. I was enthralled finally to be a student in courses that I felt utterly committed to. No longer was I standing skeptically on the outside looking in; I wanted to be a healer and I immersed myself so deeply in my practice and studies that I thought of little else. The science courses were academically rigorous and very difficult for me, but I loved the hands-on work. It was taught by people who understood how energy currents behaved as they moved through the body, and how they would get blocked when there was a trauma of any nature to the host, be it physical injury, emotional loss, or even a repeated tyranny of ideas.

In the next months, my hands seemed to recover a deep sensitivity that came naturally to them but that had been forgotten. My fingertips learned their way back to the strangely familiar sensations of energy vortices running beneath and above the skin, and my body grounded itself so that my hands could balance the various subtle pulses in the bodies I worked with. Acupuncture charts went up on my walls, anatomy texts lay open, and a massage table was brought into the house. I studied science late into the night, memorized muscle attachments and insertions over the phone with school buddies, and practiced massage, acupressure and polarity therapy in the living room on anyone who would volunteer his or her body to the cause of my education.

Likewise, I gladly volunteered my own body for my teachers' use as they demonstrated new techniques to the class. For some, working on nude bodies and undressing publicly to be worked on by teachers and fellow students was a difficult barrier to cross. The school offered the students process groups as part of the curriculum to air our personal difficulties with the course of study, and the nudity issue came up repeatedly for others. But naked bodies did not disturb me, nor did being touched; my body craved being cradled and caressed, rocked and kneaded. I recalled the first massage I ever received in the Turkish baths in Istanbul and realized I was now working to overcome the touch deficit I had discovered in myself there.

One morning in Boulder, our polarity therapy instructor, Randy, asked for a volunteer so that he could demonstrate a powerful technique known as the lymph drain. I raised my hand and was called upon. I lay down on the massage table under sheets, enjoying the warm winter sun radiating through the window upon me.

Randy had magnificently sensitive hands, and had been nicknamed Radar Randy by the students because he would always gravitate to the areas on our bodies that stored tension and emotional charge. The heat that was transmitted through his fingers magically unpeeled the layers of tension in their grip, so that feelings rose easily toward the surface for release.

On this morning, Randy began working steadily and slowly on my body, under my jawbone, under my arms, in all the places in the body where lymph nodes lie in clusters beneath the skin. My classmates gathered around the table with their notepads and pens, casually observing and taking notes. But as Randy's hands moved to my collar bone and upper chest, demonstrating his technique on the intercostal muscles, the fine netting between the ribs, I felt pierced by a pain so sharp and sudden that I repeatedly gasped out loud for breath.

"Stay with it, Tirzah," Randy spoke gently. "Keep your breath moving, real easy now." He could tell that he had hit upon a mother lode of emotional holding and knew that we were in for a ride. His fingers, like laser instruments, continued to soothe out the tissue between my ribs. I breathed to accommodate the pain, to stay ahead of it, but I had never felt a sensation like this. It was not a purely physical pain, and in this it was even more startling; it penetrated deeper, somehow, beyond my physical tissue into what I felt must be my heart, or even my soul.

Randy saw that I was breathing hard, at the very limit of my pain tolerance. His hands stopped their work and rested on my chest as if to say, *Keep going, let whatever this is come to the surface.* The searing pain in my ribs had let up, but now my emotion was uncorked, flooding me. Suddenly, a cry began to rise up from my chest for release. It was not a simple cry of vulnerability or despair. It was more like a cry for one's life, a shriek of horror and indignation that wanted to explode out of me like a volcano. My breathing was coming even harder now, and my entire body was pouring down sweat as if I were running a race. Without any thought process at all, my arms reached up desperately, as if searching for a door. They groped in the air with a reckless frenzy that matched my breath, which had turned into panting. Everything in the room faded into darkness, and behind my closed eyes I saw a moving picture with me in it, me and many other women, naked and panicking and reaching out, screaming for help, for mercy, for release.

"Help!" A word managed to escape between my panting. And then again. "Help! Won't you *help?*" Again and again I screamed for my life, the yell piercing the air around me. But there was no help to be had. I had been left, let down, abandoned. My arms finally collapsed at my sides and then a torrential downpour of tears began, the tears of giving up on life, on God, on everything that once had meaning. I drowned in those tears, choked and coughed and spat up, but they kept flowing. By this time the entire class had stepped in close around the table, riveted to what was happening to me.

Compassionate hands held me as I wept, my body racked with sobs and coughing. Randy's voice gently penetrated my sounds from the head of the table, speaking words of comfort that told me I would be okay, that everyone was here to care for me, that I was not alone. His hands were still on me, lightly now, and I felt him working to balance my energy, to soothe me. He gestured to the other students to touch my feet to help the energy move down and out. But it took what seemed a long time until I was back in that room, back in my twenty-one-year-old body, back in a school building in Colorado.

Finally I could sit up. I looked around. Everyone in the class sat or stood around me, very focused, very present. I looked into the watchful eyes of my classmates, one by one. I could see that some of them had been crying as well.

"Well, class," Randy began with a knowing smile, looking around at our exhausted faces, "this is what is known as an emotional catharsis." A relieved laughter broke out among us, but still there were some furrowed brows.

"I have to share something," Larry broke in then. "I had this experience when Tirzah was reaching out with her arms. It was like I could see everything that was going on for her. It seemed like she was in some dark place, like in a gas chamber somewhere, and she was with lots of other women, hundreds." Larry began to break down in tears himself just then, but continued to speak through them. "I could see it. They were huddled in this dark chamber and they were all crying out for their lives." Then he broke down. Others had begun to sniffle as well. Mary spoke up from the back of the room.

"I saw it, too! Something terrible was happening to her, and violent. She was in this big group of people and the air was getting thick and dark. I kept thinking about how the Nazis gassed people in the Second World War."

"Me, too!" Kathleen cried out. "What I felt was that it was somehow Tirzah, but not Tirzah. And she was fighting for her life, not wanting to die. It felt like a film I'd seen of a mass murder."

I listened with rapt attention, both amazed and relieved to hear the experiences of my classmates. Somehow their sharing made me feel less lonely. There was a lull in the room and then Steve spoke up.

"Maybe all this really happened! I mean, maybe this was a past life memory or something."

Randy judiciously kept the circle of comments moving until everyone had shared their thoughts before we broke for lunch. Ideas and theories about what had happened abounded. The only thing that was doubtlessly clear was that some deep cache of feelings in me had been evoked and released, feelings of entrapment, desperation, and despair. I was awed to hear that others actually saw something so similar to what I had just experienced, the excruciating helplessness of a tormented death, perhaps en masse and perhaps at the hands of the Nazis.

I drove back to Denver slowly that evening, feeling drained but mystified by what had happened. What if it *were* true? What if I *had* died for being a Jew in a place like Auschwitz in my past life? Was it conceivable that the experience I had had that morning could actually have been the very feelings of a person dying in a concentration camp? Perhaps fierce emotions such as the ones I'd just experienced did not die with a person but went into a sort of deep freeze with the soul, only to "thaw out" at a later, more opportune moment.

These notions seemed utterly plausible to me in that moment, despite the highly speculative nature of such theories as transmigration of souls and reincarnation. Who could ever know for sure if such things actually happened after death? Still, my thoughts and emotions continued to cascade together: It now made visceral sense to me why so many Jews like my parents were adamant, even rabid, about the topic of Jewish survival and protecting their people from the danger of annihilation, whether real or perceived. There was so much collective pain in our people, accumulated over thousands of years of enduring violence. Where was all that pain to go? How many thousands of Jews, for instance, must have gone down at the hands of the Nazis, vowing not to die in vain? And if every single Jew had experienced anything like the feelings that I myself had felt that morning, the ocean of panic, indignation, and rage that would have been generated by six million people was unfathomable! What had become of all those souls, people murdered in cold blood without recourse of justice? If souls *did* reincarnate, I thought, then it surely made sense to assume that the most passionate and unresolved feelings felt at the time of death would return with them into the next life.

From the time that I was four or five, I could remember my parents and uncles talking heatedly about our duty as Jews never to forget what had happened to us, the call of our people to survive in the aftermath of near genocide, the responsibility that we survivors bore for those who were murdered that they not have died in vain. In fact, these ideas had been repeated so often that they seemed to lose their meaning, becoming the predictable household tirade that I had learned to shrug off and ignore as a child on my way out to play. Now I understood these things in a different light; I had felt them in my own body.

Most of the world's esoteric traditions, including Jewish mysticism, do contain teachings about reincarnation and the transmigration of souls, but the existence of these phenomena is still a matter of personal belief, since, like life after death, they are unprovable. In a sense, their veracity is beside the point. Whether or not my soul actually lived through a lifetime as a Holocaust victim matters little; if the experience of it lives within me, then its power affects me nevertheless, just as if I had lived through it myself. Either way, I must respond to the "experience" by allowing myself to be affected by it.

The fact that people have powerful experiences, dreams, and images of other lives points to a powerful psychic reality that Carl Jung called the collective unconscious. Jung postulated that there is a subterranean ocean of information just beneath the roots of our personal lives which is much like a shared memory bank of human experience. The collective unconscious is the place where the drama and patterns of human history are stored and become accessible at special moments of our lives.

The concept of the collective unconscious underscores two ideas central to all of the world's mystical traditions. First, that all of our psyches are interconnected, and second, that nothing in our human past ever really disappears. Whether we are educated or not, whether we remember or not, the deepest stratum of the human psyche is a shared record of our past. It becomes clear that the trauma and tragedy of a formidable event such as the Holocaust exists beneath the surface of all of our conscious minds, whether or not we are Jewish. We may choose to deny or ignore such powerful, transformative events, but there is no escaping them. They shape our destiny.

A hot soup was on the stove when I arrived home that night. Annie had moved in with Herb and it was their night to cook. I was happy to be home in the easy comfort of this family, eager to discuss my intense experience with the household. Yet as I began to share what had happened to me, I realized that by putting it into words, the experience was becoming just another interesting dinner topic, no more noteworthy than any of the other sources of amazement typically brought up for commentary around this table. I cut myself short; my experience was far too personal to be used for parlor talk.

In bed that night I continued my musings: if that desperate woman I experienced this morning were really a former me, what would she be saying about the life I am now living? Would she approve? It was certainly not a Jewish life by any standard, but it was a healthy one, I assured myself, healthy enough to have allowed such an experience to come forward, anyway. If she had come back to live a religious Jewish life, well, she would have to wait. Doing that was not at the head of my list, and I was the one in charge this time around.

SEVERAL MONTHS LATER, the Arica household threw a party for my fellow students and other assorted friends. One of the guests was a local psychic of some renown, and I asked if he would give me a quick reading. He looked at me steadily and answered, "Let's have a cup of tea, shall we?" We sat down in a quiet corner after fishing out a teapot and two tea cups from the kitchen cupboard. Strangely, he insisted upon brewing the tea the old-fashioned way, using a packet of loose tea that he had brought with him. We poured our tea and finished it over some small talk. As I was wondering what had happened to my request, he pointed to my cup. On the inside wall of the little china dainty was a picture, as clear as life, made out of several strewn tea leaves. It was a noble-looking figure with something hanging over his head.

"You're quite an idealist when it comes to love, aren't you?" he asked me knowingly.

"You could say that," I agreed. "What are you seeing?"

"Look in the cup," he said, pointing to the figure inside it. "Can you see that it's a knight on his quest? He has a star shining over his head. You are about to meet someone who is truly unique, out of this world, you might say." Then he chuckled. "You have never known a love like this, Tirzah. Be careful."

I was amused at the incident, and bewildered. The image of a knight reminded me of what Morrie had said about my search for someone who would rescue me from my questions. But Morrie had not said this in a context of praise, rather of concern. The guest refused to give me any more details. Before he took his leave that night, he kissed me on the forehead and whispered, "Hang on. Your star is coming."

It was three weeks to the day after my tea-leaf reading that Annie brought home a character named Everlasting. She had met him at work at the metaphysical bookstore; they were coworkers there and she had been intrigued by him, by his bearing and the mysterious things he said.

Except for his hands, which were large and elegant, I did not find Everlasting particularly attractive at first sight; he looked far too serious for a twenty-eight-year-old. With his slight build, beard and mustache au naturel, and dark, shoulder-length hair, he could have posed as Jesus Christ.

"No, his name is not a joke," Annie whispered to me in the kitchen as we fixed Oriental twig tea on his first visit. "Listen, Tirzah, he comes from somewhere else."

"Like where? He seems American to me."

"Right, he is. But I mean he lives entirely on the spirit plane. It's his only orientation. *We* may *talk* about spirituality. This one *lives* it."

I peeked around the corner into the dining room, where Everlasting was sitting alone at the table. His eyes were closed in effortless meditation and the room seemed to vibrate strangely, as if he had temporarily parked his body on the zafu while flying off to meet with friends in another galactic reality. I was intrigued by his absent presence; I wanted to know where he was, and even more, where else there was to be that I should know about. I did not want to miss anything if it was important.

Annie and I returned from the kitchen with a tray of tea and rice cakes. Without opening his eyes, Everlasting brought his hands up from his lap as if in prayer and bowed his forehead to touch his fingertips. It looked like the Indian greeting, *Namaste*, but it was hard to tell whether he was saying hello to us or finishing with others elsewhere. Then he opened his eyes and smiled at me broadly.

"It's good to see you again," he said in a deep, warm voice, looking directly into my eyes.

"What?" I was sure I had misheard him.

As if reading my mind, Everlasting nodded his head reassuringly. "You heard me right. I've been expecting you. But we'll get to that later." He winked at me cryptically, then turned to Annie for his tea.

That is how my friendship with Everlasting began, with my spiritual longing and his seductive innuendo that sent a chill up my spine. Everlasting had a magnetic self-certainty that began to draw me toward him that very first day, and continued to do so over the many months that followed. Even when I did not know what he wanted from me or what he could possibly be talking about, I listened to him, believing that truth itself lay hidden in his words.

I found it thrilling that someone in the world seemed to know all about me and what I needed for my spiritual evolution. And I desperately wanted to believe him when he told me that he had done the painstaking spiritual work of securing the vital answers about the way the world worked, and had come into my life to share them with me. Being young, beguilable, and spiritually voracious, I wanted only one thing: to sit at the feet of this self-proclaimed teacher and learn from him. I learned plenty, but not exactly as planned.

Everlasting did not fit well into the Arica house. Apart from Annie, my roommates disliked him, finding him arrogant and removed.

After several visits by Everlasting, Tracy and David approached me. David began.

"You're free to bring over whomever you want, Tirzah. I mean, we're not your parents or anything. But who *is* this guy? Who would go around with a name like *Everlasting?*" They giggled. I remained serious.

"Sorry," I countered defensively. "How about looking beyond the exterior of things before you judge them? Everlasting is an extremely high being."

"That's just what I was afraid of," David shot back at me, "that this guy is so high, he's out in the ozone somewhere. How about deep? I prefer deep to high any day. Anyway, Tirzah, it's only out of love for you that I'm saying anything."

Tracy put her arm around me. "You're not falling for this guy, are you? I'm sure he's smart and artistic and all, but honestly, he gives me the creeps."

I shrugged them both off and took to visiting Everlasting at his place, which was a humble room in a boarding house, bare of all furniture save a cot and a jumble of easels and paints, papers and pens. My first visit there felt like entering another world. On his walls hung his large paintings, vivid geometric mandalas that seemed to buzz and vibrate when I looked at them, creating optical illusions that confounded my eyes. My eyes darted around the room as Everlasting boiled water for tea on his hotplate.

"Sorry I can't offer you a chair—or one of those fluffy Zen pillows you have at your house. What do you call those, anyway?"

"They're called zafus. They're meditation pillows."

"I certainly never needed a zafu to meditate," he said with a chortle. "Nor did the great yogis. It's better not to get too materialistic about one's spirituality, don't you agree?" He poured the tea and handed me a mug. Then he grabbed up a metal tool box and a pad of paper and sat on his bed. He motioned for me to sit down next to him, which I did, looking on as Everlasting's lithe hands transformed the paper, first in ink and then water colors. What flew out of his pens and brushes struck me as nothing less then miraculous. Everlasting had barely touched his tools to the paper before an image appeared—a blissful woman sitting in meditation in front of a setting sun. I was amazed beyond words by his talent and felt as if I had been transported into the space of the picture. A deep silence wrapped itself around me, a silence I had never experienced before in any of my previous meditations.

"It's not difficult," he said after a while, laughing at the expression of wonderment on my face. "All it takes is tuning in to her reality. She's a goddess."

I did not know what he meant, but I continued to watch him in open-mouthed awe as he delicately painted the final orange hues on the clouds and touched the woman's lips with crimson.

Women were a common theme in Everlasting's artwork, and watching them take form under his hand put me into a sweet, dreamlike trance that felt very satisfying. As I continued to watch Everlasting draw and paint on subsequent visits, I began to understand the beatific smile I had seen on the faces of the Virgin Mary or of the *gopis*, the female consorts who followed the Hindu god Krishna around. It was a special quality of blissful surrender that lifted them above the harsh dualities of this world. I longed to become as serene as these women, and I determined to embody this quality of surrender.

It was not only Everlasting's art that enraptured me; there was also his music. He played an old guitar, spontaneously composing songs about the world of pure spirit, roads made of light and angels on the wing. With his charmed hands, he also built small lap harps, decorating them with astounding intricacy using colorful images of Hindu gods and goddesses. These harps were tuned in an uncommon way, and as he played them, always impromptu, I would be thrown into an indescribable state of transcendent bliss.

As I look back on the scene today, it is clear to me that I was being seduced by this man, not only physically but psychologically and spiritually. As I fell under the power of Everlasting's dark charisma and exotic religion, my own sense of inner direction and strong will began to fail me. I thought I had fallen deeply in love, but it would be truer to say that I had fallen into submission.

We became lovers. I began to pass my nights curled up next to Everlasting in his narrow bed, his ardent gopi. Everlasting would enjoy me sexually, but always with an air of condescension. By day I would literally sit at his feet with my eyes closed as he played music or painted, ready for a fix of the beauty and peace I believed only he could give me.

My massage studies began to fail. But I had more than just a time-management problem; I was being torn between two opposing worldviews. From one side I was pulled by the earthy body orientation of my healing-arts studies, which harmonized with the premise of my Arica and tai chi practices that grounding oneself in the belly, the source of human health and power, brings one to wholeness. But I was also enamored of Everlasting's teachings, which, like the kundalini yoga I had studied one year earlier, focused on nothing lower than the third eye. Everlasting railed against grounding oneself in the physical body, saying it only seduced one more deeply into a false attachment that would inevitably have to be cut. Yet I had discovered an undeniable joy and aliveness through my body, and although I was falling behind in my studies, I nevertheless defended this path to Everlasting.

"I've come to learn that the physical body is a sheer reflection of the soul's inner workings," I hazarded one day. "It's a doorway into the world of energy and spirit." Everlasting rolled his eyes in response.

"You shouldn't make statements like that, Tirzah. You truly do *not* know what you're talking about. The physical body is merely an illusion that has trapped mankind into losing its spiritual identity. This earthly world is a temporary prison. Can't you *see* that?"

Oh, the internal war that ensued between these two schools of thought, the earth-bound and the heaven-bound! The newer one came by way of enchantment, mystical transmission, and not a little pushiness. It promised me security with its black and white, absolute answers. The other orientation I was taught by Everlasting to believe was inferior, tragically slow, and mired in this world of gray uncertainty. After spending a lot of time around Everlasting, I finally took refuge in the clear-cut route, clinging to his self-confidence for my security. As I followed his lead, leaving the human world little by little, I began to enter what I believed were bliss states.

"I've got to know more about this otherworldly place, you know, this serenity I feel when I'm here," I told Everlasting one day. "It's incredible to me. I mean, I wonder why the whole world isn't tuned in to this bliss."

"The whole world doesn't want bliss, Tirzah. To have true bliss, you have to surrender the fight with life. Most people don't want to stop fighting."

"Well, I do," I said with total confidence. "I am *really* ready to stop fighting with life. I want to become as peaceful and clear-minded as a goddess."

Everlasting turned serious when I said this; he looked at me squarely, placing his hands on my shoulders.

"Do you mean that, Tirzah? Because I can teach you how if you're absolutely sincere. But it would require the utmost obedience on your part. Obedience and giving up your New Age lifestyle. Could you do that?"

I paused to consider his question. "I think so. Yes, I feel like my spiritual growth has been going too slowly with what I've been doing. I want to make a leap of consciousness now, I'm ready to really change myself."

After that day, our relationship began to shift. Everlasting wore a more austere countenance, assuming the role of spiritual teacher even when we were being intimate. Only then did I begin to notice that others beside myself came to visit him for counsel and spiritual direction. I felt stung to see other young women come and go, but I chose not to bring up my feelings, preferring to calm my irritation by meditating.

Sitting in meditation with Everlasting, I succeeded in mollifying my pain. There were times, admittedly, that my gibbering mind consumed me, perhaps in a useless effort to bring reason to my soul. More frequently, though, I was transported (by what or whose power I am still uncertain), lifted to a realm beyond the mind into clear space, infinite space, peace itself. I imagined that I was visiting the mind of God, a region that rested above the dualism of my life, above the ups and downs of the body, above the cycles of pain and pleasure. I was brought to my knees to behold this territory, and to this day I stand in awe as I remember what I beheld during these meditations. I swore I would go to extreme lengths to have more of these experiences—and I did.

As I proceeded in my new role of student under Everlasting's tutelage, it became increasingly clear to me that his teachings were a package deal. If I wanted to continue to learn from him about other planes of existence, I would have to submit to his spiritual lineage, which was Hindu. He now made clear to me that everything he said or did began with his guru, Beloved, a black man from British Guyana who had revealed himself to Everlasting years earlier and for whom Everlasting had dropped out of art school. It was to Beloved alone that Everlasting submitted, receiving the guru's instructions directly, either through meditation or the mail. This submission included, some years earlier, changing his name from Paul to Everlasting, a name that would remind him of his soul's true identity.

One day, after a particularly transcendent journey to another plane, as I sat dumbfounded by what I had experienced and yet unable to move or speak, Everlasting whispered to me in a stern voice: "It is only by the grace of the guru that you have these experiences, Tirzah. What you saw today was Beloved's gift. Now go write to him and thank him." There was a knock at the door; another student had arrived and I was dismissed.

In a daze, I walked back to the Arica house where I slunk into my room, fastidiously avoiding my housemates. I did not want to be brought down into a discussion about what I was up to, nor about the fact that suddenly I had a guru, in addition to a spiritual teacher who was also, strangely, my lover. I could not bear being questioned as to why everything in my life had changed. It was clear to me that soon I would have to leave the plush zafu comfort of the

Arica world. Oscar Ichazo's teachings seemed like a feel-good Disney World compared to what I was studying now.

The doctrines of my newly adopted lineage were the Hindu Vedas and the Upanishads, in particular, the Bhagavad Gita. I was asked to pay special attention to the warrior Arjuna, who was commanded by Krishna not only to sever his ties with his family but to kill them off, one by one. Based on these ancient texts, Everlasting explained to me, it was apparent that we were all living in the Kali Yuga, the final period of decay before a great and massive destruction came upon the planet. Signs were all around, apparent to anyone who had her eyes open. Floods, droughts, and fires were already hitting this continent; couldn't I see it?

Beloved's prophecies had led him to northern Minnesota, where he had bought land and was building log houses, storing food for survival, and teaching people to live independent of American culture, whose capitalist economy would be falling asunder any time now. Everlasting told me that these geophysical and economic crashes would lead to widespread panic and violence on the part of anyone who was caught in America's materialism, and we had to train ourselves now to separate ourselves from our false attachments. He assured me that Beloved's community was the perfect haven to do this.

The day would come, Beloved had predicted, when many would flock to this land, thankful for the prescient community's preparations. But for the time being, Beloved's community consisted of him, his three wives, his children, and a handful of others. Everlasting would join them later because he had work to take care of in the outer world. I never found out what this work was, but guessed that it had to do with recruiting people like me to Beloved's apocalyptic philosophy.

Even at my young age, I could detect some grandiose thinking going on here. Nevertheless, I followed along, addicted to the blissful meditations and serenely secure in the guidance I was finding, which sounded absolute, simple, and foolproof.

"There are absolutes in this and all worlds, Tirzah. Just as there is a great hierarchy which we are all part of. Your New Age friends can try to deny these things by imagining that they can continue to let their likes and dislikes govern them. But in the end, we are not free agents in this world."

Everlasting's monologues were captivating; they both scared and aroused me. I had arrived at similar conclusions about the moral accountability of the New Age belief systems. My faith in Everlasting's authority grew. If I stuck close to him, he who obviously had direct lines to the other planes whence came absolute answers, I would be able to discern the right way unfailingly.

As time passed, I noticed that Everlasting was growing increasingly rigid with me. When we went out together, grocery shopping or to an occasional lecture or concert, he would watch me vigilantly to see if I was keeping my spiritual focus. At times I would find him glaring at me from across the room, pointing repeatedly, angrily, at his own third eye center, as if telling me: *You've lost your center again. Get back where you belong!* I would instantly comply, although I shuddered at the grimness of his approach.

Yet despite the fact that I was now following his path with increasing fervor, I was, true to my nature, still questioning. Or, as Everlasting put it, rebelling. I was struggling to reconcile his teachings with the profound emotional and physical experiences that I had had in Arica and in my healing classes with Randy. I had thought these were spiritual experiences, but according to Everlasting's teachings, they were meaningless discharges, not worthy of attention.

"You've expressed a desire to learn, Tirzah, but you continue to support all these other vacuous teachings. I'm telling you again: Unless you surrender completely to this path, you will only continue to confuse and hamper your soul. *Half surrender produces half bondage!*"

"I understand. But how can I just forget what I've learned up till now? Isn't that disrespectful to the other teachings?"

"Remember Arjuna. Let everything that came before this die so that something new can thrive."

His answer worried me. I knew what would follow. It was not only the revelations I had had in the past year that were needing to be dismissed. It was my family and my Jewish heritage that would come under Arjuna's sword next, of this I was sure. For all the pain and disappointment I associated with my upbringing, I felt physically ill to think of forcefully cutting it off.

"I'm not sure I can just jump from one lineage to another, Everlasting. As much as I love the Upanishads and all, I'm not a Hindu. I've probably been Jewish for lifetimes! You can't just give up your karmic family with a snap."

"But that is exactly what is required! Don't you see? Beloved knows and I keep telling you, you've got to release your old baggage once and for all! And that includes Judaism. It's clear to us that you cannot go any farther in that lineage. It's a dead end, spiritually; it's taken you as far as you can go. You've got to renounce it or you will never move forward."

"For God's sake, Everlasting, I'm not ready to make a decision like that. I don't think I could do it even if I wanted to."

"When will you ever stop rebelling, Tirzah? You and your stiffnecked people! You just can't let go, can you? Beloved and I cannot do the work of stepping over the threshold for you!"

I felt as though I was in a vise grip, struggling this way and that, but the pressure only intensified. I had by now moved out of the Arica house into a tiny apartment by myself. My housemates had said good-bye to me with condescending courtesy when I told them I was trying to save money to eventually move up to northern Minnesota, to Beloved's community. I did not go into such detail with my parents. They would find out soon enough that I had dropped out of the life that they had just begun to learn to tolerate.

Meanwhile, I reported in to my job at the restaurant each day trying to hold an in-the-world-but-not-of-it consciousness. I would tenaciously repeat a Hare Krishna chant or one line from the Bhagavad Gita throughout my shift, taking dinner orders from the restaurant patrons with a constant focus on my third eye, and seeing the dining room as *samsara*—the endless cycling of birth, suffering, death, and rebirth—in process before my eyes. I remained coolly above the scene, serving yet never involved, interacting with coworkers and guests as beings of light, never as personalities, invoking God's light everywhere. Then I would return to my apartment, shower and change into white, pray, and read a bit of the Vedic scriptures, and fall into an exhausted heap until the next morning. Where did I think I was going? To God, of course, and with no shortcuts.

I took a formal leave of absence from the Healing Arts Institute, telling my teachers I needed time to pursue my spiritual studies. My fellow students and friends fell away, and Everlasting became my only friend and confidant. Then one day, about a month after I had moved into my own apartment, orders arrived from Beloved for Everlasting and me to immediately disengage from each other in every way, as teacher and disciple as well as lovers. The reasons for this directive were never given, although I tearfully implored the two men to give me an explanation again and again. I was told simply to be obedient and call on my trust in the guru. Nor did Everlasting show any emotion about breaking off physical ties with me. He came one last time to return some of my belongings; thereafter he left me impersonal notes at my door with meditation instructions and a line or two of lofty spiritual encouragement.

"Beloved is your teacher now. He will take you the rest of the way."

"But Everlasting, I don't even know Beloved! You're the one—"

"That will come, in time," he interrupted. "He knows *you*, that's all that counts. My own work here is done, accomplished."

"What was that, to turn me on and then split?"

Everlasting turned toward the door. He would never engage me if I was in a negative mind-state. With his back to me, he said sternly: "I've already told you this. There is something in your soul that has been dormant for centuries. I did my best to awaken it. Now watch your attachments to the wrong things. It's time to move on." Then there was silence between us. His head bowed, in prayer or in pain, I could not tell, as he let himself out. He never turned back to face me, certainly not to kiss me—that would have been the false and sentimental attachments predictably trying to reinstate themselves. After he left, I stood there for a long time, bewildered by the sudden change in my destiny and wondering: Whose life had I stepped into, anyway? Who was calling the shots?

I rebelled against Beloved's command, sending Everlasting notes and stalking his building. But I never seemed to find him in. One cold night as I paced back and forth before his doorstep, hoping he would arrive before I froze to death, I realized that I had a choice. With Everlasting out of the picture, I could choose to reinstate my entire life with no trouble at all. My old friends would rejoice and so would my teachers; I could forget this arcane teaching in the blink of an eye. But by the time these thoughts had formed, I already had my answer. Despite the excruciating loneliness I felt, I would continue on the warrior's path. I was furious that the man whom I had deified and for whom I had abandoned the world had rejected me so lightly. Well then, I would gain enlightenment without him, by clinging even more tightly to the path he had shown me. Damned if my spiritual progress would be deterred by a man, any man!

I went home, determined to entrench myself even more deeply in my inner world, ignoring the fact that my life had become a dour and crusty cocoon, devoid of humor and sensuality. Only months earlier, I had thrived on people, enjoying all sorts of physical contact, hugs, massages, and dancing. Now all that had vanished. I was on a straight and narrow path, and would not be stopped.

So obstinately did I cling to the life of transcendence that I could not yet see the danger I was headed for. Had I only been able to acknowledge and trust my own feelings, my doubts, and my rage, even my unrequited physical desire, they would all have guided me back to my inner wisdom and a more balanced path. But I had welcomed a teaching that trained me to distrust myself, to relate to my feelings as negative mind-states that pulled down the spirit and were meant to be jumped over as quickly as possible. And so the inner guidance that might have corrected me—I had long since ignored any guidance from the outside—went unheard. I remained planted on this extremely rigid Hindu path, more determined than ever to proceed.

Two months later, I was packing to move to Beloved's community in northern Minnesota. The price of admission was twenty-five pounds each of peanut butter and brewer's yeast for the community's storehouse. As I readied these and my new boots and long underwear, a dream I'd had almost a year earlier flashed through my mind. It was about marrying a rabbi and surprising everyone, including myself. Why would I be reminded of such a dream at a time like this? I certainly had not taken refuge in a rabbi and Orthodox Judaism. I was convinced that what I had undertaken was miles from anything my parents or tribe knew, and it promised to take me even further away from them into the world of pure spirit.

But the dream was opportune. It was hinting that I had indeed been lured back to a form of orthodoxy—orthodox Hinduism. I had abandoned the "zafu life," my admittedly cushy, spiritually meandering existence, in favor of the absolute, black and white answers of an overarching authority. In this sense, I had indeed returned to the familiar psychological ground of my childhood; only the packaging was different.

For dose kind of answers and dat kind of life, you might as veil have married an Orthodox rabbi and make your papa happy! quipped a mocking inner voice with a Yiddish accent. An interior trickster had recently sprouted in my head, relishing the opportunity to make hay of my predicament. But I was not laughing along. I refused to see any similarity between my present Hindu path and the concrete morality I had been raised with. As for Judaism, it had disappeared for me (or so I thought) and the designated spiritual track I had signed up for was taking me out of the world as I had ever known it.

Everlasting or not, here I came. I flew via Winnipeg to Beloved's community that January, arriving in a snowstorm in twenty-degrees-below-zero weather. I wore a painted red dot at my third eye to protect myself. I was determined to keep my focus as high as my aspirations.

CHAPTER FIVE

WITH WINGS TO FLY

"Destination?" the voice repeated.

"Oh, uh, Roosevelt," I stammered, fumbling in my pocket for my one-way ticket from Winnipeg, where I had flown that morning from Denver. "Only I'm supposed to get off at the six-mile marker just before town." Without looking at me, the uniformed driver nodded his assent as he punched my ticket and returned it, then moved across the aisle to his next customer before climbing back behind the wheel. I closed my eyes and fell back into a languid half sleep, lulled by the overheated bus and the straight white plains passing monotonously, hour after hour, outside my window.

The bus pulled over to let someone off on the road, and the doors swung wide open to let in a rude blast of frigid air that called me to wakefulness. I shivered. It was January 1, 1977; I had wanted to start the New Year in my new spiritual home. But if it was my destiny to come to this northerly wilderness, then why did this part of the world feel so damn foreign? I opened my eyes, continuing my musing. The Mediterranean I could relate to. Stepping off a train or bus almost anywhere in Greece, Spain, or the South of France had always felt like stepping back into a picture I belonged in. But this unstoppable Minnesota whiteness was eerie and unfamiliar to me.

"Miss, this is your stop here," the driver called back to me as the bus brakes shrieked. I hoisted my bags up onto my back and shoulders and made my way toward the door of the bus. Once outside, I gasped at the stingingly cold air and began to trudge across the snowpacked road toward the log cabins I hoped were Beloved's community. The mantra I had begun repeating on my way to the Denver airport early that morning sprang back into mind and I repeated it more rapidly now: *I am in God, God is in me; God and I are one*, as if in quantity it might have a better chance of working its charm of fortification. The dense snow squeaked underfoot like styrofoam being crushed. In the distance, I saw a thickly bundled figure waving at me; it was a woman.

"Hello," she said with a courteous yet flat smile when I had come closer.

"You're Tirzah? I'm Carissa. Beloved is inside waiting for you." She took one of my bags off my shoulder. "When you need it, the outhouse is over there," she said, pointing across a small field. I squinted to get a view through the heavily falling snow. "That's the bathhouse right next to it."

I thanked her and looked around me quickly before heading indoors. The community's property was roughly the size of a football field, and the small log structures standing on it were handmade and dismally inelegant.

Oy, is dis primitif or vat? My Yiddish jokester was back, laughing at the situation. *Too primitif for a Jewish girl like you, dat's for sure. Vut vill you do mit de silks in a primitif place like dis?*

When I packed, leaving behind a cat, all of my furniture, and many irrelevant books, I had been careful not to discard my luscious turquoise silk blouse and a floor-length gold silk dress, burying them under the polypropylene and woolen winterwear in the bottom of my pack. I had not lost hope of someday going out to an opera, or perhaps listening to some chamber music after an elegant dinner. I knew in my heart that this was heresy, the material world throwing its net of maya, illusion, over me yet again. Still, the vision of myself as a beautiful young woman who would one day have a man of her own and, God help her, even enjoy the finer things of this mundane world defied my Hindu training.

Carissa led me to the main cabin, where Beloved lived with his wives and where I would have my quarters. Once inside the cabin door, I beheld Beloved for the first time. His back was to me, busily stoking the woodstove. Without turning around, he spoke.

"Good, so you've arrived."

He rattled the stove closed and turned to face me. I was taken aback by how small he was, not much taller than me and very compactly built. His skin was dark black and he wore very short hair and spectacles. There was nothing particularly exotic about Beloved from the outside; even his clothes were American.

"So here you are," he said, looking into my eyes with no hint of a smile. "Let the ladies show you around. They still have some chores to take care of before it gets totally dark. After dinner, we'll talk."

As I followed Beloved's wives around over the next few days, it was plain to see that they all did formidable amounts of work to keep their austere lives going. I bristled at the inequality of the situation. Under their husband's scrutiny and to his exacting specifications, they baked bread, prepared meals, laundered, cleaned, chopped wood, and tended their infants and the community animals. In such extreme temperatures, with neither running water nor electricity, just getting through the day seemed like a staggering task. But I heard no complaints.

Others besides Beloved's wives belonged to the community, but they, like Everlasting, were on some sort of leave, their cabins sitting vacant. My eyes circumscribed the scene. Is this what it amounted to, then? One small black man, three wives, some chickens, goats, and me, all together here in this dangerously cold weather? As the first signs of panic fluttered in my belly, I commanded my focus to shift back to my mantra, reprimanding myself for judging from the outside. I would wait for Beloved's teachings.

Later, as we sat at a tiny table eating our spartan dinner of heavily cumined dahl and rice, Beloved stood and read aloud passages for our edification from a large volume called *Krishna, the Supreme Personality of the Godhead* and from the Brihadaranyaka Upanishad: "The Atman is to be described as *not this and not that*. It is incomprehensible, for it cannot be comprehended; undecaying, for it never decays; unattached, for it never attaches itself; unfettered, for it is never bound. He who knows the Atman is unaffected, whether by good or by evil. Never do such thoughts come to him as 'I have done an evil thing' or 'I have done a good thing.' Both good and evil he has transcended, and he is therefore troubled no more by what he may or may not have done."

I looked around me at the others to see how the readings registered with them. Their faces were blank; they chewed away at their meal with eyes downcast or closed, mostly looking exhausted. I gathered that discussion was not an acceptable pastime at Beloved's table. Yet my mind would not be still; it brimmed with ideas and responses to what I had just heard. For instance, I knew that Atman was the Sanskrit word for the inner God or the Self that Carl Jung spoke of. I was developing a pet theory that the Hebraic corollary to Atman was Elohim, one of a multitude of holy names for God but the only plural name that existed in the Jewish tradition. For however many people had souls, there were that many Elohim, or manifestations of the Self, I thought. And this divinity that we had implanted within us, Elohim or Atman or Self, was eternal certainly; incomprehensible, unfettered—yes, all of these. But did it transcend good and evil? What was being implied? That our actions were inconsequential? Beloved was continuing; I tuned back in.

"Then father is no father, mother is no mother; worlds disappear, gods disappear, scriptures disappear; the thief is no more, the murderer is no more, castes are no more... The Self is then untouched either by good or by evil, and the sorrows of the heart are turned into joy."

This was utterly different from anything I had ever been taught in Judaism, where the value of one's life was determined by one's actions. Who you were was who you were in the Jewish view, and that would not change by way of mystical intervention, but by changing your own actions. If you committed some evil, no touch of God's would transform you; you had to make amends, then change yourself. For Jews, mystical experience was no license for poor behavior. This was obviously why the rabbis had stipulated that the Kabbalah be studied only by learned people forty and over. They wanted you to be firmly grounded in the world of ethics before you took off into other dimensions.

I mused on these ideas as I helped the women clean up the dishes. Before I was done, Beloved motioned for me to come behind a large batiked pink arid beige cloth. There he sat, cross-legged on a large bed.

"Sit down. I know you're tired after your long journey, so we'll be brief tonight," he said in a crisply accented English that I could not place. He was looking down as he spoke, flipping through a book that lay on the bed. "You had a question?"

Did I have a question? Sure, I had a million. For starters, I wanted to know by what standard he deemed himself to be a guru, why he had three wives, what he meant by splitting Everlasting and me up, and whether he considered women to be lesser than men, because it sure looked that way. But I went in another direction.

"The reading at dinner, when you said 'untouched either by good or by evil,' did it mean that contact with the Atman absolves your guilt even if you've done something terrible?" He looked at me blankly. It was hard to read him, and that made him scarier to me.

"Once divine knowledge is revealed to a man, he is free. In the fire of his divine knowledge, all evil is burnt away. Freed from evil, freed from desire, freed from doubt is the knower of Brahman." As a child, I had always found it frustrating when asking a heartfelt question of the rabbi to be answered with quotes from the Torah. I felt the same way now. Beloved was staring at me with squinting eyes. His tone was impatient.

"Tirzah, what is it that you desire?" The immediacy of his question stung me. I closed my eyes and tried to calm myself before answering.

"For one thing, the bliss that I was allowed to experience this year with Everlasting, and the peace of my true nature. And also the feeling of the Divine Mother around me, all of it—I want to learn how to live from there, in that space." I hoped he knew what I was talking about. "It was too hard in the world, in the city."

"Do you think I don't know what you've been going through?" he said it with a smirk. "You don't have to wait anymore to elevate yourself to God. I'm here by your request, to take you up. But you must obey me. Do you hear?"

I nodded, hoping that my fear and confusion were not showing. I had no idea who this man was nor what gave him the right to say these things. But my faith in Everlasting—strangely incontrovertible even after he had jilted me— had gotten me here, in the belief that before me sat a true avatar.

"Go meditate now, for one half hour before sleep," Beloved continued. "I will be there to help you." He waved me off and I obediently departed through the curtain room divider. Here in the main room a bed was set up for me. I climbed onto it and under the covers to begin my meditation.

I focused on my third eye where I had painted my red dot. This was known as a *bindu*, a reminder of God's residence within, like a small seed or the blue pearl of the Self. I had not understood Beloved's cryptic words and felt relieved to return to myself and my own simple mantra. *I am in God, God is in me; God and I are one*, I repeated. But my mind started up immediately: What if Beloved *was* an avatar? Did that mean he was an embodiment of God? Good grief! I didn't even know if I liked him. I needed time to study him before I turned my life over to him. Everlasting would say that was just my mind short-circuiting me again, and couldn't I just surrender for once? No! One can't force surrender; I did not feel comfortable with this man, guru or no. My teacher Randy had said in his farewell blessing to me when I left school: *Remember, no path is a true path if it's not the path of the heart.*

And so I struggled until sleep finally claimed me. If Beloved came to elucidate my meditations, I never noticed. When I awakened, the cabin was frosty; it had gone down to forty degrees below zero during the night. Through the dark hours, the wives took shifts feeding the stove. In the morning, stiff but happy to get moving, I began my karma yoga training under their direction: splitting logs, stacking wood, and tending the animals outside, baking bread and cooking inside.

I decided that Beloved's three wives must have worked extensively in meditation to bring about the kind of silent composure they exhibited throughout the day. Or was it depression? I could not tell for sure. Each focused on the task in front of her without speaking an idle word. How peculiar not to hear any womanly chatter about rough hands or new clothes, certainly not about their master and husband. As I followed them around, I brimmed with thoughts and speculations, theories, questions, and, not infrequently, judgments.

The wives were all in their twenties and early thirties, I guessed, white, able-bodied and seemingly intelligent; none of them looked Jewish. *Of course dey're not Jewish!* my Yiddish jokester could not keep from commenting. *What Jewish girl worth her salt would marry a schvartze with no money, only to come up into dis kind of cold to work herself to the bone? She'd have to be meshugge!* I hushed my mind with my mantra.

After a lunch eaten in silence, Beloved called for me.

"Let's continue with desire," he said matter-of-factly. "You didn't get far in your meditation last night, hmm?" If he was just an ordinary guy, he had uncanny abilities. "Look here, Tirzah. As your desire is, so is your destiny, because where your desire is, there is your will. And where your will is, there are your deeds. Take a regular person like you: you act according to the desires you cling to. And after death, when you go to the next world, all the affects of your deeds and the impressions of all you've gone through in your life get distilled. Those desires and attachments that are not purified build inside the soul, wanting completion." As Beloved spoke, the woman I deemed to be me in the last life flashed into mind. She was banging on the door of the gas chamber. Beloved continued.

"They pull you back into rebirth. And bang!" Beloved clapped his hands together loudly, "you're back here for yet another round of life. Vedanta, or the Vedic scriptures that we follow here, tells us that once you have experienced the Atman," Beloved continued, "once you've attached to this other realm, you can step off the train. You're free! You never have to come back to this dark world again. Once you see this, Tirzah, all the identifications and attachments you think you came back here for and all those things you crave lose their appeal, like food that's lost its taste. It all becomes meaningless, because there is something light years greater and more real." He paused here, looking at me sternly. "We are after freedom here. Do you understand me?"

I nodded a perfunctory yes. But I felt intimidated and could not help but sense that Beloved was somehow addressing that experience of death I had had in Randy's class and the realizations that had followed about my identity as a Jew. If he was who he said he was, a realized being, then he knew everything I knew about myself and more. Suddenly, trusting my own self seemed less effectual than trusting Beloved. This thought first bedazzled, then scared me.

"Are you with me, woman?" he barked. His words slapped me back into focus.

"I think so, yes. You mean that if we can let go of our personal desires and identifications then we can be released from the cycle of rebirth? And if we can't, then those become our destiny."

"You heard correctly," Beloved answered me, his voice rising. "Now apply it, don't just say the words. Is what you desire truly to be free, as you say it is? Or are you still clinging to the karmic pressures you came in with?" He was after something, but I was not sure what. "Meditate on these things. And be careful not to tell yourself lies, Tirzah."

I left his quarters confused. Did ultimate freedom imply severing all allegiances to one's religion and one's people? But what if I had signed up for a specific mission in this lifetime that required me to have an allegiance? Mine had not yet come into clear focus yet, but already I intuited that my work had something to do with repairing psychic wounds and serving spiritual needs. Surely it would be incorrect to abandon a soul's mission of service! Yet in Beloved's interpretation of Vedanta, the high road was to soar above all of that. One's identifications became flawed by virtue of their particularity; rather than being honorable, they were seen as attachments that snagged a soul on its way to the highest goal attainable, which was to become one with the infinite.

That week Beloved announced that he would take nine days in undisturbed meditation in another cabin on the property. Our normal daily practices of reading the Vedic scriptures and meditating would continue, but his absence would allow me time to think things through. I passed these days tending the animals, the fires, and the food with the other women. At first it was awkward between us. No one had said anything, but I knew indirectly that the sort of small talk that makes life more comfortable among strangers was either undesirable or prohibited in Beloved's house, and so I desisted from asking them questions or offering any information about myself. By midweek, the four of us had settled into an unusual silence, punctuated by an occasional humming or chuckle that I had not heard when the master was in.

I had taken to praying for clarity in the matters that Beloved had raised with me. What was my true path? Following him toward spiritual liberation? Or was there another mission waiting dormant in my soul? Had Everlasting showed me to the door of my ultimate potential, or had I been led dangerously astray to this strange black man in a cold white land? I honestly did not know the answer to these questions and I prayed fervently to the point of tears each night before bed for an omen, a dream, some signpost to direct me.

On the sixth night of Beloved's absence, I awoke suddenly in the black of night with a wave of fear. I lay in my bed with my eyes closed and my heart thumping loudly. The other women were silent behind their partition and embers crackled in the stove. The room felt charged with a strange sort of electricity. What was it? I sat up and opened my eyes. There on my bed with his legs crossed was the dark figure of Beloved, staring at me with eyes that flashed red and gold like an animal's at night. I gasped loudly.

"What—?" I began in horror, but was instantly silenced by a long black index finger that floated from his lips toward mine.

"Shhhh. It's all right," he whispered. "Go back to sleep."

I lay back down in bed, holding the bedcovers tightly up around my chin. When I lifted my head a few seconds later, he was gone.

The next morning I awoke with a feeling of eerie uncertainty. Had Beloved really been there in the night, or had it been an apparition, an astral projection? I began wondering what the unspoken expectations about intimacy were in this community. How had Beloved's wives been selected anyway? Whatever the case was, things were going too far. I did not want to be played with, either in mind or in body, and I had not come here to be anybody's puppet.

Moreover, if Beloved did know something about me—my karma or my soul's journey—that I did not, let him be forthright about it rather than covert and manipulative. I determined that I would level with him when he returned.

All this while, the frightful cold had not let up and the physical reality of life in this frozen white country became unbearably grueling to me. I challenged myself to surmount my discomfort. Yet even going to the outhouse and taking care of bodily hygiene became onerous tasks for me. I pushed aside the facts that my extremities were in a perpetual state of frozen numbness and that I was experiencing cramps in my lower belly on and off throughout each day.

Ignoring my body as best I could, I went about my daily chores such as chopping wood or cleaning out the goats' pen. Occasionally, the Yiddish trickster would step in to converse with me. *So don't get so carried away with dis teacher of yours and his ideas. You tink your* bubbes *and* zeides *didn't know from cold weather? Dey knew! And chopping wood, dey knew, too! Dere's nothing so new here. You tink your ancestors, those simple folk*, pashuta Yiddin, *you came from, didn't know dat dis material world is* gurnischt? *You tink dey ever let demselves* rest *in this world? Never! Der eyes were fixed on survival in dis world and some peace and quiet in the next. Don't forget dat!* In this way, my Jewish kinfolk admonished me lest I have any ideas about betraying them. But I had many such ideas.

The little cabin changed markedly when Beloved reappeared the next week—it grew serious again. In fact, Beloved's brow was now knit in an attitude of angry consternation. He spoke little and when he did speak, sharply. His wives dodged adroitly out of his way when he passed and complied with his wishes quickly. I did not dare ask to speak with him now.

When he had been back a full week, Beloved motioned me into his quarters after dinner. But I was not allowed to begin. He clearly had his own agenda.

"I've been trying to help you," he began forcefully. "But you are very stubborn, too stubborn. Your longing is strong enough, nobody would doubt that. And it's ancient, you return with it every lifetime! Now you are being given a chance, as you have requested, and yet you still refuse to let go!"

"Excuse me," I asked earnestly, "but could you tell me what it is that I'm supposed to let go of?" Beloved moved toward me until his face was only inches away from mine.

"You mean, you still don't know?" His voice hovered somewhere between laughter and anger. Then he grabbed my wrist and held it firmly, as if he would refuse to let me bolt one more time. "Listen to me! You changed your name from Miriam to Tirzah two years ago, do you remember?" I nodded, wondering what he was getting at. "When you did that, you opened a door to a karmic change. And everything is still hanging in midair since that time, waiting for you to decide. Do you know what the word *decide* means, anyway? Homicide, suicide—it means to *kill off* something so you can let something else come to be! You need to kill off your associations with your past, with all that Miriam was."

Miriam was the name I had been called by my parents and teachers, by all the rabbis and rabbis' wives who had taught me about the Jewish people and their heritage. For me, the name Miriam symbolized what the name actually meant, *bitter waters* and my rebellion against too tight a religious grip.

"You mean, my Jewish past?"

"Yes, and all the damn stubbornness that goes with it!" he yelled.

I felt hot, my hackles were up, in ready defense of a heritage that I myself had felt suffocated by. At the same time, I wanted to know what Beloved meant. Was he just an anti-Semite or did he see something that I could not about the nature of my people? I decided to collect myself and appeal to him to spell out his intention.

"Beloved, look, I'm a little slow about all this, so hang in there with me, okay? Judaism *is* another path to God—like Vedanta is, right?"

"Hold it there," he said, still stern but slowing down a bit. He had let go of my wrist and his pink palm rested in his lap. "Vedanta tells us that all reality is one single principle: Brahman. The highest goal is not to become a Vedantist, nor to be a Jew, but to transcend all the limitations that come with those names and self-identities once and for all, to realize your true nature."

"But Judaism's greatest belief is oneness, too," I said, thinking about the Shema Yisrael, the central prayer that states the Jewish credo. *Hear Israel, the Lord our God, the Lord is One!*

"Some people can go to God using Judaism as their vehicle," Beloved conceded, dropping his voice to a near whisper, as if he was telling me the most intimate of secrets. "But most do not. Most get stuck on the Jewish history of suffering and victimization, and they begin to identify with being a victim or being oppressed, or maybe, like the new Jew in the State of Israel, with being a fighter. For some, those are lofty identities and their souls will never evolve any higher for ages to come. But there are other souls who have gone around the wheel many times and were not intended to stop there anymore. Remember, the soul's nature is not to be earthbound. Your soul, for one, Tirzah, is intended for spiritual freedom. It's intended to soar!"

How I would have loved to pick up and run right then, out of the room and away from this cocky little man. Yet something inside me wanted me to hear this and made me screech on my internal brakes so that I could not move. I was affronted by Beloved's portrayal of my people, yet what he was saying about getting stuck in one's identity resounded in me as truth. My head started to spin. Something vital was surfacing from way down inside me. I put up my hand to stop Beloved from saying any more. My eyes were closed in concentration and I felt myself beginning to well up with tears and emotion.

"Beloved, you've got to know by now how much I want to make it in this lifetime, to bust through. But... what if I told you that Judaism was... well, inextractable from me? If there is truth in it, then maybe that truth lives inside of me. Why would I want to give that up? Truth is truth, isn't it? Why not just filter out the decay and the mistaken thinking of the Jewish people, and salvage the valuable stuff?"

"I wish it were that easy!" Beloved bellowed back at me, his back erect, his brow furrowed. "Besides, I'm not concerned with mining Judaism for its gold. That's someone else's work. For our purposes, let's say that it's *you* that needs mining. Imagine yourself to be a mountain, a big, solid heap of junk and mistaken thinking, sprinkled with gold dust. We need to systematically bulldoze the mountain and sift the rubble for the worth. This will take years and it has to begin quickly." Then his voice trailed off and he closed his eyes in meditation. I closed mine, too, frantically imagining what being bulldozed would feel like. Would I have to become one of his wives, God forbid? And what would happen to the rest of my life? I realized that my body was shaking. Beloved interrupted my musings sharply.

"Your wavering will not get you far, Tirzah. Cut with your past and do it now!" Then, after a moment had passed, he spoke more gently. "Enough for now. Go to sleep and don't be so nervous. It doesn't help." I thought I saw a hint of kindness at the corner of Beloved's mouth as I nodded good night to him. For the first time, I felt his peculiar brand of personal attention.

Days passed and my internal pressure grew. Beloved had set me before a spiritual chasm and had asked me to cross it, to separate myself from my past once and for all. If only I could make the leap, or better yet, if only I had wings to fly the distance, I could be further initiated into a life of god-consciousness and would have what I considered to be my highest mystical nature revealed to me. I would have escaped into meditation, but even meditating had begun to fail me these past weeks, my ability to fly high arrested by the tumult of decision making. With Everlasting, I had grown accustomed to lifting off weightlessly into infinite fields of pristine light, but these billowing journeys had been forced downward by the undertow of my dilemma.

The choice was mine: to make vows to a new karmic lineage, or else declare my weakness in the form of loyalty to my past, my bloodline, and my lower, material nature. There was no question which was the preferable, more warrior-like path, yet I could not seem to move forward. Outwardly, I tiptoed around the issue as if it had never been discussed. But nobody was fooled. At the end of my first month in Minnesota, I felt Beloved's patience with me growing thin.

One evening after coming in from feeding the animals, Beloved broke through my pretense.

"You can't sit on the fence forever, Tirzah." His words reminded me of Elijah the Prophet's when he scolded the Jewish people for being unfaithful. I knew the lines by heart in the original Hebrew: "How long will you hop from branch to branch?"

"I know," I nodded, looking down. "I've been working on it."

"You can't trick yourself into having it both ways. Your soul has already decided."

Already decided? If that were true, maybe it was just a matter of going ahead. That night I steeled myself. If I was ever going to move forward spiritually, then I would have to take Beloved at his word, and once and for all summon the Arjuna-like swordsman from within to slice through my reticence and let go of a past that kept me earthbound and without cosmic vision.

I imagined hearing a groan going up from the Jewish quarter of heaven. What about the woman who struggled for her life? What would she say about such vows? And what about all those in my own family who had perished trying to live pure Jewish lives, unencumbered by meshugas such as gurus and kali yuga? To these voices I answered staunchly: The godly essence of my heritage would always remain; what was pure and transcendent about Judaism would survive within me. I was only sacrificing my small-minded identification with it, nothing more.

The next morning I asked to see Beloved first thing.

"So, you're ready," he said matter-of-factly, as if he had been privy to my nocturnal wanderings. "It's about time. We'll go right ahead. Your oath of commitment needs to be worn on your body as a reminder that will last throughout your lifetime. It'll come in the form of piercing your ear. Just one ear, your left. Carissa can do it for you, or Helena. Julianne is too squeamish."

I had never had my ears pierced, being too squeamish myself. As Beloved spoke, a memory surfaced from the Bible, an injunction to the slave. It went something like this: "If a slave chooses not to be freed on the seventh year, but rather to indenture himself to his master, you must pierce his ear with an awl as a sign of his lasting commitment to you." Suddenly I felt cold.

"I'll do it myself," I said, trembling. No one would touch me. If I was to become a slave, it would be by my own hand; I would be a slave to God, not to any mortal man.

"All right then. I have a gold ring for you. You do it in your own way. Come back and show me when you've finished." Unceremoniously, Beloved handed me a small, black leather pouch. Inside was one gold hoop. After examining it, I placed the bundle in my back pocket and went on with my morning chores. But I did not forget it. It seemed to burn through the pocket of my overalls into my flesh, and all morning I struggled to swallow down the hot tears that crept up my throat.

After lunch, I went to Helena, the seamstress of the community, for a thick needle. I put it through my gray mitten and walked over to the bathhouse, where a tiny little shaving mirror hung on the log wall, the only place I could find some privacy. Along the way, I picked up a small but solid piece of ice. After locking the door, I pressed the ice to my earlobe. Then I made a prayer: "Holy Father and Mother. With this act, help me to penetrate all the false ideas I have about who I really am. Bind me to You even closer so I can hear Your true purpose for me. I beg you, please don't let me go anywhere but the Truth. I do this for You and for You alone. Amen."

With my final words, I jabbed the needle into my ear. I shrieked with the pain that rose up to resist the puncture, but my fingers persisted to push the needle through my flesh. My body roared out in resistance against the invading metal but I wrestled myself not to stop pushing before the deed was done. The walls of the log cabin spun dizzyingly around me.

The next thing I heard was a banging at the door and Helena's voice. I found myself lying on the bathhouse floor, and realized I had fainted some minutes before. I was dirty and wet from my fall, but I had a hole through my left ear. I crawled weakly to the door and managed to unlatch it. Helena's eyes belied her displeasure at my state though she kept her voice steady.

"Let's clean you up a bit. Then I'll put in your earring. First you're going to need some rubbing alcohol. Didn't you think about disinfectant?" I hadn't and I was glad to be in someone else's hands who was a bit more clear-minded than I.

Back at the main cabin, cleaned up but still shaky, I felt the small gold hoop in my left ear. I had done it.

"All right," Beloved said to me the next day. "Here is your first test as an initiate of Vedanta. Study this piece from the Mundaka Upanishad. Go ahead, read it aloud." I opened the book and read the first sentence as marked.

"'Like two birds of golden plumage, inseparable companions, the individual self and the immortal Self are perched on the branches of the selfsame tree. The former tastes of the sweet and bitter fruits of the tree; the latter, tasting of neither, calmly observes.'"

"It continues," Beloved chimed in. "Study it and meditate upon it. And then there is this." He reached into his pocket and pulled out a sealed airmail envelope, hand-addressed to me, care of Beloved. "Let's see which bird you will be." My heart raced. It was from my sister Laya. I steadied myself lest I show Beloved my distress. "When did it come?" I asked casually.

"Last week," he answered. "I've been holding it for you till the right time. Remember your pledge about your past. It included family, too, you know."

I excused myself and went outside. I had not heard from my family for weeks, not since I had come to Minnesota. My stomach cramped up as I read:

Miriam, hope all is well up there. I thought you might want to know that Dad is in the hospital. Some complications with his diabetes. The doctors don't know exactly what it is but his heart is affected. Tom and I are in town looking after Mom, so don't worry. Just pray for him and try to be in touch. Love, Laya.

A pale February sun had begun to burn through the morning mist. Feeling its tentative warmth embrace me, I sat down on a log, bowed my head, and wept. Here I had made vows to a new Torah and a new lineage while my own father lay in a hospital, possibly dying. Who knew? There was no way to reach me by phone in this godforsaken place, and Beloved had kept the letter from me for days. How dare he! And then to expect that I should sit like the bird who calmly observes! I was furious.

I got up and started walking. There was a farmhouse three-fifths of a mile down the road and a wary farmwife let me use her phone. Isaiah answered the phone and reported that the doctors were stumped, my dad was failing. My belly cramped sharply as I walked back to Beloved's community.

That night I thrashed in bed, alternately praying, meditating, and pleading for help. How cavalier I had been! All my lofty intentions of disbanding the emotional ties to my past had not involved my heart at all, but came purely from my head. My allegiance with my people was still intact, stronger than ever. I knew this in my guts.

When I came behind the curtain to talk it over with Beloved, he barely looked up.

"Weak of heart!"

"Beloved, my father could be dying."

"It was one of your rabbis that said,'Let the dead bury their dead,'wasn't it?" He looked up at me. "It's time for you to go, Miriam. That's really your name, after all. Why not be honest with yourself? This is the same point you keep arriving at, life after life after life. You are offered freedom, and each time, at the last moment, the material world calls you back, your family calls you back. It's always something. Okay then. So let it be."

I staggered for words, shot through by his cruelty. "Is it that... final, then?"

"Look, I made vows, too, to *my* superiors," he answered angrily, and for the first time I could feel his own disappointment with me. "I promised to take you on. So, no, I won't abandon you—I'll work on your behalf to help you to your next stop. But it will be as Miriam, the Jewess, daughter of her people. This is the identity you are choosing, after all." His face was dour, his tone set with finality. "Now we need to get you out of here. You'll leave tomorrow."

As I pulled back the curtain to leave, he added with a snicker, "By the way, there's a rabbi you'll be meeting. Go with him. You have my blessing." When I looked at him quizzically, he said, "Go now," and turned away.

That night I slept little, wrestling down my feelings of failure, anger at Beloved's dismissal, and anxiety over my father's health. I whispered words of prayer throughout the night, for guidance, protection, and clarity.

At dawn I rose to meditate. It would be a day of travel: north to Winnipeg and then back, through the secular culture of airports, buses, and cities, to St. Louis. I was afraid of this reentry into normal society and full of anxiety about losing my spiritual focus upon my return to the secular world.

After my fervent prayers, I let go and fell back onto my bed, more from exhaustion and defeat than from intention. My body fell into a quiet yet wakeful state of relaxation, and then, quite despite myself, a strong feeling of exhilaration began to build in my chest.

With this excitement came an astoundingly clear image to my mind's eye: an enormous rose-colored heart floated in midair. But it wasn't just a picture; it had a personality, a warmth and a wisdom about it that made me want to cry. Before long, the heart sprouted two huge white wings, and began to soar carefree into open space. I remained quite still, hardly breathing, not wanting to lose the vision I was having and the feelings that it evoked. As if in the background, I could hear my own self sobbing, although no actual tears fell from my eyes, and a great sense of relief moved through me.

All this time I had been so hard, so determined, but I had forgotten my heart. This experience was a powerful answer to my prayers, a message that my heart was still intact and I could trust it to lead me. The spiritual pressure that had been building for months had become a sort of tyranny, a cage around this elegant bird. Now it had burst open.

Gratitude welled up in my chest. Even if I was choosing the more earth-bound path and was bound to my people, unable to kill off my past and transcend my karma, I was following my heart. My healing had begun. I may have failed the test of crossing the chasm into new spiritual territory, but now I knew I was being guided by a vision bigger than my own and kinder than Beloved's.

Only two months had passed since I had walked into this strange and frigid reality. How fortunate I was to leave when I did before any more damage was done! In many cults, I now realize, the process of self-extrication can take years, even decades. I often wonder at my good fortune. Was it the power of prayer, of destiny, or the sheer grace of God that helped me make my quick exodus out of this voluntary enslavement?

After a bowl of hot cereal and stiff good-byes to Beloved and his wives, I set out, feeling a freedom that made me want to belt out old Joan Baez spirituals and kick around the snow and ice as I walked along the road. I carried just my pack on my back, having left some of the heavy-duty winter clothes behind for the women, and this time, I wore no mark at my third eye. I was centered in my heart now and still feeling a warm throb in my chest from my dawn experience. Yes, I was lost. But who wasn't? Something had shifted for me; I felt a new ease as I made my way back to my family home.

Throughout the day, I watched people with an unfettered mind, speaking spontaneously to fellow travelers and wishing them well or calling out "God bless you," relieved of the heavy burden Everlasting and Beloved had placed on me of judging the outer world so harshly. For the first time in months, perhaps since my Arica days, when I chanted the mantra *We are one*, I felt that I was on the same boat as the rest of humanity, no longer separated from others, no longer fighting the common current in order to keep up my rigid spiritual focus.

But alongside my newfound sense of oneness came an immense grief—the loss of what I supposed was the opportunity of a lifetime: the transcendence of one's humanity. To my critical mind, I was back where I had started, having failed to reach the timeless, boundless zones of spiritual freedom. After all the passion, aspiring, and dedication, I had no outward accomplishment to show for my spiritual work but a pierced ear, which was now infected.

What I could not see was that in allowing myself this failure, I had actually opened myself to God's grace and compassion. By *not* succeeding on this rigid path—the fundamentalist path that kept luring me back in different guises throughout my journey—my heart was able to fly open, and once again join humanity. But my head still told me that the human adventure was not good enough. I had been indoctrinated with the Hindu idea that humanity was too slow and imperfect, that I needed to evolve beyond it, to a state that was free of its baggage, into my soul's pure essence.

My very first religious training in Judaism had also smacked of a "separate and different" worldview; it too was one that judged heavily, and professed to be the one *right* way to live life. Again I had fallen for the same brand of absolutism that I had experienced in an ultraorthodox world—only the packaging was different. Both held the heart captive behind tight bars.

After years of flirting with spiritual paths that tend toward a dramatic, all-or-nothing doctrine (and I include some interpretations of Judaism in this camp), I have learned that when the path begins to look black and white in the extreme, suspicion is in order. The greatest truths of life are not so simple. Real spiritual maturity asks us to stretch ourselves so that we might contain the opposing forces of our lives, rarely to negate one by making it wrong.

In the absence of a loving heart, any form of spirituality can turn into tyranny. The true test, after all, is not transcendence but love. Along the way, it helps to ask: Does the path I am on help me to connect with others or does it separate me? Is a sacrifice being asked of me for the purpose of aggrandizing myself or the group, or of becoming more permeable to God's will? Am I being trained to listen to the voice of truth within, or am I being told what the unquestioned truth is from without?

Spiritual freedom is seldom secured in a tidy manner. It is neither grasped nor jumped into all at once, but is rather the slowripening fruit of a seasoned soul. I had been asked to pluck the fruit prematurely, to let go and fly free of a self I had not yet become. I did not realize that before I could spring out of this world and away from all that I had been given, I had to first choose to be *in it* with my whole being, body and soul—to step into life in its most human form.

Shame crushes the spirit, leaving us isolated. But humility connects people. My failures had humbled me, but having been gifted with the vision of the winged heart, I could not feel ashamed. I arrived home without the chutzpah, the bravado, I normally exhibited. My heart ached at what I had been through, yet it was open and alive. Paradoxically, through failing the test of transcendence, it had sprouted wings. In this way, I came to the hospital to visit my ailing father.

CHAPTER SIX

BLOOD TIES

WHEN I ARRIVED HOME ON FEBRUARY 28, 1977, I found my family in a similarly humbled mood, shaken by the severity of my father's condition and the uncertainty of his prognosis. I had told my family only the barest minimum about my foray into the Hindu religion, though even that was enough ammunition for them to damn me for years to come. But there is nothing like a reminder of one's mortality to silence a judging mind, and given the gravity of my father's medical situation, all I had to endure was one or two derisive comments about the intelligence of moving to northern Minnesota in January. I did not argue the point.

The days passed uneventfully. I visited my father at the hospital, where the doctors were stabilizing him on medications, listened to my mother talk out her fears, and caught up on world news. Since my return from rural Minnesota, where every day had seemed charged with spiritual intention and every conversation had crackled with meaning of karmic proportions, I had fallen into a sort of sleep state, as if resting from a soul-deep exhaustion. I had not yet begun to come to terms with the dangerous cosmic journey I had just alighted from, or its failings. Nor had I taken stock of the fact that the course of my life had been almost devastated by my turning it over to my hierophant lover and his guru for their guidance. I knew these things awaited my attention, but I could not think about them just yet. My mind was still too permeated with the sticky ideology I had been immersed in to be in any way objective.

One morning, after my first week home and some gradual improvement in his health, my father called me into his hospital room for a private tête-à-tête. I was prepared to hear him review plans for a battery of tests at the Mayo Clinic and give me orders for how best to care for my mother. But he surprised me.

"Miriam, do you remember a man named Daniel Fox?" he asked with a gleam in his eye. "That young rabbi from South Africa? He says he met you at shul just before you moved to Colorado."

Daniel Fox. I did indeed remember him. He was a swaggeringly handsome man with deep-blue eyes and a goatee. The fact that he was a rabbi and yet sexy had intrigued me when we were introduced.

"Yeah, I remember. What about him?" I answered nonchalantly.

"He's back in the States starting a new yeshiva. He called me in the hospital last week. He asked about you."

"What for?"

"Miriam, don't be stupid. He's single and you must have impressed him. Why don't you call him while he's in town?"

"I'll consider it," I answered politely, while inside I chortled to myself about how novel it would be to date a Jew, not to mention a rabbi.

What was it about rabbis, anyway, that they kept cropping up, first in my dreams, then via Beloved's ominous parting words, and now in my waking life? Why was I being tickled by these images of consorting with a rabbi—I who had engrossed myself in non-Jewish ideologies and practices for years now and had come so close to severing ties with the Jewish religion altogether? There was some message here, but it lay just beneath the surface, inaccessible to my conscious mind.

I could not yet see that something in my own psyche was leaving me signals like so many little bread crumbs along my path, hinting as to the direction it wished for me to grow in. My inner masculine side—the capable, analytical facet of my personality—was beginning to come to life. But I was utterly unaware of my own potential at the time, and I had not begun to envision myself as a person with any authority of my own. Instead, I continued to do what many women do until they step into their own worldly power: I projected my spiritual authority onto any man who fit my picture of wholeness.

Beguiled by my father's words, I found it pleasant to weave mental fantasies about the handsome rabbinic stranger. Perhaps he was a spiritual adept, I mused, a universally inclined soul who had chosen the Jewish tradition to pour into it his visions of the cosmos, while being unattached to Judaism per se. Or maybe he was secretly a student of Vedanta or Eastern mysticism, dedicated to uplifting the Jewish people through meditation, and God had put him on my path to be my mystical companion. Despite the fact that Beloved had uncovered my very visceral connection to my Jewish heritage, I reckoned it would take at least such a companion for me to want to actually *return* to my Jewish heritage. It would take someone who valued all forms of wisdom and could rise above his identity as a Jew while still being one.

Two days later, I called Daniel Fox. His voice was deep and buttery. He told me he would be in St. Louis for a few more days doing fundraising for his new school, located in a town just north of San Francisco. We made arrangements to go out on Saturday night.

"I'm enchanted that you came back to town just in time to see me," he said in a self-assured voice as we walked to his car. "I had a feeling we would meet up again." His words, reminiscent of my first meeting with Everlasting, made me chuckle slightly under my breath. Did all men use these lines, or only the ones I chose?

"Did I say something funny?" he asked as he opened the car door for me.

"Oh, no. It's really only happenstance that brings me back to town." *(He should only know from where!* my Yiddish jokester piped in.) "My dad took ill, as you know."

"There is no such thing as happenstance," he answered smugly as he revved his car and slid it into fourth gear. "Only *b'shert*—meant to be."

We drove downtown and rode the elevator up to the rooftop of the Stouffer Tower to overlook the city of St. Louis at night. It did not take me long to discover that my date was not a spiritual master. As we talked, I noticed that Daniel peppered everything he said with the names of wealthy, influential people.

"You certainly seem to know a lot of important people," I finally said.

"Not as many as I have yet to know!" he answered quickly, so smitten with himself that he missed my sarcasm.

Still, Daniel was enigmatic enough not to be dismissed entirely. He seemed to follow my discourses on karma and the evolution of the soul without flinching. In return, he told me about his plans for a boys' religious school that would integrate nature studies, sailing, and high-caliber academics into a Talmudic curriculum. Perhaps I would come sailing with him? He had just purchased a thirty-eight-foot sloop, which he would be sailing north from Long Beach to San Francisco in a couple of weeks. There was nothing like sailing, he boasted, if one wanted to experience a taste of *real* freedom. I held my tongue, embarrassed at the rabbi's show of shallowness. Yet there was something in his manner of speech, perhaps it was his smart South African cadence or his accent, that I found alluring. And then there was the fact that Daniel was playing by his own rather than anyone else's rules. That was an anomaly for a rabbi.

I saw him twice more before he left town. My father was packing for the Mayo Clinic when Daniel dropped me off at home the last time. There was a sentimental twinkle in my father's eye as he shook Daniel's hand at the front door.

After the rabbi's black convertible rental car had driven off, my father said to me wistfully, "Miriam, it would be a great thing if you could bring a Daniel back into the family."

It took me a moment to understand his meaning. So my father had his own brand of fantasies going on, too. To him, Daniel represented an opportunity to create a tidy ending to an ugly family tragedy. Even the rabbi's name was perfect: Daniel, just like my lost brother's. I could see the headlines in my father's eyes: *Wayward Daughter Saved from Eastern Religious Cult by Handsome Young Rabbi; Family's Losses Recouped Point for Point.*

I did not begrudge my father his delight. He needed something to keep his morale high, and fantasizing a healed family—that is, a family who saw things his way—was a good start. Besides, what did I know? Maybe there *was* some obscure magic at play here. As I thought about it, a sailboat trip up the Pacific coast sounded lovely, a fine diversion from my endless ruminations about how to pick up the pieces of my life. I was feeling as though I had just been thrown by an expensive racehorse, one that I had bet heavily on. I was bruised and disoriented, and had nothing left to invest. If someone wanted to give me a free ride badly enough, I supposed I would not turn it down.

My own sense of self-failure and the bind of not belonging anywhere was daily metamorphosing into a form of nihilism, the kind that looks at life's options and says, *Why not? Nothing really matters anyway.* It was not that I was enamored of the rabbi; I could see through his braggadocio quite clearly. It was rather that something seemed to have been set in motion and I hadn't the energy or the direction to oppose it. I told my father about Daniel's invitation to sail. Not surprisingly, he gave me his blessings. "I'm not kicking the bucket yet," he said. "Go enjoy yourselves."

From the moment I made the decision to fly out to Long Beach where Daniel's new boat awaited him, I dropped even the vestiges of my spiritual practice. I was skimming the surface of life and that was fine with me. I did not care to meditate; it would have put me in touch with the pain I had buried inside, the pain of losing Everlasting, of having sacrificed my relationships with my Arican friends, of my aborted studies and my failure to attain the spiritual heights that had beckoned me. I did not want to deal with any of these catastrophes, nor did I wish to hear from God for a while. I would play it cool, abandon myself to life, and lay to rest my almost rabid spiritual focus, which had gotten me nowhere fast. The rest of the population seemed to be dillydallying their incarnations away with no mind for spiritual liberation. Why should I not do the same?

What was worse, my twenty-two-year-old brand of nihilism was hopelessly tinged with my Hindu indoctrination, which told me that all aspects of life that might lure one into believing in the illusion of the earth plane must be transcended. Human warmth, the need for family, and indulging the physical body were all samsara—worldly traps to be avoided. Yet all of these were suddenly calling for my attention, especially my physical health, which was showing serious signs of deterioration.

Now that I was away from the rural community and in the comfort of my parents' suburban home, my symptoms had grown more noticeable. I had missed a couple of menstrual periods and had chalked it up to the extreme climatic changes I'd undergone. I supposed that my body was probably colluding with my intolerance for the frigid outhouse and having to heat water by hand to get cleaned up. But now I was back in civilization and my periods had still not returned. What was more, my lower abdomen continued to cramp up intermittently throughout the day, and the pain had been growing weekly.

My approach was to ignore the problem. The physical body should never control one's state of mind, I reminded myself. Discomfort was to be surmounted unless it was a crisis of life or death. I did not realize that I was heading for just such a crisis.

Just before leaving St. Louis to meet Daniel in California, I phoned Annie in Denver to let her know that I had left Beloved's and that I was going sailing with a South African rabbi.

"You never cease to amaze me, Tirzah." Then she quickly added, "I'm just thankful you're out of that guru's clutches. Do you know how many of us were praying for you?" I cringed. "You probably don't want to hear this, given that it was me who introduced you to Everlasting, but I was really worried about you. I knew you were headed for trouble when you stopped smiling. Life should never be that serious."

I told Annie a bit about Beloved's community and the rigorous attempts I had made to follow his philosophy and transcend the normal human path.

"Better that it didn't work out," she answered. "Besides, where else is there to go, outside of the human experience? Now hold on a minute, I want to check something." I heard her flip through a book, her astrological ephemeris, no doubt. "Tirzah, listen. There's a lunar eclipse coming up next weekend. And it's in Pisces, right on your ascendant. This is probably the worst time possible for you to get on a boat, especially going north against the current. I hope this rabbi friend of yours knows how to sail!"

I laughed Annie and her astrology off and promised to be back in touch with her as soon as I figured out my life. Later that week, I flew to California.

There were to be three of us sailing, Daniel reported when he picked me up at the Long Beach dock. He had invited Larry, a hefty eighteen-year-old from Atlanta and a student at Daniel's new school, to be first mate. I figured that Larry was along to satisfy the Orthodox injunction that no time be spent in private with an unmarried woman. Either way, I was glad for Larry's easy-going company, and, unlike me, he seemed undaunted by the nautical world.

Shortly after we hoisted the anchor, I realized that Daniel's self-assured-ness about his skills at sea was nothing more than a facade. Our first day out he spent sick and coiled over the deck railing, vomiting. Then he staggered to bed, yelling out some numbers to Larry and leaving us to navigate by ourselves. This was the first time I had set foot on a sailboat and I didn't dare ask Larry how much sailing experience he had. He seemed to know what he was doing, but I had begun to lose confidence in men who looked too sure of themselves.

Late that night, Daniel still below, the boat began making strange sounds. We had entered shallow waters and were periodically grounding our keel on the sandy shoals. Daniel had just come up to see what was happening when there was a loud crashing noise from the belly of the boat and we jolted to an abrupt halt. Daniel quickly radioed for help, yelling "May Day! May Day!" in a voice so shrill and childlike that I almost laughed out loud despite the tense-ness of the situation.

It turned out that we had gone aground very near a U.S. naval base. Within a quarter of an hour, a Navy crew met us with an array of security alerts, sirens, and blaring lights. We were taken into their facility like criminals, undergoing a harsh and scrutinizing interrogation until four in the morning. Shamefacedly, we explained that our captain had taken ill and we had simply gotten lost; we were neither spies nor were we invading the naval base. Our story was wacky, but they finally believed it and they helped us back onto course heading for San Luis Obispo.

The next day was beautiful and sunny, and Daniel seemed to be feel-ing better. The men laughed about our silly ordeal of the night before, while I remained silent, wary of their lightheartedness. We began to trade stories about our hometowns and Daniel spoke about life in Johannesburg as sunny and carefree. My ears perked up. I had been reading about South Africa in the news, and the utter viciousness of the apartheid regime was a well-known fact. Steven Biko, the charismatic nationalist leader, had been beaten to death by white security guards in 1977 and Nelson Mandela had already been in prison for ten years. I wondered how Daniel could speak so blithely about the situation.

"How can you call your country *carefree* when its natives have had their country stolen out from under them and are living in squalor? If it's carefree for whites, it's because they're walking around with their eyes closed!" Daniel's face grew red and his eyes narrowed at me.

"Why do all you leftists sound alike? You people love to make a fuss about nothing. We live very peacefully in South Africa. The blacks are miserable by their own doing. They don't know their place." After a dumbfounded pause on my part, he added, "And you, you're so wedded to your crazy way of seeing life, you don't begin to know the facts."

"So, if things are so lovely in your homeland, why didn't you stay there?" I shot back. Daniel collected himself for a moment and then replied.

"Simply because there are more opportunities in your country vis-à-vis Judaism. There's more tolerance for innovation. That and the fact that there's bound to be trouble for us Jews. The blacks don't like us."

Small wonder why, with an attitude such as his, I thought to myself in disgust. I said no more, shocked by Daniel's denial and hurt by his snideness. What kind of a rabbi was he, to want to defend a notoriously corrupt system? I had thought rabbis were meant to be spoksmen of justice and proclaimers of truth, even if they were not spiritual adepts.

From that point on, I held my peace when it came to discussing political views about anything. We arrived at San Luis Obispo on Friday evening and set anchor for the Sabbath. Safely bobbing, the three of us lit two small white candles and sang the Hebrew blessing as the orange sun quickly sank into the sea. Our plan was to spend all of Saturday at this anchorage; I looked forward to resting and reading my book in the sun. After a quick dinner, the three of us dispersed to our respective quarters to sleep:

In the morning, I came on deck to hear the men discussing the use of the engine to get under way again.

"But why would you start the engine? It's Shabbos," I cut in. "I thought we were just going to take it easy for the day."

Daniel's face reddened. Then he spoke brusquely. "I didn't think things like Shabbos mattered to someone like you. Anyway, we have to. There's talk of a storm hitting tonight and this way we have a chance of outrunning it. This is a captain's decision."

Larry nodded and I shrugged my assent. Together, the two men weighed anchor and powered up the engine. Of course I was not a Sabbath observer, the rabbi was right about that, but his blatant violation of the holy day rankled me and, once again, lowered him in my esteem.

Daniel's calculations were faulty. All that morning, as we made way under power, it was bright and sunny, but by noon the sky began to darken and the wind freshened, swelling the waves into peaks. The storm that Daniel had meant to outrun was already breaking loose and torrents of wind angrily whipped the surface of the ocean. I looked over at Daniel across the deck. His face was sallow and I knew he must not be feeling well. Soon he was looking gray and green, and begged off the wheel altogether to go to his quarters to rest. Larry and I took over once again.

By this time, the boat was heaving up and down in an alarming fashion. I began to grow frightened. Why was the captain of our ship below decks sleeping at a time like this? I thought of Jonah the Prophet going to sleep away his destiny as his crew mates struggled with the raging storm that God had sent on his behalf. Here the rabbi had violated the Sabbath to save time and avoid trouble, and just look where it had gotten us! We were going right into the storm! I imagined God's wrath pouring out of the heavens toward this man of little integrity, roaring out His dismay through the raging wind. "You call yourself a spokesman of Mine? Well, let me show you a thing or two..."

As our boat seethed in a tumultuous sea hour after hour, the rabbi slept below. "Get up here and face your trouble, Jonah!" I said under my breath as I fought to hold onto the wheel. Even Larry was beginning to look nervous now. It was clear that the boat was utterly out of our control, heaving about recklessly on the growing waves. Daniel finally emerged from his quarters looking aghast. He began to yell orders and threw foul-weather gear at us to put on in a hurry. When the waves began exploding over the sides of the boat so that we could no longer see, he had us each rope ourselves in lest we be thrown overboard.

Our sloop struggled to keep from capsizing, and we all fought simply to hang on. The seas were thirteen feet high now, and we were being repeatedly drenched by the heavy sheets of seawater that pummeled the deck without cease. It began to dawn upon me that we might not make it. Only God knew where we were in this vast ocean now, being cast about like a piece of straw. Now I felt ashamed at how glib I had become about the topic of death. During these last several years of spiritual questing, I had spoken of death as my friend and ally. All that talk seemed like utter nonsense at the moment. I could easily die this very night and my spirit raged against it. With blackness all around, our boat had become an unresponsive, waterlogged object that could sink under the next wave. How long until we overturned or were ripped from our lines and thrown into the cold darkness? My whole body shook from head to toe, and then I remembered my need for God. I began to cry hard, praying through my tears.

"Oh God, I've been such an idiot. Please forgive me for being so arrogant, for thinking that it was I who was in charge of my life. I admit it, I forgot You, God, I forgot that my life is in Your hands." As the boat flailed about, utterly out of control, the psalms and Hebrew prayers that my memory still held in storage rose to the surface of my mind and I grabbed onto them for dear life. Into the howling wind and hurling waters I cried out these reminders of my childhood faith, the first mantras I had ever recited. *"Hineh lo yannum v'lo yishan, Shomer Yisrael!* Don't sleep now, God, I've been sleeping, don't You sleep! Watch over this boat! *Mima'amakim k'raticha Yah!* I'm calling you from the depths, God. Don't leave us to die in this storm. I beg You, don't leave us to die in this storm. Let us live through this!"

Our battle with the gale continued for hours. I was numb with cold and fear when suddenly, out of the blackness, I thought I saw lights off our starboard bow. At first it looked like a cluster of stars, or could my imagination be playing tricks on me? Perhaps we had all died and they were celestial lights.

Then I heard the voices of my two crewmates yelling in celebration. But I was certain that it was by no skill of theirs nor by any fluke of nature that we were saved. It was by God's grace alone that our boat had found its way back to civilization. I was never so happy to see the lights of humanity; the radiant neon colors of 7-Eleven, Howard Johnson's, and Mobil Oil onshore were resplendent with life and divine meaning. The men started the engine up once again and steered their way to shore while I sat down on the soaked deck and wept. This time I cried from relief, the sobs rising from deep in my belly at the gift of life, at the miracle of my pleas having been answered, at God's presence being so palpably, undeniably close by.

My spongy legs barely supported me on land and my body felt weak from overexertion and cold. As we docked the boat, we began hearing reports of accidents at sea that night. Two fishing boats and their crews had been lost and many more had reported serious damage. I whispered ardent prayers of thanksgiving as Daniel checked us all into a hotel for the remainder of the night. It was four o'clock in the morning.

Although little more than an hour before we had been struggling for our lives, I was astounded at the sight of Daniel kibitzing lightheartedly at the front desk with the hotel manager. His shamelessly cool persona had fallen firmly back into place. Where was God in his picture? I wondered. Here was a Jonah who had never woken up. If the trip had done anything for me at all, it was to wake me up to the fact that I was lost and needed God's help. This was when I began to learn the valuable lesson that there is always more security to be found in feeling one's neediness and vulnerability before God than in faking control, a behavior that the captain seemed to be modeling.

Orthodox friends of Daniel's, Brenda and Jonathon and their new baby, came to meet us the next morning. First, we surveyed the boat's damage and Daniel made arrangements for its repair. Then we all piled into their car and drove to their small house in Santa Clara. The men left hastily to pick up vehicles and go to the grounds of Daniel's new school. I remained behind to rest.

My body was still shaking from the stress of the night before and my cramps had begun again. When I went to the bathroom, I found that I had started bleeding heavily. But it was no ordinary period, rather, a steady stream of bright red blood that did not seem to let up. I began to panic. I needed someone who could attend to me, but only the cool and reserved Brenda was in the house with her baby. I made a prayer and called Brenda from inside the bathroom for help. Blood was everywhere.

"I think you're hemorrhaging," she gasped. "Let's have you lie down." Twenty minutes passed, and with the blood flow intensifying, Brenda called an ambulance to take me to the hospital. She stayed behind with her baby.

In the emergency room, the doctors probed and prodded me but could find nothing wrong. Surely it was related to the extreme stress of yesterday's boating incident, they said. The bleeding had slowed down; it would become a normal flow, and I was healthy enough to recoup my blood losses. I was sent back to Daniel's friends with a prescription of Darvon to ease the pain from cramping.

In the morning, the bleeding had subsided, but I knew that my problem had not been resolved. I felt an urgency to leave; whatever lay ahead for me, I did not want it to happen here, where I did not feel at home. From my room, I called two friends I had made at the Arica training who lived in the Bay Area. They were happy to hear from me and gave me directions to reach them by bus. Before leaving, I sat in my room and prayed. *Whatever is happening inside my body, please dear God, let it come to resolution. Help me learn what I need to learn but don't let me die. Hold me in Your protective arms on the bus ride. I need you. Amen.* Then I made haste to depart. I did not want to see Daniel again; any illusions I had had about him were now a memory that mocked my poor judgment. After cool good-byes to Brenda and Jonathon, I traveled on.

Later that night, out at a lively Mexican restaurant with my friends, I began to feel the the warm river of blood coursing out of me again. I rushed to the bathroom, leaving a crimson trail behind me. This time the flow was more forceful and gave no sign of letting up. I sat in the bathroom imagining rows of glass milk bottles being filled up with my red life force, one after the other. I began to cry. What was happening to me? My friends had followed me into the bathroom with towels from the kitchen. I did not need to look at the horror on their faces to know I was in serious trouble. Half an hour later, faint and scared, I was in an ambulance racing to the hospital in Berkeley.

The medical staff stood around me looking concerned. They estimated that I had already lost over five pints of blood and rushed me into surgery for a D and

C to clear out my uterus and stop the bleeding. I was wheeled into surgery quite conscious. Once again, I was smitten by my fear of death and a violent trembling shook my entire body. I felt so out of control that even prayer eluded me. *Let me live, God, let me live* was all I could think. Then I threw up. The doctors finally calmed me with a shot of Valium and proceeded with the D and C.

After the procedure, as the hospital aide rolled me into the elevator, I lay awake. I was alive, yet somehow, all I could feel was shame and failure at not having been able to control my violent fear. For over two years I had been working on achieving mental equilibrium. What was meditation for if you could not use it under duress? This last week I had fallen apart several times, giving myself over to panic and forgetting that I was not my body but pure spirit that would live on even if my body drowned or bled to death. Once again, I felt that I had been tested and had failed.

With these dismal self-reflections, I was wheeled into a sunny room where I spent the next week. The doctors explained to me that I had suffered an extreme hormonal imbalance, and asked if I was aware of anything that may have contributed to such a state. I answered that I had been on a tumultuous boating trip, nothing more. Inside, I knew that the answer was far more complex than that.

Blood transfusions began that day, along with intravenous penicillin and minerals. My friends came to visit me and made blessings over the plastic sacs of blood that dripped life back into my veins. They were kind to me, bringing others from their community of friends to cheer me on in my healing. But I was rough with myself, vacillating between feeling thankful for being alive and being deeply disappointed in myself for not surmounting the physical scare and transcending into the peaceful realm of the spirit.

Midweek, I opened my eyes from a morning nap to find my polarity therapy instructor from Boulder sitting by my bed. I refocused my eyes.

"Randy? Is it really you?" I asked bewildered. "What are you doing here?" He explained to me that he had come to California for a conference and had heard through mutual friends that I was in the hospital. I had not seen Randy since leaving for Minnesota. He had been disapproving of my choice to leave school and had cautioned me to follow my own truth rather than my teacher's. *No path is a true path if it's not the path of the heart* had been his last words to me, and I had not forgotten them.

"I heard you've been having some close shaves lately," he said laughingly. "I thought you might be able to use a little love to help pull you back."

I felt tears rising. "That's just the point. I'm not sure I want to come back. It's too hard and I keep botching it up."

"Who's judging?" Randy answered me. He was already standing at the foot of the bed holding points in my feet, balancing my energy. "Talk to me, Tirzah."

As Randy worked on me, I told him how I had come to leave Beloved and the trouble I had experienced since then, all of it intertwined with my extreme disappointment in myself.

"You're incorrigible, Tirzah. What does God have to do to get through to you? Break you in two?"

"I'm dumb," I answered. "I admit it! I can't see the forest for the trees here. What am I missing?"

"It's so clear to me that you've been forcing your spiritual work, as if you were in military training or something. You're merciless with yourself! Of course you keep failing, because your expectations for yourself don't include one little factor... that you're human! Remember, human? Made of flesh and blood? Maybe it's how you've been trained by these Hindu teachers of yours. Or maybe it's your Orthodox background that made you so rigid, but Tirzah!" Here he stopped to look at me directly. He was shaking his head and looked as though he might cry from sincerity. "You've got to stop this! You haven't left any room for the *heart* in this scheme of yours. Or for God's loving compassion. Nobody can survive without that."

As he said these last words, the image of the heart with wings instantly appeared to my mind's eye. Maybe God had attempted to redirect me by means of that image, but I had quickly let His effort get drowned out by my harsh judgments.

"I was told that I've been spinning my wheels for lifetimes, that there's a hump I never quite make it over."

"Maybe the hump is learning to love yourself, Tirzah. What in this or any other world could be more of a challenge than that? I don't care how many lifetimes you can save yourself from with your austerities. If you're not learning love on the way, where have you really gotten in the end?" There was a silence between us, and his words resounded through the room. Then he added, "Where is there to get to, anyway? Life isn't a race, you know. You've heard of the Bodhisattva, haven't you? He's able to jump off the wheel at any time but *willingly* chooses to keep coming back to help others. Now that's *high*, as you old dualists would say!" I had heard of the Bodhisattva and wondered if all traditions had such an ethic. In Judaism, it was the tzaddik, the righteous one, who was often hidden away, working wonders and spreading goodness in the most invisible ways.

Randy had shifted his position and stood near the head of my hospital bed to work on my neck. My body began to relax as it hadn't for a long while. I breathed deeply.

"Your energy is a mess, Tirzah. All in tangles. You should be glad I stopped by," he chuckled.

"I know. I hadn't felt well for a while. And then all that blood flowing out of me, like a red sea. The docs said I had a hormonal imbalance. But I don't think they really know."

"What do *you* think caused it?" he threw back at me.

"The blood loss? I always thought of blood as being what connects you to life and families. You know, like blood ties. Whatever it was, losing all that blood, it felt like my connection to life almost got severed."

"You've got some work ahead, too, to tie yourself back into life. You have this body, for one thing. And it's calling out to you to live in it! Think of it like a child calling out to its mother. It needs you to tend it and love it, even if it *is* imperfect and impermanent. You can afford to be gentle with yourself, Tirzah. There's no shame in being human." After a pause he added, "Remember, you can't serve others if you haven't first learned compassion for yourself."

Then we were quiet and I slid into a pleasant sleep as Randy continued to work on me. When I opened my eyes, he was gathering his things to go. He turned to me and whispered, "Meditate on increasing your blood, Tirzah. Think of it as your humanness flowing through you." When he was halfway out the door, his tone lightened. "And next time, you don't have to go to such extreme measures just to get me to work on you!" He winked at me. "See you back in Boulder."

Now why did he say that? I wondered. I had not mentioned going back to Boulder at all. But suddenly, it didn't sound like such a bad idea, especially if there were friends like Randy there who could guide me back into life. I would need plenty of humor and touching to help bind me in my body. And I would need to reconnect with my purpose again, not the purpose I had been engaged in, of leaving, transcending, escaping the prison of life, but a new purpose that would connect me to others and make my life fruitful again. Randy had spoken of serving others as if it was already understood that this was my life purpose; his words seemed to remind me of a pledge I had been on my way to making.

I knew that I stood at a choice point. The path of transcendence had been difficult enough. Now there was another, even more difficult decision before me, and that was to say yes to life. For that path there were no teachers: Friends could invite me back, but I had to choose life for myself.

Saying yes to life is the beginning point of spiritual adulthood. As with every other passage on the spiritual journey, we can get encouragement from others, but in the end, the *yes* has to come forth from our own selves, body and soul. Making a commitment to life can't happen until we have taken a good, sober look at what we are signing up for, having surveyed some of the delectable as well as the disheartening aspects of living in this world and realizing that life is an unpredictable journey composed of both aspects. It is a critical juncture in the spiritual journey, one that is never crossed by neophytes. Because only after we have experienced what it is to live falsely, or to live in the shadows, a half-life, only after we have encountered death itself, does our choice to fully seize life take on a new dimension.

A major principle in Judaism stems from the commandment *Bachartem b'chayim*—Choose life! The Jewish toast, *L'Chaim!*, "To life!" as well as the letters spelling the Hebrew word *Chai* (life) worn as a piece of jewelry, are liberally used by many Jews, but many of us do not know the inner significance of these words or why they are so popular. Choosing life, the Torah states clearly, has to do with staying connected or aligned to God, the eternal power that is present and speaking to us at this very moment. More than just living robustly or with verve, choosing life means committing ourselves to being very much in this world while holding to something that lives beyond it. The something beyond—call it God, truth, or the higher power—allows us to live life amid all the odds that this world presents without losing our foothold. It takes being in constant relationship with a power that does not die, outwardly to the higher consciousness and ethics that the Torah provides and internally to the still, small voice of our own selves. I had no idea that this concept of life was at the very basis of the Jewish heritage.

Instead of relating to our flawed, human world as separate from the divine, I now know that life is best approached as an interpenetration of light and dark, a blend of spirit with matter and the timeless with time. Rather than pressuring ourselves to graduate from normal consciousness to ascend to another, higher plane of truth, our task is one of bringing heaven down to earth, to live life with an open heart, to walk the dark path while carrying an internal lantern.

From my hospital bed, the frail recipient of the care and loving concern of friends but mostly strangers in white, I finally began to realize that life required *relating to*, not skipping over, and that meant bringing to it not only my discipline and grit but the failed, flawed, and embarrassed parts of me as well. Nobody in the hospital seemed to mind my failures as much as I. Love, food, and medicine, were not being withheld, but rather administered with the beatific generosity I had seen on the faces of the madonnas and gopis that Everlasting had described as faces of the Divine Mother. All that was required of me was the self-compassion and humanity to receive it. Did I have the ability to do that? It felt like a far greater challenge than being the warrior self that seemed to be my nature.

My friends collected me from the hospital at the end of the week and brought me back to their home to rest. After a few days, they took me to the airport and helped me onto a plane back to St. Louis. I had called my parents from the hospital to let them know where I was and to confirm my medical coverage. Now they awaited my arrival with concerned looks on their faces and a lot of questions I could not answer. My father had just returned from the Mayo Clinic, where he had been given a new regime of medications but few answers himself, so we could sympathize with each other. The only thing about my journey to California that I could tell my parents with any certainty was that the rabbi named Daniel was about as good at sailing as he was at being a rabbi and that I would not be seeing him again.

As soon as I could, I made my way to Laya and Tom's farm, which was vacant, Laya and Tom now living full-time in St. Louis. There, among the early autumn dogwoods and fields ready for harvest, I regrouped myself and recouped my strength while I made the necessary arrangements to return to school at the Healing Arts Institute in Boulder.

As I learned to approach life in a more humane way, I was also learning that the world of divinity was not high above me in another, separate realm, but below me, around me and within all of life's experiences. Spiritual mastery was neither something to be gotten (like a consumer item), nor achieved once and for all (like a law degree), although this goal orientation pervades many schools of thought nowadays, as it did the one I had just exited. Living a spiritual life, I now knew, was a lifelong process, one that involved not only study and practice but also keeping the heart open and the body grounded. As for teachers, there was no shortage: Feelings, intuitions, dreams, and friends along the way were all there in abundance to help me stay in harmony with the great mystery of life that some call God.

I MOVED BACK to Boulder in time for the spring 1978 semester, renting a room in a house with four other students from the Naropa Institute for Buddhist Studies and the Healing Arts Institute. Being in Boulder was an entirely different experience now. I no longer looked at life there with disdain and judgment; I was too weak and humbled by what I had been through. And although I was intent upon following my studies at the Healing Arts Institute through to completion this time, I needed to pace myself, paying careful attention to my nutrition and my rest. I still had almost a thousand hours of course work in nutrition, Reichian therapy, body-mind psychology, and therapeutic massage to complete before I graduated from the program. And my old ways of mastering myself through ruthless discipline and self-judgment were no longer reliable options for me now. My experiences of vulnerability and failure had changed all that, as well as my attitude toward others.

In my clinical massage practice with fellow students and clients whom I saw under my teachers'supervision I realized how changed I was. I had grown into a new sense of compassion that was quite heartfelt toward the people I was treating and the pain they were in, whether physical, emotional, or spiritual. As I lay my hands on people's ailing bodies or listened to them talk about themselves in riddles, I no longer heard Everlasting's harsh voice in my ear judging them for their frailties of spirit or their inability to access the truth about themselves. What I did hear, coming through the voices of so many people, in ways both subtle and forceful, was the struggle to live in human form.

There were those whose ties to this world were too strong, meaning that they had lost connection to their spiritual side, the intention with which they entered this lifetime, and were in need of purification, remembering, and revisiting their original purpose. But more numerous—perhaps I was attracting them—were those who harbored secret doubts about being in this world at all. Often the tentativeness of their relationship with life came in the form of questioning where or even if they belonged in this world, or a disillusionment about the meaning of life in general, or a perceived sense of personal failing to effect change on the planet. A weak tie to this world, I noticed, was not always conscious but showed up in a physical ailment like a lack of vitality, recurring injuries, inability to digest food, or weak blood.

My own frail health proved to be a boon. I was forced to work slowly with my clients and was more present than I had been earlier in my studies. I took pains to interview each person I saw, to ask questions about his or her life and find out what was of greatest importance to each one. Being aware of my own struggles and pain and the way I had armored my own heart for so long, I developed an ability, with help from the counseling courses in the Healing Arts program, to track people's voices and gestures as they spoke about their problems. Often I would notice averted eyes or a shift in posture or a change of topic when we neared the source of personal pain. If I succeeded in gently drawing the person's awareness to the area, it would often open and reveal itself in the form of some insight or revelation.

But an even more powerful phenomenon began to occur regularly as I worked with growing numbers of people on the massage table. With the use of breathing and under the firm touch of therapeutic massage, my clients would often go through an array of emotional responses that my training had not fully prepared me for. The touch of my hands in combination with the client's breath seemed to unlock not only deeply stored physical tension but emotional pain as well. Men as well as women would release feelings in the form of tears and sobbing, waves of fear and bursts of anger. Over time I realized that these were emotional experiences that had been, for some reason or another, either blocked off or short-circuited at the moment of occurrence and had buried themselves physically within the muscles' fabric, waiting for release. These feelings often had a life of their own, and they wanted out. Words of interpretation or insight from me, although I had plenty, usually interrupted rather than added to the client's natural process of discharge. Again and again, I had to learn to put my theories aside, sit back, and trust the wise and natural process of healing inside each person I worked with.

These massage and breath sessions often brought people behind the threshold of consciousness into a sort of trance state, a fertile ground where important soul information was abundant and accessible. This state did not occur in every session, of course, but it occurred often enough for me to begin to contact teachers and look for information that would help give me a cognitive handle for what was unfolding in my practice.

One semester passed and another began. As I reflected upon my training, I realized that what had started-out to be a physical form of therapy was quickly leading out of the physical dimension of healing altogether and into areas of the soul. Not that there were any borders between the body and the soul; in fact, that was precisely the point! The body, I was seeing with more and more regularity, was a portal to a person's inner realm. Certainly my own ailments had brought me some of my most valuable life learning. Now I was being taught in more ways how, far from being a prison, the body was a trustworthy courier of the soul.

Only a fine line separated my spiritual search from my healing studies now. They were so intermingled, it was hard to discern where one left off and the other began. Besides massage therapy and related body-centered therapy skills, I poured myself into studying Bach Flower Remedies, the Chinese Five-Element Theory and the groundbreaking movement known as holistic health, the all-encompassing philosophy of the day. I marveled at the synchrony and interrelationship of all the natural healing modalities that were coming to light. Everything I studied seemed to be pointing in the same ideological direction as my discoveries from my own massage therapy practice: The human is an indivisible whole. There is a magical interpenetration of body and psyche, and the relationship between them means that information from the mind freely translates itself from the stuff of dreams and beliefs to symptoms of well-being or pathology and back again. As with a hologram, any one piece of the whole gives access and insight into the entire being.

These were exciting times, and I had many colleagues and fellow students in Boulder with whom I shared these burgeoning ideas about the interconnectedness of our bodies, our minds, and the world. As information poured in from various fronts such as cancer rehabilitation, hypnotherapy, and brain research, it seemed as if our collective consciousness, rather than any one individual, was liberating the truths that were reshaping the templates of our thinking. There were hundreds of us in Boulder at work in the fields of healing, meditation, and spirituality; students and graduates of various schools of healing who were becoming practitioners in our own right. We considered ourselves to be comrades and pioneers in this adventure of shaping a new paradigm of health, sharing our experiences, literature, and excitement with one another with no thought of territoriality.

The end of my healing arts training approached. I hadn't consciously planned what would come next, but as I took stock of my life, it became apparent that I was building a flourishing private practice: Medical doctors and chiropractors from around the area referred their clients to me for relaxation, massage therapy, and exploration of the unconscious that might reveal the origins of a given physical or emotional disorder. For the first time since I had tended sheep on a kibbutz in Israel, I was in love with my work.

Yet I knew I was already at the limits of my training. I could easily handle clients who were basically healthy. They would rise from our session revitalized, having sloughed off their physical tension or the weight of some unpleasant emotional baggage. But then there were people like Ronnie, a woman of forty-five, who came in for rejuvenation and left calling her doctor for Valium. Ronnie had been abandoned as a baby, and although she was adopted by a loving family soon thereafter, she had never dealt with this primal wound. On the outside she was well adjusted, with a prominent position in the state government and a family of her own. But our relaxation work unearthed Ronnie's buried pain, and the panic and rage that ensued scared me and left her turned so inside out that she wished she had never seen me.

Two directives occurred to me at this point: I needed more training, and I needed to continue my explorations into my own soul. The first I would need in order to be a competent and skilled practitioner in the quickly growing field of natural healing. The second was born of my inner promptings and dreams, which told me that I was ready to dive further into my own unconscious realm. I began looking into a degree in counseling, as well as searching for someone who could help me interpret my dreams and decipher my own less-than-healthy patterns of giving my power away to men and self-judgment.

Almost two years had passed since my wintery experience in Minnesota. Once again, my feet were planted on the earth. My body was healthier, I was making a good living in an area of work that intrigued me, and I was living with a spirit of openness and experimentation.

At about this time, my parents and my younger brother Isaiah emigrated to Israel. My father had been forced to retire owing to his fragile health, and the doctors could not say how long he would live. What better time to realize their lifelong dream of moving to the Holy Land? We wrote amiably back and forth about their difficult new adventure. They were relieved to hear that my life had stabilized and that nothing contrary to their worldview seemed to be lurking on my horizon, at least for the time being.

I had indeed recommitted myself to life; only my spirituality was still tentative. I rarely allowed myself to meditate, for example, lest I feel tempted to soar into the boundless zones I so loved and leave this world. What in my Hindu explorations I had experienced as the divine world had deepened me, but that depth now proved to separate me from most people. I had no way to communicate about the endless zones of silence I had grown acquainted with, or the golden bliss I had used to comfort my human loneliness. So I stood on the other side of those experiences, disallowing them but never forgetting them.

I have learned over time that the process of regaining our health during or after a crisis is often accompanied by feelings of extreme discomfort. At Beloved's community, my intrinsic health had asserted itself in the form of tormenting mental struggle that forced me to wrestle with his teachings and finally to leave them. Now on my own, my health once again asserted itself painfully, this time in the form of a searing loneliness. I pined for intimacy, to share all of myself with a partner—my earthly side as well as the part of me that was awakened to the divinity in the universe.

During the next year, I remained in Boulder, working and studying for a master's degree in counseling through a university without walls called Beacon College. I began Jungian analysis with a remarkable woman named Leif. Life was fuller than it had ever been, but I had one unanswered prayer: for someone to share it with.

CHAPTER SEVEN

TO BEAR THE BEAMS OF LOVE

AFTER GRADUATION FROM THE HEALING ARTS INSTITUTE IN 1979, I rented a clean, comfortable Victorian home on Spruce Street in Boulder with two other women: Hannah, a social worker, and Joan, a psychologist. The three of us were on a similar quest for psychological and spiritual growth. By day we worked at our people-oriented jobs, while our evenings and weekends were filled with classes, workshops, and trainings. Together we practiced tai chi and studied with Reshad Feild, the Sufi master from Great Britain. I finally had the personal sobriety—or was it battle-weary skepticism?—that allowed me to take what I needed from these teachings without losing myself in the process.

During this time, the Naropa Institute in Boulder hosted Buddhist-Christian dialogues with brilliant and openhearted thinkers of both traditions. These presentations triggered in me profound dreams and insights about the Christ spirit. For the first time, I had a small inkling of what it might be like to have an ardent personal relationship with God, and I coveted having a teacher as pure and present in my life as Jesus was to his devotees. But I knew the dangers inherent in throwing one's lot in with a spiritual teacher, even one that was disembodied like Jesus. For now, I preferred to be spiritually homeless, allowing my dreams and inner promptings to be my guides.

It had become clear to me from looking at my dreams with Leif that before I involved myself with another spiritual path, I needed to focus on more personal issues, like clearing up my problematic relationships with various family members and learning to tell the truth to the people around me. At the time, I found this personal focus to be annoyingly ordinary and wanted to skip over it (which, thankfully, I did not).

Each session, I would dutifully bring in my dream journal and recite to Leif the dreams I had recorded that week. She would proceed to ask me for my associations to the various symbols that had shown up—a brightly colored fish, a cup of coffee, a library full of books. As I related to her my associations, Leif would artfully elicit other information about my life. Often, this process evoked extreme discomfort and embarrassment. I did not wish to expose and examine those painful areas of my life to which I had resigned myself: my parents'vulnerabilities, my blundering patterns with lovers, my faltering self-image. Yet, uncomfortable as I felt, bringing such topics into the light of day to be discussed with a wise and nonjudgmental friend allowed me the freedom to let go of much deeply held shame and rethink my responses to life.

I can see now that my work with Leif was one and the same as spiritual practice and that the personal tasks she gave me would be fundamental to any serious religious discipline. Whatever path one travels, sooner or later one finds that achieving (and sustaining) higher states of consciousness simply cannot happen without first looking at the personal issues that clutter one's life. I resigned myself to this unglamorous grunt work as I continued to pick and choose from the teachings and texts of many religions. Although I longed to find my true path, I held back on any commitment for now, telling myself I belonged to no religion and simultaneously to all religions.

Leif also helped me to understand how my Hindu training with Everlasting and Beloved had affected my worldview. I saw more clearly the dangerous, dichotomous thinking that led me to perceive God and the divine world as separate from the less significant earth plane. I was learning instead that spirit and matter, mind and body were all elements belonging on one continuum. And in much the same way, I began to realize that the invisible world of spirit was not a separate place to plea for help or escape to, but a continuation of our physical world, interconnected with humanity.

As my worldview evolved, I began to look for a relationship with God that was reciprocal. I had learned from Jung's teachings that as we relate to and honor the Self, so the Self will relate to and honor us. If we ignore it, it will leave us to our own devices. But if we spend time cultivating a relationship with the divine force—for instance, by paying attention to our dreams and intuition—it will reach out to us, to fill us with new insights and help us to grow. It had proved to be true for me; to the degree that I made myself receptive, so did I receive.

Although I had little awareness of it at the time, I was also searching for a relationship with a man that was reciprocal, a mirror of the ideal partnership with God. I had experienced the others. Now I was ready for a healthy relationship, one in which I was neither fused with my partner nor dominated by him, but rather enjoyed a loving interdependence.

I longed to meet a man who shared my vision of spirit as a continuum and would join me in living life in a conscious way. I had adopted a personal goal that life in the material world would be my spiritual offering, and I wanted to meet someone who would share that goal. In this relationship, we would use every aspect of the material plane as an opportunity for worshiping God: keeping house, making love, and even making money would all be included.

However, this kind of relationship was nowhere in sight. Instead, an embarrassing pattern was becoming obvious. In my idealism, I was attracted to nonconformist types of men, exotic world-travelers and passionate spiritual seekers. But invariably, the ones I moved toward seemed to move away from me. The men I found to be attractive were hardly predisposed to my particular vision of spiritual partnership. Within weeks of falling hard for one of these deep-eyed poets, I would discover that he was on his way to a yearlong trek in Nepal, was in treatment for substance abuse, or had just taken vows as a monk. My dream of sharing a life of embodied spirituality was not coming true, and as the months rolled by, I began to grow hopeless.

It was not the case that there were no men after me; there were plenty, but most of them left me cold. Many were nice Jewish boys from good homes who had been nowhere interesting. Nowhere interesting to *me*, that is; other young women seemed to have no problem being excited by these guys. My would-be suitors were advancing steadily in their fields of interest, on their way to success in management or law or banking. I tried to reason with myself: All of these are valuable fields, are they not? Barry would obviously make a good provider, I could see that. Phil had an outrageous sense of humor and Jay loved children. If I thought that there was not enough spiritual grit in these well-groomed, dependable types, I reminded myself that it was difficult to live in Boulder without *some* interest in the spiritual side of life. I tried to spark in myself some fire of interest for these men, with whom a relationship would have been so simple. But in the end, I was not after simplicity; I wanted a spiritual adventure. I did not know it then but in my quest for my mate, I needed the unfamiliar, not the common, the dark side of the moon rather than charted territory. My own likeness would not do; I was unconsciously seeking someone who was my opposite, to help bring out in me more of who I was.

Friends would set me up on blind dates and give my phone number to eligible Jewish bachelors. I took to stereotyping. As soon as I heard an East Coast accent on the phone, or a reference to job or money, my interest would wane. I tried to explain to my friends that the familiar values with which I had grown up were nice, but they were for someone else. On dates and at parties, my eyes roved endlessly, seeking to exchange looks with someone different, someone whose face blazed for me with mystery, someone who would take me on a trip into unknown regions.

I tried to settle for the familiar, forcing myself to date the brotherly, well-intended men who sought me out. There was Jerry, an earnest soul who believed that persistence was his ally in his attempts to court me. He brought me flowers regularly and was ever available at my beck and call. For my birthday, he lavished on me an extraordinary dinner at the Flagstaff House, the most expensive restaurant in town. I was duly flattered. Like me, Jerry had just begun therapy; he was reading *Love Is Letting Go of Fear* by Gerald Jampolsky and wanted to share his insights with me. But as he spoke to me over our candlelit dinner of the changes that were taking place in his personality, the neuroses in his family of origin and how he could finally laugh at his Jewish background, I had to wrestle down my boredom.

I flashed back to my latest sessions in analysis. Leif had been challenging my attraction to shady, unconventional types, men who would not come through for me, while I continued to dump the grounded, practical types—like the sincere and homey one now sitting across the dinner table from me. I had to admit that my track record showed a pattern of startlingly poor choices—men like Ron and Everlasting—a Jewish mother's nightmare. Was I trying to sabotage myself or was my wiring faulty? I wondered. As Jerry continued to express his predictable revelations, I was visited by my Yiddish trickster, whose finger wagged at me admonishingly:

Tirzah, dere is absolutely nothing wrong with dis one! Just look at how sincere he is! Better you should run after some twisted soul than a mensch like this? For what? I groaned. The voice would not quit. *So who are you to be so picky? The Queen of Sheba? You're twenty-six already! You want you should be alone for the rest of your life?*

I did not want to be alone. And I had not come so far in my spiritualization process that I no longer worried; I was full of worry. How could I be sure that my Yiddish trickster did not know more than I? Could I trust my own instincts here and wait for someone who was both mysterious *and* a mensch? But try as I might, I could not manage to push myself against my almost visceral distaste to go any further with Jerry or the likes of him. There was simply no passion to be found with these men, and I could not bring myself to fake it. I continually refocused on my work. And every morning and night I prayed fervently for my mate to appear.

At this time I had a big influx of new clients coming to me for massage and relaxation therapy. They had either been advised of my work by their friends or referred by various doctors around town for help in reducing pathogenic stress. I had an office in my home and booked appointments with people around the clock, often not knowing initially much more about them than who had referred them.

One wintry day I had four new clients scheduled. By the last hour, I was feeling spent, having already attended to a grieving widow, a Vietnam veteran suffering from Agent Orange toxicity, and a cancer patient. I cringed to think of what more the day had in store for me. At three o'clock, with the sun already quite low and the fire in the woodstove blazing to keep off the early evening chill, I opened the door to greet my last client of the day. There stood a man with the glowing face of a sprite, in a lean six-foot body. He had full, blushing cheeks, long blond hair, and eyes that gleamed the same electric blue color as his down jacket.

I was taken aback by how unveiled, how uncommonly open this man's face was as he introduced himself. I reined in my delight at the sight of him and asked him in. His name was Fredrick Hodkins and he lived in Longmont, the next town over. He had been suffering from digestive problems and had been referred to me by his doctor for stress reduction. We sat down in my office for the initial interview and I felt my ebbing energy spring back, my limbs tingle, and my own face grow flushed with curiosity.

At the onset of our interview, Fredrick made clear that for me to understand his physical problems, I would need to know certain particulars about his work. He was now the minister of the United Church of Christ in Longmont, a liberal Protestant denomination, although he had been raised a Southern Baptist. Fredrick was a voracious scholar of the classics and the sacred texts of the West, and also loved the Upanishads, the *Tao Te Ching*, and the sacred poetry of Rumi and Kabir. He spoke ecstatically about his work in the church—not the conventional work of being a minister, but the opportunities he had to awaken people to their own spirituality. He waxed eloquent about giving Sunday sermons on roller skates and dressed as Ralph Waldo Emerson, about blowing the minds of his youth groups on nature treks and ski trips. He was teaching his congregation to meditate and a select number were even studying kundalini yoga with him. He had introduced a lecture series in Longmont and over the last four years had brought in Virginia Satir, Elisabeth Kübler-Ross, Ram Dass, and Father William McNamara. I listened to him, taking notes for my intake file and struggling to control my personal interest.

"Just about anything that points to God, I will devour," Fredrick continued without pause. "I have this strange job of translating the untranslatable, boundless exquisiteness of spirit to cynical teenagers and small-minded adults. But heck, if spirit is really coextensive with matter, then it shouldn't be that hard, right?" There was a pause and our eyes met. At that moment I sensed that Fredrick, too, was intolerably lonely to share his vision of the spirit. He was an overflowing cask of life, looking to share his bounty with someone who could appreciate the vintage.

"Excuse me for being presumptuous," he finally said, breaking the silence before I could. "But from what Dr. Will tells me, it seems that, in a way, you're in the same business as I am. The business of translating spirit, that is. Only we're coming to it from opposite directions. I start from spirit and pontificate about how everything in life is an embodiment of God. And you start from matter, and read the body as the message bearer of the spirit dwelling within it," he stated cheerfully, delighted with his equation and awaiting my response. "Would you agree?"

I was taken aback. It was exactly how I saw what I did, in words I had not considered before. But being appreciated like this by someone who could see and articulate my vision unsettled me. I felt as if the tight cork on all my pent-up longing had begun to swell and shift out of place, and I feared it would burst out under the pressure of my own desire. I held myself back. Fredrick looked at me with raised eyebrows, waiting for my answer.

I stammered, "Coextensive with matter, did you say? Are those your words?"

"No, that's Teilhard de Chardin speaking. He says that God is coextensive with matter, the same fabric as spirit, you might say, only denser. The Hindus say that this world is an illusion, but I don't buy it. It's so clear to me that this world resounds with God, everything, the light and the dark. What I like to say is that this whole beautiful mess we live in is not an illusion, but an *allusion*. The whole world *alludes* to God, everything, light and dark." As Fredrick spoke, the famous vision of Isaiah popped into my mind: *Holy, Holy, Holy, God of hosts, the whole world is filled with His glory.*

"So you're saying, the whole world *is* His glory. Even to say *filled with* is too much of a dualism."

"Exactly." Fredrick had picked up my train of thought instantly, and was thundering ahead. "I'll tell you my pet theory: In the same way that God is coextensive with us, just as we grow and learn and struggle through our lives, so God is also growing and struggling, in and through us. We're here for God to use, like a laboratory for the evolutionary process. God expresses Himself through us, and we play out God's drama. In other words, my suffering is not mine alone. God is using me, and all of us, to cook and evolve Himself. Excuse me, Herself—language is so inadequate. Anyway, that notion makes me feel less alone when I am up nights with this burning pain in my belly. It helps me to know something important is going to come out of this pain."

My mind was racing. I knew of the idea of transubstantiation from my Christian reading, and that God in the form of Jesus took on the human experience to take part in the suffering of the world. I had just finished Carl Jung's controversial book, *Answer to Job*, which had gone so far as to say that God was in need of the human experience to learn compassion for His creatures' suffering, having stagnated into being a merciless deity who was out of touch with their pain. I wondered if this idea of God living through our experience existed elsewhere, maybe in Judaism. Despite my excitement about our topic of discussion, I forced myself to reel in my attention and refocus on the session. I asked Fredrick about his symptoms.

"Dr. Will says it's colitis." Fredrick put his hand on his belly. "I've been working on it with nutrition, acupuncture, and yoga. But I know what it is. My life is about to fall apart."

Fredrick was a radical: He was on fire with the spirit and had no patience for the petty congregational politics that seemed always to be running at cross currents with his excitement to impassion people with God's immediacy. Trouble was also festering with his church board over his outspoken political views. My eyes dropped to the gold band on Fredrick's left hand, before I even knew I was looking for it. My heart sank. Now he was telling me that his marriage of twelve years had begun to disintegrate.

"All I can think of is getting a sabbatical and having some time for myself," Fredrick was continuing. "I would love to go monastery hopping, for instance, from cloister to cloister, to chant with the monks, be in silence, to read myself into oblivion. Small wonder that I fantasize about monasteries, huh? A clergy's life is public property."

I noticed that our time was quickly advancing. I managed to shift our discussion back to present tense. I decided to lead my client in a guided relaxation instead of massage, for there was something about touching this man that seemed far too personal and inappropriate. Fredrick seemed quite adept at going inward, and at the end of our time he arose, looking refreshed yet peacefully silent. I too felt a deep quiet come over me. After he made an appointment for the following week and I saw him to the door, I sat in front of the fire and fell into an easy meditation until my roommates came home.

Around the dinner table that night, Joan, Hannah, and I shared stories from our day: the frustrations of working at the city-run social services, the child abuse that was turning up at the junior high, the last ravages of the Vietnam War that were just now coming to light.

"But my day was redeemed in the end," I announced. "My last client was utterly beautiful. All my energy came pouring back to me during that last hour. After all the jerks I've met lately, and all the mama's boys, this is one guy I could imagine being with."

"Whoa, Tirzah!" Joanie replied. "Who is this that you would be interested in if he were not a client?" We all chuckled as we dug into our blueberry cobbler.

"Don't worry. Not only does he live in another town, but he's married, *and* he's a Christian minister."

"A triple curse!" Hannah droned, raising her arms in a feigned trance, playing the wise family oracle. "Think no further of this man, nor allow thy fantasies to make a fool of thee! Thy parents, not to mention thy venerable ancestors of Jewish antiquity, will never find favor with such a one as him."

"Hail to thee, O Great One!" I played back. "And thanks be to thee for telling me once again that which I already know! Still, allow me some small delight in the exchange of worthy ideas with this mere Christian mortal."

And delight I had, but it was no small delight. On his second visit, barely disguising my appetite for further theological discussions, I asked Fredrick to speak more about the idea that God was evolving through him, and the resultant tension in his body. He answered eagerly.

"I've put to rest the notion that God is a fixed entity or some predetermined goal toward which we're all moving. Inasmuch as He—or She—is unknowable and transcendent, I'm convinced that God lives inside of us, this very moment. But living with that kind of mindfulness, what I now call 'radical amazement,' is a difficult way to live—at least in Longmont, it is. I'm sure you Boulderites have an easier time of it," he said with a laugh. "But my people resent me for reminding them that fundraising, accounting, building maintenance, all of it is God's arena and needs to reflect holiness!" Again our eyes met. I was regaled to hear him put into words my own vision. "And as if that wasn't enough, I've been getting railed at for being a blasphemer and a heretic, because I preached about God as a great process, not a personality. People don't like that, somehow. It makes them feel less secure."

Without stopping, Fred began opening his leather satchel and leafing through his papers. "As a way of showing you the tension I'm experiencing in my life, I wanted to share something with you. You know sometimes Christians take on a hyperhumble posture—which I personally can't stomach—that our lives are a one-way gift. Here: I used these lines in a sermon last week and my parishioners went berserk: *'God is everywhere, in man, in politics, in daily life, and he is imperiled. He is not Almighty, that he might cross his hands and thus await his certain victory. His salvation depends on us.'*"

"Hey, isn't that Kazantzakis?" I cried out. "*Saviors of God.* One of my favorites!" Up until this point, I had been able to maintain my professional persona, but now I could not restrain myself. He was hitting too close to my pet ideas.

"Listen," I launched in, "I much prefer to believe in a God who's in a reciprocal relationship with me, a God who's growing toward wholeness Himself, rather than one already perfect and without need. Can I share this with you?" I asked, casting professional boundaries to the wind. Fredrick nodded animatedly in response. "I've had this hunch ever since I was a kid in Hebrew school. When Moses stands at the burning bush, and asks for God's name, remember? The name that God gives, Eheyeh Asher Eheyeh, is usually translated as 'I Am That I Am.' But that is an *awful* mistranslation! The name really means: I will be what I will be. God is saying, in effect, I'm in process, too, so don't try to put me in a file folder. I'm changing and *becoming* through this process of human redemption, too." Fredrick grinned as I spoke.

"I totally agree," he said when I had finished. "And it's a very becoming name," Fredrick punned and we both laughed. After a moment, he looked at me and declared, "So you're Jewish! No wonder all this comes so easily to you!" My smile had faded; I was taken aback.

"What does being Jewish have to do with anything?"

"You must be kidding," he answered with his eyebrows raised. "'All of existence is the body of God,'" he quoted. "I believe your Rabbi Kook said that. Your religion is filled with these ideas—or so I thought—that creation is an extension of God Himself, but that it's not complete and that humans are needed to complete the work."

I must have been looking at Fredrick with a stunned expression, because suddenly he stopped. "Why are you looking at me like that? I'm sorry. Have I misspoken?" I was feeling highly uncomfortable but did not know why.

"No, I mean, I can't say. I wasn't aware that any of these ideas were Jewish." Now it was Fredrick's turn to be surprised.

"I thought all Jews knew them. I've always envied the lack of schism between God and humanity in Judaism. I had the good fortune to study with Abraham Joshua Heschel at seminary. He's the one who coined the phrase 'radical amazement.' Now, he was *radically amazing* himself! But, look, it's all over your literature."

"You know, I've all but given up on the Jewish tradition. It felt too narrow."

"Anything but!" Fredrick chortled. "Listen, do you know the creation myth from your Kabbalah? It's a perfect—"

"Why do you keep calling it *mine*? I told you I gave up on it. It's more yours than mine. You obviously know more about it than I do." I did not understand why I was suddenly so filled with intense emotion.

"I'm sorry if I touched a raw nerve there, Tirzah. But I personally do love it. When I was a student I realized that Christianity is inextricable from its Jewish roots. I called myself a Judeo-Christian. Anyway, do you want to hear this?" He did not bother to wait for my answer. "I think it's Lurianic Kabbalah that tells of this great shattering of vessels at creation and how light got scattered all through the world, hidden just beneath the surface of creation by broken shards?" Again I looked at him blankly. I had never heard of Luria or of this story. But there was no stopping him. "The sparks of light are waiting to be released back to God. But only we humans can do that through our words and deeds and intentions. It's a marvelous metaphor, don't you think?"

Fredrick was so overjoyed to be sharing the ideas he loved that he was practically singing, gesturing with his hands as he went on. But I had begun to grow sad listening to him, as if I had been left out of a party. Why hadn't *I* learned these things? Didn't this knowledge belong to me as a Jew? Within seconds, my sadness began to turn into a stinging, hot anger. Why was it that I often felt out of the circle when it came to Jewish matters, as if there were secrets being withheld from me? Why was it that I had to come by these ideas through Kazantzakis and Jung, and now I needed a Christian minister to tell me that they were in Judaism all along? Waves of feelings rose and fell within me. I attempted to swallow them down and concentrate on the lively and provocative client sitting opposite me in my office.

After that session, in which we focused on Fredrick's physical symptoms for a mere fraction of the time, I realized that I was in trouble. Contact with this man was compelling and called to the surface so many of my own questions, needs, and feelings (not to mention my longing for personal time with him) that it was impossible to consider working with him for his benefit. Of course I wanted to help heal him, but I had a greater urge to speak with him as a friend for more hours than were possible, to pick his brain and library, to share my own books and poetry and confusion. What was more, Fredrick was adorable to me, a deliciously alive human being. No, there was absolutely no hope of my pretending to be professional with this client. I determined to tell him the following week that I was not the right practitioner for him and that he would have to find someone else for treatment.

On his third visit, within minutes of his arrival, Fredrick announced that our sessions had proved to be an enormous release for him. He felt deeply comforted to be able to disclose his soul, to have someone to discuss his most passionate ideas with, an equal who understood what he was talking about. He was also gratified to be able to remind me of the greatness of my own religion. He had barely taken off his jacket before he was diving into the theological discourse for the day.

"So I've been thinking about it, and given what you've said about reciprocal relationship, you must have read Buber. But have you studied his Chasidic tales?"

"Wait a second." I finally asserted myself, cutting off his stream of words. "Before launching into a discussion of Buber, don't you think we should focus more on you and your problems?"

"I thought we were. Indirectly, of course. Is there something wrong?" He looked miffed and slightly hurt. "Look, I love the relaxation, too, but our talks are heaven for me."

I explained that I enjoyed them, too, but that I felt we were not attending to his health. If we were to continue working together, we needed to stay more focused. Out of my own discomfort, I insisted that he lie down on the table and keep his active mind quiet, long enough to follow me on an exploratory journey of his organs. He did so obediently. But my idea turned out to be a wholly unsatisfying venture, dry and overcontrolled.

After Fredrick had gotten up and was reaching for his appointment book, I said to him, "Look, I don't think this is working very well. I apologize, but I don't think I can continue seeing you." Fredrick's eyes widened. "Not that I don't want to!" I assured him. "It's just that there is so much I want to talk about. And I doubt I am doing you any good at all." His retort was quick and forceful.

"That's not *at all* the case! Where are you getting that idea? I need these sessions. I can't believe you're turning me away! Why?"

"I think I'm just too interested in the things we're talking about. And I can't listen to you neutrally and apply my therapeutic skills because I get too excited myself. There's no hope asking again. I've decided. I'll give you some other names."

Fredrick left looking abject. And I too was miserable. What had I just let go of? A rare spiritual comrade, a lifeline to the world of ideas, an unabashed lover of God with whom I could share my hunger! I tried to cut my losses. Weeks passed and the world seemed grim. Then, as if with the first scents of spring, I got the idea to go to church. I gathered up Hannah the next Sunday morning and together we drove across the Colorado plains to Longmont. Fredrick's church, on Francis Street, was an enormous institution that took up the better part of a block. As we parked the car and walked toward the front doors, I was taken aback by the number of crisply dressed, conventional-looking parishioners also arriving for the ten o'clock service. "This is positively mainstream!" I said nervously to Hannah. How could the radical free spirit I had met possibly be conducting an institution like this? I braced myself for disappointment.

I had not been inside a church this size since frequenting the cathedrals of France and Spain. Those had been mostly formidable historical structures, and the masses I had attended were stiff and impersonal. I had gone there to experience the architecture and the music, to experience what had gripped the devotion of Western culture for so many centuries. Only rarely had I been moved to pray. Now, as we entered the modern brick sanctuary, Hannah and I were welcomed and ushered to seats in the middle of the large congregation. A huge cross loomed at the front of the room. I bristled with discomfort. What was I doing here? The organ began to sound from somewhere overhead and people rose to sing the first hymn. All in the spirit of adventure, I told myself.

Then Fredrick arrived, gliding down the center aisle with a huge smile on his face and the same high color I had found so appealing. He wore a hooded cassock of natural linen, with a heavy cord around his waist and a colorful Guatemalan stole around his neck. Instantly the auditorium warmed. Once at the pulpit, he opened his arms and greeted his congregation, bidding them to move up closer to the front so that he would not feel so lonely. Then with the same vivacity that I had witnessed in our sessions, he leapt into a sparkling performance that began by his captivating his audience with proclamations and jokes, shifted into passages from Scripture, and included personal disclosures, wild hand gestures, and dramatic questions of the congregation. In preparation for Easter, his topic involved the role of Judas Iscariot in the crucifixion. Fredrick's voice boomed emphatically.

"We must not go into the holiday one more year, reading the story of the Passion one more time, without asking ourselves: Who is Judas? Jesus lives within me, yes. But, then, doesn't Judas? And where are the repugnant Pharisees if not within myself?" The congregation was listening now in rapt silence. I looked around. Hadn't these people called Fredrick a heretic? At least for the moment, it seemed that everyone was under his spell.

"No, the betrayer is *not* on the outside!" he was proclaiming. "We do not get to sit smugly in this church accusing Judas, or the Jews, or the *other guy*, any other guy, for killing our Lord. There is no other guy! The betrayer is all of us. And until we own that dark part of our soul, we will never inherit the light!"

I was dumbfounded. Here Fredrick was working with the New Testament in the same manner that I was learning to work with my dreams, using the Biblical characters to find the relevant archetypes within. I was elated; this was the same man with whom I had removed the heavy stone from the well of universal wisdom and had drunk so deeply. I wanted more.

After the service, Fredrick stood at the open doorway of the church, shaking hands and hugging his parishioners as they filed out into the breezy spring day. When he saw me in line, his face blanched and his mouth opened wide. Rather than hug me, he reached his hand out to shake mine. Then he laughed nervously.

"Don't tell me you've been here the whole time! Did you hear what I said today?" he asked like a little boy after the class play. I nodded and placed my hand on my heart.

"They were very deep words, Fredrick." And then, before stepping through the doors, I added, "Listen, if there is any way I can ever be of service to you, let me know, will you?" I did not know what I meant exactly, but the words had come out of me as if they themselves knew their own importance. Two weeks later, Fredrick called.

"Don't worry, I'm not calling for an appointment," he joked. "But you asked if you could help me, and there is something. Would you get together with me to talk about some ideas? I need a sounding board." I was thrilled and agreed to meet him that Wednesday, his day off.

I met with Fredrick once a week for the next three months. We spent our time, usually three or four hours, walking in the hills, he with his satchel and me with my backpack, brimming with papers and books. Then spreading an old blanket in the sun, we would plop ourselves down on the ground get comfortable, and read aloud to each other; first drafts of sermons, passages from Scripture, quotes from Carl Jung, C. S. Lewis, and St. Teresa of Avila. In between we would share a sandwich and water to keep ourselves going.

Often, Fredrick would coax me to translate a Hebrew passage, or to offer my views about a Christian tradition that may have Jewish roots. I was surprised to find my knowledge of Hebrew and Jewish history still fresh, and I was enthralled to be able to offer my appreciative friend a new insight or twist for his upcoming sermon, gleaned by looking at the etymology of a Hebrew word or by contrasting the *gematria* or numerological value of two phrases. Voraciously we pieced together theories about life in Jesus' day, the prominent rabbis that could have influenced his thinking and the politics of the Sanhedrin, the Jewish high council, and the Temple that affected him. We laced together theories about the various underground communities of the new millennium—the Essenes and the Gnostics and the burgeoning movement of new Christians—and imagined what life was like for these revolutionary ascetics. Fredrick read to me the writings of the Desert Fathers and I recounted to him tales of the Sinai Desert, its bedouins and the remote monastery of Santa Catarina that I had visited on a backpacking trip in Israel.

Beyond our stimulating intellectual exchanges, however, I was particularly moved by the curious habit that Fredrick had of spontaneously breaking into prayer during our meetings. Right in the middle of an exuberant talk, without warning, he would close his eyes and talk to God.

"O Mother-Father-God," he would often begin. Then he would simply speak from his heart, saying something like "My heart is breaking open with joy at this moment. I know You can feel it because it is Your heart as well. I thank You for this soul companion with whom I partake of Your spirit, the delight of my life." At first these outpourings embarrassed me. They were so pure hearted, so guileless, that I felt as if I were eavesdropping on lovers. But slowly I learned to appreciate these prayers as moments of ritual that collected our overflowing joy and offered it up to the one God we both believed in. I pined to be able to pray like this, with neither structure nor form, straight from the heart. Over time I was able to join in. These were the moments of greatest passion for me.

My housemates were certain that Fredrick and I were having an affair and were escaping to make rapturous love in some hidden annex. They were wrong, although our exchanges were as passionate as the best lovemaking on earth. Fredrick and I were escaping the driven world of work and schedules and responsibilities and were diving into sheer pleasure, which for us was the delicious world of ideas. We joked that our meetings were a contribution to the plumping of the "noosphere," Teilhard de Chardin's term for the growing repository of ideas that enveloped our earth. At the time, I did not identify myself as a Jew, but Fredrick did. He was certain that by virtue of our friendship an invisible bridge between our two lineages, the Christian and the Jewish, was being built in the ethers, bit by bit. One day it would become manifest, serving the world as a template for unification between religions.

Often when I came home from my meetings with Fredrick, my entire being would be vibrating, the closest thing I have ever felt to bursting with love. But it was not only with a personal love for my friend that I felt my soul to be swelling. It was also with a love for God, for the world, and for all the individuals who searched for truth, dedicating themselves to breaking free of the constraints of conventional consciousness to reach beyond to the world of spirit. My relationship with this man felt eerily connected with my life's mission, which up until this point had remained opaque but was now becoming more apparent: to reach beyond the patterns of history that would define me by the particular dimensions of my people's fate and break through to a life of worship that united rather than separated, a life of spiritual essence rather than one choked by religious forms.

Meeting another human being who speaks the language of our soul and has the ability to see us in our essential beauty is one of the high points in a lifetime. Suddenly there is an infusion of new meaning and vision into our lives, and we feel a nourishment that is soul deep. Sometimes our life's mission is spurred by meeting this other person, and through him or her we can see who we might become. I believe this is because the contrasexual partner reflects for us our other half—for a woman, the animus and for a man, the anima—the half that is waiting in the Self to become a part of us. This is why meeting our "soul mate," an external likeness of the Self, can be one of the most spiritual experiences we ever have, because it is, in a very real sense, an experience of coming home to our potential wholeness. However, it is important to remember that our beloved is an *other* person who reflects our Self but is not us. Nor are we them. This differentiation is where the challenging work of relationship comes in.

Meeting Fredrick stimulated new preoccupations for me. Along with the sacred poems of Rumi and Mirabai, I began to be drawn to an old copy of Psalms that I had kept since childhood, and my brother's dilapidated prayer book that had traveled with me to Minnesota and back again to Colorado. Without realizing that I was reconnecting to my own ancient lineage, I opened these books in secret, and often, as tears streamed down my face, I prayed from them, allowing the Hebrew words to run through me like a river of gratitude and devotion for God's mysterious ways, for what was unfolding in my life, for what I was learning was called grace. The world was full of God's grace, and Fredrick was teaching me that God probably had nowhere near the need for the harsh judgments and serious outlook on life that I brought to bear on mine. God's love was abundant and revealed itself to the degree that we could open ourselves to receive it.

After several months of meetings, there was a kiss, delicate and grateful, the fruit of our long waiting. The longstanding problems between Fredrick and his wife had culminated in separation, and the arduous process of a divorce awaited him. But I was not thinking of that. I was thinking of the fact that here before me, in my arms, was precisely what I had ordered, a spiritual partner given to living life exuberantly, on as many levels as was possible. I wanted our relationship to go on. This rapturous moment of bringing our bodies together was exactly what I had prayed for, but who was I to deserve such bliss? I struggled inside and finally came out with my feelings of unworthiness to have been gifted so richly.

"No, of course you don't deserve it!" Fredrick answered with a chuckle. "Nor do I. That's not what this is about. This is about grace, Tirzah. It's neither our worth nor our entitlement but God's grace that this is happening."

Grace. It became my watchword. Each time I would catch myself constricting, pulling myself down out of the experience of love from a lack of faith or sense of self-worth, or from fear, I would calm myself and remind myself of God's grace that could allow all things. During this time, I could almost feel my soul stretching to contain the experience of joy and fullness I had. And I would recite the statement of William Blake over and over again: *We are put on earth for but a little while that we might learn to bear the beams of love.*

It was far from the case that Fredrick and I were living a saccharin existence. His divorce was pending, and the uneasy politics at his church had escalated. He decided to take a three-month sabbatical from the church, during which time he would reevaluate his position as minister. From my side, I was convinced that I had found my true love, the one with whom my soul had been destined to live out this life, and I began to come to terms with the fact that my Orthodox Jewish family would have a fit when they heard my happy news.

When my parents first moved to Israel, I wrote them all about my studies and practice, my friends, and my plans to start on a degree in counseling. Although they knew I was not living a Jewish lifestyle in any fashion, they were proud of my professional accomplishments and my ability to support myself. But having lived through years of family strife resulting from my sister Laya's relationship with a non-Jewish man, I dared not tell my parents or my siblings about Fredrick. As our relationship deepened, I continued to put off the inevitable.

It was now 1981. Fredrick, who was thirty-six, was going through a major midlife change, submitted his resignation to the church the following year and moved to Boulder to open a private pastoral counseling practice. I was twenty-seven and ready to make a leap myself. We rented a little house together, with a deck to sun ourselves and a rose garden in the back. There was no need to speak of marriage. Living together was commitment enough, the next step in a natural progression. We had found true love and we believed that life would unfold as God willed it. But we were not naive. We both knew that with our commitment would come struggle. The dark fear that I had harbored since Laya and Tom's wedding—that someday I would stand in my sister's place, having to choose between my true love and my family—had now come to light. Now I was the one who was beginning to live a life straining between two worlds.

Meanwhile, Fredrick prompted me to drink in the deep teachings of

Judaism, bringing me books and articles that pointed toward the essential wisdom of its practices and its inherent holism. I shared at length with him how constricting traditional Judaism had been for me, how it had seemed that devotion to form had overridden the original intention of bringing holiness to the world.

"But you're your own person now. You're free to go back into your tradition and take the best and leave the dross. You and I have been touched by grace, Tirzah. And that allows us to wade deep into our respective traditions without drowning." Fredrick sensed far more accurately than I did just how vital my connection was to Judaism. What he knew intuitively took me years to realize: that it would be necessary for me to return to it in order to unlock my wholeness.

"I do believe that eventually, God's grace will lead us beyond all traditions. But until then, all forms reveal essence, Tirzah, even Jewish forms. What's required of us is to break them open." I knew he was right, and that opening of the tradition to its deeper meaning could not be done in anger and frustration, but required an open heart.

In my pugnacious desire to unburden myself of the onus of my heritage, I had also rid myself of great beauty. Fredrick and I, now living together, began to light Sabbath candles each Friday night, and I realized how radiant they were, their light filling our house with a particular kind of holiness. Likewise, the fragrant, braided Sabbath loaf, which I took to baking myself, seemed to nourish like no other bread. I found that the Chasidic masters were, in depth and paradoxical wit, the equals of the Zen and Sufi masters, and I pored over their stories along with the new texts of Kabbalah that were being translated and published.

My deepening connection with my Jewish roots remained an extremely private affair. Yet I knew that Judaism was a community-based religion. I had been programmed to be part of a body bigger than myself. I made a reticent attempt to hook up with the Jewish community in Boulder by looking in the religion section of the newspaper. There I found a small congregation advertised which sounded somewhat warm and inviting. They held their services in a nondenominational chapel on the University of Colorado campus and were congregation-led. Perhaps I could find something there that I had not been able to see during my rebellious years. In a small, self-led group there were bound to be spiritual seekers like myself. I steeled myself for reentry into the world of Jewish communal prayer.

The following Saturday morning, I put on a skirt and blouse and drove across town. I slipped inside the sanctuary timidly and sat at the back of the pews. As the service progressed, I was surprised to find how little had changed since my synagogue experiences as a child. The Hebrew prayers were still spoken in mumbled fashion and the tunes were the same lackluster melodies I had learned decades earlier. I sang along and prayed quietly to myself, in tandem with the congregation, happy at first to hear the familiar phrases and tunes, but feeling dull and disenchanted by the end of the almost three-hour service.

Still, I returned to services on and off for several months despite my disappointment. I wanted badly to believe that there was something in my own heritage that was worth coming back for. The occasional church services I attended with Fredrick were lovely in their own way, even moving at times, but decidedly foreign to me, not my home. Synagogue was home, but an uninspired, even chilly one. I became superficial friends with a few of the elderly women in the congregation; no one else approached me.

So that my experience would be less lonely, I finally built up the courage to invite Fredrick to attend with me. I reminded myself that he had a knack for seeing and calling forth the beauty in my tradition far better than I could. Maybe he would appreciate these services and help me see them through fresh eyes.

We arrived one Shabbat after the morning blessings, and the *gabbai*, or deacon, took note of us sitting together in the back. This man had seen me plenty of times before but never formally introduced himself. Sitting together as a couple suddenly rendered me more visible and apparently gave me more clout than a single woman had. Trying to include and welcome newcomers into the community, he came over to us, warmly shook our hands, and wished us a "Shabbat shalom."

Then he whispered to Fredrick.

"Would you like to receive the honor of taking the Torah from the ark?"

Fredrick blushed with surprise. "I'd be delighted," he answered, deeply moved to be included. Even Fredrick knew that holding the Torah was no small task; to handle the holy scroll one had to be both able-bodied and devout in spirit. He sat erect and attentive.

As we waited for the right moment, I saw a young woman flag the *gabbai* over and agitatedly whisper something to him. This was followed by a flurry of hand gestures, shrugs, and more whispering on the part of several congregants. They peered in our direction. Within seconds, the *gabbai* marched back over to us looking annoyed.

"Forget that," he said to Fredrick curtly. "Only a Jew can touch the Torah." Then he ducked away to continue the job of assigning tasks.

I squeezed my partner's hand. I did not need to look into his eyes to know that he had been deeply hurt and I ached for him. Fredrick had had his first taste of the Judaism I knew so well: seemingly warm but, at the core, utterly exclusive. I registered this experience in my mind as emblematic of the giant obstacle that barred my way from reconnecting with the Jewish tribe.

We slipped out of the service early. As we drove home, Fredrick made light of what had happenèd.

"Well, now I understand why you had doubts about inviting me! But look at it this way: I would have been a lot more offended if the service had been less dull."

"Spiritual rudeness is one thing and boredom is another. What does one have to do with the other?"

"Just that now that I feel so unwelcome, it's easier for me to admit the truth, that the service felt empty to me."

"There wasn't much spirit there, was there?" I answered sadly. "I thought maybe you would be able to appreciate something that I was missing, some meaning that I couldn't find "

"Nope," was all he answered. Fredrick had a stalwart public demeanor, rarely showing how deeply affected he was by the behaviors of others. But now I knew that it would be a long while before he would venture into the Jewish world again.

And this was true for me as well. I was discovering that religion and spirituality were two separate things. My allegiance was to my growing spirituality, which was a matter of the heart, and after this experience, I was even more jaded about exposing it to anyone but my partner and God. I would still pursue my Jewish studies, but I was now further away from reentering formal Judaism, or any religion so partisan that it fostered the notion of separateness. As I saw it, this was clearly missing the point of the game, which was to move beyond personal allegiances to an expanded heart, one that knew no boundaries.

Fredrick, now free of institutional responsibilities, pored voraciously over the mystical texts of his own religious lineage. He began studying and then teaching classes in the Course in Miracles, the Gnostic Gospels, and the works of the Christian saints to growing circles of students. We continued to share ideas and to pray and meditate together in a way that was common and comfortable to both of us. And although we never actually went monastery hopping, we made pilgrimages once or twice a year to visit spiritual teachers such as the Hindu guru Baba Muktenanda, the Carmelite nun Mother Tessa Beilecki, and the Sufi sheikh Pir Vilayat Khan. We also visited a variety of Carmelite and Benedictine monasteries for personal retreat. One of our favorites was the monastery of Christ in the Desert in Abiquiu, New Mexico.

Christ in the Desert was tucked into a steep, red rock canyon. A long, tortuous dirt road led into the tiny settlement of simple adobe buildings. Entering the monastery grounds, we would descend into a state of quiet reverence. This was holy ground; the monks lived in silence except for their prayers and there were no other human voices to be heard. There was only the sound of the river flowing at the bottom of the canyon floor, the cawing of crows, and the whipping of their wings that echoed off the looming rock walls around us.

The first time we visited, the guest warden showed us to our humble accommodations, then conducted us around the garden and to the dining table, where we were invited through hand gestures to eat with the monks. As we all sat eating our simple bowl of vegetable stew, one monk read aloud an inspirational reading for the day from the writings of the Desert Fathers. I was reminded of Beloved's community: the same rural life, the same austerity, the same table practices. But this was a place of the heart, where God's presence was communicated not through stern doctrine, but by the earnest faces of the monks, the power of the cliffs and river around us, and above all, the blessed silence.

The next day we woke before dawn, put on all of our clothes against the stark morning chill, and tromped over to the chapel to join the monks in prayer. Fredrick wrapped himself in the black and white woolen tallit, or prayer shawl, that I had given him as a gift, as was his custom whenever he prayed or meditated. We entered the candlelit chapel and found the monks chanting the psalms in English, accompanied by guitar.

Psalms had become my personal form of prayer, and although I was partial to the original Hebrew, I was deeply moved to hear the monks' chanting. Like voices from antiquity, they seemed to sing with the same purehearted intention as the poet King David himself. Listening to them, I was moved to sweet tears. The words that I had loved so well since childhood and to which I had returned only recently were dissolving me, bringing me face to face with that old, familiar longing, the soul-deep yearning for a reconnection to God. I wanted nothing but to be able to purify my life so that it could become a vessel for the purposes of the spirit. I wept and wept throughout the service.

It was Sunday morning and other guests began to arrive from Taos and Sante Fe as the day brightened, entering in silence and seating themselves in the back of the whitewashed chapel. At the end of the long service, the doors were opened onto the sunlit day and the monks and guests poured out together. I had emptied myself in prayer and I rejoiced to see the pure blue sky and greet the new day. From somewhere in front of me, I heard a strident voice, like that of an angry crow.

"You should know better than to wear a tallis before a Cross," the voice screeched. "And look, you're letting the tzitzit touch the ground!" Fredrick and I had gotten disconnected in the crowd, and now I dodged in front of others to catch up with him. I spotted the angry face of a female guest, obviously Jewish, who was picking up the holy fringes of Fredrick's prayer shawl and kissing them indignantly. I cringed. Another display of manners from my tribe, at a monastery of all places! "You obviously don't know anything about Jewish law!" the woman finished with a voice full of spite and stomped away.

I walked up to Fredrick's side and clutched his arm. He had chosen to maintain silence, seemingly unruffled. He turned and winked at me, as if to say: There's nothing like capping off Sunday morning prayers at the monastery with a lecture on Jewish law!

Later in the week, as we drove away from the monastery on the rutted mud road, we laughed at the incident and the contrast between the soulful Christian service and the strident Jewish voice of criticism. What was a law-abiding Jew doing at Christ in the Desert Monastery, anyway? I joked. But I knew the answer: Jews were everywhere. Wherever a teacher was presenting the dharma, a teaching of truth, or a community was living it, there Jews abounded. Certainly in all the spiritual arenas that I had frequented, whether it was Baba Muktenanda's ashram or Sufi whirling dervish classes, Jews were there. Jews are a spiritually voracious people, but our spiritual longings have often gone unsatisfied by the lifeless ways in which Judaism has been transmitted in modern America. And now that the boundaries dividing Jews from other peoples are looser than ever before in history, we have gravitated to other quarters of the spiritual world, to seek nourishment wherever it is to be found. But sadly, we do not always succeed in taking in the spiritual riches being offered without also revealing our frustration, irritations, and pain, often in the form of discourtesy to others.

During my years of spiritual explorations, I had grown accustomed to this sort of rude or brassy Jewish behavior in groups. It embarrassed me deeply and I tried my hardest to avoid these people who seemed all too familiar to me. Their disturbances tended to pull the group down, coming in the form of hostile questioning of a well-meaning presenter, bickering that some portion of the presentation was inadequate, or looking for others to take responsibility for their own discomfort.

After years of simply wanting to steer clear of these people, I now feel compassion, convinced that such behavior is an unconscious cover for spiritual confusion and the misunderstanding that somebody *out there* is responsible for our pain, that somebody *else* owes us comfort. When the questions are not

answered and the pain is not alleviated, often these people get angry. Like a
tired or hungry child who whines and throws tantrums instead of being direct
about her needs and taking action to get them met, these spiritually hungry
adults have misplaced their own responsibility, masking their deep neediness
with rudeness.

I still wonder about these stereotypical Jewish behaviors. Perhaps they
stem from our long history of the world going crazy on us. Often someone
out there really was responsible for our pain (hosting countries unexpectedly
throwing us out; assumed friendly monarchs and whole segments of popula-
tions turning into vicious enemies in what seemed to be the blink of an eye).
For centuries Jews had little control and could not take complete responsibility
for their lives, being at the mercy of so many wild forces. Could we still be
reacting to our tragic past by trying to overcontrol the present-day situations
and relationships of our lives? Have we adopted a style that attempts to compensate our tragic history? Unfortunately, we have gone too far if we are putting relationships of goodwill at risk and poisoning the atmosphere around us.

I did not need much more proof that the Jewish world was uninviting. Yet
I also knew that to cut myself off from my people would cause a commensurate
pain. I could not help but think about Fredrick's and my future together. What
was next? Laya and Tom's choice of conversion would not be ours, that was
clear. Fredrick was wedded to his path, and to denounce it would do a violence
to his soul that would be unfair and difficult to heal. Asking him to become a
Jew when I myself was so ambivalent about my birth religion did not portend
well for our relationship.

We continued living our lives, putting the question "What's next?" on
hold. My resolve not to venture back into the Jewish world was based on my
fear of the stigma of our mixed-faith union, and the expectation that reentering the community without lying about who we were and what we believed
would result in our being shamed or shunned. Fredrick said he simply did not
care that much. He had a love for the principles of my religion, but not for
belonging to it.

In our second year together, Fredrick and I attended a conference of the
Association for Humanistic Psychology. We signed up for an inspiring class in
Kabbalah taught by a traditional rabbi. Heady and excited by the teacher's
ability to wed the psychological and spiritual worlds, we went up to him to
introduce ourselves at the end of the day. The rabbi was warm and jovial with
us, until we told him that we were life partners devoted to our respective paths
and intended some day to marry. I felt his body stiffen.

"I applaud your intentions," he said tersely. "But you're doing an impossible thing, trying to join a household of two religions. No rabbi, including myself, would ever give you his blessing. You may as well not bother to look." He then turned to leave.

Once again I felt dejected. How was it that all afternoon this erudite man who had expounded upon the universal principles of the psyche as contained in the Kabbalah was now telling us that people were essentially different and should not be mixed? Fredrick and I fell into silence as we walked to our car, feeling both hopeless and defiant. Through these repeated experiences of alienation, the bond between us was growing fierce. We were becoming love warriors, holding high the standard of our universal beliefs, and growing increasingly self-righteous as we grew isolated from the communal world of Judaism.

You will never have to choose between me and Judaism, Fredrick had said to me early on as he coaxed me back to my roots. He had meant that he was not intimidated by my reconnecting with my heritage. Now I was discovering that I was! It was a world that did not seem to have changed nor grown since I had been away, a highly conditional world that was guarded by a multitude of gates, rules, and laws. And if the principle of love lay at its core, it seemed so well hidden, even from its gatekeepers, that I began to wonder why anyone would ever bother to look.

I stopped making efforts to reconnect with the external Jewish world and instead threw my energy into my healing work and my studies toward my master's degree in counseling. Our friends, all avid in their own spiritual practices, supported us unconditionally, as Fredrick and I continued to weave our lives together. With the same aplomb with which we began our relationship, we remained loyal to our faith in the great mystery that stood far beyond the forms or even the theologies of either of our religions. This was our God: one who was both personal and unknowable, growing and transforming us ceaselessly, and willing, despite all of our man-made roadblocks, to gift us with the grace of loving acceptance.

CHAPTER EIGHT

THE WAY OF THE ALEPH

I n 1983, after Fredrick and I had been living together for two years, we began to discuss marriage. Still avoiding the topic of my love life with my parents, I realized that now it was I who was playing ostrich, withholding the most important news of my life and hiding myself from their inevitable dismay. Finally, after months of deliberating, I composed a letter that explained my love to them. "Please try to understand that Fredrick is a good influence on me—he's helped me become more, not less, connected to Judaism." But my defenses were useless. My mother's warm and chatty letters from her new home in Israel quickly turned terse and professorial. I had not even mentioned marriage to Fredrick, but she smelled it coming.

"Intermarriage," she lectured me, "is the one boundary which, when crossed, cuts a Jew off from the People of Israel, immediately, and with no recourse. The continuation of the Jewish people is simply not possible when intermarriages occur. You cannot live with a goy and delude yourself into thinking that you are adhering to your people and remaining a link in the great chain of the Jewish generations!"

Her words seemed almost too heavy for the flimsy tissue-paper aerogram on which they were written., I answered my parents brazenly, describing Fredrick, his love of Judaism, his passion for books, what a mensch he was. These were their values, after all; he deserved their respect.

"Regardless of the sort of fellow your friend is, we cannot accept him" came the reply in short order. "It isn't personal. He may be quite wonderful, as you say. But as a non-Jew, he will never be anything to us."

I left off trying to reason with them and simply wrote of other things: my graduate studies, my therapy practice, my new puppy. The outward conflict with my parents subsided, but the tension within me grew. Only part of my life was acceptable to them and only that part could I share.

Having now worked with hundreds of interfaith families, I see clearly that "marrying out" of a family's religion, ethnicity, or culture is a phenomenon that presents everyone involved with a challenge, rarely a painless one. In choosing a mate from beyond the family's boundaries, the child is actually taking an important psychological step toward becoming his or her own person. But this step can be seen as a betrayal by family members, one charged with huge emotional implications (such as dishonoring the ancestors or putting one's people into peril) far beyond the youngster's intentions. Instead of celebrating their newfound love, the couple is suddenly freighted with feelings of guilt and responsibility, and often find themselves scrambling to appease the hurt feelings of relatives.

The children's discomfort is matched in many cases by the distress of their family members, who are now faced with a choice that is bound to bring irrevocable changes: The family must choose to expand its boundaries to include the outsider or be faced with the ominous task of tightening its boundaries and rejecting its own member. Either choice means that the family must redefine itself.

If a healthy family unit is to be maintained, open and respectful communication is required, in which all parties can speak the truth as they see it without fear of attack. Listening and sharing from the heart, however, are skills that take time to develop and are not easily manufactured during a crisis. As in any time of tension, a family's weakest traits come to the fore when its integrity is threatened. A neutral facilitator, either a family therapist or an unbiased pastoral counselor, can greatly help the process.

When intermarriage does occur, the most psychologically healthy response that I have witnessed is when family members are able to speak frankly about the changes awaiting the family (both the disappointing and joyous aspects) without condemning or manipulating one another. Openly acknowledging and including the feelings of each member—even disagreement and hurt— allows the family to take the next step together: to stick together and expand itself by including the newcomer.

None of this was my case. I tried to look at the situation through my mother's eyes: I would always be peripheral to the mainstream Jewish community if I remained with this Gentile—unless, of course, he converted, which would cut *him* off from *his* spiritual lineage. And my relationships with my siblings as well as my parents were already cracking. My brother Ezra, who was now an ordained rabbi himself, wrote me a pedantic farewell letter saying that my choices did not allow any further contact with me. ("Didn't I know that Jews and goyim were like oil and water and did not mix?") And my sister Laya and her husband Tom bristled with discomfort at the very mention of my partner. A cloud seemed to hang between us in our letters and phone calls, and behind their terse and restrained voices I imagined I could hear their unspoken question reverberating: What gives you the idea that you can bypass the agony *we* had to go through to get married?

It was not a question of bypassing agony. I was already *in* agony to realize that my choices were not resolvable. It was an issue of survival. Would I be able to survive the consequences of my choices? For now they were rejecting only Fredrick, but one wrong move—marriage—would lead to their rejection of me! Could I bear being cut off? Or would I, like my sister, break under the pressure of ostracism and return to the fold?

I had bumped into a paradox: sharing my life with Fredrick *did* cut me off from my tribe, and I already felt the psychological danger of this. Yet it also connected me to Jewish spirituality. How ironic that precisely this forbidden partnership would inspire me to rediscover my roots! I was not interested in connecting with the Jewish people, that was true. It was the spiritual teachings underlying the religion that interested me, and Fredrick shared in my interest.

My dreams made it clear that there were riches to be mined in my own ancient heritage. In one dream I found myself in an ancient city in Europe, standing outside the formidable cast-iron entrance of a Jewish temple. I was overtaken by a longing to enter, but could not find any way over or through the locked gates. As I paced back and forth on the cobblestone street trying to figure out what to do, I noticed something sticking out from under the stones. I kneeled down and pulled out two manuscripts: One was entitled *The Collected Works of C. G. Jung*. The other was a treatise on the mystical nature of the Hebrew alphabet. The dream ended before I found a way into the temple, but I had already found what I was looking for outside in the street. The dream told me that the wisdom of my deeper self (symbolized by Jung's writing) lay buried side by side with the wisdom of Judaism. I would not come to these treasures in the conventional way, through the gates. I would have to dig for them, but I did not have far to go.

Only a few weeks after this dream, a woman by the name of Chava came to town. She herself was a renegade from an Orthodox home and a student of a rabbi from Europe named Zalman Schachter-Shalomi. Chava was an artist and a student of Kabbalah. She was a mysterious soul who seemed to commune with the divine forces through her artwork, remarkable bead sculptures that depicted the Hebrew names of God. I was mesmerized by her unabashed Jewish spirituality and approached her at the opening of her show. Could she teach me the mysticism of the Hebrew letters, I asked timidly? Chava's intense gray eyes peered at me warily. For a long while she said nothing. Then she fired questions at me. Did I know that the Hebrew letters contained within them all the forces of the cosmos? Did I know that the human drama of the Bible was only a facade for the cosmic interplay of archetypes, which danced in the bodies of the Hebrew letters? Did I think I could submit to the rigor of such study?

I did not have to think long. I said yes. For the next four months, until Chava suddenly left town, I submitted, not without criticism for my sloppy discipline, to her lessons on the holy letters. Under Chava's tutelage I drew them, chanted them, combined them, added and multiplied their numerical values. The Hebrew alphabet had been familiar to me from the time I was six years old, but I had never been instructed in their mystical power. On the macro level, each of these twenty-two letters represents a dynamic state of cosmic energy. And on the micro level, the human level—humans being the mirrors for the cosmos—the letters designate stations on the human journey that we all make, such as innocence, revelation, and impoverishment.

The words of the Hebrew Bible, made up of these powerful little ideograms, are not just words, I was finding out, but dynamic energy configurations that mean a lot more than any English translation could ever transmit. For example, the Hebrew word "Adam" which connotes both the male and female of the human species, is composed of the unknowable, uncontainable power of divine consciousness (t), which resides within the simple constraints of the four elements (s), but which has the potential to continuously renew and transfigure itself in the cosmic waters of life (n). What would normally be translated as "man," I now saw, was the expression of our highest function as humans: the transformation of energy.

I brought my letter studies home to share with Fredrick. Together we read Carlos Suares, Lawrence Kushner, and Jorge Luis Borges, all scholars of Hebraic mysticism. We bantered back and forth about the etymology of phrases in the Torah, the variety of God's names, and the correspondences between the twenty-two letters, the major arcana of the Tarot deck, and the Kabbalistic pathways on the Tree of Life. Fredrick's facility in Greek and Aramaic made our conversations even more outrageously stimulating.

Throughout our discussions and meditations, we returned repeatedly to one letter that depicted for us the life we wanted to pledge ourselves to. This was the aleph, the first letter of the Hebrew alphabet, the one that was ungraspable because it danced beyond human concepts, wedding the opposites of life. The aleph not only designated the number one, it *was* the place of oneness, the silent source from which all else sprung.

The aleph's form (t) shows a long, bridgelike body that connects heaven and earth. Like a whirling dervish, perfectly poised between the upper and lower realms, the aleph is a dynamic transformer that channels the cosmic forces. Its upper hand is raised, openly receiving its power from heaven. Then carried down through the body and channeled into the earth through the lower hand, the power is transmuted into a different, more usable form. The aleph began to represent for Fredrick and me not only bridging opposites, but using opposites to bring about transformation. This, of course, was our highest aspiration: to wed our Jewish and Christian lineages to bring about change, perhaps a new way of thinking in the world. I surprised Fredrick with the gift of a large stained-glass window with a glowing aleph at its center. We hung it in the window of our meditation room over the altar, and in time the aleph became our personal symbol.

One Friday morning, as I came in the door from classes, Fredrick was waiting for me, looking pale. He took me by the hand.

"Come here, Tirzah. I have something to tell you," he said ominously. "Sit down."

"What is it?" I asked, growing alarmed.

"Something strange happened while you were at class. There was a phone call. I think it was your mother, only the woman wouldn't say who it was."

"Okay... what did she say?"

"She said, 'Tell Miriam her father is dead.' When I tried to get more information, she hung up on me." Fredrick began to cry into his hands. "I think it was your mother, only she wouldn't talk to me. I can't even say if the news is true or not!" he sobbed.

We held each other, and I too began to cry, knowing in my heart that the news was true. This would have been my mother's way. Unable to deal with my non-Jewish lover over the phone, she had no choice but to dump out her terrible news and run. I was furious with her cold disrespect at such a time, but within minutes, grief had blanketed my anger.

After the first waves of emotion had passed, I went to the phone to call Laya. Yes, she confirmed, it was true. Dad had died early that morning. And because it was Friday and already early evening in Israel, he had already been buried before the oncoming of the Sabbath. My body began to shake with the shock. I was not prepared for my father's death, even though I had known it could come at any time. He had died giving out sweets to poor families before the Sabbath arrived, something he loved to do. After being rushed to the hospital and declared dead, his body had been prepared for burial in the holy ground of the Mount of Olives overlooking Jerusalem, wrapped in his prayer shawl. Now there was nothing to separate him from the land he loved best.

I made hasty plans to free myself up so I could fly to Israel the following week. I vacillated between extreme efficiency and torrents of emotions. It was very difficult to contain myself in a small airplane seat for twelve hours. When I finally arrived at my parents'apartment in Netanya, Laya was already there caring for our distraught mother and beginning the arduous process of going through financial and legal papers. I said nothing about how the news of my father's death had come to me, nor was my life and love in Colorado ever mentioned. All that was beside the point now. My mother was in crisis and we were all in deep grief.

After I rested a bit, I began the work of going through my father's drawers and closets. I took down his suits and coats and folded them into piles to give to the needy. Handling the personal items in his drawers, I was overcome by my father's familiar smell, sweet and musty, the one I had known since I was a little girl. By the end of his life, he had stopped writing me; perhaps he had finally given up on me once I had broken the news about my lover. Now I had no way of explaining to him the spiritual opening that was transpiring for me, and there was no chance for reconciliation.

My father's top bureau drawer had always been the one I had loved to pick through as a child. Whatever was in his pockets at the end of the day got tossed here: toothpicks, odd key chains, ticket stubs, and loose coins. As I pored nostalgically over the sweet-smelling drawer, I came across a slip of paper with my father's writing scrawled on it. It had been folded into a tiny square, like a *kvittel*, a personal plea that one would slip between the stones of the ancient Wailing Wall in Jerusalem. I opened and read it. "Ribono Shel Olam, I beg you to return Miriam Tirzah to the path of her ancestors."

I sat down on his bed in a daze. This then was his last will and testament to me, a prayer. He had made clear to me all through my adult life that his estate would go only to those of his children who were living a Jewish life. I had taken myself out of the running with my news about Fredrick, and I was left with this prayer.

"Is it so unallowable, Daddy, to follow my heart?" I spoke out loud to him as if he himself were looming over me rather than the frosted light fixture hanging from a cord. My frustration and anger burned in my chest. "Is there no room for the path of *my* heart here, only yours and the ancestors'? You know, it's this kind of narrow-mindedness—even more than the path itself—that makes me want to leave altogether. But you've never been able to see that."

Over the next week, my sister, mother, and I traveled to Jerusalem to visit relatives and distribute my father's clothing and personal items to Orthodox charities. My father had a widespread reputation for his charitable acts, and as his next of kin I was greeted with respect. But with my relatives who knew the direction my life had taken, all personal inquiries about me were avoided. I was offered pat words of condolence and then the family's conversations went on to more agreeable topics, veering away from any reference to me or my flawed American life. I began to feel as if I had some dread disease that must not be discussed.

My discomfort grew daily. Who was I here? In this Jerusalem society, where the Orthodox lifestyle was unquestioned and every person's role was prescribed, I felt altogether invisible. In this conventional society, as a holistic health practitioner or a devotee of the mystical letters, as a lover of the sacred paths of the world and a partner to one on the Christian path, I was nothing.

I began to ache for Fredrick, for his humor, the way he had winked at me when confronted by the Jewish critic at the monastery. As I went through my daily activities, being jostled by belligerent crowds on the street, shoved out of line at the bank, and criticized in shops for not having the correct change, saying the right Hebrew word, or wearing the right clothes, the impressions of the Israeli culture that I had had as a twenty-year-old flooded back to me. Now I knew that it was not only my youthful sensitivity that had made me want to shake people for their rudeness to others. I was convinced that there was more objectivity to my original perceptions.

Here in the Jewish state, many people seemed to be carrying around their own version of the rancor that Fredrick and I had encountered at the monastery. In the silent canyon, the woman's uninvited remarks had seemed crude and out of place; in Israel, this harshness was commonplace. An impatient anger, similarly abrasive yet even more judgmental than the Jewish behavior I had observed in America, seemed to fill people here. It seemed mostly to be directed at people doing something incorrectly, against the rules. I wished I had Fredrick's aptitude for observing this critical behavior with compassion and humor, but it disturbed me deeply. I remarked to myself that I would have to cultivate tolerance for the lack of tolerance in my own people.

On the afternoon before leaving Jerusalem, my mother, sister, and I took a bus to the Mount of Olives to visit the site of my father's grave. Throughout the ages, Jews have held this mountain to be the mythic spot for burial, believing that when the Messiah finally came, a resurrection of souls would begin with those buried there. It was my father's greatest dream to be buried on the Mount of Olives.

I placed a rock on his grave, as is the Jewish custom. I did not bring a written *kvittel* of my own to leave tightly tucked into his earth. Rather, I knelt down and whispered my prayer: "Rest well, *abba*. Try not to worry about me. I may seem distant to you, but trust in me. I'm not abandoning you, or our faith, I promise."

Fredrick collected me from the airport the next day. I was exhausted but elated to see him. He nursed me through the culture shock back into my life of clients and graduate studies. And there was good news while I was gone, I had received an invitation from the Healing Arts Institute to become an instructor of Reichian therapy, a body-centered therapy based on breath and emotional release. I gladly accepted it. This would be my first chance to put forth in words the remarkable information and insights I had been collecting since my graduation.

FREDRICK AND I lived together for the next two years in a state of unresolution. We wondered at the mystery of a union that felt as wholesome and fertile as ours, but that seemed to create so much conflict. It was a fact that our coming together had created pain and rifts for my family members, and marriage without conversion hailed even darker consequences for my relationship with them. We considered the option of remaining unmarried, but that seemed cowardly. Besides, we wanted children. I felt impelled to go forward and make my choice to be with Fredrick official. Marriage was the inevitable next step.

"You know, you could convert to Judaism and still just be who you are. Nothing would have to change."

"My God, Tirzah! You're really grasping at straws now. Everything we stand for is about living in the world authentically. Isn't it?" He looked me in the eyes. "I wish I could convert and mean it. I know it would make things a lot simpler for you, but it's not right for me to become a Jew. I'm moving toward the universal. I don't want yet another form to live up to."

"I know that. And I don't want you to become something you're not, just to placate the wrath of the tribe. I'm not even sure I could love you if you were Jewish," I joked. "You would remind me too much of what I've been trying to escape!" We laughed but there was something ominous in the air. "Look, I'm nervous," I told Fredrick. "Even with all my high ideals and convictions, I'm scared of what's going to happen to me if I cross this line."

"The line of marriage?"

"No. Somehow, marriage is only the outer taboo, just a symbol of breaking away. There's something even bigger, like a huge *Thou Shall Not* hanging over me. Thou shall not be different than us, think different, act different, or dare say that you can do it on your own. *You can't do it on your own!* That's what the voice says in my head. That I won't be allowed to break away from the tribe and if I dare try I will be pulled apart. Just look what happened to Danny and to Laya when they tried! Remember what the rabbi told Danny? *Go in this direction and you won't live past thirty.*"

I had just turned thirty. Did the rabbi's curse hold true for me, too? It was feeling more and more that way. No longer was there a funny Yiddish trickster who occupied my head, spouting witticisms and cheery counsel. Instead, a vengeful rabbi with a pointy black beard and beady eyes had moved in. His voice taunted me from inside, issuing warrants for life and death, laughing at me sadistically for the audacity of thinking I could marry a goy under a *chuppah*, the Jewish wedding canopy, feigning holiness outside the prescribed Jewish formulas. "Not with your kind did we Jews survive for three thousand years!" he would scoff. "Traitors get their due, you wait!"

Fredrick tried to console me. Intermarriage happened all the time, didn't it? I would be fine; I would be liberated; we would live a fine life together. My analyst Leif, likewise, advised me to stand up for my choices, to go my own way, even if it meant being condemned."

"Leif, I know it's irrational, but I'm scared that my soul will get cut off from its source and rot. I guess Catholics would call it eternal damnation or something."

"Tell me, is your source the tribe? Or is it God?" Leif pressed me. Then she looked me deeply in the eyes. "Tirzah, nobody on earth can cut you off from your true source. And if you are afraid that following your own life path will cut you off from your heritage, then please remember that Judaism has been going on, with many variations, for thousands of years. There is no singularly right way to be Jewish. Everyone must find their own way. This is yours."

My weekly explorations with Leif deteriorated into pep talks that buoyed my spirits for a day but left me thrashing about at night. Often I would wake up trembling, feeling all alone in the dark, without the personal fortitude to forge ahead into uncharted territory. Once again I felt that I was on a stormy sea at night in a pilotless sailboat, not knowing if I would make it back to dry land.

At Leif's suggestion, I went in for an additional hour per week, all I could afford, but even then, I felt myself floundering. I prayed for God's guidance, but wondered if God, like my family, had turned away. When I could sleep, my dreams served to remind me of the dangerous terrain ahead. In one dream, my house flooded in torrential rains and all of my Jewish books were ruined. Fredrick entered the room and, seeing me weeping over the now illegible pages, said: *There are more important things in life, Tirzah. Cut your losses and move on!*

I tried to move on; we set a wedding date in October. As I busied myself with caterers' menus and wedding apparel, my distress lurked just under the surface. In my daily meditations I would cling to the image of the aleph for strength and solace. The aleph was a Hebrew letter, yet it seemed impartial to religious politics, dancing beyond the opposing voices of my dilemma, reminding me that the truth about life was never fixed but constantly changing. It seemed to tell me that I alone could not heal the huge ideological rifts around me; I could only work on myself, healing my inner rifts and holding tension with the opposing forces that lived within me. The outer conflict was unavoidable if I was to continue to be myself in this world. All I could do was to be more and more who I truly was.

To allow the aleph's wisdom to spring forth in our relationship meant to give ourselves over not to each other, but to something beyond both of us. Fredrick and I pledged our marriage to the unnamable power of transformation that would change us both in the process of our lives together. We took a poem of Rumi's that spoke to us of this intention and put it on the inside of our wedding invitation.

> *Out beyond ideas of wrongdoing and rightdoing,*
> *there is a field. I'll meet you there.*
> *When the soul lies down in that grass,*
> *the world is too full to talk about.*
> *Ideas, language, even the phrase "each other"*
> *doesn't make any sense.*

A couple of dear friends helped us design an aleph with Celtic braiding (to signify Fredrick's Welsh heritage) running through the body as a symbol of both of our heritages meeting, which we used on the outside of our invitation and as an insignia on our wedding rings.

After our painful encounter with the rabbi at the Association for Humanistic Psychology Conference, afraid of being rejected and shamed, we did not dare to ask a rabbi to officiate at our ceremony. Instead, we busied ourselves with cocreating our own nondenominational ceremony, and we asked a close friend, John, to preside; Colorado state law allowed lay wedding officiants. The wedding service would be held in a lodge up in the mountains and would include various rituals drawn from Jewish and Christian as well as Wiccan wedding rites, Fredrick having become immersed in the nature-based, goddess-centered Wiccan religion.

Once we had mailed out the invitations, my terror increased. There was no turning back now. I felt that I was sliding into quicksand and thrashed about for some feeling of control. Fredrick and I fell into power struggles, arguing hotly and meanly over the arrangements and rituals surrounding our wedding.

"Let's have wine and challah as communion," he suggested. "Then everyone can come up and—"

"Stop!" I yelled. "We will *not* have holy communion!" I declared, "nor will Christ's name be mentioned under a *chuppah* at *my* wedding."

"You know, I am sick and tired of being bossed around by you, Tirzah, and by your family. My family has always treated you well, but yours hasn't had the human decency to acknowledge my existence, yet they're running the show in absentia!"

"It's not them, it's me! If my entire family boycotts my wedding and me for the rest of my life, I am going to need *some* support! This is my wedding too, and I need more representation of my heritage there! Outside of standing under a canopy and breaking a glass, there is none." I thought of a real Jewish wedding and how the bride and groom were celebrated by the community with wild dancing and Hebrew songs. "How could you understand what I'm needing? You're a WASP!" I ran out of the room crying.

We had been in a relationship for almost five years, struggling for permission to be together. Now, on the verge of making our marriage vows, we were fighting to be separate. I had no other thought but to salvage my individual identity, which included my Jewishness.

Fredrick too was doing his own version of fighting for control by asserting not only his Christian but his Celtic roots, selecting several Wiccan rituals. One was casting the circle, creating a sacred space at the wedding site by sprinkling water, circulating incense and ringing a bell around the circumference of the room at the beginning of the ceremony. Another was hand-fasting, pledging loyalty by binding our hands together. Seeing how important these acts were to him, I agreed.

In working out a relationship, it is easy to get caught in the cross current of psychic impulses. On the one hand, we are in love and are drawn by an almost visceral urge to merge, to attach to our loved one and thereby find our wholeness. And because one's lover reflects an aspect of the Self and we humans are ever in pursuit of the wholeness that the Self presents, there is a very strong gravitational pull to the beloved. At times, this attraction would have us lose ourselves to our lovers; drifting into their orbs, we find ourselves adopting their viewpoints and politics, sometimes even their mannerisms and gestures.

But another force, the force of differentiation, pulls us in the opposite direction. I believe that we are not here to merge, but to become more fully ourselves, the most complete individuals we can be. This opposing pull, back to our own individuality, usually makes itself known some time after we have bonded with our new love. We may have had to overcome great external resistances to be with him or her, and these challenges strengthen our resolve to stand firm as a unit. Only then does the more fundamental challenge present itself, this time from within: the pull of our souls to individuate, to become separate and whole individuals.

Ultimately, for a relationship to succeed, both of these forces are necessary, the pull toward and the pull away from one's lover. When both forces are recognized as natural and are not feared, the tension that they produce can lead a couple into an energizing rhythm. We then have a double mission, to be joined while being our independent selves, and to be our own selves while in union. At this level of relationship, boredom is a rarity!

Not understanding all this, I felt as though I was treading water in a most tumultuous ocean. I had resisted the outer pull, my family's protestations, giving in to the first delicious urge to merge with my love. Now the time had come to establish my independence from Fredrick, and create a differentiated self from which to relate to him. But this differentiation could not be accomplished by moving back to my family and their ideals; I was struggling for my independence with them as well! I had to find a new refuge—neither my family nor my lover, but myself.

Sending out the wedding invitations became a symbol of the second struggle for independence, or, rather, my declaration of it. I mailed them out to my entire family, including my mother in Israel. My mother's response was silence. But it was a loud silence, a screaming din of indignation and fury—I could feel it. Then a letter from my Aunt Ruth arrived, a jeremiad, eloquently voicing the family's disdain. "How do you dare to send your mother an invitation or to think that anyone in the family would want to be party to this event? It is an undeniable fact that intermarriage is regarded, not only in our family, but in all authentic, loyal Jewish circles as a violation of the inner core of our faith and of the continuity of our people." Never before had I felt the full impact of coming from a line of orators, but I was determined to go forward and suppressed my feelings of devastation.

A week later my sister Laya called. "I got the invitation, Miriam. And Tom and I discussed it. Someone from the family should be there."

"Not necessarily. Not if you can't be happy about this. I have really dear friends here. I'll be fine."

"Listen, I know you think I'm opposed because of the Jewish issue. But it's not that. I'm just wondering if Fredrick is the right one for you."

"You know what, Laya? At this point, I'm not interested in your appraisal. I've been through too much to get here."

"Well, I'm coming to your wedding. I'm your sister, after all."

"Listen, Laya, I appreciate the gesture, but—"

"No, I've made up my mind. I'll come in right after Yom Kippur."

YOM KIPPUR, the most solemn day in the Jewish calendar, fell on the Sabbath that year, just two days before the wedding. When the sun rose, I went off into the foothills by myself to spend the day in prayer. Fredrick stayed home to clean the house and greet his family, simple and kind Midwestern folks who had driven in from Missouri together in their camper. (Fredrick and I had always joked about the irony of both of our families'coming from Missouri, yet living galaxies apart.) I came home before sundown, having dozed and daydreamed in the hills more than prayed, feeling the depth of my exhaustion.

As soon as I stepped through the door, the celebration began. Fredrick's family was truly happy for us. Lib and John, his parents, were relieved that we were finally tying the knot after living out of wedlock for five full years, and were already busily at work, arranging colorful centerpieces for the banquet tables, untangling ropes of little white lights, and decorating the bamboo poles of our wedding canopy with ribbons and flowers. My spirits lifted. I had Fredrick's family to buffer me, to fete me, to treat me like a bride. And my women friends began to drop by with funny wedding items, sexy garters, fancy cosmetics, and good-luck crystals. This was supposed to be fun, and the fog of the last few months of psychic tension began to clear to make way for rejoicing.

The next day, my sister Laya arrived. She acted warmly toward me, bringing me beautiful gifts and asking how she could be of help. But I could tell it strained her to have to celebrate a marriage that she did not favor. It was exactly ten years since Laya's own crisis, which had reversed the course of her life, and now she had come to watch me as I walked over the threshold that she herself had almost stepped over but could not. No mention was made of her own shaky decision, the angst that had led up to her partner's conversion, or the extreme fragility the years of ostracism had wrought. All of that seemed to have slid under the surface of her consciousness, dissolved into a decade of living out her choice to create a traditional Jewish family with her converted husband.

The conversation that two sisters might have had about the course of their lives—each having played out opposite sides of the same coin—never happened. Instead, Laya and I took our respective positions: I played the defiant younger sister who blithely announced that my wedding would be full of pagan rituals, and she played the retiring elder, wearing the entire family's disapproval on her stoic face.

The night before the wedding, friends who lived in the mountains hosted an American Indian sweat lodge for Fredrick and me as a purification ritual. A huge bonfire was already burning when we arrived and all of our dearest friends were sitting around it singing songs. In the middle of the fire, twelve round stones gleamed like radiant red jewels. The sweat lodge, an igloo-shaped hut built of bent willow branches and canvas, was twenty yards away; water jugs for drinking and fresh sage bundles for incense sat ready at its door. As the men continued to tend the fire, a group of eight women undressed and knelt down to crawl through the flap. *"Mitakuye-oyasin!* ("All my relations!") we were each bade to announce as we crawled on our knees into the earthen womb, declaring our connection to the family of life, our relatives, friends, and all the peoples of the earth. I was struck by the bitter irony of this proclamation on the eve of my wedding, when my heart ached from the broken connection to my own family.

Once we were all inside the lodge and huddled around the empty center hole, the fiery stones were brought in one by one on a shovel. Each stone sizzled with heat as it hit the damp, bare earth. Our shivering bodies began to warm. We laid sage branches on top of the stones to give off cleansing properties and fragrance. As the heat built and sweat began to roll down our bodies, my friend Shar led the first chant to the spirit behind the four elements. We sang and sang, intermittently drinking water and sprinkling the stones to create steam. With our sweat flowed our prayers, and as the heat intensified, so did our feelings. Our voices rose spontaneously out of the darkness.

"I pray for our sister Tirzah as she crosses this threshold," chanted the voice of Patricia. "May all of her sacrifices to be with her man bring her great rewards." All of the women answered *"Ho!"* in affirmation.

"I pray that the Great Mother bless this bride with the ability to let go of her past and embrace the future as she builds a new family." *Ho!*

"Holy Father and Mother, thank you for this gathering and for our community of friends. May we truly know how connected each of us is to all of creation, regardless of religion. My prayer is that Tirzah and Fredrick be able to open their hearts wide and receive all of our love. And that the soul that I feel is waiting to come in as their child be blessed at this wedding, too!" *Ho!*

Again, we chanted. The heat rose. And then we heard a weeping in the hut. I knew it was Laya. The rest of us sat silently, feeling her pain. Finally, she spoke.

"Miriam. There is so much I want to say to you." Again, she began to cry.

"Laya," I responded out of the darkness, "you are like the last glowing embers of this stone in the middle of our circle. My only connection to the family. Thank you for being here."

"Don't let the light go out," she responded emotionally. "Please don't let it die! There is so much here for you, waiting for you to claim as yours. And, my little sister, you will always be Miriam, don't ever forget that." I began to feel lectured.

"Miriam means 'bitter waters.' I've left her behind. I'm Tirzah now.

"Miriam is your heritage! You can run from it, but you won't be able to hide for long."

Shar, feeling the tension building between us, broke in with a chant. "Ancient Mother, I hear you calling..." The women joined in quickly, and I sang, too, but my body was rigid with tension, wishing my sister had come with simple love rather than as an envoy of the Jewish people. I had to resist her pull back to the tribe. If ever I did find my way back, it would be done on my own terms and in my own time.

Shortly afterward, the women crawled out of the hut, hot and refreshed by the night air. It was the men's turn then, and the women bundled themselves in towels and sat around the fire, chatting in low voices as the men's laughter and singing rose into the night air.

The next evening, Fredrick and I were married. The ceremony began with the casting of a sacred circle around the room, using water, incense, and flower petals. Then Fredrick's family walked proudly down the aisle. Fredrick and I followed them, arm in arm, accompanied by Samuel Barber's passionate and somber Adagio for Strings. We had chosen this unconventional entry to make up for the fact that no parents were there to "give me away."

The wedding canopy, the *chuppah*, was supported by three friends and my sister Laya. Laya's face was dour, the one island of reserve in the sea of delight and love generated by our friends. I avoided looking at her. Meanwhile, my knees were knocking violently together under my simple yet elegant white floor-length gown. I walked to the altar and lit one candle for each member of my family who was not represented at the ceremony. Although sixty of our friends surrounded us, their smiling faces did nothing to quell the thundering energy that was moving through my body.

This was a moment of destiny. As Fredrick and I stood facing each other, I knew that our wedding pledge to the divine forces of transformation meant stepping into holy fire. We were willing to be burned by it, transfigured by the pain and exaltation of relationship, and worked over by God's design for us, a design that we could not yet see.

"Why are we so different from other lovers?" Fredrick touched me with his words. "Because we choose to adore God through loving one another. Because our love is more like prayer. Because our marriage has eternal consequences, since the destiny of our souls hangs in the balance. Tirzah, I cannot separate my relationship with you from history, the destiny of the race, the plight of the planet, the shape of the universe. We are not isolated from anything and I cannot love you apart from my participation in history. I cannot consider you without thinking of my mission, our mission. While others are victims of fate, we are seizing our destiny. And only as I feel my compassion growing for the planet, do I know that our love is healthy."

Our wedding rings, two glowing alephs, were passed through the earth, water, fire, and the smoke stream of incense that had been set out on the altar. This Wiccan ritual symbolized that our marriage was blessed by the elements but not subject to them. We then recited Hebrew blessings over wine and bread, followed by the Lord's prayer. When we exchanged rings, John performed the hand-fasting, binding our hands together in a sacred cloth to signify our pledge to be spiritual friends and helpmates to each other, wherever we found the other through time and space, in this and all lifetimes to come. I was still trembling when, finally, a small glass was placed at Fredrick's foot.

"This part of the ritual comes from the Judaic tradition," our friend John announced. "A glass is smashed at the end of a wedding to remind us that even at the moment of life's greatest joy, there is great brokenness in the world, which we must continue to repair. May Tirzah and Fredrick strengthen each other in their love so that their healing influence in this world is profound!"

Fredrick raised his foot and stomped on the glass. A loud crunch was heard. At that moment, my tension broke and I burst into sobs of joy and relief. Several friends yelled out *"Mazel tov!"* John wrapped Fredrick and me tightly together in a new rainbow-colored tallis, and our friends came crowding around us. I was still crying hard as their hands reached out to touch us in blessing. John raised his voice high.

"By the power of God vested in this holy community of friends, we now pronounce you, Fredrick and Tirzah, husband and wife!" A great roar of voices and applause went up from the crowd as we kissed long and hard. Then we were escorted to a private room to have a few minutes to ourselves. We had been fasting all day in preparation for the ceremony, and beautifully decorated plates of food awaited us. We sat, hugging each other and feeding each other stuffed grape leaves and strawberries, giddy with relief. We had passed over the threshold and had survived.

We emerged from our antechamber into a dining room sparkling with little white lights, candlelit tables, and loving faces. A string quartet played our favorite chamber music in the corner, and our guests enjoyed an extravagant vegetarian dinner as Fredrick and I roamed from table to table to visit with friends and relatives. Even Laya seemed to be in better spirits now, mixing freely with our friends and smiling for photographs. After dinner, the tables were cleared and a klezmer band set up to play. My Israeli friend, Nava, led us all in the hora and other Israeli dances. My life felt complete. Fredrick and I left for our honeymoon in New Mexico the next day.

As I had surmised, my wedding meant that I had heard the last from my family. Apart from Laya, there was no more contact from anyone in my family, not even a letter voicing disdain. I never asked my sister whether my mother sat shiva, the seven days of mourning for me, but I did not need to. I knew that I was effectively dead to her. When her brother died the following year of a sudden and terrible disease, I called her in Israel to tell her of my sorrow. She hung up on me. I went on with my life with a pain buried deep in my heart that masked itself as anger or indifference. Every so often it would rise to the surface and I would ache for family, for the people whom I had known since my child-hood and who had brought me into the world. I filled the void as best I could, relying heavily on Fredrick and my community of friends to be my family.

ONCE I HAD completed my degree in counseling, I received several invitations that began to shift the course of my public life. One was from a local college to teach a course in Kabbalah. I was taken aback. My knowledge was too sparce in this area, I told them. I had only read books, and books do not a Kabbalist make. But the mystical Hebrew alphabet, which in a sense lay at the root of the esoteric tradition, was a vital experience for me, something I had interiorized deeply. The letters I could teach, and I did. Many of the students who showed up for the aleph-bet class were part of a newly formed nondenominational Jewish community in town, dedicated to the study and practice of Judaism as a spiritual path. They called themselves a *chavurah*, a fellowship, with the name Gesher Or, which means "bridge of light."

It was at this time that I first came into contact with Rabbi Zalman Schachter-Shalomi. I had held this man in my peripheral consciousness for years, having studied with his student Chava and having purchased a col-orful tallit from his organization, P'nai Or (which means "faces of light") in Philadelphia. Perhaps I had been waiting for the moment of my own readiness to encounter his teachings. That moment came when I was lent a copy of his book, *Fragments of a Future Scroll*, an eccentric cookbook-style guidebook to Kabbalah for the modern seeker, replete with cross-references to humanistic psychology, Zen Buddhism, and Hindu yoga. Here I found passages of Sri Ramakrishna, the Buddha, and the Maggid of Mezeritch expounding their teachings all on one page! And in newly translated teachings, Rebbe Nachman of Bratslav and Rebbe Pinchas of Koretz discussed the interconnectedness of all souls and the human dilemma of living in the mundane world after intense revelation. Here, right in my own tradition, was the depth I had hungered for.

I was intrigued even more by the book's author than by the wisdom it contained. Clearly, this man stood far beyond Jewish partisan politics, beyond judgment of the Jew who sought spiritual teachings elsewhere. The author of this book seemed to have one goal in mind: to help his reader understand the universal depth of the Jewish mystical path, while building bridges to, not renouncing, other traditions. I felt grateful that such a rabbi existed. Reb Zalman was the kind of scholar I had been waiting to meet, one who was steeped in classical Jewish learning and who knew the rationalist Orthodox world as well as the mystical world of the Chasidic masters. While holding these in reverent tension, he had gone further yet, talking with Sufi masters, Catholic monks, and Native American elders to find the common thread in all of their traditions that connects us with each other and to the cosmos. This rabbi had chutzpah! What Fredrick and I were doing on a domestic level, Reb Zalman was doing globally.

I asked around and various people told me Rabbi Schachter-Shalomi's fascinating story. He had been born in Poland and raised in Austria and during the war had been imprisoned with his family by the French Vichy government in an internment camp in France. In 1941, they were able to flee Nazi-occupied Europe and arrived in New York. There he continued his Judaic studies in the ultra-Orthodox Lubavitcher yeshivah. After he was ordained as a rabbi by the Lubavitcher rebbe, Rabbi Yosef Yitzchak Schneersohn, he was sent out, along with my cousin Rabbi Shlomo Carlebach, to the universities and colleges of North America with a sacred mandate from the rebbe to help bring Judaism back to life on American campuses. This he did, but not before entering into the mind of the students and the cosmic experiences revealed to them by the mysticism of the East and the psychotropic drugs of the West. Reb Zalman, as he is called by his students, studied with Sufi masters and Buddhist lamas, Native American elders and transpersonal psychologists. His explorations and studies—he went on to earn a doctorate in Hebrew literature—and his own mystical experiences became the basis of his teaching for thousands of spiritual seekers.

Fredrick and I were fascinated by this man who seemed to embody so much of our own journeys. That year, together with a non-denominational congregation in Denver, we had an opportunity to bring Reb Zalman to Colorado. We planned to attend his Shabbat retreat in the mountains, and on Sunday morning bring him home with us to rest before a Sunday-night lecture in Boulder. I fretted over how a rabbi would deal with the facts of our intermarriage and a house with Greek Orthodox and Celtic crosses hanging opposite the stained-glass aleph, mezuzahs on the door, and texts on Jesus peppering the bookshelves. Would the broad leeway he seemed to give to all religions hold up in the flesh?

The retreat was held at a dude ranch in the foothills of the Rocky Mountains. Reb Zalman entered the lodge on Friday evening looking like a jovial bearded grandfather with a broad grin and a twinkle in his eye. He was wearing an embroidered cap, a zip-up kaftan, and slippers. "Shabbat is about comfort," he announced to the group of seventy-five formally dressed adults. "We have to be easy with ourselves in order to allow in our additional soul, the higher Self known as *neshama Yeteyrah*, which wants to emerge when we light the Sabbath candles. See? I'm very comfortable. Now you do the same!" As the group proceeded to take off shoes, find pillows to sit on, and rearrange themselves to form a circle, Reb Zalman came up to Fredrick and me and shook our hands. *"Gut Shabbos,"* he said with a keen smile. "I see you have a Talmud with you?" He pointed to Fredrick's large leather-bound journal.

"No. I write a lot," Fredrick responded, opening it to show him the handwritten pages of his tome.

"Oh! So you're writing your own personal Talmud! Later, you'll tell me what you wrote down!" he said with a chuckle.

But there was no simple way to write down our experience of this man. The weekend proved to be like a mystical journey on his stream of consciousness. Over the course of Shabbat, he wove the group in and out of prayers, through tales of Hindu saints and Sufi fools, meditations, personal anecdotes and teachings from Torah. Life was multidimensional for Reb Zalman, and by means of his teaching, I was able to revisit other teachings I had assimilated and to put them into perspective. As he spoke of the enormous pull each soul has for the "world to come," I flashed on the transcendent dimension I had frequented with Everlasting and Beloved. Since that time, which had split me off dangerously from the world, I had beaten down my urge for the mystical realms. I now realized that by disallowing my experiences of higher realms, I was still caught in the same nasty dialectic. I had split heaven and earth into an either/or choice. Reb Zalman brought in a third way: to ascend to spirit and descend into body simultaneously.

"What's more important than ascendency, simply going up, is how to make the soul go up and at the same time keep the body grounded!" He then proceeded to take us through a meditation from the thirteen-century Jewish mystic Gikatalia, using the unpronounceable four-letter name of God, also known as the Tetragrammaton, which was embroidered on a velvet hanging on the wall behind him, to help us visualize each step:

"Breathe out completely until your lungs are contracted and small. This is the first letter, the yud [h]." We followed his order, holding still for several seconds. "Now breathing in through the mouth, expand your lungs. This is the breath of the upper hay [v]. Now hold that holy breath inside you remaining quite still, and circulate it up and down your spine and limbs: This is the letter vav [u] in you. And when you have done this, exhale the breath out of your mouth. Haaaaa. This is the last letter, the lower hay [v]. Now begin again."

For several minutes we meditated in this way, contracting, expanding, and circulating the four holy letters in our bodies. The whole room swelled with energy.

"Now rest," said our guide. "Let the exercise go and allow the soul to lift off." A deep silence overtook the room. I had the strange transcendent sensation of passing through the normal gates of consciousness, while at the same time being firmly rooted in my body.

Reb Zalman let us rest in this blissful quiet instead of rushing back into the Sabbath prayers. Never before had I experienced such a deep silence at a Jewish service, nor had I ever known that ancient Jewish meditations such as these existed. I was elated.

When the moment was right, Reb Zalman had us join him in the 148th psalm, which he sang as a call and response to the melody of "Michael Row Your Boat Ashore." The entire group rose to its feet and harmonized *"Hallelujah"* as ecstatically as a resonant gospel choir.

As I blended my voice with the group's voice, I watched our leader, who was overflowing with life. With his head thrust back and his eyes closed in ecstatic song, he remained in perfect connection with us, his students, while also appearing to be in direct union with the source of all life. Here was a teacher who, in every way he could, aimed to heal the split in our dualistic thinking. For him, the body and mind were one finely tuned vehicle that had the ability not only to experience the divine but also to embody it.

When we had finished that segment of prayer, Reb Zalman continued. "The Holy Name is one of the clearest maps of reality. Each of the four letters stands for a specific realm of divinity called *olam*, or world, which is also a realm of human consciousness—the Four Worlds. And each dimension of consciousness, or world, is interrelated to and encapsulates the one before it." Once again Reb Zalman pointed to the velvet wall-hanging on which the name's four-letters were positioned vertically. This time he began at the bottom.

"The lower hay represents the World of Action, our corporeal existence on the earth plane," he began, grounding his legs and pelvis, showing their similarity to the two-legged letter. "This world is the sphere of physical manifestation: houses, money, physical health and activity. These are our earthly vessels, with which to contain the holy forces. The higher dimensions need these vessels, and without them, the Shechinah, or female principle, cannot find a *dirah l'mata*, a dwelling place, below. Acting servicefully in this World is known to Jews as *gemilut chasadim*," he said, adding, "but you might be more familiar with the Hindu term, karma yoga. And the science of tuning our breath and bodies in order to carry the force of the upper worlds is, of course, hatha yoga.

"This letter represents the world of the heart," Reb Zalman said, pointing to the long torso-like letter vav. "The joy and the pathos that we experience in the world is not ours alone, but is shared with all of creation. One who serves God from this place of pure devotion is known as the *bhakti yogi*, the dweller of the World of Formation. Ramakrishna lived in this world and so did the Buddhist saint Milarepa. And in our own tradition, King David is one who shows us the way into the heart of all hearts, with his psalms. For example"— here Reb Zalman chanted a beautiful melody—"'*Barchi naphshi et Adonai, v'chol krovai et shem kadsho!* Oh my soul, bless God, and all my innards, bless the holy name.' Notice that King David is singing to his own interior soul, but the word he uses for 'innards'—*krovai*—also means relations, every being connected to me. So what does this tell us? From thousands of years ago, our Jewish tradition had the same connected worldview as the Native American, who chants '*Mitakuye-oyasin!* All my relations!' when he enters into prayer." Several in the audience, including me, let out sounds of surprise to hear this fact. Reb Zalman grinned at us. "What, you were never told about your *bubbes'* and *zeides'* heritage?" he chuckled. "So," he said continuing with the second world, "it is in this World of Formation that we realize that our individual hearts and what they feel are a part of something much greater than we have been trained to know."

Reb Zalman paused to take a drink of water and then, glancing my way, continued. "On yet another level, we know that our feelings and relatedness to the world and others around us are inseparable from what we believe. If your mind is coded, for example, with the belief that this world is rotten or that the physical vessel is a place of imprisonment, how can your heart rise up in song and thanksgiving? I have had both young and old seekers come to me, after having lived in an ashram or after imbibing the teachings of the East, and they ask me, 'Zalman, teach me the best way to transcend life on earth.' And I say, 'I'm sorry. This I cannot do.' Where is there to go? We must see that all levels of creation are mirrors for consciousness and can be raised up! The saintly Ba'al Shem Tov taught us to use everything—our sexuality, our earthliness, even our evil inclination—to serve God. There is no jumping over life, only moving through it, making it holy as we go." Again Reb Zalman looked in my direction, this time with penetrating eyes. My insides did a flip; how could he know that these were my issues?

"The world of our beliefs is in the upper hay," he went on, again pointing to one of the four letters. "This is known as the World of Creation, and one who lives in this dimension, disciplining the mind to penetrate the mysteries of life, is also known as a Raja yogi. Krishnamurti was one, as were many of our great rabbinic sages." Reb Zalman then looked out into the crowd, careful to read the energy in the room. "Stay with me a minute more. If you can, be placing these letters in your body as we go through the worlds. The lower hay in your legs, the vav in your torso; the upper hay in your arms and shoulder girdle. Take a deep breath! Ahhhh!

"And now we come to the yud, the small, head-shaped letter, with the curl on top that draws down for us from the Endless, infinite source of light. The yud signifies the World of Emanation, or Atzilut, which is known to our Hindu cousins as Advaita. In that culture, the school of *jnana* yoga trains the yogi to perceive the world of pure being, far beyond the dualities of the mind and body. In this blissful space, we are who we truly are, one with God. But we cannot live in this place forever. The Holy One wants to be known, to reflect Her face through ours, and through our minds and emotions and actions. This is the purpose of creation.

"*Nu?* Where are we going with all this?" Reb Zalman laughed at us as we struggled to keep up with everything he was saying. "What we are aiming for with all of this is integration. Our spirituality needs to be integrated into all of these dimensions of our selves. If it is, then even the simplest, most mundane action holds within it the key to the universe! 'To see a world in a grain of sand and a heaven in a wildflower,' as Reb Blake would say! This is why the Chasid who comes home from visiting his rebbe and is asked what secrets he learned can say that he learned from his master how to tie his shoes! For the one who can see, even the tying of shoes reflects a cosmic experience!"

By this time, my head was throbbing. Reb Zalman was putting into words an area of my deepest personal commitment: spiritual integration. I had arrived at this goal on my own, after experiencing a string of disappointments and confusions on my quest. Now I was hearing that it was a founding principle of my own birth religion! How was it possible that I had never heard this before? Had it been deliberately hidden, and if so, why? I closed my eyes to sort through the thicket of emotions I was experiencing: anger at having been left out, excitement at what lay ahead for me, and compassion for a tradition that had become dangerously cut off from its own depths. A whole generation of American Jews had been fed a stale white-bread version of a profoundly nourishing diet. No wonder we had rejected it!

Reb Zalman had made clear to all of us that at its core, Judaism provided a model of spirituality that was healing to the modern psyche because it included all realms of human experience. Whereas Beloved and Everlasting had opened the door for me to the upper world of pure being, there was an intrinsic lack of integration in their model: It had no stability in the other worlds. Under the guise of a nondualistic cosmology, their teaching was flawed by a dualism that held the material and feeling worlds as lower realms to be escaped. For this reason, when the door to the upper realms had shut on me, I was thrown into an abyss of failure, feeling as though my very life was a mistake. Through the lens of Reb Zalman's Kabbalah, it was plain to see why unintegrated spiritual teachings were so dangerous for the initiate.

We finished out the Shabbat on Saturday evening with singing and dancing, and the next morning Fredrick and I packed Reb Zalman and his bags into our little Honda Civic and made our way to Boulder. By this time, I had warmed to this man who seemed to encompass the deep wisdom not only of our common tradition, but of the world. I felt no trace of inhibition with him. We chatted intimately about ourselves, and Fredrick and I recounted the story of our paths'crossing, our marriage, and the aftermath in my family.

"I'm sorry for you. But *nit gezorgt!* Don't worry!" He looked at me with his wise eyes, then smiled. "You're not alone. God is mixing up the human gene pool as never before in history. So is it a tragedy or is it an incredible opportunity? We Jews have a propensity for doomsday thinking! But if we think we're going to hold back the trend of intermarrying, then we're trying to hold back the ocean. It can't be done. The Shechinah, the holy presence of God, is at work behind all of our hyphenated lives."

"Hyphenated lives?" Fredrick echoed.

"Yes, the joining of disparate parts, hyphenated. I use the term when two religions meet within households like with the two of you, but also for the intrapersonal. How many of us who are questing spiritually have hyphenated identities? Nowadays we are Jewish-Buddhists, Zen-Catholics, Hin-Jews! It's the age of the permeable membrane! I would be a different man had it not been for the time I spent with the Trappist monks. It broadened me immeasurably in the area of my devotional service. And sitting in meditation with Baker *roshi* in his *zendo* silenced me in ways I could never have experienced within Jewish settings."

"That I believe!" laughed Fredrick. "The meditation you led us in yesterday was the quietest I've ever seen a group of Jews being!" Fredrick was delighted to have this wizardly comrade sitting beside him, someone who, like him, was both firmly rooted in his tradition yet able to embrace the bigger spiritual picture.

"We're learning!" Reb Zalman quipped. "We have to learn from our brothers and sisters of the East! Why do you think there is such a cross-germination?" Then he dropped his voice. "Reb Shlomo Carlebach gave a teaching based on the Iszbitzer rebbe that, in short, goes like this: After the Holocaust, there was such mass confusion. Just like when a family loses a loved one, but multiplied by millions. The leaders of our people were also thrown into chaos and, more, into rage! Who wasn't raging at God after the Holocaust? The whole Jewish culture had been nearly obliterated, and with it, our greatest and holiest teachers. Who would guide the next generation? Everyone was numb, as if frozen by the shock. And then the next generation was upon us with questions, asking the why and what and how of spirituality. But in this frozen rage, we could not point the way. The rational stuff could be passed on, but the heart's fervor was not available to be given over. What was given over was frankly flat, without substance or taste. And then the sixties came and with it, an explosion of spiritual teachings from the East—Satchitananda and Baker *roshi*, Yogi Bajhan and Alan Watts—and so many more. They had the clarity and equilibrium and also the fire that we had lost. And it was to them that thousands of our *yiddelach* went for the dharma."

"But now some of us are coming back to take another look and say, hey, it's got to be in Judaism, too!" I added.

"The hyphen we were talking about is really just a sideways vav," Reb Zalman sang in Talmudic singsong. "Always joining, always bridging opposites, so that one can empower the other. Just like in your marriage. You goad one another to grow. And where do you think *Hashem*, God, resides?"

"Everywhere, of course," I answered.

"But especially in the hyphen!" he said with a grin.

I was happy yet somehow unnerved to hear a rabbi speak this way. He seemed to take my intermarried lifestyle so lightly. Yet I had gone through so much pain in relating to the dogmatically bound religious world. Reb Zalman saw it in my face.

"Tirzahla," he said softly to me, as if he were my own *zeide*, grand-father.

"You are still taking it personally—your choice, your pain, your mother's pain. Of course, and you should. But looking at it through another lens—the wide-angle lens—what's clear is that the holy Shechinah is moving through you and your relationship. And through us all. She is agitating the birthing efforts of the planet. Sure, it's painful, but it's pain that we are all enduring together, the pain of change and renewal."

That night he lectured to a packed audience in Boulder on the topic of the emerging renaissance in the Jewish religion. The evening was an uproarious success, ending with the crowd standing together prayerfully singing "Dona Nobis Pacem" in several languages (including Hebrew and Arabic) under Reb Zalman's guidance. Immediately afterward, I whisked him to the airport.

"You know, Tirzahla, there is a good group here in Boulder." I myself had been surprised by the turnout. All of my students from the mystical aleph-bet class were present, as well as many other spiritual seekers, Jewish and not, whom I had never met. "Listen to me. You're doing a good job of bridging with your husband, and I can tell you are gravitating to the right things in your studies. But I can see how lonely you are. You need *mishpacha*, family!"

"So what can I do?"

"I think you have it! Right here. There was a community there tonight and *oy!* what prayer! Tonight's group will not come together again, but I can feel that there is a community here waiting to happen. And you need to know that there are thousands of people like yourself, a whole network from all different backgrounds, who are doing the work of Jewish renaissance—Jewish Renewal. There's family waiting for you... only not like the one you came from. Trust me!"

I dropped Reb Zalman off and said good-bye amid warm embraces. I turned his words over in my mind many times in the following months. I had great reluctance to get involved with a Jewish group, even one that was pluralistic and dedicated to Jewish spirituality. My experiences with the Jewish community had been so disappointing that my cynical voice told me that I'd better steer clear of Jews in groups altogether. Yet my yearning was great. Judaism was a community-centered religion, and I was tired of celebrating holidays alone and trying to explain their meaning to Fredrick.

What was more, Fredrick and I had just discovered that we were expecting a baby! I needed help in sorting out what kind of legacy I would give to my child. I did not want my child to grow up in isolation from the Jewish world just because of my choices, yet I did not want to submit my child to a standard Jewish upbringing to which I myself could not subscribe. I knew I would need support to sift these matters out, and in the absence of family with whom to do it, community was becoming a dire essential.

Not long after Reb Zalman's visit, I received a phone call from the *chavurah* Gesher Or. They were formally establishing a chapter of the national Jewish Renewal movement in Boulder. Would I come to be a part of the first think tank? I accepted, almost despite myself.

CHAPTER NINE

WEAVING WORLDS

Our daughter was born in the spring. The birth was unexpectedly long and difficult, and as at other times of physical duress, I felt humbled by the impersonal nature of pain and my difficulty in coping with it. A band of strong women friends coached me through the labor and Fredrick stayed by my side throughout, keeping up my courage and sense of humor.

When the moment of delivery finally came and the doctor lay my baby on my chest for the first time, I exploded with emotion. I had family now—blood family, something I had been without for years. My husband and my dearest friends were also family, but my daughter and I had a physical bond, a connection that had been painfully absent from my life. Something opened in me at that moment that allowed love to flow into the center of my being from some deep and hidden source, filling the hollow carved in me by my family's rejection. I wept with joy.

The tiny creature whom we named Emily seemed to beckon me into another dimension. As we glided back and forth in the rocking chair or gazed into each other's eyes as I suckled her, time disappeared for me and I followed her into a world where all of life was about veins and passages yielding to the liquids of love—blood and milk and water—where everything from flowers to furniture seemed to pulsate with light.

Up until Emily arrived, the word Shechinah had been only a concept to me, used loosely to signify the feminine face of God. Now the Shechinah became real, an everyday presence from which I was not separate, but in which I seemed to be living, like a diaphanous state of consciousness that enveloped me. I knew something had changed for me as a result of the new experience I was having: For the first time in my life, I knew without question that I was loved and that I was meant to be alive, doing exactly what I was doing at each moment. My normal state of mind—rushing, judging, comparing myself and my situation to an ever-rising standard—was now gone, leaving in its place a more contented state of being, with softer edges and a more compassionate heart. The new consciousness had everything to do with the baby I had been gifted with—she had opened me to it, as I had opened myself to her—yet it was not dependent upon her, but upon a divine force that was making itself known to me more clearly than ever. And although I felt personally warmed and comforted by the feeling of being deeply loved, I also knew that the love I was receiving was not exclusive to me, but that I shared it with all living beings.

I came to call this experience Shechinah.consciousness, and it was filled with all manner of mind-bending paradox. For example, as much as I was open and defenseless to the creative powers that had poured through me, I also felt unstoppably fierce in guarding the little being that had been entrusted to me. And although I was singularly focused on my baby, and present to the minutest detail of life at hand, my body seemed to be coursing with the pulse of all life, feeling the plight of all creatures, from stars to starfish, parsley sprouts to banyan trees. The unarmored power of the feminine principle that I had been following in my Jungian studies had come alive for me and in me. No longer an idea, the Shechinah was living in my reality. Or was it that I was living in hers?

After her first few months, Emily began to come to life. She was still tiny and delicately built, but now she seemed to wake up to the scene around her, squirming about and grabbing with tiny fists everything in sight. At the same time, I too began to feel a restlessness growing within me. Something had begun to shift for me. Still bonded with my baby, my mind was growing hungry for stimulation, to converse, to read, even to return to work. Yet I despaired of leaving the softer world that I had discovered and going back to my former fast-paced life. Discussing my divided feelings in Leif's office one afternoon, with Emily at my feet in her wicker carrying basket, I was drawn by the title of a book on the shelf behind Leif: *My Schism*. Now that was the book for me! I anticipated the author's personal wisdom about living a life divided. After the session was over, I went to reach for the book, but there was none to be found by that name. Instead, a volume entitled *Mysticism* sat in its place. I stood there startled, realizing how my inner conflict had become the lens through which I was seeing the world.

Soon thereafter, I dreamed of three otherworldly visitors with whom I felt absolute comfort and friendship. We danced together in rapturous harmony throughout the night, and I felt completely at home with them. When the dawn broke, my friends announced their departure. I was shocked by this, and proceeded to weep and plead for them not to leave me, sure that I would never again find such companions with whom I felt so beloved. My friends comforted me compassionately, but departed as planned when the sun rose, leaving me bereft and lonely.

Leif helped me to understand that the dream heralded changes ahead. The Shechinah consciousness that I had been gifted to experience in its full force had begun to wane; this was nature's way. The time was coming for me to return to another rhythm: of people, activities, and work. I prayed to be able to bring my experience of loving interconnectedness with me, to bear witness to the Shechinah's life-giving power, which lay beyond the surface of a frenetic and fragmented world.

As I began to reenter the realm of time, I began to wonder how Fredrick and I would bring up our daughter. We were both overflowing with love for her, but what form would our love take? I began to grapple with the challenging reality of raising an interfaith child. How would we train her to know God and to live in this world? Who would be her spiritual family?

"Tirzah, she's a child of God. The last thing she needs right now is religion."

"I know she's fine right now. But don't you think we should start thinking through how to raise her?"

"I'm not into worrying about it," he replied. "Between the two of us, she'll get everything she needs religiously. She'll have plenty of time to choose her religious identity later on."

But I was not satisfied with Fredrick's casual approach. We had both grown up in structured religious communities with solid religious education. Fredrick had been raised with a rigorous church education, easily as devout as my Jewish education. And even though I had railed against the narrowness of mine, at this point of my life I was beginning to see how it had shaped me in positive ways. As one example, learning Hebrew as a child had served me in countless ways later in my life. I was not about to wait for Emily to tell us she was interested in learning; by then, precious time would be lost.

But what religious training would we give her? The more I stewed on these questions, the more I realized that there was another, more pressing issue to be dealt with: my ambivalent relationship with my own religion. I loved Judaism; it was Jews I had trouble with. And given how community-oriented Judaism is, I knew it would be a tough road ahead to hand down a more Jewish life to my daughter while keeping my interactions with Jews to a minimum.

As an experiment, I began to participate in a series of visioning sessions with a small group of people—the new *chavurah*, or fellowship—who wanted to further Reb Zalman's work of Jewish renewal in Boulder. I had to admit I actually liked these people, even though they were, without exception, outspoken and opinionated Jews. Our meetings were lively and idealistic—and, more important, fun. The group was full of fresh ideas and was bent on creating a warm community that would nourish us spiritually.

In our initial meetings, it became clear that we had all brought with us loads of baggage. Not one of us had passed through our Jewish upbringing unscathed. But unlike other eras of Jewish history, the scars had not been inflicted from an anti-Semitic outside world. They were spiritual and psychological wounds and rose out of the unsatisfying American rendition of our own religion. Before we could begin to shape a new community, we needed to clear out the negative experiences of our Jewish past. This would help us to prioritize our needs and clarify our vision.

We began with twelve people in our group. There was only one Jewish couple among us; the rest were either single or intermarried. All of us were well-educated professionals ranging in age from thirty to fifty, and all had at least a smattering of Jewish education deriving from the Reform, Conservative, and Orthodox denominations of Judaism.

At one of the early meetings, at Davida's house, we went around the circle, sharing our negative experiences with traditional Judaism. Our discontent was not difficult to identify. Many in the group reported suffering boredom and fragmentation during Jewish rituals. The prayers, they said, seemed to have no relevance for them. What was more, God had been reduced to a *He*, some distant commodity, spoken to in ponderous titles such as "Lord of the Universe" and "King of Kings." The Jewish prayers, especially as they were translated into English, tended to alienate with their stiff tones and concepts that separated humans from the divine.

Others of us shared the experience of being disconnected from our bodies and from one another during Jewish rituals, being kept inactive except for standing at the prescribed times. As children, holding our restless energy under wraps had been especially difficult. "It wasn't that there was no warmth," Teddy said, "Jews are certainly affectionate enough, and always there for one another when trouble hits, but during temple prayer, I always felt isolated, off in my own little world."

"And *oy* on you if you didn't fit in!" Zev said, wagging his finger sarcastically. We knew what he was talking about, because most of us hadn't fit in. You had to look good, with two perfect parents named Siegal and always achieve the highest honors in school. Having a respectable amount of money and wearing it was also important, at least in the temples that we belonged to. But if you were unmarried, intermarried, or in any other way deviated from the mold, it was like being handicapped. People didn't know what to do with you.

The women in our group spoke of an overriding sense of being second-class citizens in the synagogue, rarely or never offered privileges such as coming up to the Torah, chanting, or blowing the shofar. The more traditionally raised among us, including me, shared what it was like to be relegated to sitting behind screens or curtains, removed from the men who were leading the services and doing the "serious" *davvenen*, or prayer.

After everyone had spoken his or her piece, a marked shift occurred in the group. The atmosphere among us lightened. What a relief it was to share our disappointments in a group of Jews and not be condemned for them! After all, we were not out to judge the religion, but to reclaim it, to salvage its innermost essence and redress its outer forms.

I had spent years feeling disaffected from the heritage I had grown up in, writing off my losses in smug disdain. Now I saw that escape was the easy route, perhaps the one I had to take until I found the maturity to go back into the fold and speak my truth. That was when my life began to change radically.

"Bashing the system" from which we came, be it a family or a religious organization, is a popular approach nowadays. But it serves no purpose except to tighten us into a position of self-righteousness. This makes the ego feel good for a while, but smugness rarely produces growth. The more difficult choice is to face the pain of our disappointment, then stay in there long enough to share with others what's wrong and make an effort to make things better.

At this juncture in history, when the structures of so many spiritual and community organizations (not to mention families) are breaking apart, we need to recognize how malleable our society is, and how much we really can do to revision the very things that have hurt us. If we dare to bring our intention and our focus to bear on a situation, rather than turning our back on it, *change can happen!* And when we unite in groups that commit themselves to be forces for creative change, rather than agitation circles that pull down what is dying, we become servants to the creative forces of the universe.

What appealed to me about this group was that it was both creative and pure of heart. We were committed to building an intimate, inclusive community, using the Kabbalistic model of the Four Worlds. This meant that we would include our bodies, emotions, beliefs, and spiritual aspirations in our return to Jewish ritual and prayer. Unhampered by normal synagogue politics, fund-raising, or denominationalism ("my brand of Judaism is better than your brand"), we felt free to pursue a direct religious experience in the tradition of the early Chasidic communities. But unlike these eighteenth-century groups of men, we would not be restricted by gender divisions.

Our visioning meetings were anything but dull. All of us were outspoken

Jews, and our voices clashed and collided with excitement at the opportunity to unburden ourselves of our pasts and recreate a spiritual community based upon real needs. These first meetings fueled the group to create forms and structures that would bring us back to the essence of Jewish ritual: spiritual growth and intimacy with God.

In modeling ourselves upon the values of the original Chasidic communities, which were inspired by a tzaddik, or holy man, known as the Ba'al Shem Tov, we took as our guiding principles the very ideas that this great leader had taught: Correct motivation (*kavvanah*), God-consciousness (*devekut*) and ecstasy *(hitlahavut)*. But the inevitable question arose: How bound by tradition would we be?

Unlike members-of the contemporary Chasidic world, we did not hold stringently to *halacha*, the legal praxis of Judaism. We decided to follow the adage of Rabbi Mordechai Kaplan: *Tradition has a vote, but not a veto.* We would use tradition and history as a springboard, while referring for inspiration and guidance to our own sensibilities and other spiritual models we had been exposed to along our journeys. Several of us in the group had experienced Reb Zalman's services, and proposed incorporating his heartful style of praying and meditating while seated in a circle so that the process of relating to God could be reflected in the faces of those around us. Sacred dance and vibrant song were hallmarks of the Chasidic movement, and many of us were enamored of the melodies and robust style of Rabbi Shlomo Carlebach.

Both men and women in the group voiced a need to be utterly egalitarian and democratic. No gender and no person would take the exclusive lead; we would all lead services in rotation, which would require each of us to study and prepare. We planned to celebrate Friday nights together twice a month, bringing in the holy atmosphere of the Sabbath by lighting candles, singing prayers, eating, and studying together. After one year of strengthening ourselves and our practices, we planned to open our membership to anyone who shared our values.

I arrived at my first Friday evening get-together with Emily in my arms. The group was small enough to meet in a living room and this helped us feel like a family. The leader for the evening led the group in a pre-Shabbat meditation, candle-lighting songs, and evening prayers that involved body movements. After an abundant pot luck dinner, the group acted out a hilarious impromptu skit based on the weekly Torah portion. I ached with laughter as I watched a group of people enact Jacob's bickering inner voices as he struggled with his mother's orders to dupe his brother. We were all in hysterics, even as we were in awe of the depth of learning that was taking place.

As I sat nursing Emily in the corner and watching the group interact, I reflected on what was making this *chavurah* work so well together. The intimacy factor was perhaps the most important. We were small enough—twelve people and some spouses—to feel like a family. There was safety here; everyone had agreed on the same spiritual principles at the outset, and all voices were listened to and respected (which is not to say that there were no arguments). There was a clear sense of pride in bringing the best one had to offer. I noticed that everyone had contributed something, whether it was homemade challah, song sheets, or steps to a new dance. The comfort level was also due to the fact that members who were married or in a couple had brought their partners, primarily non-Jews, and all were welcomed openly. I had brought Emily, but Fredrick had chosen to stay at home and have time to himself.

Several months passed. One Friday night, after returning from a particularly innovative Shabbat service, I described to Fredrick how we had gone into nature together to greet the Sabbath, each of us composing a haiku poem along the way in praise of the holy forces in nature. Later, we had sung the traditional Sabbath psalms interspersed with our own poetry and dance. Fredrick could see how excited I was by the experience. "You're definitely invigorating the tradition!" he laughed. "What Matthew Fox is doing for Catholicism, Reb Zalman and all of you are doing for Judaism," he said, referring to the Catholic priest whose movement, known as Creation Spirtuality, is designed to revitalize Christian faith and practice by means of reinvestigating the roots of Christianity. I too was beginning to realize that what we were involved in was part of a much larger movement of worldwide spiritual renewal.

"Why don't you join in?" I asked. "You aren't afraid of being shamed for not being Jewish, are you? Over half the couples in this group are intermarried."

"No, no, it's not that," Fredrick answered quickly. "I just have no interest in a new spiritual group. I guess it's too many years spent in church. I left the church because I lost my taste for organized religion."

"Well, how about disorganized religion?" I joked. "We're anything but organized! I'd really like you to join us. It's more fun as a family."

"Maybe at some point I will," he answered from behind his book. "For now I just enjoy having a quiet house to myself."

I waited for Fredrick to change his mind, but eventually accustomed myself to doing communal Jewish events without him. This made me sad, but I could not fault him. He was getting his spiritual needs met through the community that was building up around his classes. Fredrick was teaching the Gnostic Gospels and alchemy privately and at several small colleges, and though he shared these teachings with me, I did not venture into his community either.

Our roads had begun to diverge, but I could not see this yet. My eyes were set on other things.

Over the next few seasons of meeting twice a month on Friday evenings and holidays, the Jewish Renewal group grew in strength and knowledge. We also developed an amazing support system that went into place immediately when a crisis occurred. Child care, meals, and emotional support were provided for any member who was in need without their ever having to ask. Likewise, weddings, births, and other joyous occasions were planned and carried out enthusiastically.

Like me, many of the *chavurah* members had sampled a variety of practices in their search for a viable spirituality. Miriam had lived and worked with Native Americans in Oklahoma, and although she had been raised with a strong Reform Jewish upbringing, prayer had never come alive for her until she was inducted into sweat-lodge ceremonies. Davida had spent years in the Sufi community, and nothing in her Jewish background had moved her like the Sufi *zikhr* practice—intensive group prayers, rhythmically chanted to specified movements. Others of our members were practitioners of Thera-vedan and Tibetan Buddhism, as well as twelve-step programs.

Now we were all in the business of breathing new life into Judaism, creating a Judaism that was open to the deep wisdom and universal practices of other traditions, just as our teacher, Reb Zalman, had modeled for us. Yet we found that a Friday-night service based on the Native American pipe ceremony felt diluted, certainly not Jewish and as if we had done both traditions a disservice. And chanting in Sanskrit before candle lighting was also decidedly not *shabbosdik*, or in keeping with the flavor of the Jewish Sabbath. On the other hand, some traditions worked. We found that half an hour of Vipassana meditation before Jewish prayer was the perfect remedy for a harried entry into Sabbath, as was resounding a crystal bowl, or chanting a Hebrew chant in *zikhr* fashion, to help us make the transition into holiness.

Where was the line? Our mission was to penetrate to the essence of our tradition, and from there to take our nourishment. At times, the outer clothing—the forms and rituals—needed changing, to better reflect a broadened worldview. But this led to a debate: Where did the essential body leave off and the clothes begin? Many of the laws now seen by Jews as inviolable, as if they were the body of Judaism itself, had been prescribed by rabbis who lived in a world radically different from ours. Yet these men had themselves sat at the cusp of an era, like us, deciding what behaviors were relevant and necessary to keep the tradition alive. We were after the same thing, only our worldview was very different.

Our criteria for answering the many questions that arose out of this next stage of our development were not necessarily the same as those of other Jewish groups; tradition for the sake of tradition did not necessarily bind us, nor did *halacha*, the legal codes of Judaism, although we studied them to learn more and to find a starting point for our discussions. "Tradition is a deposit we made in the last incarnation so we wouldn't have to learn from scratch in this one," Reb Zalman had said. "We don't want to throw it away, God forbid, but not everything can be adopted whole as it is." In all of our discussions, the touchstone was the spirit that was engendered by our actions. Did the ritual in question increase our experience of holiness? Did it bring us further into our hearts? Did it promote the viability of the tradition? These were our rubrics.

In the same way, it was ours to decide how porous to other traditions our services would be. After much deliberation, we decided that Judaism stood at the center of our spirituality. If the non-Jewish contribution augmented our prayer—say, by quieting our minds or preparing us to open our hearts to God—then it would be deemed kosher.

Another area of potential conflict arose around leadership. It was naive of us to think that we would all be leaders of equal caliber. Certain individuals stepped more naturally than others into leadership roles, particularly those with a strong Hebrew education or group facilitation skills. Yet we were committed to a rotation of leaders so that everyone would be challenged to learn and grow in their Jewish skills. The pyramid paradigm in the synagogue that many of us had experienced as children, with the rabbi (or, worse, the president of the board) at the apex and the broad level of recipients at the base, was anathema to us. We were all rebbes, we told ourselves, or could be, and the fact that some of us had no experience in leading prayers would have to be surmounted some- how, but not by having the same leaders lead all the time. It helped to institute pair leaderships, whereby the more educated in Judaism were coupled with those more talented in other areas. But the struggle continued, the shadow side of democracy asserting itself, our services at times sinking to the lowest com- mon denominator of the group rather than rising to the highest possible level.

While the *chavurah* filled many of my growing needs for spiritual connec- tion, my appetite for studying Judaism was still growing insatiably. I needed to continue learning, to see how other Jewish Renewal communities were han- dling common issues, to immerse myself in Reb Zalman's modern-day trans- formation of the ancient Jewish teachings. It was becoming clear to me that my own personal renewal was intertwined with that of my religion. The pull toward Judaism was a pull toward my own self. I could not resist it. Yet I intu- ited that I would be leaving Fredrick behind if I continued in this direction. I was clearly becoming more Jewishly active than he cared to be. I chafed at my conflict for some time and finally brought it up for discussion with Fredrick.

"There's really no problem if our love is strong, Tirzah. I think you're just getting hung up on form again."

"But form is important, too. It's fine to say we are each following the path of our hearts, but then what do we have in common?"

"God. Our faith and our vision. Isn't that enough?"

"Yes and no," I answered, feeling frustrated. "If we don't *enact* our faith together and if we don't share our rituals, our vision is going to fall apart."

I was in a bind. Undeniably, I was being drawn back to my native religion, one that my husband loved in theory, but that he clearly had no interest in practicing. It was not difficult to deduce that problems in our marriage might follow. Yet I could not hold back the evolutionary tide that pulled me toward further involvement in Jewish Renewal. We were both committed to living with integrity and the truth was apparent: For me there was no turning back, and for Fredrick there was no following.

As a rabbi and therapist, I now work with numerous couples who are wrestling with this particular issue: How can a marriage stay strong when each partner is involved in a different tradition? It is not an easy question and there is no easy answer to it. In fact, when an unmarried couple comes to me already struggling with such a problem, I do my best to make clear to them that they are embarking upon something truly difficult—too difficult for many. I have learned over the years that people are by nature so individual, and creating a successful marriage is so challenging, that to enter it without sharing a common direction in life is asking for trouble. And I know from experience that the bigger the role one's spiritual path plays in one's life, the more distance is created if this path is not shared with one's partner. Even well-matched couples change in the course of a marriage, and although the process of staying close when both are on different paths is possible, it takes ingenuity and commitment. Simply showing up at each other's events is rarely enough to bridge the gap.

The magic ingredient, I have found, is space—not his or hers, but a third space born of the overlap of the couple's passions and spirituality. It takes an active process of creation to discover the shared space between two people who are on different paths. Often the key lies in what shared love brought a couple together in the first place. Praying from the heart together, walks in nature, reading devotional poetry to each other, and shared community service: all of these can become intimate rituals that express and strengthen the holy universal ground between two people.

As Fredrick and I turned it over, we agreed that our own family

rituals—spontaneous prayer before meals, singing together, and candlelit meditations—worked well to strengthen us, more than my attending church with
him on Christmas Eve or his coming to Friday-night services. The rituals we
did together were neither Jewish nor Christian but were based on the tenets of
both: faith in one source. They were our humble ways of bringing together our
respective spiritual paths.

Fredrick, having just turned forty, was going through his own process of
renewal. To connect with his own lineage, he made a trip to Great Britain to
study his family tree, walk the land of his ancestors in Wales and visit sacred
sites such as Glastonbury Tor, Stonehenge, and the island of Iona. He returned
invigorated and stronger in himself. No longer Fred or even Fredrick, he was
ready for a new name, and took Evan, a family name more distinctly connected with his roots, as his first name. The name change seemed to mark the
next phase of my husband's life.

I resisted this change, taking a full year to get used to it and only then with
reticence. Repeatedly, I would annoy Evan by calling him Fredrick, thereby
summoning his old self, the one with which I was secure and which I was not
ready to leave behind. My discomfort, I know now, was really fear. I intuited
that Evan's name change signified a movement into territory that belonged to
him alone. We were both venturing into new areas of our lives, and I was afraid
of the subtle but growing schism in our relationship.

The next year, I followed an intuition that took me away from home. Out
of his collaborative friendship with the renowned psychologist and human
potential pioneer, Jean Houston, Reb Zalman had designed a Jewish Mystery
School, an experimental journey into the mystical body of Judaism, led by him
and his senior students at Fellowship Farm, a Quaker facility in the country
outside Philadelphia. This was a nine-month intensive course that consisted
of much personal independent study, and meetings one weekend a month at
Fellowship Farm for group classes. I heard about it just after I had weaned
Emily and had experienced yet another level of the grievous separation from
the blissful state of connectedness her birth had brought me. The upside was
that I was now free to travel. Evan encouraged me to attend the Mystery
School, which began in November, 1987, and volunteered to be a full-time
parent during the weekend each month when I would be away.

As soon as I signed up, I was besieged with ambivalence about putting
myself into a group that was exclusively Jewish. It was fifteen years since I
had been part of a large group of Jews, and all of my anti-Jewish biases, accumulated over the years of being an outsider, were hitting me in the face. I
was afraid of encountering the loud, rapid-fire speech, the critical nature, the

"never-enough" mentality so seemingly prevalent in Jews. I wrestled with my prejudices, telling myself that this was an opportunity to face my projections, to get over my own brand of anti-Semitism. There was no other way to heal my aversions than to examine them.

Another strong incentive for me to persevere and overcome my resistance to my people had to do with reclaiming that which was mine. I was stuck with a Jewish family problem that could not be worked on directly. To my relatives I was no longer a member of the tribe or the family. In cutting me out of their consciousness, they had tried to disavow my share in the Jewish legacy. But I *was* alive, and so was my connection to the heart of the Jewish tradition, if not to the mainstream Jewish community. Attending Reb Zalman's Mystery School along with eighty other students from around the United States was a declaration of my belonging to my people.

I found the hills of Pennsylvania full of life and fragrance even in the winter. The quarters that lodged our school were in part a small animal farm, and the animals' smells and noises brought back memories from my stay on kibbutz in Israel. But little time was spent out of doors; the program was packed with classroom material. Each month was dedicated to one Chasidic rebbe and his teachings. Through lectures, guided meditations, and the study of texts in pairs, the students entered into the thinking, concepts, and teaching style of each Chasidic master. Reb Zalman's staff, composed of men and women rabbis and other specialists in the field of Judaica, helped us to absorb the abundant information through journaling exercises, panel discussions, and small-group exchanges. I ate the teachings up, worked fervently on texts, and took copious notes. I knew this world of study well and began to realize how much I had been longing for it.

But in my fervor to devour information, I could barely stay in touch with the quiet Shechinah presence I had discovered within me. I was grasping for wisdom in the form of information, in a rush to excel in the name of spiritual achievement. When I was honest with myself, I could not help but see in myself the very qualities I had criticized in other Jews. In an effort to get as much information at these meetings as I could, I too was now rushing, reaching, and grabbing for something outside myself.

Yet I had just stepped out of a graced period of early motherhood, in which I had experienced God's potent presence from within! The Shechinah had infused me and I had made a solemn pledge to bring my experience of Her into my life. This meant to go slower, to be in the present moment, to stay in contact with the felt sense of Her. Now I was having trouble keeping my pledge. And despite the fact that the Mystery School staff worked hard to make these weekends of study multifaceted, punctuating them with meditation, music, and prayer, I began to lose myself to a chafing internal conflict.

The Shechinah was here, I knew that, as She was in all places. And it was clear that we had all come together to the Mystery School in Her pursuit. We were attempting, here and in all facets of Jewish Renewal, to reclaim the more feminine, mystical sensibilities of our religion. Yet the Jewish study hall, the texts, and the Jewish ambiance—fast-paced, loud, a bit pushy, and highly mental by nature—made that difficult. For me, and for many others I could see as I looked around, Judaism was associated with an unquiet, sometimes driven sensibility that focused on external reality and an external God to provide answers to life's questions. As if there were some final answer to get from the outside, some wisdom that one had to drive oneself toward, Jews seemed to be engaged more in the *pursuit* of spirituality than in the practice of it.

Certainly nothing dishonorable was going on—on the contrary! The Mystery School was vitally alive, filled with the excitement of people wanting to study, and the learning techniques were innovative and participatory. Yet a piece was missing here, the same piece that had been missing and that I had craved in my earlier experiences of Judaism: a recognition that what we were looking for was also inside us, that going inside ourselves was in itself transformative, and that quiet walks, being out of doors, and listening within were all ways of opening to the other side of holiness.

I realized the changes that were taking place in me when I returned from Pennsylvania every month to my quiet home with Evan and Emily. After the first weekend when I arrived home, I raced through the front door yelling for my family. I found my husband sitting quietly, feeding our daughter; gentle music played in the background. Without noticing their peaceful atmosphere, I ran over, gave them both slurpy kisses, and proceeded to launch into a frenetic report of my new training. Within minutes, Emily had begun to cry and Evan was giving me looks of dismay.

Having been in the new environment, I had begun to talk louder and move faster, mentally racing from idea to idea. Each month it was an effort to get back into rhythm with my sweet-spirited little girl, to consciously slow myself down so that I could meditate more deeply on the ideas I had encountered, talk them over with Evan, and apply them to my life.

To stay in the Jewish world, I knew I would have to bridge this externally focused, fast-paced milieu with my inner one, which required quiet listening, tuning in to the body, and unstructured time. For me, the quest for information had to be balanced with a quest for transformation or it was worthless. To maintain this balance of what one might call the masculine and feminine faces of religious experience became for me the guiding principle of being a spiritualized person in the modern world.

The image I had read about in Kabbalistic texts of a tree with roots in heaven now made sense to me. Each of us is such a tree. If we could but remember our divine origins we could live both sensually and fruitfully on earth while manifesting our holy essence.

Over the months, as I slowly got more comfortable with being in this Jewish environment, I could see more clearly that Reb Zalman and his students were modeling a process of taking the Jewish tradition and molding it so that it could meet today's needs. While always honoring the sacred texts, they brought Judaism to life in their hands because they used it not as an end but as a template for spiritual unfoldment.

Prayer became a new adventure. The prayers and their traditional order were revered in Jewish Renewal, but they were enhanced by melodies, movements, and intentions that brought out their depth and personal relevance. For example, the central credo of Judaism, the Shema Yisrael, is a proclamation from Moses to the people of Israel to remember that at the source of all creation is the one God. *Hear O Israel, the Lord our God, the Lord is One!* In most synagogue settings, this prayer is recited quickly, leaving one oblivious to its profound mystical meaning. In Jewish Renewal services, we slowed the prayer down and used the six holy words as a meditation.

One such meditation that moved me deeply was led by Reb Zalman. He asked us to recite the Shema four times, with four *kavvanot*, or intentions. The first time we slowly said it, we heard it through Moses' lips, as an injunction to us as a people to raise our consciousness. We paused to absorb the message. Next, we were asked to recite the Shema by placing our own name in the place of Israel ("Hear O Tirzah...") and saying it through the voice of our own highest Self; suddenly it became a personal reminder of our inclusion in the wholeness of the higher power. The third time, we recited it substituting the name of one with whom we had a fractured relationship (here I called upon my mother) to lay the foundation for healing and wholeness in the world. Again, we paused to feel the power of what we were doing. And the last time, we were asked to recite the Shema Yisrael as if we were on our own deathbeds, preparing for our final transition into the world where all is clearly one.

I was shaken by this way of praying. It was entirely different than anything I had ever experienced in a Jewish context, and much more akin to the in-depth meditations I was used to from the world of Arica and other psycho-spiritual practices. My exposure to these liturgical innovations began a long process of releasing me from the narrow view I had previously held of Jewish traditions.

I had internalized the legalistic voices of the tradition that kept such a tight vigil over the "right" way things were to be done, and sometimes I would initially bristle when Reb Zalman's students took liberties with the ancient prayers. My crotchety inner voice would resist and I would hear disparaging comments such as *This is Judaism? Who're you kidding?* But if I opened myself to the new experience long enough, it became clear to me that what the rabbis were doing worked! These imaginative alterations were done in service to the prayers' very essence, and almost invariably took us more deeply into the experience of holiness.

It was not always comfortable to grow. When Reb Gershon led us on the guitar in the *Lecha Dodi*, the Friday-night prayer that welcomes in the Shechinah's presence, to the tune of "Ancient Mother," I felt indignant. Was he joking, to put this sixteenth-century mystical song to a Native American chant sung in the sweat lodge? But when I let go of my judgments, I realized that "Ancient Mother" is the invocation of the Shechinah in Native American culture! Reb Gershon was able to bring forth the true intent of the prayer, leading it with all the wistful sincerity of one who has experienced the feminine presence and knows how difficult it is to maintain contact with Her. His intention caught on with the group and led to an ecstatic Sabbath eve.

I was being turned on to Judaism as I had never been before. Studying the Chasidic masters, I realized that there was indeed a *bhakti* path—a devotional path—in Judaism as in Hinduism. Because I had facility in reading the sacred texts from my knowledge of Hebrew, I was paired up to study with a woman rabbi named Shoni, also from an Orthodox background. Shoni had been ordained by Reb Zalman two years earlier. We had great fun together as we unpacked the holy teachings of the Ba'al Shem Tov, Reb Schneur Zalman of Liadi, and Rebbe Nachman of Bratslav, cross-referencing them with our knowledge of other mystical traditions, scientific research and back again to the Jewish world.

Shoni broke the mold of rabbi for me. Coming from an Orthodox background, I had never met a woman rabbi before my Mystery School experience. Many of my Judaica teachers had been women, the wives and daughters of rabbis—pious, studious, modest, and sometimes brilliant. I had imagined a woman rabbi to look something like these women, demure and mousy. But Shoni was unabashedly outspoken and glamorous, down to her elegant flowing dresses and long red nails. One Sunday, as we were being driven to the airport together, I remarked that I was amazed to have met a women rabbi like her.

"It's time you broke open your images of what a rabbi is, Tirzah, my sister," Shoni responded. I had been watching her as she artistically applied her eye shadow and lipstick. Shoni snapped her compact shut and looked at me hard. "In our lives, we are in the business of weaving together worlds that have been separate for centuries. Men don't have a copyright on righteousness, you know, or on scholarship. You and I rocked the limits this weekend with our studying, as good and better than any man, right?" I nodded my assent. "So why shouldn't we step into these roles and do it in our own way?"

"Right. I agree with you," I answered. "I just don't have very many pictures of women, I mean, feminine women—not just women aspiring to be men—in traditional male roles."

"Guess what, Tirzah? There haven't been pictures till now. You and I are *making* them right now so that our daughters will have them," Shoni retorted. "That's our job: to fill the roles of leadership and do it with all the gifts that the Shechinah gave us women: beauty, sensuality, connectedness. Look out, world!" she said laughing. Then, in a more somber tone, she added, "The planet depends on the feminine vision, Tirzah. We're in a terrible mess. The masculine approach is clearly not working."

Meeting Shoni gave me even more permission to continue the work of marrying the seemingly opposing forces of my life. The process had begun with falling in love with Fredrick, and bringing together two religions under one roof. Now this urge to unite opposites was reaching to the very bastions of my ancient heritage, while at the same time inching into the domain of my new vision of the feminine. Could there be an alliance between the old and the new? Was this heresy or simply hubris? I did not know. But here I was in the midst of the Jewish world again. This time, however, I was not checking my beliefs at the door when I entered; my marriage, my feminist sensibilities, and my politics were now all part of my Jewish involvement.

Before saying good-bye at the last Mystery School meeting, Shoni and I made plans to rendezvous at her home in Florida. Then she surprised me by placing her hands on my shoulders and striking a serious tone.

"You're going to be a rabbi someday, Tirzah. I see it." My response was instant laughter.

"You've got to be kidding!" I cried. "Not me. Never. I'm not cut out for it." Shoni recognized that I was dancing as fast as I could away from her comment, but her gaze remained steady.

"And when it happens, I'm going to be there, *b'ezrat hashem*, with the help of the Shechinah!" I shook my head at her, gave her a hug and climbed into the airport van. But her words stuck with me. What a preposterous idea! I had been disowned by the self-appointed sentinels of the religion for transgressing the most serious of religious boundaries. To think of going even further into their domain—and in a role of authority, yet—when I was already such an outcast was unthinkable. I convinced myself that Shoni's comments were a joke and nothing more.

Yet I was on fire with the new possibilities that had been opened up for me, the unoccupied margins surrounding the Jewish tradition. And there were so many more like me than the stalwart Orthodox camp seemed to know, thousands of souls who had been disenfranchised of their Jewish faith because of the sterile or narrow ways in which it had been passed down to them. I had met these Jews along the well-trodden road of the American seeker, in ashrams, spiritual retreat centers, healing arts trainings, and therapy offices. I had been one of them myself; hungry for the spiritual roots that had been denied me and loathing the constraints, the politics, and materialistic focus associated with the religion of my childhood.

Religions are like living organisms. The source that brings each individual being into life, blessing each with a task and the energy to carry out that task, is the same source from which all religions flow. Like the wakeful individuals who must periodically renew their contact with the source of their vision, religions also experience (on a grand scale) cycles of growth and decay, and at great intervals, the travails of rebirth. The personal experience of having our life structure crumble or our belief systems fail is a grueling one, but it inevitably leads to reorganization at a higher level. In much the same way, our religions—humanity's collective road maps to the life of the spirit—are at this point in history undergoing a revamping period, which feels chaotic and unsettling but which will ultimately make them more meaningful and relevant to our modern needs.

The malaise in Judaism has reached a critical mass, and out of it the movement for Jewish Renewal was born. I sensed how vital it would be to the multitude of Jews who had given up on their religion. But sadly, at the end of the 1980s Jewish Renewal was still a well-kept secret, a grass-roots effort that had not hit the public at large. I was fortunate to have come into contact with Reb Zalman, and to have my own small community of like-minded Jews in Boulder, willing to experiment and innovate.

I returned to my *chavurah* from the Mystery School with an abundance of energy and ideas to share. These were enthusiastically embraced by my growing community.

TWO EVENTS IN the next year shifted my self-concept dramatically, allowing Shoni's prophetic words to seem slightly less absurd. The first was a marriage ceremony of two dear friends, Daphne and Bruce, which Evan and I were asked to perform together. Evan had married dozens of couples in his capacity as minister. He viewed marriage, as I did, as a sacred event in which the priest or officiant calls forth the divine powers to witness and bless two souls who are crossing a major threshold in their lives. I felt bashful about participating at first, never having been behind the scenes at any but my own wedding. Still, I was open to the idea, and happy to follow Evan's lead. Neither Daphne nor Bruce was Jewish, and although they were active in the Boulder spiritual community, they were not affiliated with any church. As Evan and I had done in creating our own wedding ceremony, Bruce and Daphne selected the prayers and rituals that spoke to them, choosing freely from an array of possibilities that we made available to them in our meetings.

The wedding was held at the end of August in a large country grange. As soon as the processional began, I felt seized by the power of the event. Here were two individuals coming together in the face of all their previous disappointments and loss, openheartedly saying yes to an ongoing process of revealing themselves to each other, of giving themselves to love and all the consequences of that love. As Evan and I surrounded them, facilitating the various parts of their ritual and holding them, as it were, in our care, I felt for the first time the transcendent nature of ecclesiastical service. I felt Daphne's and Bruce's souls towering over us at the wedding altar, huge luminous presences that did not fully merge, but rather flickered together like two flames dancing.

Evan and I were not only calling forth God's transcendent blessing on the couple. We were also calling on the imminent presence to pour through the community around them, to create something that felt like a soul container, a vessel to support them in both their bigness and their vulnerability as they crossed into marriage. Such an intimate event this wedding was, and yet so exalted!

Evan and I spent long hours the next morning talking about the wedding ritual and what it meant to be "a person of the cloth."

"There are a few moments in a person's life that are like perfect gems. Last night was one," Evan mused as we made the bed together. "When the focus is there and all the necessary elements and people are in place, then people can open themselves up to the powers of transformation. That's what happened last night."

"Now I understand the Jewish teaching that says that any prayer made at a holy event like a wedding has special potence. Because everyone gets changed somehow, not only the bride and groom."

"Transformation—that's what sacred ritual is about. It has less to do with religion and more to do with opening heaven's doors so that the soul can grow."

"And the ritual leader, what a powerful role! I felt both myself and not myself last night. In service to something much bigger than one man and one woman. The Shechinah, I guess."

"Right," Evan said. We were both sitting on top of the bed now as we continued talking. "Being a clergyperson is like being a standin for the holy forces. But it's dangerous work, too. It demands that you be in constant surrender to God. Otherwise you get either disgustingly inflated, or you run around trying to please people all the time and burn out. Either one will kill you. You have to give yourself over, not to people, but to the God within people." I took his words in deeply, sensing that I would be calling on them again in the future.

The following summer, another significant event occurred for me. I attended the international conference of Jewish Renewal, known as the Kallah. The conference took place on the Bryn Mawr campus outside Philadelphia and drew over four hundred people from around the world. I brought Emily, who was now a sensitive little three-year-old with big blue eyes and soft blond hair. Throughout the week, I divided myself between classes that shook my world and looking after my timid daughter. The experience was overwhelming to us both. This time I had less ambivalence about being in a group of Jews. The ambiance was bubbly and joyous. I had never met so many Jews who were so happy—happy to be Jewish and happy to be sharing a vision of Judaism that was so vibrant.

I had already been inducted into the new traditions of Jewish Renewal through Reb Zalman and the Mystery School. But I had not been fully aware of the force of the women in this movement. Among the general participants at the Kallah, scores of female rabbis and community leaders, composers, and choreographers had come together to meet and exchange ideas, to sing and pray together. In awe, I studied these women from a distance as they communed, led prayer, chanted, and taught from the Torah, enchanted by their sure-footedness, their verve, and the sisterhood among them.

It was my class with a feminist scholar, Rabbi Sue Levi Elwell, that turned the tide for me. Her class in Jewish Feminism put in conceptual language ideas and feelings I had harbored for years. There was a missing voice in the Torah, she taught, the voice of women. The traditional Jewish texts of Torah, Talmud, and Midrash were clearly directed to the menfolk. Listening to Sue speak, I thought back to the story of the giving of Torah at Mount Sinai. It had always been a painful story to me: Moses is told by God to tell the Israelite men to separate themselves from the women for three days in preparation to receive the revelation. The separation itself was never the problem for me; it was the direction of the voice. Clearly it was not to the womenfolk. The text does not say how the women were to prepare for this greatest of events. Were we included or left waiting in the background? Were the quaking earth and the sound of the shofar audible to us as well as the men? And the great voice of revelation? We might fill in the story with *midrash*, but the text itself is clear: Women were not included in the directive, not at Mount Sinai and not at the giving of most other teachings of Jewish law. Women were spoken *about* rather than *to;* clearly the normative Jew was male.

I had known this since I was a child, poring over the journeys and stories of the forefathers, lists of male generations, and admonishments of male prophets. The women were there, just behind the surface of the story, but the texts and their redactors had most always silenced them. For many women, this silence had been internalized as a statement of our being of lesser worth. The models of strength we needed were few and far between. How could we learn from our foremothers if their stories were absent? And what of their dances and chants, their recipes for midwifing into and out of this world? In this light, the cut that I suffered with my own mother was just a small part of how cut off I felt from the lineage of women in our tradition. In this bigger severance I was not alone. The entire culture suffered.

"We women have been socialized to take on the experience and voices of others," Sue declared in front of her overflowing class. "Isn't it time we took on our own experience, our own voices? If our sacred texts are blueprints for norms of behavior in the Jewish culture, do we not need a new collection of texts and teachings to make the feminine vision visible?"

At the end of the lecture, a bold female voice rang out from the back of the crowded lecture hall. "I'm a non-Jewish guest at this conference, raised Catholic. But I have to say that women's voices have been silenced in *all* religions and cultures, not just Judaism. I'm studying to convert to Judaism and one reason is that I feel more hope for women in this religion. I have found the women to be incredibly sassy and to know how to take charge." Several women laughed and applauded at her unexpected compliment. Hands shot up around the room to share other viewpoints.

"If Jewish women are strong and feisty, it's *despite* all the marginalization we've endured. We never would have survived as a people had it not been for the ferociousness of us women. It's about time we got out from behind the scenes and made our voices count for something!"

Several other students added their fervent comments before the teacher reigned the class in.

"The passion and compassion that burns in us is how the divine presence speaks through us," she proclaimed. "This voice—which is our voice—needs to be heard and integrated, because it, too, is part of the living Torah."

The women's Torah, it was becoming clear to me, was found in our life stories, in women's call to consciousness, in the essential female experience. The poetry, prayers, and insights gleaned from our centuries of pain, all of this begged to be told and incorporated into the story of our people.

The Torah, if it is to be a living body of truth, has to reflect the whole, has to embrace rather than censor the stories of those who have not been part of the accepted Jewish mainstream. Ironically, that includes half the Jews! But along with the women, there are other camps who have been disenfranchised from the whole along the way: homosexuals, people who have converted to Judaism, Jews who are intermarried or have adopted other spiritual disciplines but still want to identify with their people.

That same week I studied with Arthur Waskow, a Jewish Renewal scholar who, without ever saying it directly, was dedicated to bringing out and strengthening the feminine principles of the Jewish religion. Arthur brought in the planetary connection. He taught about a new view of kashrut, the ancient Jewish dietary laws that teach us both discipline (by restraining our desires) and compassion (by regulating how we butcher our animals) regarding what we put into our bodies.

Arthur took kashrut a step further. He spoke of an ecologically ethical kashrut known as eco-kashrut, premised upon Jews' connection to the rest of the world rather than our separation from it, which magnified Jewish law to take responsibility for the earth's welfare. The discipline and compassion implied in Jewish law had to be extended to encompass how we treat all aspects of life on our planet.

"Ask yourself: Is it eco-kosher to eat fruits and vegetables that have been grown by drenching the soil with insecticides and giving cancer to the workers who pick them?" Arthur asked in a bellowing voice from the head of the class. "Is it eco-kosher to drink your Shabbat wine out of nonbiodegradable plastic cups?" The class murmured in recognition. "We've got to ask ourselves these questions or as Jews we are living only a partial truth! The earth has been given to us as a precious gift to steward. So is it or is it not within Jewish law to stand by as great forests are destroyed? Or to become so addicted to our automobiles that we don't even notice that the carbon dioxide we are sending into the atmosphere is endangering life on our planet?"

His questions resounded in me. Bringing Judaism forward into the twenty-first century, I learned, means waking up from our Jewish isolation, as well as from the narcissism of the culture around us, and taking responsibility through our actions. Guidelines for living were given to us in the *mitzvot*, the commandments, but we need to update them so that they reflect our modern consciousness. Failing this, our tradition is in danger of becoming an empty shell rather than a way to connect with a living God.

Arthur himself was a visionary who taught the Jewish prophets as if they were contemporary social activists hell-bent on repairing the world, and the Jewish cycles and laws as an organic whole by which we could heal our modern lives. Studying with Arthur, I realized that the path of Jewish spirituality was not only personal but political. There was no longer a need to separate my love of the earth and nature or my global concerns from my Judaism. Judaism was no private, small-minded affair; it encompassed every passion I had.

Nor was Judaism as monolithic as I had been trained to believe. At this conference I was reminded that it is a living religion, and that in every period of Jewish history, and throughout all the cultures and climates it has been placed in, it has developed and changed. By virtue of its adaptability, Judaism has survived.

BY THE END of the week, my mind was spinning with new ideas. Fortunately I had a little companion, Emily, who helped me keep my focus on the here and now. Every night as I read to her in the dormitory, we heard the most wondrous music wafting down the hall and through the walls, voices singing ecstatically in several-part harmonies. The music, melodious Hebrew rounds and canons, exhilarated us both. In my mind, I waxed poetic about this being the voice of the Shechinah that had been submerged for centuries by the overpowering masculine voice of our tradition. It seemed that these evening concerts were nothing less than the burgeoning feminine that was being drawn forth by the numbers of us who were ready and listening for her.

One bedtime in the middle of the week, Emily and I left our room to follow the sound. Peeking through a door down the hall, we found a group of young women rehearsing for their post-Shabbat performance. In our pajamas, we crouched down to listen. It was Vocolot, a small choir of women from Berkeley, and their leader, Linda Hirschhorn. I crept in with Emily and sat in the corner with her on my lap. The women smiled our way and continued singing. "*Miriam, come to us quickly now; please teach your daughters your sacred dances,*" Linda's voice entreated Miriam the Prophetess. Miriam, the name I had discarded years earlier, had reemerged with a new, positive association as the connection to the women's lineage that had been broken, for me personally and for so many other Jews.

These women were calling across the generations to the wise woman of our people, to come forth in spirit and guide us, to teach us the ancient wisdom that had been lost and buried, to make our lineage whole again. Their songs were my prayer, too. For the first time in my life, I was ready to actively take my place in the long chain of the Jewish people. Now I had hope that I could come back to my own tradition in a way that was truly meaningful.

CHAPTER TEN

THE CALL

For months Shoni's prediction that I would become a rabbi gnawed at me. On the one hand, I could not take her words seriously because my own image of rabbi was not large enough to contain someone like me. Certainly not me as my real self, with all my history of doubting, searching, and trying out other systems of belief. After all, wasn't a rabbi a person squarely planted on the firm ground of Jewish faith? I had been exposed to vital women rabbis, but they obviously were not bound by the sorts of inner pictures that held me captive. My inner screen was still set on the rabbinic channel that showed my Orthodox uncles with their graying beards, furrowed brows, and Talmudic maxims ready on their lips. On the other hand, I simply could not rid myself of a strangely resonant feeling that spread through my chest whenever I allowed myself to imagine stepping into the role of rabbi.

Trying rationally to figure out my dilemma exhausted me. Finally I let it go. I was content with my life in Boulder, with my small family, a thriving private practice, and my *chavurah*, with which I shared the creative process of renewing Judaism. As one in the group who had a stronger Jewish background than others, I taught various classes on scripture and prayer in the Jewish Renewal style. And now that the children of the *chavurah* members were growing up, I helped to prepare them for their Bar Mitzvah rituals, week-long initiation processes that combined lively Torah services with challenges in nature, community work, and personal ritual. I was at home in my life; I did not need more. Or so I told myself.

The morning of my thirty-fifth birthday, I awakened early with a sense of urgency that I had never before experienced. I felt as if my soul was on fire. Alarmed, I lay very still in bed. Within minutes it occurred to me that this feverish experience had nothing whatsoever to do with my body, but came from another, inner realm, the realm of the Self.

As if listening to a far-off animal call, I worked to identify the message behind this fiery sensation. *You have no time to lose*, it seemed to be saying. *You*

are ready to travel the path. Now move! The message was referring to the path
of becoming a rabbi; that was plain to me. I began to quiver. Why now? This
urgency would have me begin studies this very moment and I had not even
said yes yet! Didn't I have a choice anymore? Besides, how could I be sure that
the voice of this experience was trustworthy? Perhaps it was hopelessly out of
touch with the world, and its plan would steer me into disaster! Yet with all of
my ego's bantering, I knew that I had already consented with every cell of my
body.

We have many voices playing inside us. Perhaps the most important work
of a spiritual initiate is to discern which voice is speaking to us at any one time.
Is it the voice that goads us, not kindly toward our new edges, but into proving that we are inadequate? Is it the voice of our past, drawing us back into
repeating old patterns? The voice that comes from the Self is recognizable.
Listening to it leads us into our hearts, never into self-loathing. This is the
true test, because the Self may sound harsh, but it is always loving. With just
a few words, it can lift our cumbersome mental baggage and redirect our life's
course.

I lay in bed watching the light filter in through the shades. With this one
stroke from heaven, in the form of an inaudible voice, everything changed for
me. The wall that my mind had formed over months to protect me from a territory I did not believe I could enter on my own was now gone. Suddenly, there
was no internal obstacle in the way of my becoming a rabbi, but there was also
no shelter from a destiny at which I quaked.

Later that day, as Evan and I climbed into the foothills for my annual
birthday hike, I told him about the surprising voice I had experienced early
that morning.

"It feels ferocious inside of here," I told him, describing my inner environment. "Like a fever's burning in me. The message is so insistent, even if I didn't
agree with what it was telling me to do, I probably wouldn't have a choice in
the matter."

"Well? *Do* you agree with what it's telling you?"

"I do," I answered. "In some ways it makes no sense at all, and in others,
it's what my whole life has been leading up to."

"Well, Tirzah," said Evan, putting his hand on my shoulder, "I believe
you've received the call."

Like a dream that builds like a tide and forces itself over the threshold of
our consciousness, the call arrives one day to each of us, if we are listening. It
rushes to us from the Self in a completely unfiltered manner, delivering its message without bowing to our personalities. When we hear this voice, we know it.

It vibrates with the other world, setting our bowels to water or our heads into a fever. For a split second, we are able to see with all of our soul's clarity why we are here and where we must go in this lifetime. Thank God for such moments! It is vital to use this light to orient ourselves while we have it, because what follows is often a period of difficult challenge.

Although we may have desired God's guidance, and even prayed for it for some time, the answer we get is numinous, and like God's hand, cannot be forced. It comes on God's schedule, not always convenient to us humans, and what is asked of us may make no outward sense at all. Often, it sounds treacherous, because it beckons us to journey into the fateful zone of our soul. It is the will of God coming to destroy our too-small egocentric system, pulling us toward our destiny by means of exactly those struggles that our ego has been trying to avoid.

That evening, I went to the phone to call Reb Zalman. Surprisingly, I got him in person.

"Reb Zalman, it's time. I want to start studying for ordination."

"Good," he replied almost lightly. "I've been waiting for this." Then he grew silent. When he spoke again, his voice was more serious. "You know, we'll have a lot of opposition, given your marriage to Evan. Much of the world will not be ready for an intermarried rabbi. Give me some time to think things over."

Reb Zalman called me back later in the week.

"Tirzah, I have no problem with you being a rabbi. But others will. You'll get used to that in time, just as I have. For as many revile against you, there will be just as many that need you." I was silent, absorbing the impact of his words. He continued. "The rabbinic curriculum and standards are all outlined in the ordination packet. I'll have the office send it out to you. Now listen to me. Apart from what you study with me and the Renewal rabbis, I want you to go back into the traditional Jewish community and set up classes with rabbis in Denver; find out what's out there. We don't need insulated rabbis in Jewish Renewal. Klal Yisroel, the Jewish people, needs cross-pollination."

I shuddered. Already, my life's course was leading me back into a world that I had assiduously avoided. Now came my first test: Could I enter the mainstream community and hold my beliefs intact? Or would I fall prey to the Jewish consensual reality which declares that there is one right way and many faulty ways to live? Would I be able to hold to my own center, referring within for the direction in which I needed to travel, or would I once again lose the delicate balance of external and internal learning?

Certainly, there was no rabbi in town who blended the worlds of spirituality as Reb Zalman did, no one who was as interested in the influx of the Shechinah in all walks of life. It would be up to me to immerse myself in Jewish learning and then distill the teachings that I felt were ones to live by, ones that led to the path of the heart. If I was to be a rabbi one day, I knew that I would need to translate Jewish teachings into a language that was applicable and meaningful to people who were not necessarily living Jewish lives. Reb Zalman was my mentor and rebbe, but I would have to rely on myself to do the work of integration.

My official training began. Under the tutelage of Reb Zalman, I undertook what would become a four-year journey. Because the Jewish Renewal rabbinic program had no official seminary site, I set up as many of my own learning projects with local rabbis as possible, interspersed by trips back East. Local rabbis at that time meant Denver rabbis because Boulder's Jewish community was still small. I enthusiastically jumped into classes to learn Mishnah and Shulchan Aruch, Jewish law, and I was overjoyed to find a woman to teach me the ancient art of Torah chanting. The notes came quickly, as if they were a familiar language I had simply forgotten along the way. I spent hours commuting to and from Denver, joyfully chanting passages from Torah and singing the liturgical melodies that I was studying.

As the first year of my program passed, my knowledge base increased rapidly. But once again, I began to have a gnawing feeling inside that something was missing. The authors of the classical Jewish texts whose works I was studying, male rabbis from various eras of Jewish history, all shared the same approach to Judaism. It seemed that they were all answering the same two questions: how must one perform the Torah's commandments flawlessly and how must one think about God and the Jewish people. These, however, were not my questions.

It was not that the texts were uninteresting to me. Maimonides' *Mishne Torah* astounded me with its rigorous precision, and I took on the scalp-tightening legal discussions of the Talmudic tractates, or treatises, as a personal mental challenge. The facts, practices, and moral prescriptions that I studied engaged my rational mind; the problem was that they did not seem designed to lead to spiritual experience or an opening of the heart. If the mitzvot, the commandments and laws, were the most important ingredient on the Jewish spiritual path, I assumed that they were founded upon a consciousness of oneness, as declared in the Shema Yisrael. But I wanted to know whether practicing them would lead one *back* to that consciousness. Further, what was written about those dark times of life, say, periods of personal misfortune or when one is wracked with doubts about life's meaning, when the Jewish prescription for faith was not so easily followed? And what had the rabbis taught about cultivating a more individualized relationship with the divine forces?

In the meditation practices that I had learned from other traditions and through my study of dreams, I had been trained to transcend my normal rational functions and open myself to other planes of consciousness. These practices had brought into view the bigger scope of the soul's journey, and had taught me to detach myself from the details of my life in favor of resting in simple awareness and heartfulness. I had certainly found this transcendent view to be a strong focus in Jewish Renewal practices, and I could not believe that it was totally absent from the practices of the rest of the Jewish world. The Kabbalistic systems that Reb Zalman had transmitted in his teachings were surely being lived somewhere in the Jewish world, and I was determined to find out how and where.

I poured myself more ardently into my studies. Like a blind woman groping for a door in a wall, I knew there must be an opening to the inner world somewhere in this mass of Judaic tradition, a little-known passageway that would lead me through all the outer laws and practices into the inner states of silence and communion with the divine that were shared by all traditions. But I could not find that opening, and the part of me that had bailed out of the Jewish world so many years before was beginning to get frustrated once again.

Just at that time I heard that the singer Yisroel Feld had just moved to Denver. I had been given a tape of his Jewish music years earlier and had not forgotten it. Yisroel's baritone voice was unusually warm and resonant. His songs were based on passages from the Prophets, Jewish liturgy, and his own poetry about the soul's search for God. Something in them, in his voice, in his expression stirred me to my core.

The first time I put on a tape of Yisroel's music was one Friday afternoon, soon after Evan and I had begun to live together. By the third song, my soul's deep longing to come home to its Jewish roots had swelled to the surface. Evan came in hours later to find me dissolved in tears. It had been one of the signs that told us that my severed connection to my Jewish lineage was rising to consciousness to be healed. Yisroel's music had elicited a longing that ultimately led me to decide to become a rabbi.

I told myself it was God's design that had brought Yisroel Feld to Colorado, no coincidence at all. I asked for his number and called him. He was difficult to reach. After much persistence, I was able to set up a meeting with him. When I saw Yisroel for the first time, I was surprised to see that he was about my age, thirty-seven. His appearance amazed me—the depth of his blue eyes, the angelic shine of his brow and cheeks, his long gold and red beard. He spoke to me in a quiet, deep voice, with a cadence that lulled me, softened me. He looked at me penetratingly, almost seductively, as if seeing something that I myself could not be aware of. But the next instant, his eyes were elsewhere, distant and unapproachable. He told me that he performed his music and taught around the country but actually preferred to meditate and study in quiet. Still, he consented to begin a small class, which I promised to organize, based on the teachings of Rebbe Nachman of Bratslav.

Though it was apparent to me that Yisroel was an Orthodox Jew, I was able to override my instinctive aversion to Orthodoxy by convincing myself that he did not act like any Orthodox Jew I had ever met. This man sparkled with an inner connection. Surely he had discovered the conscious, more connected way of living that traditional lifestyle. I was compelled to discover the secret to God's plan for living an authentic Jewish life, one that would lead to an enlightened state; I believed that Yisroel could show me the way.

Each of Reb Yisroel's classes began with music. We met around a table in his basement on Sunday evenings as his wife put the children to bed upstairs. Yisroel accompanied himself on a vibrant-sounding twelve-string Martin guitar. I watched intently as he sang one and then another of his compositions, his face angled toward heaven, his clear brow gleaming. There were few of us on those nights, perhaps half a dozen or less. Sometimes we would join in, singing lightly and clapping a rhythm. But mostly Yisroel sang alone. It was his rapture, the unabashed love of God pouring through his voice and hands, that captured me. At those moments, listening to him sing, watching his uninhibited ardor, I was utterly and completely present. Suddenly, there was no other place on earth, no other thought, no other moment than the present one before me. And perhaps it was by virtue of inhabiting it so totally that the moment became eternal, vibrating with life.

When the music ended we would all fall into an awed silence that seemed to last an eternity. During these periods of meditation I would often experience wave upon wave of a pulsating bliss. It was closest in sensation to an orgasm but was not sexual. Ripples of warm, radiant light convulsed through my body. Sometimes, as we transitioned from sound into silence, I dissolved into a weeping so deep that I imagined the longings of lifetimes were being dislodged and washed up from the bottom of my soul.

After a time, Reb Yisroel would begin to speak, often with his eyes closed, always in a slow and penetrating voice. My mind was engaged by his stories of holy men and miracles, but more often I was led inside to a deeply meditative sort of listening. I felt the presence of God here. I was in my rightful place, a perfectly contemplative environment, absorbing the teachings of Judaism I had longed to hear.

He began one Sunday evening lecture by quoting Reb Schneur Zalman.

"The alter rebbe said this: 'Meditate on the greatness of God to the point that it burns in flames of emotion!' If your meditations are without fire, if your davvenen does not have passion or voice, then where will it reach? We must use fire to burn through our *katnut.*"

He was speaking about burning through the *mochin d'katnut:* the small mind, the pettiness of our personal selves to reach the *mochin d'gadlut*, the great mind, what I knew as the Atman, or the Self. Here was the moon, as it were, to which the fingers of all religions pointed: the need to give ourselves over to something bigger than ourselves, thereby *becoming* bigger than ourselves. Only the how to varied from tradition to tradition. In Judaism, the mitzvot or commandments were given as the way to transform ourselves, to move from *mochin d'katnut* to *mochin d'gadlut*, and thereby create holiness in the world.

"Every *mitzvah* is a conduit from this world to infinity," Yisroel continued, his eyes closed, his body swaying slightly forward and back in his chair. "Every time we perform a mitzvah, we have an opportunity to unite with the infinite and draw down from it. And however much *devekut*, or God consciousness, you hold at the time of doing a mitzvah, to that degree you become a container for *shefa*, divine abundance. You know, God only wants to pour delight upon the human soul. And our job is to make of ourselves containers that are both strong and hollow so that we have something to collect the *shefa* in."

I leaned forward in my chair waiting for his next words. Yisroel himself was focused inward as if in a trance. His spine was straight, but now his swaying became more fervent.

"*Isarusa d'tata*, as we arouse God from below, the Holy One responds to us from above," Yisroel continued. "This means that if we utilize the power of our mind and connect it with our longing, we can create a tangible experience of our meditations. If we empower our thoughts with passion, there is nothing we cannot reach. Nothing!" Reb Yisroel slowed himself down. His eyes opened and fell on me. "What one thought are you holding on to tenaciously in your mind? And how persistent can you be with it, how deep can you go with that one passionate thought?" I felt the teacher's eyes penetrating me; I flushed under his gaze and looked away. I knew the answer to his questions instantly. My passion was to know and feel God in this world. And I could go very, very deep. I had proved that with Beloved and Everlasting, and before them, at the Kundalini ashram.

The room suddenly felt charged with tension. My underarms tingled with a cold sweat. I was now home, back in the Jewish world, and I had put myself in the position of being confronted with the same question posed to me on every leg of my spiritual journey: Could I give myself entirely to my desire to know God? And now I heard a new question ring in my head: Could I give myself over completely to a strictly Jewish way of life?

I looked at Yisroel at the end of the table. Here was the teacher I had wanted to meet, a true mystic of my own Jewish lineage. Reb Zalman was certainly this, but his grounded, grandfatherly presence in my life had grown secondary to that of Yisroel, and for this younger teacher I had a different, more emotional kind of feeling. Tears of ecstasy and relief flooded me. I felt that I had found something here for which my soul had been searching for centuries. I wanted to stand up and declare myself ready, to shout, *Yes! I want this! I am ready to give my being over to God now, right now!*

My goal—connection to God—had never changed, but now this teacher became the way to the goal. If I imitated his life, I decided, adopting everything he had adopted and behaving as he behaved, then I would achieve it. But, as soon became apparent, in the process of following Yisroel my own unique connection to God fell by the wayside.

The desire to make a radical change in one's life, to give oneself over wholeheartedly to a cause, is a tricky business. We long to fall in love, to find a person or teaching of such value that we can permit ourselves to take a plunge, to supersede the skeptical voice of reason that so tightly rules our lives. Yet there is an intrinsic flaw in this yearning. Too often, it is based upon a premise that what we have within ourselves is not enough. Then we follow others out of sheer desperation that our own inner knowing is insufficient, that we must become something other than who we are. But this road is beset with danger. To the degree that we feel inwardly inadequate, desperate to change, we are prone to make choices that are black or white, all or nothing, often throwing our relationship with ourselves away for another.

Sitting on the small metal chair, I struggled to compose myself. I was determined to continue on this course, to sit at the feet of this holy man, to follow what he followed, and to go to the inner regions that he inhabited. I had absolutely no awareness that I had projected upon this shining rabbi the very face of God.

When I reached home that night, I found Evan on the couch and shared with him my fantasies about changing my lifestyle.

"Yisroel is an Orthodox rabbi," Evan cut in. "Aren't he and his wife what you would call ultraobservant?"

I nodded. I knew what was coming.

"As I see it, you came from that world," Evan said in his slow and even tone. There was nothing about him that would ever appear flustered. "It didn't work for you in the past. Why should it suddenly be different?"

"No, it didn't work for me. I admit it. The Orthodox world seemed vacuous and narrow. And definitely sexist. But any system can lose its spirit. I found that out in the Hindu world, too. The difference is that now I'm back at my roots and I have a chance to do it right, but I've got to throw myself into it completely. Otherwise, it would be a lie. Why do you think Yisroel just happened to appear at this juncture in my life? He's a teacher who can lead me through the straits. If Yisroel can find his way to holiness in this tradition, there's hope."

"I thought Reb Zalman was your rebbe."

"He is, definitely. But he's so engaged in the work of bridging. I want to know what it would be like to fully immerse myself in an unadulterated Jewish experience. I want to know if it can be a formula for union with God."

"You know, Tirzah, I can't help thinking that you may be slightly nuts right now. So prove me wrong, okay?" Evan had closed his book, *The Creative Mind* by Henri Bergson, and put it down on the floor near the couch where we sat. This meant he was concerned. "What's it going to take to follow this path? And more importantly, can you do what it takes?" Evan had been raised in a Baptist house-hold, but he was fully abreast of the rigors of the Orthodox Jewish world.

"Let's see," he began. "It would mean keeping the Sabbath strictly. It would mean rejoining a community in which women and men are separate and unequal. It would mean dressing in a way that would not attract attention—for you that would be the hardest of all," he chuckled. "And what are you going to do with your goy husband?"

"'Love me, love my goy,' I'll tell'em." Now we were both laughing and shaking our heads at the strange twist that God had brought to our lives. After that late-night conversation, Evan said little and watched warily as I proceeded.

During the following months, I was carried toward Yisroel as a fish is carried downstream. I wanted only to be close to him, to his way of life. Suddenly Boulder's population looked paltry; even my Boulder *chavurah* looked pale and uninteresting next to the passionate new world that was opening up to me. I fantasized about moving to Denver to be closer to Orthodox Jews. I imagined rearranging my life to allow ecstatic prayer three times a day. I saw myself sitting on the women's side of the *mechitzah*, the synagogue divider, my voice lowered and my hair covered with a scarf or hat in the custom of religious married women. I did not see exactly where Evan fit into all this, but in my euphoric thinking, being married to a non-Jew was no obstacle.

Adoring my teacher as I did had transformed my way of seeing. Suddenly the world I had so adamantly rejected glowed in a different way. Utterly smitten—maybe even in love—with the holy man I had put before me, I had lost my own vision.

I accepted several invitations during this time to join friends in Denver for prayer and meals on the Sabbath. Evan was rarely included in these invitations; it was as if he or my marriage did not exist for my new friends in Denver. He would stay behind making a peaceful Saturday with four-year-old Emily of television, reading, and bike rides, while I donned hats and ankle-length dresses and rushed off to sit through lengthy prayer services at the synagogue where Yisroel prayed. There I prayed fervently, keeping my voice quieter than usual among other women with lowered voices. While they chatted after services, I would sit studying Chasidic interpretations of Torah, poring over the *Sefat Emet, Degel Machaneh Efraim*, and other texts. It was understood by all that I was preparing to become a rabbi, but nobody mentioned this or any part of my personal life. I was not there, after all, to socialize. I was on a quest for the holy life, and the Chasidic path had opened to me as the door in the wall I had been groping for.

There was a certain familiar comfort in these Orthodox surroundings. I was cultivating a rabbinic personality modeled to me years earlier by my uncles and male teachers, and more recently by Reb Yisroel. I became stooped over my books. Sometimes I caught myself playing with my chin as if it had a beard on it.

During this period, as my spirit soared, my body became a stranger. My back and hips began to ache and I had great difficulty sleeping. Something inside was deeply disturbed, but I could not make conscious that once again I was losing my own ground and center as I reached for a mystical system that was not organically my own.

One Sunday I asked my old friend, Annie, to drive up to the Indian hot springs with me, about an hour into the Rocky Mountains. Annie was the one who had introduced me to Everlasting over a decade before. She had watched me emerge from that intense episode into a healthier, more joyous woman. She herself had just returned from Nepal and India, where she had visited Hindu and Buddhist holy sites. As I drove, I told her about my dream to become a rabbi and of my burgeoning Orthodoxy.

"Look, I'm a wandering Jew, too," she said matter-of-factly, looking out the car window at a herd of buffalo grazing in a field just off Highway 70. "Just be careful you aren't walking into a trap," she said, looking over at me seriously.

"And what trap is that?" I asked, bracing myself for what would come.

"All the form in Judaism. Jews take their forms so seriously. Form has got to serve what is beyond form, otherwise it becomes an idol."

I felt myself get defensive.

"Look, you Buddhists have your concepts, too. Right action, right livelihood, and all your prostrations and bells. It's not all that different." We drove in tense silence for some way. Then I felt my heart reopen to Annie, and I allowed myself to express some of the concerns I'd been keeping bottled up.

"The truth is that most of the Jewish practices I've taken on have to do with a very socialized form of Judaism. The problem is that it's not my society or my style. I can't stand holding myself back, sitting behind the partition in clothes I don't feel comfortable in. I want to belt out my prayers, to dance, to carry the Torah for myself! And my life has gotten so cut off from nature. I pray better outside. But in the Jewish scene I'm in now, it rarely varies: always indoors, always following the same order of prayer and food. Men act like this, and women—"

"So, why do it, Tirzah?" Annie cut in.

"Well..." I was beginning to feel cornered. "I have this incredible teacher, Yisroel. I believe in him without question, and it's his society. It works for him, so I'm trying to make it work for me. Annie, this man is a holy man. He's for real. I would follow him anywhere. Yisroel is truly on fire for God."

"Oh, I get it. Yisroel is on fire for God and you're on fire for Yisroel! Jesus, Tirzah, are we going to have to repeat that one again?"

I looked at Annie in horror.

"Didn't you get it with Everlasting and Beloved that you've got to follow your own self? God made you a beautiful woman with all the fire you need right inside of your woman's breast. No man is going to get you there, however holy he is."

I felt stung, my cheeks growing hot. I had never drawn a parallel between my Hindu teacher, Everlasting, and my Jewish rebbe, Yisroel, but now it had been drawn for me. I turned my eyes away from the road toward my friend, my assailant. Annie's silver hair was wild, her green eyes set on me, sparking with intensity.

"Is it really so clear as that?" I finally managed to ask in a slight voice.

Annie raised her eyebrows and shrugged.

"Hey, I'm your sister." She said no more.

A few minutes later I replied haltingly. "I'm trying to take in what you said. I hate you for putting your finger on the pulse so glibly like that. But, God, maybe it's true. I have such an investment in this teacher. Why?" Tears rushed into my eyes, blurring my vision. "Why do I have this blasted heed to follow someone outside myself, and always these men! What do they have that I don't?" Now I was crying hard.

As my feelings came to the surface, I became aware, of the deep stabbing pain lodged in my back and shoulders. Annie's left hand intuitively slid to my shoulders and she kneaded the muscles as far as she could reach. "I've been hunched over too many books," I explained, cringing, trying to bring some breath to my back. "Sometimes I feel like I might wake up with a beard if I don't watch out." We laughed, but I had more tears waiting at the surface.

"I think it's time for a trip into the earth mother," Annie said softly. "Look, right on schedule!" she exclaimed as I pulled into the parking lot of the Indian hot springs lodge.

Something shifted in me on that journey into the mountains. As Annie and I walked naked into the dense, steamy air of the underground tunnels, I felt a sort of homecoming. Lowering myself into one of the hot pools of underground water, I reached out to touch the chiseled stone face of the cave wall. It is a holy act to return to oneself, I thought, and maybe one of the greatest *mitzvot* of all to consciously release the ideas and patterns that have held you back from your own self.

A blessing sprang to my mind just then and I spoke it to myself, with the cave, the vapors, the healing waters as my witnesses: "*Brucha at Shechinah, Eloheynu Ruach Ha'olam, matira asurim.* Blessed are You, Shechinah, holy presence, who fills the world with Your living spirit, You have helped me to release that which bound me." And I slipped under the waters. With this journey into the belly of Mother Earth, aided by my sister in spirit, I began the return to my own center and to the feminine wisdom I had pushed away.

A few nights later I had a dream. *I was in a very old city. A Torah was brought out by old men and carried about on stilts at an enormous height. There was much weaving and swaying and fear of its falling. Why didn't they simply carry it in their arms, against their chests? I wondered. Then I looked down to find that my own chest had become enormous. I had breasts like Dolly Parton's. I was shocked. My breasts began to let down enormous quantities of milk. "Oh God, what will I do?" I cried.*

I knew this was an important dream, one in which my unconscious showed its conflict with my new direction. Leif helped me to understand the dream's message. The Torah, the dream was saying, was being held too high above the people, like some strange icon, rather than being held close to the heart. I needed to bring the Torah and her teachings back down to a level that was more human and based in the body. And if I doubted that I had my own feminine wisdom and nourishment from which to draw, the dream came to set me straight. I had plenty. It was coming from inside me and I'd better get used to it. *Come back to what you know*, I was being told. *You know plenty.*

I began to write in my journal again, to tap my inner voice. I *did* know plenty. I knew that the Torah, read literally in unchanging exactitude, was like an aging, untouchable idol perched on stilts. The Torah's teachings and her mitzvot, indeed the conduits to holiness that my teacher said they were, needed to be touched and handled, made personal and meaningful for each of us. It occurred to me that I could no longer follow exclusively the dictates of Judaism as prescribed by the long lineage of male rabbis; from now on, practicing Judaism would have to become a more personal process, one in which I regularly referred back to my own feelings and wisdom.

The next Sunday night I arrived at Reb Yisroel's home for class, two weeks having passed since the last class, owing to his travel schedule. I walked in with a different posture, taller and more alert. No longer the docile girl nor the hungry young Chasid, I sat down as a woman, having deliberately cleared myself of judgments, holding myself open to the currents of the evening. Reb Yisroel sang just a short song before we fell into silence. Then he spoke.

"A drop," he began, "just a tiny drop from the infinite source, the *Eyn Sof*, falls into this world and fuels all of life here in our world. And that drop is the Shechinah, the feminine presence of God. But the very source that feeds the Shechinah is blocked. It has stopped flowing directly and freely. The Shechinah, just like us, is in *galut*, in exile. Just as each of us has an innate yearning to go home, so does this feminine face of God. Just as we cry out for reconnection, so does the Shechinah cry out to be reunited with the Infinite. And, God willing, this reunion will happen and the abundance will flow again. When? When the Messiah comes and the next *Beit Hamikdash*, the third holy temple in Jerusalem, is built. Then the entire world—all peoples—will be transformed, *bimheyrah biyameynu*, soon and in our time, may it be."

I had never heard Yisroel speak about the events of the outer world in such a way. I was surprised. Although questions were unusual at this point in the talk, I lunged forward with a new daring.

"Excuse me, but what will finally bring all this about?"

"Us," the teacher replied simply. "The Jewish people and their holy acts." I looked at him quizzically. He looked directly at me and proceeded. "It is a Jew's destiny to fulfill this mission of spreading light to the world." Then he began rocking back and forth, his eyes closed, his gaze inward. "Our people have access to higher powers, higher energies than others do. That is one of the Jew's central functions here on earth, to draw down the flow of *Hashem's shefa*, God's infinite abundance, to correct the break in that flow, and to reconnect the Shechinah with the ultimate source of that energy."

Like so many times before, it felt as though the rebbe was speaking directly to me. But what was he getting at? Evan, who had accompanied me on many occasions to Reb Yisroel's classes, was not with me that night. Would the rebbe say these words in Evan's presence? I felt defensive, as if I were being taunted.

He continued. "The *Mashiach*, the holy Messiah, will come at the point of our people's readiness. Not to be worshiped, God forbid, but to help with the final stages of reconnecting the *Eyn Sof* with *Malchut*, the highest plane with the lower planes of manifestation, so that we can have direct revelation."

"Who is 'we'?" I blurted out again.

"'We' is the Jewish people."

I was feeling hot. "What about the rest of the world?"

"The rest of the world can benefit. They, too, to a more limited degree, can partake of the revelation, the connection of high and low that is to come. But although there may be a few exceptions, the rest of the world was not given the same potential as Klal Yisroel, the Jewish nation, to redeem the world. And that is because we have the mitzvot, the Torah, which step up our capacity for transformation a thousandfold."

I tried to collect myself to consider my own beliefs. Perhaps the Jewish people did have a special mission, but God had created a world teeming with rich civilizations and cultures, and each one had its own intrinsic holy purpose, distinct and special unto itself. Light could be shed in many ways. All peoples shared the holy function of fixing and healing what was broken, of drawing down God's abundance into this world of ours.

No, I could not subscribe to Yisroel's spiritual politics. In his doctrine, all other nations seemed largely irrelevant. We have come much too far in world history to believe that the Jewish people are the saviors, God's solitary choice through which all the world will benefit. The problems unleashed by such magical thinking and the shadowy human reaction against the Jews' perceived conviction of superiority had been monstrous. Wasn't that apparent to everyone in the modern world? The stakes had been high, I had lost my family in the process, but I had wagered on another way of thinking, that all of humanity had equal spiritual potential.

As the evening wore on, the teacher continued talking about the special role of the Jewish people. His words passed by me like the throngs of people on their way into the holy temple, all moving methodically in the same direction, while I moved in the opposite direction, against their flow. When the class was over, I rose from my seat, faced Yisroel squarely, and wished him good night. Then I walked up the basement stairs for the last time.

Many possibilities coursed through my mind that night as I drove back to Boulder. I had come to class differently, that was true. Was it my imagination that Yisroel was also different that night? Or was I hearing him with different ears, ones that heard the disparity in our thinking rather than agreeing with everything he said? Could the teacher, with his uncanny ability to read the interior life of his students, have stated these ideas, which he knew were counter to my own beliefs, in order to help me disengage from him? Had he been testing me? Or was he, after all, oblivious to how offensive his words had been?

I never answered these questions to my satisfaction. When I arrived home, all the lights were out. I crept upstairs to my study and wrote the following letter.

> *Dear Yisroel,*
>
> *Tonight it was not appropriate for me to speak out any more than I did. But now I must tell you who I am and where I stand. I have been grateful to meet and study with you; you gave me hope that the devotional path in Judaism is alive, and that the way of ecstasy is possible. Yet I can go no farther as your student, nor can I continue on the Orthodox path. It is your path to follow, not mine. I am devoted to the Jewish tradition and have pledged myself to help it thrive, but Judaism must thrive in a new way now. I reject the theology that you put forth tonight, that would have us hold ourselves as being metaphysically superior, that sees Jews as having greater spiritual potential than the other people of the world. This sort of thinking creates dangerous insularity, if not wars. Everything that I am striving for in Yiddishkeit runs counter to such thinking. I am committed to working for oneness, not more separation. Besides, what do you think would happen to my marriage if I adopted such a belief? Can't Jews hold to our own spiritual path and see that others, too, have a holy purpose if they choose it?*
>
> *I must say that although I have learned much from you, I have felt my spirit, perhaps it is the spirit of my womanhood, squeezed out in the Orthodox setting. It has been difficult to find an outlet for my own voice or spontaneity. My relationship to God, which is also prompted by its own dictates, the inner Torah, if you will, has suffered greatly.*

Finally, and this is perhaps the most difficult to express, I have (or some part of me has) gotten lost in the Chasid-rebbe relationship with you. Your ecstasy has inspired me beyond words, but ultimately I have to kindle my own fire; I can't keep warming myself at yours. I am glad for our differences after all. They remind me to return to myself to search for the "chelek eloha mima'al," my divine Self, which will guide me onward.

If I have been disrespectful to you or erred in any way at all, please forgive me. I wish you only joy, inner and outer, in your life.

Tirzah

I heard from Yisroel within two days. He said he understood what I had said, and that we should stop meeting in order to meditate on these issues. I thanked him for calling and we hung up. It was the end of an era for me.

I was not interested in restoring Judaism to its pre-Holocaust status, despite the tug of nostalgia to return and rebuild what once was. Instead, I was happy to rededicate myself to what Reb Zalman called "reformating" Judaism to fit the reality maps that are appropriate for use in our era. To live with the worldview of even the wisest people of Krakow or Belz in the 1920s is neither appropriate nor useful to us now. The perilous state of our planet, for example, is a fact that was not in the consciousness of our forebears; only now do we know how vital it is to join forces across national and religious boundaries to promote peace and share resources, material as well as spiritual. Likewise, to think that one race or tradition, or one sect of one tradition, has all the truth bestowed upon it is no longer fitting. The modern world has been riddled with such triumphalist thinking on the part of many peoples and nations, and often destruction has come of it. In our day we are called, rather, to honor one another, to guard the integrity and wisdom of our lineages while sharing them with others.

Now I harked back to my rebbe, Reb Zalman, and the things he had said about this topic. In his lectures on a reformatted Judaism, Reb Zalman shared the model of a living organism with many parts to it, each necessary for the overall health and functioning of the whole. The organism is the earth, Gaia. And each individual nation or people on the earth is a particular system, or body part, like the liver or immune system, making its own vital contribution to the whole. Each one is necessary and irreplaceable and must keep its integrity so that the entire body can function.

In the days after my final interaction with Yisroel Feld, I had the uneasy sensation of driving a car for the first time without the driving instructor at my side. I felt excited and also a bit shaky. I was drawn to return to my dream of the Torah on stilts. As I sat in meditation, I felt empowered to imagine myself taking the Torah down and holding her against my chest. The love and connection I felt while doing this was exhilarating. I imagined the Torah speaking to me.

"I want devotion, yes, but I want earnest relationship even more. Do you understand? *Relationship to you.*" I was surprised by such an idea and curious to discover what might be implied by having a relationship with the Torah.

I decided to go slowly, to take one mitzvah at a time, to be reformatted and healed for myself. It was easy enough to observe the outer mitzvah scrupulously, for example, to pray at prescribed times, or to eat in strict adherence to the laws of kashrut, but then one risked being solely preoccupied with the exterior form of the law, while ignoring the inner environment that each mitzvah could produce. I was certain that each commandment had its own potential, its own interior soul, which needed a relationship with a person to give it full life.

I chose the mitzvah of observing the Sabbath as my first experiment. The Sabbath is about stopping, surrendering our normal routines, behaviors, and even thought processes for one day a week in order to host the Shechinah, the feminine presence of God. But in practice, it can itself become a day filled with mechanical actions, its scheduled prayers and meals and naps ordinary and rote. In my experience of observing Shabbat in various Orthodox circles, the day seemed to me to beg for more spontaneity, for a deeper listening.

I began by watching throughout the week which activities and behaviors were most automatic for me. Keeping a frantic pace, trying to accomplish more and more in a set amount of time, worrying about money and being a slave to the telephone were the habitual modes that kept me from listening and feeling the deeper pulses within me. For the Sabbath to become a bridge to my inner holy self, it would have to be a day in which I did not unconsciously submit to these and other automatic behaviors; it would be a day in which I stayed awake to the subtler energies of the Shechinah.

Unlike the Sabbaths I had observed with my Orthodox friends, each one predictable in rhythm and activity, each Sabbath I now observed was like no other. Every one had its own energy or personality, and if I listened carefully, it would signal me when and how much to retreat, to pray, to be in nature, to eat, to study Torah, to be with friends. The Sabbath became the time in the week's cycle when I returned to myself to regenerate, the day when I practiced opening and listening to the inner voice of my soul.

The Sabbath desired of me much unstructured time for letting go, listening, praying, and reading. I naturally started to let go of the activities that burdened me and left me numb during the week—answering the phone, running errands, and listening to the news. Instead, I was led to follow my own energy for an entire day, as if it were the Shechinah Herself guiding me. Being out of doors, visiting with friends, and singing became a new and integral part of each Saturday. The fact that my husband was not by my side in my new Shabbat endeavor troubled me, but not enough to throw me off my course.

I was still focused on the same thought that Reb Yisroel had addressed months before, holding tenaciously to my love of God, wanting to know and feel God in my life. But something had shifted dramatically. I was out of danger now. I no longer feared losing my self, because once again, God was appearing in my life from the inside.

One of the greatest tests on the spiritual path is to open oneself genuinely to new learning without losing one's own power to a teacher or teaching in the process. But failing in this regard and losing one's self is not only a normal phase in spiritual development, it is at times necessary for our growth.

The process is called spiritual transference, when we literally transfer onto our human teacher or guru the superhuman qualities of God. When a transference is broken by losing one's teacher—to death, betrayal, or disillusionment—it can be extremely painful and humiliating for the student, not unlike the pain of a broken romantic relationship. So much energy and hope have been invested in the relationship that its breaking is like the shattering of a precious vessel. But if we can stay true to ourselves and our experience of loss, we have the possibility of recollecting ourselves and growing more intimate with ourselves. Out of our disillusionment, we are thrown back on our own resources. Ultimately, the experience can be used to help us detach from the external provider of guidance and begin to listen to our own innermost voice, which brings us one step closer to inheriting our own spiritual power. It becomes clearer through one of these shattering experiences that the only guidance we can truly count on is on the inside. The voice of the Self—which is both us and far bigger than us—is ready to guide us as soon as we have ears to hear it.

I returned to my rabbinic coursework with many of my questions answered. Yes, Judaism *does* have a strong ecstatic as well as meditative branch. And yes, many of its masters have taught how to cultivate an intimate relationship with God. I also was learning that Judaism is designed to come alive through its mitzvot, or practices, but that those practices must be done with an open, listening heart if they are to lead one into an elevated consciousness. Actions that are done automatically, outside an active relationship with the living God, can grow dead and useless.

As much as I needed the Torah for direction and an influx of divine abundance, I now saw that the Torah needed me as well, needed each of us, male and female, to hold her closely and attentively, to bring our humanity to her teachings. For the first time since my rabbinic studies began, I felt truly inspired to be a rabbi. I vowed never to be afraid of the questions or conflicts of my fellow seekers. I would empower others to bring forth their individual wisdom in making Judaism a vital spiritual path in the modern world.

CHAPTER ELEVEN

UNDER ONE ROOF

FURTHER ALONG IN MY RABBINIC STUDIES, the bizarre reality of my life began to dawn on me. I could certainly see the cosmic humor in my situation and even appreciate it. But I also fell into pits of despair whenever I dwelled on the fact that apart from my Christian husband, I had no family to support me in my new role of Jewish leader.

I had written to my mother many times to spread the word of my renewed allegiance to Judaism, but had never received an answer. I imagined that my family's silence signified their contempt. First of all, to most Orthodox Jews, women rabbis were anathema, but worse was the fact of my intermarriage. My becoming a rabbi was surely a mockery to them. I could hear their voices in my head: *How dare she call herself by such a holy title after having humiliatingly betrayed the tradition?*

Evan, who aligned himself not only with the Christian mystics of his own lineage but with the mystics of all traditions, remained supportive of my rabbinic studies (apart from his disgruntlement about my having less and less time to share with him). Together we declared our commitment to the mystical underpinning of all religions. Despite the politics and small-mindedness that tend to surround them—and Evan had certainly had his fill of those from his church—we believed that all religions sprang from the same source. We knew that, as the great Sufi leader Chazrat Inayat Khan had said, there was no Jewish mysticism, Christian mysticism, or Sufi mysticism. There was only one mystical truth that was found when one went deeply enough into any tradition: the common ocean of God's silent, loving presence. This truth is what I was determined to promote as a rabbi.

In the Jewish Renewal world I could hold my head up high, knowing that I was among like-minded Jews. But as I imagined myself going through rabbinical ordination, I was frightened of declaring myself a rabbi to the mainstream Jewish world, which held little if any regard for a universal ocean shared with the goyim. And how many Jews had ever been honored for pointing to the universal spirit within and beyond Judaism? Besides, I was a woman. Who would listen to me? In the thousands of years of Jewish history, how many woman had been given a mandate for leadership?

My despondency was countered by the hearty encouragement of others who stood on the sidelines—teachers and clergy members of many sects, congregants and friends—who assured me that my becoming a rabbi would be a transformative event for many Jews who had lost their way.

"*Davka* because you *are* a woman, Tirzahla," Reb Zalman said, assuaging my fears one night on the telephone from Philadelphia, "and precisely because you *are* married to a non-Jew and *do* carry these beliefs, you will be a trusted rabbi. There are so many, *oy*, so many Jews that no rabbi can reach because they see themselves as having gone too far away. You will be able to go into places that neither I nor any other rabbi can go into. Just wait."

His words helped me; I clung to them when I despaired. I knew that I myself had been one of those very Jews not long before, and that there were many more like me. Yet this was little consolation to me in my own marriage. Despite Evan's remarkable ability to encompass my new direction in life, there were clear signs of marital distress as we continued our experiment of uniting two religions under one roof.

One Sunday morning in December I sat studying Talmud with my tutor, Monte Eliasov, a middle-aged man from South Africa who had come to Boulder to study Contemplative Psychology at the Naropa Institute. Like me, Monte was from an Orthodox background. In fact, years earlier, he had studied at the Telshe Yeshiva in Cleveland, the same one that my brother Danny had been sent to.

The surface of the oak dining table was covered with large tomes of Talmud and Torah, reference books, articles, teacups, and tangerines. On the floor beneath and around us was the disarray of a living room being prepared for Christmas: boxes of ornaments spilling with gold moons and stars, cinnamon sticks and cherry red baubles.

Monte and I were in the middle of a lively discussion about the original source and meaning of the custom of breaking a glass at a Jewish wedding. Just then the front door blew open. It was Evan, rosy-cheeked and dressed in his tweed suit and corduroy hat. Sunday mornings he went to Mass.

"Ho ho ho! Merry Christmas to all yeshiva students present! Would anyone like to help me bring in the Christmas tree?" I looked over at my Talmud partner.

"Monte, tell me. What's wrong with this picture?"

Our eyes met and we burst out laughing. But despite our hilarity, I felt pain underneath.

What indeed *was* wrong with the picture? Here was my scholarly husband, a good mind, a loving father, a real mensch who was God-fearing and gave *tzedakah*—all of the things that my parents had raised me to look for in a husband. Only the religion was wrong. A tiny flaw, I would joke to my friends. And on my better days I could laugh. But each winter, as the house was draped with garlands of evergreen, wreaths, and lights, and as my daughter grew more and more excited by the Christmas fervor, my tension mounted.

Throughout my twenties I had been a vociferous universalist, holding all the world's customs and rituals in the same neutral veneration. Santa Lucia's Day and the winter solstice, May Day and the Chinese New Year; all were meaningful and equally worthy of practice. But as my identity as a Jew began to reemerge, my own religious heritage clamored for a more prominent place in our household. Suddenly the Christian artifacts that were commonplace in our home and that I had loved began to irritate me.

In fact, as my Judaism was awakened, my intolerance seemed to grow to irrational proportions. I myself had no personal reason to be so hostile to Christianity. I did not realize at the time that what was coming through me was not so much my own negative feelings as those of generations of insulated, justifiably frightened Jewish ancestors. The Yiddish trickster was alive and well inside my head these days. He would cluck and sigh at the milieu in which I lived, especially the side-by-side existence of Jewish and Christian artifacts. "How can you hang a mezuzah on a doorway that leads into a room where dere are crosses and a picture of, excuse me, dat man wearing a crown of thorns?" he would rail at me. When the humor of my ironical situation failed me, the trickster's and other internalized critical voices grew louder in my head.

That evening was one of the humorless ones. As Evan stood on a ladder in the living room stringing lights, I broached the subject.

"Not bad," I offered. "Little white lights are definitely better than the colored ones you see everywhere. But they're still so un-Jewish." I couldn't stop myself from continuing. "You know, it's hard not to think about all the Jewish ancestors who gave their blood unwillingly to help make this beautiful Christian world of yours."

"Tirzah, you're getting snide," Evan retorted.

"I'm sorry. But we've been through this a million times. Every year you try to make Christmas more lovely and meaningful, and every year I get more annoyed. I almost feel an *obligation* to bring out the dark side of the season.

People never want to hear about the other side of the Norman Rockwell picture of a Christian lifestyle. Do you know, for instance, how many Jews your Martin Luther slaughtered?"

"I didn't hear about it in seminary, but I assure you, I know. You've told me often enough. And you are right. I'm not arguing with you. In the name of all the misguided Christians who have come before me, I humbly and sincerely beg forgiveness, from you and from your people. Truly I do." Evan had come down the ladder to speak to me, eye to eye. "But, Tirzah," he continued, "we've got to build a new world, out of all the old separation and suffering. If you and I can't do it, who in the world can? Please, let's move on."

But I couldn't move on. I was astute enough to realize that the dynamic we kept falling into was not merely about religious differences; it reflected our personal power struggle. I was struggling for my own voice alongside a man who was a self-assured, polished spiritual leader, who often seemed to sermonize to me rather than speak to me as a partner. Typically when we argued, Evan would take the noble and wise posture, the hierophant, while I found myself looking for every opportunity to burst his smug attitude.

At Christmastime, as the streets and malls filled with frantic shoppers and the media bombarded me with Christmas cheer, I felt as though I was fighting a losing battle. I was chafing from the conflict that I had willingly signed up for by idealistically marrying a devout Christian. I had signed on with a man who was a ticket to freedom from my insular Jewish background. Now I was fighting the very freedom he had brought me.

At the same time, I was clear that I could never again recede into a purely Jewish world where I would be sheltered from Christmas by people calling it the goyim's madness. I thought of all the ways that my parents and their friends would separate themselves from the mainstream Christian culture in December. No trace of holiday decorations was ever to be found in our house, not even for Chanukah. Our menorahs were the only outward signs of a winter holiday, one for each of us, lined up on the dining room window sill. Only one small gift was given to each child on the first night of the eight Chanukah days, lest we be seen as giving in to the non-Jewish consumer frenzy. Nor did we exchange greeting cards at this time of year; those were sent in the fall before the Jewish New Year.

Now after leaving and then recommitting myself to Judaism after all these years, I found my house aglow with Advent candles on the dining-room table (next to the menorah candles), a huge pine tree sparkling with ornaments that dated back to my husband's childhood, and evergreen rope twined with white lights riding the redwood rafters of our living room. As I looked around me, the lights flickering together magically, I had to admit to myself that despite the conflict it brought me, I also loved the colorful beauty of this season. I noticed the guilt at my enjoyment, wondering which of my rabbinic ancestors would be turning in his grave next. I would talk my rabbinic uncles through it in my mind with a discourse that went something like this: "These decorations are not even Christian, Uncle Theo, they're strictly pagan. Now I know that doesn't sound all that terrific to you, either, but think about it this way: bringing greenery in from out of doors was a gesture of faith in the great power—*Hashem* to you."

Evan and I hadn't always put up a Christmas tree. For the first years of our life together, my early anti-Christian indoctrination had barred any outward sign of Christmas in my house. During that period, it was exactly that: *my* house. As the holiday approached, Evan's spirit would recede day by day, until by Christmas, he would be as sad as a lost puppy. Finally, his psychological strength asserted itself. "We've got to figure this one out, Tirzah. It's my house, too." We could not continue pretending that one of us was not a devout Christian.

At the beginning of our courtship, we sought to deny that there was any difference between us that our love could not bridge. Love was the ultimate medicine; the world's fractured way of viewing things was the disease. Again and again we were confronted with statistics and literature (coming largely from the Jewish world) that advocated that only one religion be practiced in a household. But, as Evan and I had realized years before, his adopting my religion to create a unified spirituality in our home was out of the question. His own religious faith was so strong that to do so would have compromised his personal integrity. We both knew that personal integrity is the sine qua non of any spiritual quest.

It was plain that our quests were now taking us into different territories. Evan and I openly struggled over how things should be run in our common home. Fighting seemed to be a healthier alternative than hiding or curtailing our deepest spiritual longings for the sake of the other.

Of the hundreds of interfaith couples I have met and worked with over the years, only a small percentage went into their marriages with both partners actively pursuing individual religious disciplines. More often I have found that one of the partners is very committed, while the other is either uninterested or happy to share the ride. This seems to be a more workable dynamic. As Evan and I discovered, it is quite a difficult task to consciously create a household that hosts more than one tradition, in which both partners are devoted to their respective spiritual traditions. This is especially so when children are involved.

It was ironic to me at this time, considering the tension of my own married life, that my psychotherapy practice was overflowing with couples needing help. Many of these were interfaith couples who, knowing of my rabbinic pursuits and of my own interfaith marriage, sought me out as someone who could give advice on the gnarly particulars of intermarriage.

One problem that I saw often in my practice developed when a couple closeted one of its religions. I observed great pain in families where one partner in a marriage had converted to the religion of his or her spouse, not with a clear directive from their inner voice, but rather as a way of ameliorating a thorny family situation. Years later, many of these individuals uncovered resentment and rage at having "sold out." As Sandra, a converted Jew of five years, confided, "No love is worth leaving your tradition, if it's still alive inside of you. I didn't think mine was anymore, so I forgot about it, but it sure didn't forget about me." Sandra dreamed of ashes being smudged on her forehead, and of Mother Mary coming to help her with her childrearing.

I understood her. When I had tried my hardest to put my faith aside, I too had been signaled by my unconscious that it would not be done with me so easily. I had tried to cut myself off from any connection with Jews and the Jewish cycle of holidays, but for years I awoke on Yom Kippur or Passover morning with Hebrew prayers and melodies ringing in my head. When I would trouble to check the calendar, I would realize that the inner clock of my being was still set on Judaism.

I counseled Sandra and other individuals who had converted out of their birth religion for the sake of their marriages to listen closely to the inner self. For all of them it was necessary to begin to honor their birth traditions in some small way. This did not mean recklessly abandoning their new faiths, but rather to have an "and also" approach. Religions need not be seen as diametrically opposed to one another. Nothing is exclusive in God's mind, and since we are made in God's image, I believe there is enough room available in our psyches to contain paradox rather than flee from it.

Later, as a rabbi, I learned to be careful when performing a conversion ritual to discourage the new Jew from negating his or her roots. I stressed the importance of maintaining good ties with the family of origin, of respecting their ceremonies and being careful not to adopt a holier-than-thou attitude. The culture that had helped call them into being must still be held in reverence. In becoming part of the Jewish tribe, the new Jew is being stretched and molded into something bigger; she is becoming Jewish *in addition to*, not *instead of*, her birth religion.

Then there are the children, the blessed fruit of mixed-faith marriages, innocent pioneers into this vast experiment of mixing races and creeds. Increasingly, we are seeing members of the next generation being stretched to include two and three cultural identities, what Reb Zalman called hyphenated identities. How these children will express their identities as adults remains to be seen. But if at first you feel no tension at housing two ethnicities or religions under one roof, have a child, sit back, and wait.

By the age of three, our daughter Emily had taken to polling her young friends with the question: How many religions do you have in your house? Evan and I would try to listen unobtrusively from the side. Remarkably, her little nursery pals seemed to know exactly what she was getting at and would proceed to enumerate the various religious affiliations of their parents. It was hard for an adult eavesdropper not to chortle in amazement. A typical answer from a Boulder preschooler would go something like: "My daddy is Christian and my mommy is Buddhist but she used to be Jewish, like her mommy and daddy. And I'm everything."

At the age of five, Emily threw me into a conundrum with her answer to the question from one of my friends.

"Well," she said, tabulating carefully, "my daddy and me are Christian, and my mommy and me are Jewish."

"Is that so?" I could not resist remarking, amazed at how she had so gracefully hopscotched over her family's complexity.

"Yup," she nodded with assurance.

I said no more. But I was stung. Until that point, I had not realized how important it was to me that my child know that she was, beyond a doubt, Jewish. For too many years I had brainwashed myself into thinking I was truly a universalist and that Judaism was a dispensable part of my identity. Now I wondered how Evan and I had arrived at parenthood without ever discussing the religious identity of our own child. We had gotten only as far as a naive determination that she would benefit from both of our religions; we celebrated every Jewish and Christian holiday possible.

Soon thereafter, I broached the subject with Evan.

"We need to talk about Emily's religious identity, Evan. You know, kids do need a firm identity when they go off to school."

"Emily is doing just fine. It doesn't seem like she has any problem being both Christian and Jewish," Evan answered matter-of-factly. He was doing housework as we talked.

"But Evan, it's not okay with *me*. I want my daughter to know that she's a Jew. I want her to know she has Jewish blood in her veins."

"'Jewish blood'?" Evan dropped the broom. He looked at me dumb-founded. "I hope you're just being poetic," he declared.

"I am and I'm not. In Jewish law, *halacha*, the child draws from the mother's lineage. It's called matrilineal descent. That means that Emily is Jewish by law. That will never change." I was talking fast, dreading what would come next.

"You amaze me, Tirzah, you really do. Why, all of sudden, do you draw on *halacha* as if it were your time-honored friend? When it comes to the way Jewish law treats women in every other instance, you rant and rave. *You* taught *me*, when it comes to *halacha*, women don't even have legal status, they're no better than children or slaves—only slaves get freed, and children grow up. You said that yourself. So why do you tout the Orthodox rabbis when it comes to Emily and her matrilineal descent?" I tried to cut in to defend myself. "No, you don't." He had pinned me with his smugness. "You haven't got a leg to stand on. Even Rabbi Hillel would agree with me that you can't have it both ways, so ha!"

Evan was becoming a dangerous adversary. He was a quick study and he often caught me at my own tricks. I saw the error in my thinking. And I felt humiliated to admit that my present line of thinking, or feeling, as the case may be, smacked of the very racism that I had rebelled against when it had come from my teacher, Yisroel Feld, just months before.

Yet this was a matter of my guts, not my thinking. I was sensing with growing urgency just how much I wanted my daughter to know the precious-ness of being Jewish, what a miracle it was to have survived the Holocaust, what a rich culture she came from. I tried to articulate this to Evan, even as my feelings rose to the surface.

"I want her to know her Jewish family, her ancestry—"

"Tirzah, look." Evan's voice broke in, but softly. "You can give her all the Jewish riches in the world. But you can't give her a family. Your family cut her off before she was born." It was true—my mother had never acknowledged the letter announcing Emily's birth, nor had my siblings, aside from congratula-tory cards from my two sisters. Besides me, my daughter had no Jewish family. Evan now pulled up a chair next to me. He could sense the tears waiting to fall.

"Look, I know how emotional this is for you," he said with all the com-passion he could muster. "But Emily is a child of God. And the truth is that neither of us will ever be able to control what she will or won't be. We can nurture her spirit and teach her good ethics; we can show her how to pray and open up to God. But to determine that she *will* be this or *will* be that... it's hubris, Tirzah. It's your ego taking over."

How could I answer him? He was absolutely right. And yet he did not understand at all. Of course Emily would become what she herself would ultimately determine. But I knew that Judaism was more than merely a set of beliefs; it was her heritage, it was in her blood. And she was *my* blood, the only blood family that I was now connected to. Because of this, I clung to my determination to transmit to her the depth and beauty of Judaism. She might chuck it all in the end. But it would live on in her somewhere, as it had for me.

Most interfaith families have an easier time of it than Evan and I did. But even in a less extreme interfaith household than ours, rearing children is a complex matter.

To nurture psychologically healthy children and grandchildren of a mixed-religion or mixed-culture marriage, it is important to realize that the child, while being a whole person, is a composite of two halves. Ignoring either side or speaking of it in hushed tones sends the child a message that there is something shameful about that portion of the child. Even if parents agree on raising the child or maintaining the household within the framework of one religion, the other religion must never be hidden or put down. It is vital for children to know about and honor all of their roots. In this way, they learn to know about and honor all of themselves.

Some people fool themselves into thinking that religion is a non-issue. I have found that this is never the case, even if religion is not practiced nor spoken about in the home. Children who are told "You're nothing" when they ask, "What is my religion?" are not only being diminished, they are being cheated of an identity that is rightfully theirs. Even if the parents are not at all interested in religion, every family has some form of religious or cultural heritage with a richness and quality of its own. This heritage serves to connect the child to his or her lineage and gives the child a valuable sense of continuity and of belonging to something much bigger than his or her self.

Another common strategy nowadays is the "they'll decide later" approach: This is when parents give their children a smattering of information from this tradition and that, hoping that it will satisfy them until "later on," when they'll decide for themselves what religion or brand of spirituality to adopt. But children need more help from parents than that. After years of working with interfaith families and adult children of intermarriage, I see clearly that the practice of leaving children to choose for themselves later in life does them an enormous disservice.

The precious first years of a child's life are the most fertile for learning. What we fail to give our children then—languages, stories, and spiritual practices—will never be as easy to pick up later in life as they are in these first formative years. Furthermore, allowing children to decide for themselves gives them unsuitable amounts of responsibility, which, I have observed, translates into unhealthy pressure, resignation, and regret later on in life.

After many years of watching and studying the phenomenon of interfaith families, I now see that choosing one primary religion in which to train one's children is indeed optimal. If other rituals are being practiced in the household that do not belong to the primary religion, it is best to talk about them openly, explaining what they represent and why they are important. A child easily learns curiosity and respect for the many ways people worship God if adults model such an attitude. At the same time, I believe it is vital for children to have a solid religious identity of their own. When children are clear about who they are (and identifying labels are important for youngsters'development) they have a surefootedness that helps them negotiate their increasingly complicated world.

I was not alone in my passionate desire to provide my daughter with what was good and deep in my lineage. There were many Jewish parents in town who had disavowed mainstream Judaism who shared my need. That year I began directing Beit Sefer Chadash: the New School of Hebrew and Living Judaism. Despite our personal tension, Evan cheered me on. I was excited for Emily to receive a positive Jewish education and Evan was content to teach her stories from the New Testament before bedtime.

Beit Sefer Chadash, catering to children from nonaffiliated and mixed faith homes, opened with six kids and grew rapidly to forty-six within three years. Whether these children were considered Jewish according to *halacha* was not my concern. Their parents wanted to give them a spiritually Jewish background. Had they belonged to synagogues or churches, they would have partaken of programs there. But they did not. They were disaffected Jews and non-Jews who wanted to nurture their children's spirituality and sense of tradition.

In establishing the school, I realized that there were numerous families waiting on the fringes of religious life, avoiding involvement with anything that reminded them of the politics and emptiness of the Jewish institutions of their youth. Talking to the parents, I found that for many of them, their religious upbringing and education had been marred by a sense of boredom or isolation. Some reported that Hebrew School had bombarded them with information that felt irrelevant and out of date. Others claimed that their real spiritual questions were never addressed; rather, they were fed with the unquestioned standard Jewish doctrines. Instead of receiving valuable information, they had left their training with a sense of alienation.

Once out from under the wing of their synagogues or religious institutions, many of these parents had experienced a spiritual awakening of some sort. In recounting their histories to me, they reported having been deeply touched in their world travels or by service in the Peace Corps or the inner cities, by a guru or a meditative practice. In many cases there had been some transformative spiritual event that profoundly marked their lives. But they had felt no strong need or desire to fit back into a religious mainstream—until their offspring arrived. Then the mild discomfort of alienation became an aching need to reconnect to their heritage.

"Jake is asking for a Bar Mitzvah," a mother tells me in an urgent voice over the telephone. "It came out of the blue. What do I do now?"

Another typical call came from a newcomer to the area. "We have a three-year-old and another child on the way. My wife was raised Protestant and I was raised Reform Jewish. I would never want my kids to go through the sterile Sunday school routine that I did. But we do want to give them something. You know, a sense of life's mystery."

Yet another Jewish father, married to a practicing Buddhist, mourned the fact that he could not give his six-year-old daughter the deep feelings for his faith that had been transmitted to him by his Polish grandfather. "Those feelings won't come in a typical synagogue. I need help giving her the magic I felt on the Sabbath or when I climbed under his tallis as he was praying."

I was delighted to listen to these kindred souls and to create a network for what I realized was a vast subculture of disenfranchised Jews. But I was even more ecstatic to work with their children: kids from six to fourteen, pure in heart and mind, their native spirituality untouched by formal religious education. Most of them had never been told of Abraham or Sarah, the parting of the Red Sea or the giving of the Torah. But they were open to the mystery of ceremony. When I held up a big tallis and gathered them under it, they naturally knew how to reach into their hearts and pour forth with spontaneous, soulful prayers. Emily and her little friends loved to hear Chasidic stories portraying the wise rebbe, and would come to life when I told them how King Solomon could speak to the animals. Emily especially loved to hear the stories of Elijah the Prophet, who would show up to unsuspecting families at times of need dressed in rags, or as a duke, always leaving behind the perfect treasures for one and all. And she, along with the others, would sing her heart out, especially when it came to the Shema Yisrael. I wondered why.

"So what are we singing about? Whatever could it mean that God, our God, is one?" I asked her class one day.

"It means that God made a lot of us, but there's only one of God."

"It means that God started all the religions so we can all sing to Him in different languages. He likes that."

"It means that God knows where you are, even if you get lost. And you can pray to Him and He'll find you."

I let the masculine-god language go for now. I liked the answers. I liked the natural spunk and spirituality I found in these kids. They had not been indoctrinated; they were pure in heart and open to learning.

I committed myself to running a Hebrew School like I had never experienced before, founded on joy, not on duty or guilt, open to questions of all kinds, never espousing a correct form of Judaism or a hierarchy between religions. If I had my way, the Judaism of these children would never be associated with stuffy, overheated rooms; I organized walks and picnics and technical rock-climbing events for the whole school. The kids discovered the magic of Shabbat on overnight retreats, when we would climb up into the Rocky Mountains as Saturday morning was just dawning to pray and sing while the sun rose and the moon set. We took field trips to visit Jewish families that had just emigrated from the former Soviet Union, and gathered food for AIDS patients. I brought in stories of miracles and modern-day saints, and rock songs—like "(God Is Watching Us) From a Distance," sung by Nanci Griffith, and "(What If God Was) One of Us," sung by Joan Osborne—that cut to the core of our modern lives.

As I sang passionately with the kids and helped them draw out their beliefs and questions, I was often moved to tears. I had created this school in order to pass on to my daughter her Jewish legacy in a nonexclusive way. But it had become much more than that. In only a few years it had become a place that interfaith families could come to breathe easily, to ask their questions without shame, and to learn to build bridges for their offspring that could connect the family back to its Judaism without compromising their inner spirituality or other traditions. During this time, many questions came my way.

"How do we bless our new baby in both of our traditions without hypocrisy?"

"Is it appropriate to include both sets of families in our son's Bar Mitzvah? Can non-Jews be called up to the Torah?"

"Many of my wife's relatives have been hostile to her marrying a non-Jew; a lot of her family perished in the Holocaust. How can we let them know that in our home her ancestors will be remembered and Judaism won't be lost?"

As these requests for help and advice about life's passages came to me, I felt myself in a position that seemed to be novel in religious history. I had the image of sitting at the point of confluence of many rivers that had never before shared their waters. Would the rivers all flood their banks, washing together into one indistinguishable torrent? I wondered. Or could they enrich one another and still keep their individual integrity?

Sitting at this point of confluence was formidable; I took on the role of answering people's questions with humility and awe. Not only were lives being shaped, but traditions were being reshaped. I would try to sift out the religious particulars to hear the need behind the words. What I discerned most often was a plea of the heart to find understanding and self-expression, to connect across the lines that separate us from love. From the thicket of daily American life, I heard the call for a deeper meaning: "Help me to get behind the outer appearance of things! Help me to hear my heart's inner voice! Please don't fence me out; I too want to belong. I want a connection to the great mystery that is in my heritage."

To answer these people with honesty, I often had to refer back to my own life and my home with Evan and Emily, which was my laboratory for the great experiment of blending currents. And there, religious conflict remained, giving way to psychological struggle.

It was dawning on me that not every intermarriage was as difficult as my own. I watched as many intermarried couples around me flourished. Like Evan and me, they were partners who had been drawn together precisely *because* of their different natures. More than complementing one another, they actually served each other as foils, by drawing out the unique characteristics that contrasted with their own.

Unlike us, however, most couples had more room to bend, while Evan and I defended our own territories staunchly. The interfaith couples that were happiest seemed to fall into three categories: There were those who chose not to raise children at all. There were those who raised their children with a mutually agreed upon religious identity. And there were those to whom religion was mostly an unimportant relic, not a way to God, to be practiced lightly if at all, now and then and in varying modalities.

But Evan and I did have a child, and we did not agree upon her religious identity. More important, we were both in prominent positions in our respective religious communities, and faith and spiritual practice were of paramount importance in our lives.

Our particular situation took a lot of work. Sometimes we left each other behind. Each year Evan and I would attempt as best we could to share our respective holidays, translating the traditions associated with them in ways that made them relevant and meaningful for our partner and other guests. Easter was a time for spring picnics and family outings. Evan would create rituals and songs to teach the theme of life ever returning in new forms, unvanquished by death. Although his personal devotion was to Jesus, he was sensitive not to make Jesus'resurrection the pivotal point of the holiday. For Passover I would focus on the universal theme of liberation, both for nations and individuals. I would create a seder replete with songs in Hebrew and English, inviting our guests' stories and spontaneous poetry about their experiences and struggles with freedom.

With each religious holiday, Evan and I were confronted with the challenge of opening our rituals and traditions enough to bring forth the essential, universal meaning that lay within them, but not to the point of overtranslating and thereby diluting the true flavor of the event. The balance was precarious. I often felt homesick for the traditional observances I had been reared on, but I believed deeply that all our efforts were essential to pioneer the new landscape of bringing traditions together to worship the one God.

By the time I was a rabbinic student, I was in the custom of clearing the house of all *chometz* —breads, crackers, and yeasted foods—for the eight days of Passover. This laborious preparation had always been an important, if arduous, part of the holiday as I grew up. Now, however, clearing out old food and shifting my diet to spring greens and matzoh was symbolic of an internal process of freeing myself from old winter patterns, necessary for a deep Passover experience. The importance of this ritual was lost on Evan, however; he put up with it each year but resented the empty breadbox and cereal cupboards throughout the long week. Moreover, when Easter and Passover coincided, which often happened, what was he to prepare for his special picnic? It was up to me to compromise my standards, not an easy task for me.

Matters were made worse by the fact that Evan's birthday fell in mid-April, which, depending upon the Jewish year, often coincided with the *chometz*-free week of Passover. In a home that was cleaned out for Passover, how does one bake a bona fide birthday cake? Passover cake mixes were anathema to Evan. It was difficult for him not to feel shut out.

"I feel like an outsider with all this ritual of yours," he complained one spring as I was housecleaning. "In fact, I'm beginning to feel just like the *chometz* you're cleaning out, like I don't belong here."

His comment stunned me. Perhaps I was going too far with my return to Jewish ritual. I spoke about this to several friends, weighing the question heavily. That year, Evan's birthday fell on the day before the first Passover seder. I made a beautiful birthday meal for him, but since the house was already cleared of all flours and baking goods, there was no cake; I brought out a fruit compote for dessert, with a candle stuck in the center. Evan looked decidedly cranky at the sight. Just then, our friend Andrea marched into the house with a big box. She walked right over to Evan and held it out to him.

"Look, I'm Jewish myself. But some things have got to come first," she said with a big grin. "Go ahead, open it."

Evan did so. In the box stood a homemade triple-layer chocolate cake with chocolate frosting. On it were the words HAPPY BIRTHDAY, CHOMETZ! We roared with laughter and I brought out matches to light the candles. Andrea was a gourmet baker and the cake was a glorious testimony to the universal ritual of birthdays. But the next morning, Passover eve, my rigidity was back. As I came into the kitchen to prepare the *charoset* and matzoh balls, traditional foods for the seder, I saw the remaining two thirds of the *chometz*, cake staring at me on the counter. I despaired of throwing such a beautiful creation out, but it had to go. Luckily, Evan's spirits had returned.

"Don't worry, I'll handle it," he declared, and the cake was gone from the house. I wondered about that delicious chocolate cake, even coveted another slice, but never mentioned it until after Passover.

"Whatever happened to your birthday cake?" I queried. "No person on earth could have managed to eat it in a day, not even a chocolate fiend like you."

"No, I savored it, bit by bit. I knew I had to get it out of the house, so I kept it on the passenger seat of my car along with a knife and napkins. It lasted for five days. I had some every time I drove somewhere. I've never enjoyed not sharing my birthday cake more," he said with a sly grin.

I felt guilty that my husband had to sneak around me to enjoy what was rightfully his. It also pained me to see that we were not sharing the traditions that were so important to me.

When our differences seemed so insurmountable that even laughter could not help us across, we prayed. Both Evan and I were raised with prayer; it was integral to both Christianity and Judaism as a means of creating a relationship with the source of life. Spontaneous prayer, spoken from the heart rather than from the prayer book, had become our daily family tradition, a third and neutral way to spiritualize our lives at just about any moment.

Before meals we would help Emily light the dining table candle, and with food on the table we would all pause, hold hands, and take turns praying about our day.

"I have so much I want to thank You for, God. I love my family and my home. We are so lucky to have one another and all the bounty on this table. Help us to remember the needy, to share, and to serve others."

"I had a lousy day today. A speeding ticket and a sprained wrist. I'm grumpy about it. But please help me go beyond it and not let it ruin our evening together."

"God bless Mommy and Daddy, and thank you for spaghetti."

Before bed, Evan and I would take turns praying with Emily. I had taught her the Shema Yisrael as her bedtime prayer, a reminder that despite the different approaches held in her household, there was ultimately one God that we all believed in. Then we invoked the angels to come and surround her bedside and take her into a peaceful sleep. If anything was troubling her, Emily would tell the angels about it and ask them to carry it for her during the night. In the morning, of course, problems always looked a little better after the angels had handled them.

And Evan and I prayed. Sometimes at the coffee table in the living room, sometimes in the bathtub together, and often in bed, holding each other. Little was needed but a lit candle to symbolize our focused intention. We would both close our eyes and talk to God, each of us bearing witness to the other's pain, gratitude, struggle. Invariably, this simple ritual brought us out of our hard-line positions into surrender. Solutions did not drop from heaven instantaneously, but they were more likely to occur to us once our hearts were softened and humbled by coming before a power greater than ourselves. No matter what the mood or how difficult our differences had become, we could always pray for help to get us around the gnarly complexities of our lives together.

What compassion these arduous years engendered in me! In my innocence, I had not fathomed what difficulties I would meet along the path of intermarriage. But my own lessons were instantly translated into my work with families. Sometimes I was hard-nosed with the starry-eyed interfaith couples who came to me for premarital counseling. They would bristle and resist my recommendations to look ahead openly and examine the potential problems that often disrupt an interfaith household, such as differing views on childrearing and life-cycle observances. But then I would explain to them the mistakes I myself had made, born of idealism and of not taking the time to think things through. My personal disclosures tended to provoke sincere receptivity on their part.

As Evan's and my challenging journey continued, Reb Zalman's words bore out their truth: It was precisely *because* of the very difficult state I found myself in that I could inspire others deeply. This difficult stage was characterized by wrestling with and resolving issues, both within myself and on behalf of those I served. But all this was just a slight hint of the overwhelming struggle that still awaited me, even before my ordination as rabbi.

CHAPTER TWELVE

OUT OF BOUNDS

My REAL PREPARATION FOR BECOMING A RABBI CAME NOT FROM STUDYING BUT from doing. By the third year of my rabbinical training, all the texts and theories in which I had immersed myself had begun to collect around me like a body of stagnant water. It was valuable and rich information, but I wondered about its applicability to real-life situations. Reb Zalman could see this. Like a master diagnostician, he knew that I was ready for another, more personal level of study, one that would put my feet to the fire. "It's time for you to go to the hospital," he said quite unexpectedly during one of our phone meetings. "Go sign up for chaplain training. The hospital clarifies life priorities better than any *musar* text I know."

I cringed at his directive. How had he known that I felt nauseated by the very smell of the close, sweet air of hospital corridors? Inwardly I both cursed and rejoiced at the fact that my teacher could see through me so plainly. No book in the world could walk me through my distaste for physical illness and my fear of the dying process like Reb Zalman's assignment, and I knew it. It would take planting myself in the rooms of the sick, learning how to pray with them, and experiencing many deaths in order to get familiar with this part of life that I had kept myself from encountering and that I would be encountering more and more as a rabbi.

In January 1990, I began an internship with the chaplain at the Boulder Community Hospital. Chaplain Will Reller was a salty ex-Catholic priest who could face death squarely and find humor in just about any situation. At first, Will led me gently by the hand to the rooms of kind, withering ladies and ailing old college professors. Only later did he introduce me to the leukemia patients who were my own age, the accident victims in intensive care waiting to be taken off life support, and the families in the emergency waiting room who needed to be informed that their child had been pronounced dead on arrival.

What did I have to say to these people? Who was I to enter these rooms and profess any wisdom at all? At first I would pace nervously up and down the hallway outside the patients' rooms, preparing wise introductions and pithy comments about their diseases. It did not take long to learn that neither my truisms nor my ego had any place here. All that was required of me was my complete attention, the ability to empty myself of my frantic thoughts and sit with the patient for whatever length of time was appropriate. This meant giving up my speeches and discovering the feelings waiting in the silence. Often, I had to confront rage and helplessness at the situation, both the patient's and my own.

Religion had little to do with these meetings. When death is lurking and form is falling away, the brand of religious stripe one wears seems to matter little, much less than being there wholeheartedly, to clutch a hand or say a prayer that can cut through the fear. Most of the patients I dealt with were not Jewish. Rarely did it matter to them that I was a rabbi-in-training. People simply wanted to talk, to spill out their questions, to hear a word of hope and know that someone, anyone, was listening.

Outside the hospital I was finding myself in positions of leadership that were also both gratifying and uncomfortable. Through my therapeutic practice, classes, lectures, and Hebrew School, I had become more visible in the community. I willingly stepped into new roles of power, enjoying the ways I was being stretched by the questions and needs that people brought my way. But visibility and power bring with them the burden of responsibility. My words and actions seemed to mean more now, and people looked to me for answers, whether I had them or not. Often I would have the feeling that I was swimming out in the middle of the ocean, far from the safe shores of my private life where I was responsible only to myself and my family.

During this time, the number of requests for rabbinic services I received from nonaffiliated interfaith families was growing rapidly. People unknown to me, both Jewish, and non-Jewish, called for spiritual guidance as well as for officiating at marriages, baby blessings, Bar Mitzvahs, and funerals. Most of these requests I had to decline because I was not yet a rabbi. But I was concerned about these callers. They were largely people who cared about spiritual ideals but were nonsectarian and not affiliated with any religious institution. They could have gone to other clergy, but did not want the boilerplate ritual that was standard in most synagogues, nor an appeal for membership in an organization to which they were not connected. It did not seem to matter to these callers that I was not yet ordained; people associated me with Jewish spirituality (as distinct from the Jewish religion). They knew that I would not impose a formula on them and would allow for creativity in their rituals.

The need for connection, for tradition, for community in Boulder swelled, pressing in on me. I responded to as many of the requests as I could, but had to turn many away. I got a secretary to help me handle the work, but what was really needed—a community infrastructure—did not exist. Where were all these people coming from? I asked myself. Yet I knew—these people were no different than I. I understood the people who were coming to me because I too had felt disenfranchised from organized religion yet had yearned for the spirit of my tradition. I, like many of them, knew how it felt to be an outcast because I had not followed prescribed rules, and knew what it was like not to be able to find leaders in my own religion who would listen to me and take me seriously. I too had been estranged and had hungered for teachers and community who would validate me and my search for meaning. And my search was not over, either.

I was learning what every spiritual guide and clergy knows, that at transitional times of life, marked by life passages and important holidays, people come out of their shells for more light. Jews who are not interested in praying at any other time somehow sense the archetypal power in the air at the Jewish New Year and at the time for the Passover seder, and come forth to connect with others to celebrate. I am certain this is true for people of other faiths as well. And on a grander scale, at the universal life junctures such as marriage, birth, and death people often express willingness to deepen their lives in ways that may never have interested them before. This is so because at these transitional times our normal defenses are lifted and we are shown a more expanded way of being.

I took it as a privilege that people were turning to me during these powerful moments. The next phase of my own calling was upon me, there was no question about it. I called Reb Zalman to apprise him of my situation.

"I'm not surprised. The need is so great," he said over the phone. "If you feel ready, it's time that I deputize you." I stammered something in response. "It means that before you are fully ordained," he continued, "I give you the authority to carry out life-cycle rituals. You are not acting as a rabbi, because you aren't one yet, but as my initiate."

Over the next weeks I studied and reviewed with Reb Zalman and other rabbis various questions I had about Jewish ritual law, covering everything from adopting babies to funeral rites. Reb Zalman sent me a document stating that I was his deputy and was authorized to carry out rituals in his absence. All of this helped to prepare me to jump into a much needed role.

The most valuable figure in this preparatory process, however, was my husband, the minister. Evan was on hand daily to discuss with me both the nitty-gritty details and the etiquette of the duties that every rabbi, minister, and priest must learn but that are mostly unpublished. He answered behind-the-scenes questions such as: How do you work with recalcitrant parents and estranged family members at a wedding rehearsal? How do you deal with a screaming infant at a baby blessing? And how do you create a prayerful atmosphere at a ritual gathering where God is looked upon as a joke by the participants? Evan patiently worked with me before every ritual I performed. I showed him my notes, told him my plans, outlined the family dynamics. After I got back from the ritual, I would debrief with him.

Nothing shocked Evan. He had married couples whose dog had been their best man, and had known a minister who had accidentally slipped into the open gravesite at a rainy funeral. He himself had blundered, had mixed up names during ceremonies, had failed to read the newspaper to learn about a flood before preaching to a group that had been devastated by it. Evan knew all the potential pitfalls that clergy face and had the ability and the humor to transcend them. His teachings were both funny and profound.

Evan was helping me to become a leader who served not a religion but a universal ideal which seemed to be the yearning of all people: to rise to the high ground in their lives, to be made whole through connecting with one another and God. This yearning transcended the particulars of any religion. I learned from Evan that the most important skill to be learned as a rabbi-in-training was how to penetrate to the very heart of those I was serving, how to give wings to the heart as I had been shown in the vision years earlier at Beloved's community, that mysterious bird which I now knew lived within each of us.

One critical ingredient was missing in the spiritual diet of the people who called upon me: community. Many of those who called me for help were living in spiritual isolation, with no support at times of grief and often with no family around. Rituals are transformative in helping us across life's thresholds, but nothing can carry us over like loving people to witness and bless our passages.

"I'm being called again," I reported at the next *chavurah* meeting. "This time not just to study, but to act. There are so many Jews out there in need. What we've got in our little group is sustenance. We've got to spread it around." I looked around the circle. "Would you support my vision to take what we have to a larger number of people?"

The group was unanimous in their support of my vision, although as we discussed opening our ranks to the broader community, several members bemoaned losing the intimacy we had built together. Even though the *chavurah* would continue having its own meetings privately, we knew that after opening up our doors for our group to be viewed and sampled by others, we would never be the same again. All of us felt a sort of grief over the changes in store, the loss of our innocence as a small group with its unself-conscious air we had grown used to. Nevertheless, the group was willing to go forward.

We discussed the financial risks of renting space, advertising services, and providing child care and decided to begin slowly, offering one Friday night community service a month. I volunteered to plan and lead each service with help from others. I purchased a hundred Sabbath prayer books from a well-established Jewish Renewal group in California known as the Aquarian Minyan. Their prayer booklets were beautifully designed and contained traditional prayers in Hebrew, transliterations, and inspiring gender-neutral English translations.

Having watched with concern the growing number of calls and requests coming my way, Evan put his energy behind this project as well. I was delighted when he agreed to play guitar to accompany the musical prayers. We rented the Unitarian church in Boulder for the third Friday night of every month and advertised the services as follows: *Heartfelt singing, dancing and prayer. Open to all who want to enrich or rediscover their Judaism, including interfaith families and Jewish participants of other spiritual disciplines.*

It was clear that a need had been tapped: the response was enormous. I was shocked at the number of people who came out for these Friday night events; often we had well over a hundred people.

The first few services began with a few opening words from me to set an intention. Then everybody joined at the empty center of the large room to welcome in the Sabbath queen, the mythical Sabbath guest who brings with her our higher souls. Circle dances and songs helped us make the transition from our normal, workday consciousness into another state of mind, one more open to the divine energies. In a quieter mood, we kindled the Sabbath lights, each individual and family coming together to light their own candle. Before singing the blessing, we held silence. These were the most profound moments; not a word was uttered, but so much feeling was in the air. Often tears were shed at these moments, and hands reached out to connect with other hands. People edged in closer around the table filled with holy flames. I imagined that the almost palpable feeling in the room was one of relief and homecoming; a long-lost tradition that had been waiting to return to life, in many cases for years, was finally being reclaimed.

The moments of silence led into the candle blessing, and then bubbled over into lively singing and dancing around the room. People would sing loudly, clapping and spinning in a childlike manner, then greet one another with the blessing for Sabbath peace: "Shabbat shalom!" Joy flowed freely, a holy joy that hitherto had had no place to be expressed. Evan accompanied the dancing on guitar and helped me learn when to rein the group in and when to allow it to keep flowing. Music proved to be the most important ingredient of these services, both wordless melodies and prayers set to tunes. Music was the common language that helped create a sacred environment in which our group—composed of a wide variety of people, both Jewish and not, from Boulder, Denver, and in between—could pray. Many participants were interfaith couples who felt comfortable with our inclusive approach to Judaism. In this setting people could be themselves; they could come with their gay partners, their non-Jewish spouses, their Buddhist or agnostic or feminist beliefs, and not feel out of place. Some people knew all the prayers and some knew nothing of the tradition at all, but wanted to connect with others, to feel a spark of holiness kindled and bring it home with them. Here I became acquainted with an increasingly large circle of people struggling with their identities as Jews in a non-Jewish world.

After a half dozen or so of these community events, I stood back to evaluate them. A lot of creativity went into their organization, and people seemed to enjoy them immensely—more and more were coming to each service—but something felt amiss. The spirit expressed was one of open universality. But there was a nondescript mushiness in these services that was disturbing to me. The environment we created with singing and dancing seemed to make everyone feel warm and loving, but an intellectual grit was lacking for me. Important spiritual issues demanded my attention—prompted in part by the very public that was showing up for these services yet were going unaddressed—topics such as maintaining spirituality in a secular world, the challenges of living in an interfaith household, and getting beyond the idea that there is one "right" way to be Jewish. I knew that these issues were of interest to many others besides me.

I decided to give sermons at the Friday-night community services. This was risky for two reasons. First, I was now standing out from my *chavurah*, clearly seizing the reins of leadership even more and saying, "These things are important; we must go in the direction not only of enlivening but of educating." Even if other group members agreed with my sentiments, I knew that my actions would be difficult for some of my cohorts to accept. After all, had we not committed ourselves to a purely democratic, leaderless structure? The choice to pursue rabbinic studies was mine, not theirs. They did not necessarily even want a rabbi, whose presence would automatically signal structural changes to our egalitarian democracy. Now one member was forging ahead, stepping into a leadership role, one that seemed to resemble the synagogue structure we had all decried.

I understood the betrayal that this might represent. Yet I had to hold the bigger picture in mind: the growing needs of a larger community were waiting to be met. In knowing these needs so clearly, I felt responsible to raise the level of our gatherings intellectually so that people would leave not only feeling good, but carrying with them ideas that would enrich and stimulate their lives.

The second risk was less personal. It was simply that I myself hated being preached to. I was a seeker on the path, and did not presume to have the solutions to other people's questions. Even if I did, people are rarely interested in someone else's answers (I had found out as much during my hospital rounds). But they do want help discovering their own. What I knew would be most essential was raising provocative questions, imparting information, and the process of grappling that inspires growth, not a pat answer delivered by another.

I decided to speak simply and from the heart. If a topic had deep personal meaning to me, if I myself had been wrestling with it and could identify my own anguish about it, then perhaps others would find interest in it as well. I wrote my sermons as a fellow seeker on the path of spirituality, not as an authority. Many of my sermons were self-disclosing of my own personal history, describing my own love-hate relationship with Judaism and the problems I had with coming back to it as my spiritual path. The response to these discourses was overwhelmingly enthusiastic. Although I would never let Evan read a sermon before I had delivered it, he too encouraged me to continue writing them and to allow myself to be bold, to speak from my heart, to let my notes go and to fly.

One night as we sat debriefing after a service, Evan surprised me by saying, "You know, Tirzah, I think you're creating a monster. Have you noticed how many people are coming each month?" I had to think about it. We were forming a community; that was clear. But we had no organizational structure in place to contain it, which we both realized could lead to problems. There were Jewish Renewal communities around the country, but Jewish Renewal was a grassroots movement, not a denomination. Reb Zalman had guided us to see that Judaism was not in need of yet another denomination like the Conservative or Reform branches to further fragment the whole. Instead, we called ourselves a post-denominational Jewish community. This meant that we would not have the benefit of an established parent organization, neither the "recipe book" to follow nor the funding that made mainstream synagogue life easier. We were admitedly free of restrictive bylaws and organizational hierarchy, but we would have to create our own community infrastructure. For now, my *chavurah* companions and I decided to wait and watch for a signal indicating our next organizational step. We steadily expanded into a loosely structured community without formal membership that gathered monthly and for Jewish holidays and that operated on donations and volunteer services.

Meanwhile, I was coming into contact with more and more unaffiliated young people. Ken and Nancy were a couple who had come to a community gathering. Like many others who called me, they were engaged to be married and were looking for someone to officiate at their wedding ceremony.

I asked Ken and Nancy to come to my office to meet with me. They were a handsome couple, both in their mid-twenties and full of robust, cheerful energy. I learned that Ken was from an assimilated Jewish family in Chicago, and that Nancy was from a devout Catholic one. In fact, she had been brought up in a liberal, socially conscious church in Boulder. Nancy cried when she told me how important it was to her to be married in the church where she had prayed all her life. She had a priest who was very dear to her named Father Pete, whom they had asked to marry them.

"We wanted to ask you if you would consider co-officiating with Father Pete in a joint service. We've told him about you and he's considering it." My shoulders tensed. This couple was taking me into new territory. I looked over at Ken. He was looking lovingly at the passionate young woman by his side. Then he spoke, his eyes filling up with tears as well.

"Please understand, I've never been too religious. We didn't practice Judaism much at home. But since I've met Nancy, my own religion has become more important to me. She's very religious, as you can see, and that's begun to rub off on me. But I don't think I could live with a purely Catholic ceremony." He put his hand over his face, fighting back tears. Mastering himself, he continued. "I'm not Catholic, I'm Jewish, even though I don't know much about it. And it really matters to me that my wedding shows my faith."

I was touched by this couple and wanted to help them. It was no fault of his that Ken had not been given a religious foundation. Like so many other Jews that came to me, Ken was approaching the biggest juncture of his young life, and he realized that something was missing—his spiritual heritage. Had his fiancée matched him in a lack of tradition, Ken most likely would not have been aware of what was missing. He and Nancy would have gone off blithely to a justice of the peace and been married in a civil ceremony, like so many other secular Americans. But Nancy's connection to her religion had awakened something in Ken, much as Evan's had inspired me. And the significance Nancy placed on the religious aspect of the wedding ritual had opened Ken's eyes to his own yearning.

"We are taking a prenuptial course at the church. Of course they'd like me to convert," Ken confessed, "but that's out of the question. We're working on them to waive the papers that make us promise to raise our children Catholic."

"That wouldn't be fair to Ken's side of the family. We're committed to giving our children both traditions," Nancy chimed in.

I cringed, knowing the struggles that this couple had ahead of them. Like Evan and me, they would have to undergo the arduous process of deciding how to keep a constant balance in passing down two religious heritages to their children—only Ken did not have the benefit of knowing his own. I gave them books to read on intermarriage and asked Ken particularly to make time to study his own religion. I wanted to see how committed he was to his own lineage. I found later that, like many couples, Ken and Nancy's interest in religion was focused more on the ceremony than on the years of married life that would follow.

Before they returned for our second meeting, I received a call from Father Pete. His manner was convivial, but even over the phone I could sense that Ken and Nancy's situation was causing him great anxiety. We met for coffee that week.

Father Pete was younger than I expected, a round and jovial man with compassionate, doelike eyes. I felt comfortable with him at once. He explained to me that even in his very liberal church, an intermarriage in which the non-Catholic party was determined to hold on to his tradition was considered problematic. And the need to symbolize such autonomy by sharing the wedding ritual with a Jewish co-officiant was unheard of.

"This is hard for me, Tirzah," Father Pete explained to me, beads of sweat breaking out on his rosy cheeks. "I've known Nancy for years and I really want to help them, but I'm getting a lot of heat from the church for trying." I in turn shared my own conflicted feelings. I explained that I wanted to represent Ken, not leave him out in the cold. There was no other rabbi in the area who would even consider talking to him about this marriage; he had tried and been refused several times. I felt that he was stranded and reaching out for help. How could I refuse? I myself was attempting to balance my own interfaith marriage; I knew how lonely it could be. To have been blessed by a rabbi—even by a rabbinic student—at my own wedding would have meant an immeasurable amount to me.

On the other hand, the idea of marrying a couple in a Catholic church unnerved me. I could see my Yiddish trickster running around in circles, pulling at his hair, and screaming at the thought of it. *Do you know how many centuries our* yiddin *were devoured by dat very church?* he shrieked. I did know, all too well. But we were ushering in a new age, I reasoned, when priest and rabbi could finally come together in mutual respect, without trying to change (or kill) each other. Father Pete and I would be coming together to uphold the universal truth of God's divinity, and the human need to align with it. I saw the problem as a psychological one; holding the ceremony in the church seemed to unbalance the scales. But I was overly focused on the wedding itself. What I did not recognize was that if Ken and Nancy genuinely wanted to base their family on two lineages, they would have to work much harder for Ken's Judaism not to be eclipsed. I could not see clearly then how difficult this would be.

Father Pete and I were brought together by the ironic fact that we were both agonizing over the exact opposite problem. He worried about Nancy's home being diluted by a non-Catholic force, and I worried over Ken's ability to hold his own in a family with heavily Catholic influences. As the priest and I met over the next weeks, continually mirroring each other's fear and protection of tradition, there were moments when we simply stopped to laugh at ourselves and the gnarly situation. Together we decided to pray for guidance, on our own and with the couple.

Finally, Father Pete and I agreed to marry Ken and Nancy jointly. The next several meetings were held in my office and the four of us continued the process together. We hashed out a ceremony that bespoke the spirit of both religions, without compromising the integrity of either. At the beginning and end of each of our meetings, the four of us closed our eyes and entered into prayer, asking that God help guide us in our attempt to break through the religious strictures that bound us, and inspire us to initiate a truly spiritual marriage. Father Pete and I especially voiced our concerns and our fears: that the ceremony not be misunderstood by others, nor that it put out the wrong message to our coreligionists. We both knew we were walking at the edge of what was permissible in both of our traditions. I naively thought Father Pete was taking a bigger risk than I.

The day of the wedding arrived and the couple were in a state of euphoria. Amid great pomp they proceeded to the altar, where Father Pete and I stood together. We both wore ceremonial robes; Father Pete wore a colorful stole and I a hand-painted prayer shawl. Both of us spoke and quoted passages from Scripture about the power of love. The name of Jesus Christ was not invoked during the ceremony. Instead, the Lord's Prayer was chanted, first spoken by me in the original Aramaic, and then recited by the congregation in English. This prayer, the mainstay of daily Catholic worship, had always struck me as a profound expression of basic spiritual principles, and my research had led me to information that it was originally an early Jewish prayer. Ken and Nancy lit a unity candle to represent their two lineages merging into one family. They spoke their vows to each other in their own words, and Father Pete and I blessed their union in words that were nondenominational, stressing neither Judaism nor Catholicism but a third, common path, which was born of their respective traditions and their love of one God.

After the service, Father Pete and I embraced and thanked each other for the hard work and sincerity we had both put into this joint effort. We bid each other farewell and God's blessing. As I walked out of the church that day, I sighed heavily. I felt emotionally exhausted and could only hope that what we had done on that day would come out for the best.

About six weeks later I received a call from Father Pete.

"I went through a tough time with my higher-ups," he reported. "So now it's your turn." I did not know what he was talking about and told him so.

"The wedding we did. It seems that it got into the papers, and there are some very unhappy people looking for you."

Father Pete and I had asked Ken and Nancy not to print an announcement in the paper so as to avoid creating a stir in the community. Nevertheless, an article was printed by one of their well-meaning relatives announcing a Jewish-Catholic wedding performed by Father Pete Schumacher and *Rabbi* Tirzah Firestone at the Catholic church in Boulder.

I did not know from which quarter the next blow would be coming. That night I received a call from Reb Zalman.

"The rabbinical council is all in a fury," he said. His tone was unusually calm, even cheerful. "You knew about the ban they set up on interfaith marriages?"

"Of course I did. But I didn't include myself in the ban; I'm not ordained yet. Zalman, how could I not feel for these kids, being married to a Christian myself?"

Reb Zalman explained that the president of the Rocky Mountain Rabbinical Council had called him directly in Philadelphia to ask him—my rabbi and mentor—to exercise his authority over me. The council, composed of rabbis and chaplains from all Jewish denominations throughout the Rocky Mountain region, was a nonprofit group dedicated to promoting Jewish unity. Ten years earlier they had instituted a ban on rabbis of any denomination performing interfaith marriages in the region. They had not heard about the previous interfaith weddings I had performed; hence, this was the first time I had heard from them, albeit indirectly.

"They're floundering," Reb Zalman said. "They're looking for some way to stop you and they have no one but me to run to." My body had started trembling. I could not understand how Reb Zalman could be so calm.

"What did you tell them?"

"I told them they should thank you! You're doing them a service! Thousands of couples are getting intermarried every year, and these rabbis are so 'holy,' they won't speak to them until the deed is done. After the wedding, they'll consent to take them in as synagogue members, and they think they keep their hands clean like that. It's too easy. And the losses are too great." I mentioned to him that many of the dozen or so intermarrying couples who called me every week reported getting my number from Denver synagogues.

"They'll deny that they're passing these people on to you, of course. As well as the fact that you are doing their dirty work for them by working with these couples. Some things you'll have to get used to, Tirzah."

I was so upset, I could barely concentrate on what Reb Zalman was telling me. My thoughts swarmed around my head, pulling me into their downward spiral: the shame I had brought my rebbe, the negative light my actions would cast upon Jewish Renewal, the way I would lose credibility in the Jewish community. I was not even a rabbi yet, but already I had managed to stumble into a political and emotional minefield. My career was clearly over before it had ever taken off. I was shaking and on the verge of tears.

"Reb Zalman, I'm so sorry this happened. Does this make you... are you afraid?"

"Tirzahla," he answered, "by my age, I've gone through too much to be afraid. I used to be afraid of this kind of attack. Now I serve the truth, not people. Trust in your own judgment. Stand tall and go talk to these rabbis directly."

I put off the call to the president of the rabbinical council until the next day. By then I had begun to feel anger at not having been respected enough by the council to have been called directly. The rabbis had called Father Pete to verify that he had indeed performed the marriage with me, and then had made inquiries behind my back to find out whom I answered to. There was nothing direct about their communication whatsoever; they did not even take responsibility for their wrath, expecting my rebbe to carry out their reprimand for them. I could not help but wonder whether the same condescending treatment would have been used on a man in my position.

I reached the president in his office. Within the first few minutes of our phone conversation, it became clear to me that Rabbi Fey's position was set and that he was not particularly interested in hearing another viewpoint. I knew this because he asked no questions of me, but spoke the entire time in a

rapid-fire, disdainful voice. He told me that the council had met and had unan-
imously denounced my action. By marrying this couple I had defied the hard
work of many community leaders. In fact, he said, I had torn down what he
had personally taken pains to build over an entire decade, a clear-cut policy in
the Colorado region that sent one distinct message to the public: Intermarriage
is not acceptable.

"We need to bring our kids back to the fold, not sanction their leaving!"
he told me passionately. I knew there was something missing in his thinking:
the reason that young people were leaving Jewish institutions in the first place,
and the plain fact that his policy was failing to bring them back. But I held my
tongue as he continued. "Performing these weddings makes it far too easy for
Jews to remain on the fence about their religion. Let them make a stand for
Judaism for a change! As rabbis, we need to educate, not give them passes out
of the school."

Before he hung up, the rabbi made it clear to me that my future in the
Denver area had already changed. "People in our city will not want to hire
you or to hear what you have to say. If you find doors closing on you, don't
be surprised. The last rabbi who defied the council's ban was run out of town
on a rail." This knocked my breath out of me; I felt contrite, indignant, and
tongue-tied. I mumbled something about understanding his position and said
good-bye.

For days after that phone call, I vacillated between fear and rage. There
had been no forum in which to express my thoughts, and I felt too fragile now
to demand one. I received much support from my community in Boulder, but
what I faced in the larger arena terrified me.

The rabbi's words were borne out in the weeks to come. All the while that
I was building a community in Boulder, I had also been accepting invitations
to speak to the more established Jewish community in Denver. My name had
spread as someone who presented Jewish ritual in a spirited way, one to whom
young people responded. True to the rabbi's word, the lectures and presentations I was scheduled to do in the Denver area were now being canceled, one
by one.

One of the groups was a Jewish women's center in which I had found the
women to be open-minded and creative in their approach to Judaism. Meeting
with one of their leaders to discuss the issue, I listened as she shared the viewpoint and statistics I had heard so often. The consensual belief was that intermarriage was a dreaded phenomenon because it presented the most serious
danger to the Jewish people: dissolution. Jewish life, the thinking goes, will not
survive if such pluralism is tolerated.

I realized that the proponents of these views could not possibly know, as I did, how many young Jews were already lost, and how many more were being turned away by this very mind-set, which was so unappealing in its narrowness. I knew firsthand that if the only way Jewish life could survive was to adopt such an isolationist sectarianism, many Jews would elect not to participate in this narrow parochial world at all.

From the outside, it is a strange problem that makes no logical sense: There is so much fear about the Jewish people's dissolving that the rabbis are turning youngsters away in an effort to keep the Jewish ranks solid! I think that is because the place from which our policies arise is clearly not a rational one, but rather a highly charged emotional field. Sitting between the two worlds of Jew and non-Jew, I can see that the issue of intermarriage has become like a lightning rod for the great distress that the Jewish community feels about its future.

After centuries of pogroms, evacuations, and massacres, the Jewish people have just survived a near genocide, and the trauma is still in our system. Now, two generations after the Holocaust and living in a rapidly shifting society, the psyche of our people (just like that of an abused individual) is still wounded and attempting to heal. Like a rape victim who pulls in tightly in order to recover her violated boundaries, remaining contracted long after the attack, so the violated boundaries of our people are still taut in an effort to compensate and heal the brutal invasion into our lives. Fifty years after the Holocaust, the very topic of "Jewish survival" is, for some, enough to trigger anxiety and even hysteria. It jabs at our wound: the senseless loss of so many.

Intermarriage is a graphic example of relaxing our boundaries to the outside world, boundaries that are still healing. For this reason, some Jews automatically equate it with the evil that came when we last trusted the outside world enough to relax. To many Jews, the idea that Judaism can survive intermarriage—the very concept that intermarriage does *not* necessarily spell further death and destruction—is enough to start the warning signals, the overprotective mechanism of a traumatized body flashing red alert.

But the truth is that intermarriage is here to stay. The blending of cultures and religions is an unprecedented communal phenomenon in America and elsewhere, and for Jews, it is a paradoxical answer to our prayers, an inevitable consequence of our success and integration into Western society. No quick solution or sweeping policy will eliminate this blending or the problems it brings with it. Still, we can avoid being stupid by continuing to dialogue, instead of preach, thereby controlling the self-inflicted damage on our own people. If we are to survive as a unified people, we must find a way to make peace with intermarriage, and to capitalize on what benefits it might offer us.

Yet I am not naive. The experience of many individuals creates trends in society. If, as statistics show, only twenty-eight percent of the children of interfaith marriages are being raised with any Jewish identity (the percentage of those brought up with a Jewish education is far less), the trend of intermarriage is clearly not leading to a renaissance of the Jewish people. This troubles me deeply. Jews have fought to be able to make personal choices and live in a free society—just as we fought to break out of a ghetto existence—but our choices have taken us away from what is genuinely precious, our rich heritage.

Yet in most cases I do not believe that intermarriage is the true culprit in keeping us from our legacy of meaning. In a sense, it is the other way around: The absence of spiritual depth in our upbringing, among other factors, is what has sent us out on a search for renewed meaning, a search that typically leaves Judaism behind.

Relaxing our boundaries has not been an entirely bad thing. I believe that intermarriage can create a positive irritation—in my case, a crisis—that compels a Jew to seek out a deeper spiritual meaning in Judaism, a search that marriage to a Jew would probably never have provoked. As rabbi of a growing congregation, I have met scores of interfaith families whose participation in Judaism has been inspired and perpetuated by their non-Jewish members. The "stranger in our midst" often gives us Jews impetus, curiosity, and a new set of eyes through which to view our heritage and rituals freshly.

Open boundaries have been useful to the Jewish community in yet another way: They have helped us find nourishment in the form of ideas and spiritual meaning that seemed to be absent from our diet as Jews. These ideas—although unkosher to some because of their foreignness—have challenged Jews as individuals and as a community to rethink who we are and assess how our own values and teachings measure up.

The concept of grace, for example, the free gift of God's love, is one that runs throughout Jewish scriptures. Yet it first took looking at these scriptures from a Christian perspective, that of my husband and my Christian colleagues, for me to see that grace, or *chesed*, even existed as a concept in Judaism. You would never find a sign in a synagogue saying "God loves you!" Jews think of such adages as being strictly Christian. Yet the idea that God's love follows us everywhere is a very Jewish one.

In the same way, the tremendous influence of Eastern mysticism upon our culture as a whole has challenged Jews to ask: Does Judaism have a contemplative side? Is there such a thing as Jewish meditation? What is in our own mystical heritage? These questions have prompted a surge of Kabbalah teachings and Jewish meditation trainings around the world, as well as the long-awaited translation of numerous classic Jewish mystical works. All of these have served to enrich our Jewish lives.

As for our children and their choices, it is not enough for Jewish children to be taught that they must not cross religious lines. They need to know why they should remain Jews! They need to know what is inherently worthy of keeping in their heritage. The Jewish community has to be a place that is spiritually sensitive and intellectually compelling, a place where the questions of young people are met with interest, not fear. If our synagogues were alive and people found within them a genuine search for God and spiritual truth (in fact, answers are less important than the search), there would be a natural tendency for many more young Jews to become involved.

Further, we may push for Jews to marry Jews, but these unions do not necessarily create a rich or even sustainable Judaism. For Judaism to survive, more than numbers must be counted. It is our spiritual survival that is really at stake, and spirituality is not a quantifiable commodity.

But what indeed constitutes spiritual survival? Lighting Sabbath candles, attending a Passover seder, even studying Kabbalah, may enrich our souls but does not necessarily make us better, more ethical people. Throughout Jewish history, Jews aspired to be models of exemplary moral behavior, infusing their actions with holiness and dedication to God in the midst of a corrupt world. Perhaps we must remind ourselves in our time that, more than mere ritual observance and study, our survival as Jews depends upon how we treat one another. We must continue to strive for lives of spiritual dedication and moral high ground.

As a psychotherapist, I have studied the profound impression left on the unconscious mind by interactions with religious figures, be it priest, minister, or rabbi. Any bit of warmth or personal understanding put forth by such an authority becomes a treasure in the psyche that is long remembered. By the same token, a cold shoulder or a hasty judgment on the part of the religious authority can be devastating, producing damaging effects that seal themselves deep within the psyche and sometimes last for generations. A dismissive roll of an eye has the power to block a person from any further attempt to reach out for help or to grow spiritually.

There is an enormous amount of spiritual cynicism in young people, generated by unresponsive or judgmental leaders in our culture (although certainly the responsibility is not theirs alone). Sadly, I have seen this in numerous cases of intermarrying couples who have endured rejection by rabbis who would not take the time to talk—or, more important, to listen. I learned that when one steps into the role of spiritual leadership, one must be extremely cautious and aware of the responsibility involved.

It took me time to recompose myself after my unpleasant introduction to the rabbinic community. Once I got over my fear of being "run out of town on a rail," I realized how privileged I actually was to be in a position in which people who had nowhere else to go could call upon me, could entrust to me their stories and needs. I would not give that honor up lightly.

Oddly, it was not the admonitions of the rabbinical council that made me reconsider my policy about performing interfaith marriages. Rather, it was a dream I had later that year.

In the dream, Ken appeared. He reported to me that he was very happily married. "I've started going to church with Nancy," he told me. "It's easier that way; it allows us to be together more. In the end, I don't mind living like a Catholic."

I awakened in horror, sensing that the dream had probably given me a true glimpse into Ken and Nancy's life together. How could it be otherwise, after all? Ken, who was a deeply feeling man, was strongly influenced by his wife's devotion to her religion. He had nothing substantial in his own Jewish reserves, only sentiment, which was not enough to maintain the necessary balance. The books I had lent him had been returned to me unread owing to lack of time, and Ken had no Jewish community around him to anchor his delicate sense of religious identity. I had been naive to think that our wedding efforts would turn his life around.

At the key moments in our lives—births, deaths and other such transitions from one cycle of our development into another—the influx of energy from our psyches is extraordinary and doors to the divine world spring open. We feel alive in a different way, more in touch with our potential and what is most important to us in life. At these archetypal passages transforming our lives is most possible. If we use the insight and clarity that comes to us at these moments to make changes, our lives will be deeply blessed.

However, the period of time in which our more potent lives are revealed to us is quite limited. The honeymoon is over and we go back to work. The baby is born and we try to find time to sleep. Our loved one is buried and the open, raw space in our hearts eventually closes up again. It takes enormous discipline to hold on to the heightened experience we were granted and let it guide us to real changes.

This was Ken's experience, and that of many others who open themselves to moments of profound change like marriage. I learned from these couples and individuals in transition that the person must capitalize on the robust energy of change by means of discipline if he or she wants to implement changes that will deepen his or her life.

Now, when I see couples for premarital counseling, I ask them to make a commitment to do a serious piece of religious study with me. This means doing readings and exploring their feelings about religious and personal topics alike, then coming back and discussing them with each other in my presence. The attitude that love conquers all, which I myself had believed years earlier, usually dissolves once the work begins. Some couples realize that too many potential problems lie ahead and decide not to marry at all.

It is wise for both members of a couple to study themselves, to get to know their sacred landscape and to share it with their partner. It was important, for example, for me to recognize (well before I reentered the Jewish community) that every autumn at the time of the Jewish New Year and most especially at Yom Kippur, I needed to do some internal spiritual work. If I did not give myself this time for introspection, I would get sick or become sullen and irritable, and eventually take it out on my husband. I learned to share this need of mine, enlisting my partner's support. We marked the calendar throughout the year with our respective spiritual needs, thereby helping ourselves and each other stay in tune with our souls.

Talking openly about these subjects in advance of marriage can be sobering to the relationship because it accentuates individual needs at a time when the couple wants only to think of togetherness. But in the long run, these talks create the structure and mutual respect for a much deeper sort of intimacy. I have had many couples return to thank me, well after their marriage, for inviting them to think these things through in advance.

I also learned in my work with people who are in lifecycle transitions that community is necessary. In all my years spent traveling from one belief system to the next in the course of discovering my individual self, I never dreamed that I would one day value community so highly. I was too busy moving around and carving out my own individual path.

The need for community is in large part a developmentally linked issue. When we are younger, we try to move away from our family to find out that we are distinct from it. Once we know a bit more about ourselves, we want others to know us as well. Putting down roots in this life means intertwining with others, growing together, nourishing, and being nourished in the same soil. Our society would have us think that revolving-door relationships can give us what we need. They don't. Real relationships take work and commitment, but without them, our spiritual unfoldment stays two-dimensional.

I began to realize the deep satisfaction of building community by cultivating long-term relationships with the couples and families I was helping. I learned that it is an unsurpassed blessing to be there for a couple as it matures into a family, as it goes through times of trouble and celebration alike.

For a couple, knowing that the same person that blessed you on your wedding day will be there to celebrate a new child or help in the passing of a parent gives a sense of continuity and safety necessary for a healthy spiritual life. Likewise, a Bar or Bat Mitzvah cannot be done in a vacuum. Children need community and are supported when they know that consistent figures will be there for them throughout their development. This community, though it will undoubtedly change, serves as a psychological safety net to a youngster growing up in a chaotic and alienating world.

As I went about learning these lessons, my own community continued to grow. It became a huge extended family for Jews and non-Jews who were ready to connect with other seekers. Now as people came to me with questions and needs, I would ask them to plug in to the network of our community, which provided much more support than any one person could offer.

It was during this period that I truly stepped into my power as a leader. I found that developing the skills of leadership necessitated making mistakes. I fell on my face again and again, and finally began to grow into my leadership skills while accepting my imperfections. But how else do we learn good judgment if not by exercising bad judgment first?

The mistakes I made were born out of my naïveté and an unseasoned impulse to help. The fire I had to endure from opponents of my vision tempered me, forcing my leadership abilities to mature. I learned to slow down and provide those who sought me out with a more realistic sense of their options and the work ahead of them. I also became more sober and less attached to the outcome of my work. I did not expect as much from people, realizing that true change happens slowly and over time.

As Reb Zalman had hinted, what I learned in the hospital was more precious than any text. The teaching came in the form of one question that emerged for me as I confronted the suffering and fragility of life and that never ceased to haunt me: *What is truly worth living for?*

As I exercised more and more authority, and the pressure from those in the mainstream for me to give up what I believed in intensified, I repeatedly returned to this question to help me clarify my situation and rediscover the big picture. My commitment was to serve people as a sort of midwife, helping them to open and birth themselves spiritually in the context of community. I learned fairly quickly that the world does not necessarily reward one for maintaining one's integrity; those rewards need to come from the inside. My job was to hold tenaciously to my vision of spiritual integrity, not only for myself but for others. All of my lessons prepared me for the next difficult level of initiation, which arrived sooner than I expected.

CHAPTER THIRTEEN

THE CANARY'S SONG

UNLIKE TRAINING IN A PUBLIC THEOLOGICAL SEMINARY WITH ITS ESTABLISHED schedules and deadlines, my rabbinic training had been guided in a more mysterious manner by my rebbe and other rabbinic mentors from around the country. In our ordination program each student covered the curriculum at an individual pace and was supervised in like manner. There was neither a fixed time for graduation nor a projected date of completion. What was understood by all of Reb Zalman's students was that ordination into the rabbinate was an initiation based upon spiritual readiness as much as one's mastery of Judaic material. We counted upon Reb Zalman's uncannily clear vision to determine our readiness to become rabbis.

In the fourth year of my studies, 1992, two words from Reb Zalman let me know that ordination—known as *smicha*, the laying on of hands—was in sight. "It's time" was all he said, and electricity shot through my being. I quickly demurred, stalling and bargaining for a few more months. My mind raced. Had I even come close to encompassing all that a rabbi was required to know? I was not ready to call myself by the same title as that given to Simon bar Yochai, Rashi, and Nachman. The mocking voice and gnarly, pointing finger of my interior Yiddish trickster came after me once more, this time joined by a multitude of fellow Jews and rabbis who bellowed at me, *You* dare to call yourself *rabbi?*

"The simple truth is that you are ready, Tirzahla," Reb Zalman said quite matter-of-factly.

"But… but I haven't gotten the word yet. Let me wait for a sign or a dream, something that tells me it's time. I'll let you know when it comes, okay?" I had trusted Reb Zalman's remarkable seeing powers all this time; his guidance had never failed me. Yet now, at the critical moment, I could not take the leap to follow him. In his wisdom, he allowed me to procrastinate.

"For a while," he said.

But no sign or dram came, only increasing pressure, pressure to move forward despite the disdainful voices in my head that attempted to bar my way. I called Shoni, who was now on my council of rabbinic mentors and served as an overseer of my overall progress. She assured me that I would never feel entirely ready—no rabbi did, not even Moses—but that I could afford to rest in Reb Zalman's judgment.

"Set the date, and then get very quiet," she advised. "Block off time every day to meditate. That's where the strength will come from. Books and activity aren't going to give you what you're needing now."

After listening to Shoni, I realized that once again I had gotten caught in my old trap of rushing around, amassing information, and creating projects for myself, all in an effort to vanquish my inner doubts. But it was a losing battle. There was always more to be learned, always a new way to prove myself. As soon as one goal was accomplished, new ones sprang up in its place. There would be no end to what I did not know, or would need to prove, before the dark and disapproving force within me was satisfied.

When our destination is blocked by the shadowy figure of our inner doubt it is easy to get detoured off our path. Some people fall into paralysis at this point. Others get hoodwinked into taking on more and more tasks, each promising to yield the requisite proof of our worthiness to move ahead. But the tasks can be endless, and trying to fullfill them requires energy and effort that often distracts us from our deeper mission.

Sometimes the more powerful response is disengagement, to simply stop trying to appease this dark angel, to stop wrestling—reacting, proving, defending our worth—and sit still. By not reacting to our inner beasts, neither fighting nor trying to disprove them, we create an empty space in ourselves. This empty space of nonaction is critical on the spiritual path. Just as water requires an empty container in which to be collected, so the Self requires an empty space in us into which to pour its guidance.

There is a striking passage from the Talmud: *"Eyn makom panui l'lo Shechinah:* Wherever there is an empty space, there the presence of God is found." When we are full of fears and anxiety—or even self-certainty—we make it difficult for the divine forces to enter our lives. But when we empty ourselves, God's presence comes to fill the space.

I created two one-hour blocks each day to sit still in my study. I began each session by turning off the telephone, lighting a candle, and praying to let go of the noise in my head—the whining fears and negative fantasies—so that I could open to God's guidance. Then I simply breathed, focusing upon each outbreath to release the unnecessary chatter, and each inbreath to open myself to what I needed to know. It was amazingly difficult to simply sit and do nothing. Yet each day I grew calmer. I had no mystical experiences or cosmic revelations. Instead, a most wonderful sensation of inner peace began to come over me, filling me with deep relief and joy.

Sitting in silence had an unusual effect upon my own frantic state of mind. The very act—or nonact—of receptivity brought the active, go-getting function of my personality into balance with what I call the feminine principle, the receptive part in all of us that is naturally connected to the source of life and to our life's purpose. In many cases, this connection is accessed not through doing but through simply being, something that our male-oriented culture does not advocate.

It is clear to me now that many of the central Jewish practices—devotional prayer, keeping the Sabbath, and lesser-known meditation techniques—were devised to help strengthen this very receptivity within us. In fact, the tradition has within it many of the components we need for balancing our feminine and masculine sides so that we can restore our psychological health. But just as in the larger society, the feminine side of Judaism has become eclipsed by the more active, masculine aspects of the religion. Its intrinsic healing potential is there just under the surface, ours to unmask.

As I sat each day, methodically slowing myself down and opening myself up to guidance, my purpose for becoming a rabbi got clear again, along with the inner knowing that I had something vital to share. I realized that the masculine-feminine balance I was striving for within myself was exactly the balance that was needed in Judaism. As soon as I realized this, I saw an image.

A vivacious woman with dark, glistening eyes was sitting behind a screen. A multitude of people on the other side of the screen anxiously awaited the woman, yet she had been out of view for so long that there was an awkwardness about what to do with her when she arrived. In the picture, I was among those who carried her on her chair, like a Jewish bride, out into the public domain. The beautiful woman sat composed all the while, despite the confusion and fear around her, a symbol of all the radiance, creativity, and depth that had been missing for the people.

Like the image of the Torah that had spoken to me years earlier, saying: *Relate to me!* this woman, the beautiful feminine side of our tradition, wanted to come out from behind the scenes and be related to and, above all, integrated into the tradition. My mission was coming into focus: I had to "carry out" the missing femininity in Judaism. I was now ready to step into the role of bringing forth for others the life-giving nature of my heritage.

It *was* time to be ordained. I realized that mastery of Judaic knowledge would take a lifetime, and that my training would continue well after I became a rabbi and was knee-deep in real-life situations. In the meantime, I knew how to use the resources of the Jewish tradition, to look up texts, to access information, and to ask the right questions.

What was most important was my commitment to serve. Beneath all the ambivalence I had for the Jewish people, I had discovered a soul-deep love for this, my tribe. Years earlier at Beloved's community, I had been challenged to drop my karmic attachments to the Jewish lineage and I had resisted, not knowing exactly why. I had intuited even then that my life's mission had something to do with repairing psychic wounds and serving spiritual needs. Now it had come clear to me that this mission had a focus: providing this healing for my fellow Jews desperately in search of it.

It was summer and Reb Zalman and I set a date for my ordination in early November. Because I had such a strong community of friends and colleagues in Boulder, we planned for the ceremonies to be held there; my council of rabbis, those who would actually ordain me, would fly out for the occasion. Steadied by the practice of sitting in silence every day, I began to work toward the goal of readying myself to receive the laying on of hands of my council of rabbis, the powerful transmission of rabbinic authority. This included studying for my final oral examination with Reb Zalman and cocreating rituals designed to cross me over the threshold of being a rabbi. Throughout all of the active work of studying, writing a speech and working out the details of the various services and ordination festivities, I still had no idea what transformation awaited me.

November arrived and the tension mounted. As I struggled to handle all the last-minute details, Emily came down with chicken pox, and the inevitable commotion began as friends started calling and coming into town for the event. I began to feel overwhelmed at the stress of it all and at being the center of so much attention.

I had sent out announcements to friends around the country, and to the two relatives whom I felt closest to: my sister Laya and my dad's sister, Aunt Lilly from Kansas City. Vivacious, seventy-year-old Aunt Lilly had continued to be warm toward me, despite family politics. She was active in her Jewish community, yet it had never occurred to her to condemn my marriage. In fact, when Evan and I traveled to Missouri each year to visit his parents, we would travel across town to visit with her.

Aunt Lilly called to congratulate me and to tell me when she would be arriving. I was incredulous. As she fumbled with her papers over the phone to give me her flight times, I burst out crying. So much time had passed, I had forgotten what it was like to be unequivocally supported by blood relatives. In the eight years since my marriage, I had not heard from my mother, my brothers nor any of my extended family in Israel, despite my return to Judaism. Being a rabbi meant nothing—or worse, sacrilege—to them, since Orthodox Jews have yet to sanction women as rabbis. Now, even though friends were flying in from around the country and my *chavurah* community had gone all out to create a phenomenal celebration, I grieved the absence of my family. Aunt Lilly's presence helped me begin to heal that pain.

Various ceremonies were scheduled around the ordination: two large Sabbath services and, typical of my Boulder culture, an American Indian sweat lodge. The actual "hands-on" ordination, however, was a small ceremony that took place on Friday morning at my home. It was led by Reb Zalman and my council of rabbinic mentors, Shoni, Gershon and Akiva.

As always, Shoni added a distinctly feminine air with her flowing hair and keen dark eyes. She had never failed to tell me the truth as she saw it, and for this I was filled with gratitude. Watching her move elegantly across the room, I remembered how her beauty and honesty had impressed me during our first study sessions together, and the prescient remarks she had made about my future, which had helped initiate a process now coming to fruition.

Reb Gershon was a Talmud scholar of great brilliance who, ironically, had been my brother Ezra's yeshiva roommate decades earlier. Reared in the Orthodox world and ordained in Jerusalem, he became a renowned author of Jewish historical fiction before he grew disillusioned by the rigidity of Orthodox Judaism. Convinced that Judaism was not about laws and blind obedience to an ever-demanding deity, and that it involved far more than supporting Israel and the local synagogue fund, he had removed himself from the mainstream to become a circuit-riding rabbi, serving Jews in rural communities, prisons, and college campuses. Disillusioned with denominational politics, Gershon called himself "flexodoxic." His teachings were always filled with humor and irony, focusing on how modern Jews had strayed from our ancestors' simple lifestyle of good deeds.

Like all of us, Reb Akiva also hailed from the Orthodox world and he still served it. He was the associate rabbi of a large synagogue in Denver when I met him, and was a devoted student of both Rabbi Shlomo Carlebach and Reb Zalman. Akiva was a handsome man with a deep, heartful voice. He brought to life the Chasidic rebbes with their stories, their teachings, and their music, which he sang, accompanying himself on the guitar. He had not been on my council originally, but had stepped in as a colleague and dear friend in support of my ordination.

We gathered in my living room early on Friday, the morning light streaming in through the ficus trees, and Orpheus the canary singing his morning song in the background. The house was filled with the delicious aromas of an elaborate breakfast prepared and served by Evan.

After eating, we sat in a circle to sing an after-meal blessing. Then the four rabbis gathered around my new prayer shawl and proceeded to tie the holy knots at its four corners. The prayer shawl, of hand-painted silk, had been made by a spiritual sister in Oregon and was inscribed with my favorite passage from Psalms: *As the deer yearns for the brooks of cool waters, so does my soul long for Thee.* As each tassle was measured and the number of knots carefully counted, Reb Zalman spoke about the various ways in which Jews in different parts of the world carried out this "sacred macramé," which spells out *God is One.* Each rabbi in turn wove his or her blessing into the fringes, as well as the blessings of the ancestors, telling marvelous stories of the men and women who had guided our lineage.

As I donned the finished tallit accompanied by the appropriate blessings, Akiva played a mournful, wordless tune on his guitar, one that Shlomo Carlebach had written when he traveled to his native Eastern Europe for the first time after the war. The devastation that Reb Shlomo had met there—the vestiges of death camps, the shells of holy communities, and worse, the general denial that a Holocaust had ever occurred—had inspired his sad song. We sang along with deep feeling. After he was done playing, Akiva spoke.

"Tirzahla," he said, looking at me, with moist eyes, "the joy that we all feel today to welcome you into the rabbinate is tinged with other feelings, too. It's a difficult job, being a rabbi, one of the hardest. It's freighted with the burden of the great sadness of our history, as well as the spirit of greatness and joy." Akiva's words seemed to be coming from the very soul of each rabbi present. "We've been an oppressed people, and this oppression has had a strange effect upon us. To speak the truth to this people won't always be easy, Tirzah, yet you must hold to the truth like a lioness. To work tirelessly is also a requirement. Understand that once you become a rabbi, nothing you do is for your own gain anymore, but for the healing and welfare of the whole. Yet your efforts will be misunderstood by some, and by others you will be unappreciated." An ominous chill ran through my body. Akiva began to strum his guitar as he continued. His words were slow and somber and full of care.

"We Jews are at a crossroads. Some would say that spiritually, we are at the nadir of our history. Some would say we are wandering in a wilderness. Either way, you must bring your beauty and your spirit forth, even into such a wilderness." He continued to strum. By this time, my eyes were closed, sealing his words in my mind, taking in the preciousness of this singular moment, surrounded by the comfort and compassion of my teachers. For this one moment, I felt safe, as if being embraced by my spiritual parents before going out into a storm.

All this while, six-year-old Emily, her face covered with the remnants of tiny red spots, sat coloring at the edge of the room. She looked up at intervals, surveying the scene with a look of deep calm. Our friend John Dally, an Episcopal priest from Chicago, was also observing the ceremony, alternating between wide-eyed interest and silent prayerfulness. And my husband, Evan, seemed to have been born for this day, utterly at home with these rabbis, men and women of the spirit. I mused to myself that the fulfillment brought by this day was perhaps one of the reasons our souls had come together. He had helped me heal so many layers of my crusty cynicism, pain, even antipathy toward my own people. Without a doubt, he was as much my mentor in becoming a rabbi as any rabbi in the room.

Reb Zalman then unscrolled two large documents, one in Hebrew and one in English, and read them aloud. "Ordained, affirmed and commissioned to serve in the sacred capacities of rabbi, teacher of Torah and preacher of God's word, liturgist, counsellor and guide for those who seek.... She is an excellent spokesperson for our tradition and has shown great genius in interfaith relations." At this last, he chuckled robustly and we all laughed. The rabbis gathered round to sign. But as the pen passed to Akiva, I overheard Reb Zalman say to him in a serious tone, "Akiva, think first." Nevertheless, Akiva proceded to sign the documents. Reb Zalman persisted. "Akivala, are you sure?"

"I know exactly what I'm doing," he replied. "I need to stand up for what I believe. I'm here to support this ordination." Then he nodded to Reb Zalman. "But thank you anyway." I was puzzled by their exchange but let it pass.

With the documents signed, I was asked to stand in the middle of the room as the rabbis placed their hands upon me. The room grew quiet, and I felt Emily's small body come up close to mine, hugging me around the waist. She had demanded to sign my ordination documents with her newly learned signature. Her request had been gently denied and I held her close to me now as the warm pulsations from Shoni's hands bore down upon my shoulders. Perhaps Emily was aware of the power of the transmission flowing through the room. Reb Zalman stood at my back and Gershon and Akiva's four hands lay upon my head. Reb Zalman spoke softly.

"May the power of the Shechinah flow through our hands into your being, strengthening your heart, guiding your judgment, illuminating your mind to the inner depths of Torah. Amen!" The ancient Hebrew maxim followed as a call and response between the rabbis.

"May she teach?"

"She may teach!"

"May she judge?"

"She may judge!"

"May she permit?"

"She may permit!"

The canary broke out in song. I was a rabbi.

The next morning was Shabbat, and we readied ourselves for the large community service. Just before leaving the house, I glanced at the open newspaper on the breakfast table. There was a long article about me and my work as a female Jewish leader: *Reaching out to interfaith families, to women, to disenfranchised Jews.* My body began to tremble. All week long, the phone had rung endlessly with calls from friends and acquaintances congratulating me, wanting to speak with me, wishing to take part in the Saturday morning service and to bring others along. For reasons that I could not see at the time, people were coming out of the woodwork over this event, and I was feeling crushed by the excessive attention.

"Reb Zalman," I said, close to tears, "this whole event feels like it's getting out of control. I mean, it's getting so big... too big for me."

"Tirzah, listen to me," was his stern reply. "It will be as big as the Shechinah needs it to be."

I said no more. With his few words, the entire event was altered. It was no longer about me and my accomplishment (although that in itself was something to be celebrated). Reb Zalman had deftly shown me that there was much more going on than met the eye. What looked like a personal event—one woman's ordination—was in truth a stage for a much grander scene. People were sensing in my ordination, the first female rabbinic ordination in Colorado, the emergence of the long-obscured feminine side of Judaism.

I was not alone in my perception that the radiant female presence was being carried out of hiding, not only at the event of my ordination but in many ways and many places. Wherever women took their rightful roles as leaders, wherever religions acknowledged the connectedness of all beings, wherever joy and vitality were infusing the old forms, there the feminine presence was breaking out onto the scene. And as people sensed her advent, they were brought into touch with their longing for another side of their spirituality, the more vibrant, feminine side, which they may not have even known they were missing.

I walked into a packed room at the Unitarian church that Saturday morning, with Reb Zalman on one side and Evan and Aunt Lilly on the other.

Emily, her hair in French braids and wearing a green velvet dress, went to sit with friends in the front. I looked around the room. My *chavurah* family was scurrying about, setting up and ushering the event. Friends from all aspects of my life had come: Buddhists from the Naropa Institute and a Carmelite sister who had driven in from her hermitage in Crestone, Colorado, Jungian analysts with whom I had studied in Denver and Christian clergy who had helped me along the way. These last all wore their colorful religious garments: Chaplain Will from the hospital, Father Pete (my Catholic partner in inter-marriage crime), and Reverend Hood, whose First United Methodist Church had housed my Hebrew School free of charge for years, against the anti-Jewish policy of the church's insurance company at the time.

I was surrounded by loving faces as the Sabbath prayers began, led by a variety of rabbis; the service was filled with ecstatic singing and sacred dance. Before the Torah service, Reb Zalman rose to speak. He looked regal in his long blue kaftan and colorful tallit. His thick gray hair poured out from under his knit yarmulke and his eyes twinkled. He stood for a long time at the microphone before he spoke, looking from me to the community and back.

"You know, ordination is not something we do on Shabbat, since it's a contract which needs signing, sealing, and bearing witness, and we don't do these things on the holy day. All of that happened yesterday. But the celebrating is another matter! And so I introduce to you Rabbi Miriam Tirzah Firestone." Applause broke out and I blushed.

"Today," he continued, "I take a leap of faith in making a connection between the people and tradition of the past and the voice which is trying to bring us into the future.

"This is especially difficult because the model that we have of transmitting our tradition is for teaching men to become leaders, not women. When a woman comes to me and says, 'I've heard the call and I want to answer it,' we *both* have trouble. She has trouble because there are no good models to train women rabbis. Some seminaries—may I be forgiven for saying this—are creating women eunuchs, so to speak. They train the woman to act like a man, preach like a man and become a male rabbi. But the priesthood of women is different, and the guidance for this priesthood we men cannot always supply.

"I, too, have trouble. Because I have to take the teachings and the trust that my teachers invested in me—and I'm sure that if my own teachers had been able to see the events of this day at the time they signed my documents, let's just say they would not have signed! So I have to do some mighty god-wrestling—this is the meaning of the word 'Israel'—with my teachers and the tradition of the past, as well as with the vision of the future, which calls to us, saying, You cannot just run a religion by looking in the rearview mirror! You have to look ahead, too, and be guided by the prophecy that says: *'On that day, God's house will be a house for all peoples,'* and *'On that day, God will be one and God's name will be one'!"*

He asked me to stand, and pulled out a small vial of sage oil and annointed me on the forehead. "May your inner sagacity and vision come alive. I look forward to sitting at your feet and learning Torah from you!" Then he took the gold pendant from around his neck and placed it around mine. On it the words of the Talmud were inscribed in Aramaic and English: *Harachamana Liba Ba'ee: The Compassionate One seeks but the heart.*

I was already feeling overwhelmed, but the blessings did not stop there. The members of my *chavurah* stood up and drew me forward by the hand, surrounding me and reading aloud a poem they had written in my honor. A powerful and loving testimony, it was a poem about what was happening to each of us in this passage—we were all being initiated into a higher level of spiritual community. I was so moved by their affection that I wept like a little girl.

Our friend John Dally, a priest, then stood and asked to be heard. He asked me to face him and with great feeling, recited a powerful oration.

"What shall I say, my sister, my friend?' Congratulations on your ordination'? The words die on my lips, fitting as they may be. Yesterday noon, as the pale autumn sun filtered through the plants in your living room window, words of power were spoken, quietly and with great love, and you became a rabbi. The canary raised a racket, as though he alone grasped the situation, and I was reminded that canaries were once used to warn miners of impending death. Death is impending for us all, of course, but most of us are not so foolhardy as to rush headlong to meet it. But you are not most of us, Tirzah. So here is what I have to say to you:

"On Thursday night, as we prepared ourselves for the sweat lodge, I looked into the bonfire which we circled, and saw something more than I should have seen. I saw the blazing remnants of an annihilated culture, a holocaust of the people who got (to this land) first. We seek a word of wisdom from them now, but we carry that word back to houses built on their graves from coast to coast.

"As our dance grew faster, the singing louder, the fire blazed a greater story: not just the vanished Indian nations whose secrets we gobbled up, but a cast of millions glowing in the light of a myriad bonfires: witches, Jews, homosexuals.

"What kinship I felt with you, our flesh pressed together for warmth in that drafty little hole, recalling that just so, your people and mine were herded together—naked and shivering—to be gassed and burned. Not fifty years ago, on this very planet, not far from cities much like this one, we might have been introduced at a very similar function—you with your yellow Magen David, I with my pink triangle... consigned to the bonfire, the gas chamber, the ovens.

"Those fires are not out, my sister, my friend. They smolder still, world without end. And all their living coals were heaped upon your head in your ordination yesterday noon so that you may glow with their fire and speak a word of truth to the world before their heat consumes you.

"So heed the warning of the canary, my sister, but remember this as well: It was in a blaze of fire that Elijah the prophet ascended to the throne of God. Speak in the power of the fire, and draw us into heaven in your wake."

For a long while after he spoke, the congregation sat in awed silence; many were in tears. Having not expected these darkly poignant words, I myself sat stunned, feeling that John had brought a profound truth into our midst. We had witnessed a darker side of this event and there were no more words to be spoken, except in prayer.

THE GIFTS I received during those days seemed endless, and I had to stretch myself to truly receive them all. Songs were composed, paintings were painted, blessings were made on my behalf. Evan and the *chavurah* presented me with a leather-bound set of Talmud, and many charitable donations were made in honor of the occasion. The event of my ordination was both intimate and transcendent; it was about me and about no one person at all—an indescribable quickening in our midst that created a magical field around us all.

During the weeks that followed, I was deluged with hundreds of letters, cards, and calls. People poured out their wishes for my success and offered their own stories about their spiritual quests and disillusionment. I was overwhelmed and smitten by the collective outpouring, an intermingling of love and need and yearning.

Many people were drawn into the Jewish Renewal community during this time and a second *chavurah* was formed. Some of the original members were still wedded to their concept of egalitariansism, and for them I was *a* rabbi, not *the* rabbi, of the community, even though I was leading services and lifecycle rituals. I had not been elected as a spiritual leader, nor was I being paid. Still, the fact that there was a new woman rabbi within the Renewal community seemed to have an impact on outsiders, who flocked to services and called me for all sorts of counsel.

Exactly a year after my ordination, a feature article about me ran in the large regional Jewish newspaper, the *Intermountain Jewish News*. I had blithely given information about my ordination to my interviewers and they had written a very favorable article about me and my endeavor to reach out to disenfranchised seekers. Only days after the article came out, the rabbi of a large synagogue in Denver called to congratulate me.

"What wonderful work you're doing. I'm very impressed. Would you be willing to come to our shul to speak?" I politely explained how busy I was but said that I would try my best to make time.

"That's great," he said jovially. "By the way, in the article you are quoted as saying that you had a *beis din* of several rabbis. Would you mind telling me who they were?" I answered him frankly, though I was growing increasingly uncomfortable.

"And I was just wondering one more thing. Is it true you're married to a non-Jew?"

"That is true. What exactly are you after, rabbi?"

"Just wondering. Thanks so much for your time. I'll have my secretary call you next week to line up a lecture."

The secretary never called and there was never any follow-up to the rabbi's bogus invitation to speak. But within days, I got a troubled call from Reb Akiva, who now lived on the East Coast and was serving as rabbi of a large Orthodox synagogue. In great distress, Akiva told me that his synagogue board had suddenly fired him. The rabbi that had called me under the friendly guise of support was a political opponent of Akiva's during Akiva's brief tenure in Denver, a hateful man who resented Akiva's too liberal Orthodoxy as well as his popularity. After he had verified the facts with me, he had called across the country to the rabbi emeritus of Akiva's synagogue, reporting to him the news of Akiva's complicity in the act of ordaining an intermarried woman. Orthodox Jews do not accept women rabbis and certainly not one married to a non-Jew! This was precisely what the rabbi had been waiting for: an opportunity to put Akiva in his "rightful" place, namely, outside the Orthodox community. Political pressure was applied and the ax had fallen. Akiva, the father of five children, was out of a job and was left devastated. His support of my ordination had effectively banished him from the Orthodox community, and a livelihood.

Now I understood Reb Zalman's prescient warning to Akiva at the signing of my rabbinic documents. He had foreseen that the Orthodox community might misunderstand the purehearted support that Akiva had given me, condemning him for furthering the cause of women's leadership. Akiva had resisted the warning, though he himself had intuited the possible repercussions of signing. Both his words and his music on that day had hinted at the vein of mean-spiritedness within the Jewish community, and the necessity to walk through the fire of hatred if need be while holding to the truth and serving it, come what may.

I was devastated that someone who had gone out on a limb to support me had been made to suffer for it. In vain I tried to network with colleagues across the country to find Akiva another job, a synagogue who needed a truly spiritual rabbi, one who was willing to stand in the truth of his convictions. That hot grave of hatred to which John had called our attention the day after my ordination had already made its appearance. The fire of hatred this time was not kindled by the world's ugly anti-Semitism, but blazed in our own interior.

This event sobered me. Nevertheless, I moved forward, teaching a new spate of classes in Boulder, deepening relationships with people who had come forth at the time of my ordination, and becoming a member of the international board of Aleph: Alliance for Jewish Renewal.

I was less innocent now, sensing that the heat of the bonfire was never far away, always listening for the canary's song. But my commitment, like Reb Zalman's, Akiva's and that of many other people of the spirit, was to god-wrestle, to hold tension between the tradition of the past and the voices that pulled me toward the unfolding truth of the future. And even though I had committed to serve my people, my greater commitment was to stand in what I knew to be the truth, whether or not it burned.

CHAPTER FOURTEEN

SIDE BY SIDE

MONTHS PASSED AND MY FIRST YEAR AS A RABBI CAME TO A CLOSE. On the first anniversary of my ordination, I took time to look back on my journey and study the changes that time had wrought. I was stirred to recall the sheer intensity of the path I had traveled, and awed by the hidden intelligence that had guided my life to the clarity of purpose I now enjoyed.

The dramatic upheavals to which I had grown accustomed in my twenties and thirties had finally given way to the steadier rhythms of middle age. But the life questions and the search for integrity begun two decades earlier with the death of my brother and the apparent betrayal of my sister still blazed in me. No longer acted out in high dramatic form, my questions now occupied a more interior stage, taking the shape of contemplations and musings about the twists and ironies of life, about what truths must not be tampered with and the kinds of changes we must work at all costs to achieve.

As a rabbi I was now in the position of helping families come together in celebration and reconciliation as they passed through the chapters of their lives. Sacred moments such as birth, marriage, and death present a tremendous opportunity to melt away the grievances and rancor that can build up over the years within families. I knew that a ritual carried out with openheartedness and good humor on my part, and one that empowered participants by including them, could lead to monumental changes for a family. As a facilitator of these moments, I was determined to derive as much spiritual mileage from them as possible for the participants. Often tears would flow, walls between people would collapse, and the healing that had been dormant for years could begin.

Throughout my first year as a rabbi, I had noticed with wry amusement that my work with families, in particular, with parents, had a kind of magic about it. In fact, my relationships with parents of all ages—of a marrying couple, a Bar Mitzvah, or a newborn—came with an ease that was almost peculiar. It became a private joke between me and my Yiddish trickster how every set of parents I worked with seemed to fall over themselves with appreciation for what I had to offer. Yet appreciation was the last thing I experienced from my own family, with whom I still had no contact. To them I remained invisible; my own mother would not acknowledge that I was alive.

A few years earlier, I had unexpectedly seen my mother in the Miami airport. I was seized by the incredible synchronicity of the situation, certain that this was the divinely given opportunity for a breakthrough in our communication. I dashed in her direction, calling out to her, but she did not respond. She had apparently not noticed me.

"Mom, hey, Mom! It's me," I said, tapping her on the shoulder. As she turned around, I looked into her face for the first time in eight years. For a second I studied the many changes time had wrought in her. Then I noticed that she was not looking at me, but at the wall behind me, as though I were not there. Flustered and out of breath, I kept talking.

"Mom, isn't this... well, this is too *be'shert* to be passed up. Don't you think...?" Still no response. My mother stood there like a mannequin, staring straight through me. I was stunned, but managed to stammer a few words of congratulation about her upcoming seventieth birthday. Yet the woman who stood before me refused to acknowledge me. Mortified, I quickly said good-bye and walked away, barely able to breathe for the crushing pain I felt in my heart. For the first time, my being dead to her was not just a figure of speech. I actually felt dead, utterly cut off from her in every sense. I could not imagine any experience more devastating than to be ignored by one's own mother. I was shattered.

The airport scene had lasted less than two minutes, yet the image of my mother's stone-cold face staring past me stayed with me for weeks. I resolved that I would never put myself in such a devastating situation as that again; it was too eerie and painful.

Nevertheless, as the years passed, my resolve wavered and the hankering to heal my wounds returned. How could I dismiss my own case of a broken family when my whole life was devoted to healing the larger family of my tribe? The disparities in my life rankled me. After many thwarted attempts at making contact with my mother, and after years studying my dreams and feelings of rejection, I knew better than to think that my woundedness would ever be magically healed, especially by means of a physical interaction with her. Yet I still could not give up hope.

It was easy to cast Emily into the situation as well, projecting upon her the sad loss of a grandmother. It was true that Emily had little Jewish family, but then she did not seem to miss it. She was a happy little eight-year-old with many nonbiological aunties and grandmotherly types who fawned over her and assured her of her lovability. Certainly she was not suffering from the rejection that I was.

After sitting with my discomfort for what seemed too long, I began to talk myself into a trip to Israel with Emily. It had been well over a decade since my last visit; time to go back, I told myself. I had dear friends in Jerusalem and in the Galilee, and I would take the opportunity to visit my mother, if she would see me, and introduce her to Emily.

I discussed the trip with Evan, who questioned the soundness of my motives. Was I not being too idealistic, even setting myself up for rejection? And what about Emily's well-being? Would she be caught in an ugly emotional crossfire?

Evan had no interest in making the trip to Israel himself, not wishing to take time out of his teaching schedule to come along. He had started his own institute, called The School of Alchemy, where he taught classes pertaining to Western esoteric traditions, such as Gnosticism, alchemy, and Christian mysticism. Since my ordination and the increase in my rabbinic responsibilities, Evan and I seemed to be traveling in different orbs of life. What engaged and compelled me—the needs of my congregation, and disseminating the beliefs and practices of Jewish Renewal to a broader audience—were now further than ever from what compelled Evan, who was immersed in his scholarly work. At the time, he was translating Coptic texts, using his knowledge of Egyptian hieroglyphics and ancient Greek. His study brought him profound joy. Our worlds were diverging more and more.

Compounding Evan's ambivalence about my taking a trip to Israel (besides the disappointment he foresaw with my mother) was the mounting tension and violence between Palestinians and Israelis. A crazed American-Israeli named Baruch Goldstein had just unloaded his hatred on scores of Muslims as they prayed in the Cave of Machpelah, a site holy to both Jews and Muslims. Israelis were bracing themselves for the Palestinians'inevitable response in the form of suicide bombings or other terrorism. Evan was worried for Emily's and my safety in such a violence-torn country.

Oddly, I was much more afraid of meeting my mother than of any Arab terrorist. Being unrecognized by her was the worst form of violence that I knew, one that felt dangerous not to my body but to my soul. From my growing anxiety levels I intuited that I was indeed walking into a minefield with this trip, especially if I expected any favorable resolution with my mother. Nevertheless, I allowed myself to be commandeered by the interior voice of my Yiddish trickster and his traditional family values: *Vat kind of daughter— not to mention a* rabbi—*tinks of sitting in Colorado content vit her life vile her mother is far away having* tzuris *over her? You owe her to try everything. After all, you're de one who married de* goy *and put her in dis position in de first place!*

I wrote several letters to my mother beforehand to make sure that she knew Emily and I were coming. She surprised me by writing a card back, stating formally that she would indeed like to meet her granddaughter and for me to call upon my arrival. My hopes were buoyed; at least a brief visit was in store. I would not hope for much more, but human recognition would be immensely healing. My friends and community members sent me off with many blessings and prayers for reconciliation. Their support and optimism helped me believe that maybe this time healing would occur.

Emily and I arrived in Israel the week before Passover. The orange and grapefruit groves were in full blossom and I reveled in the warm, fragrant air. Friends picked us up at the airport and we spent a couple of days acclimatizing ourselves to the time change, the new foods, and the foreign language. Emily, who had had a rough time on the long plane flight, was happy simply to be on firm ground again.

Once we were settled in, I called my mother. Her voice was stiff. Yes, she was expecting a visit from Emily. If I would bring her at eight on the morning before our departure, I could wait in the sitting room of her apartment until she and Emily had finished their meeting.

I was shocked. Although my mother was speaking to me, she was still not relating to me as a human being. I felt certain that I did not want to repeat the experience of our nonmeeting in the Miami airport. Not only did I not want to endure such inhumane treatment, but I did not want my daughter to witness her mother and grandmother relating so coldly to each other.

"Mom, it feels like you're throwing away an opportunity," I said, trying to hold myself together. "Please don't close the door on our relationship."

"No," my mother stopped to correct me. "You and I have no relationship. Nor is there any possibility of having one. It is you who made your decision to marry a non-Jew years ago. *That's* what closed the door."

There was nothing left for me to say and I hung up shortly, shaking with rage and grief.

My daughter and I never visited my mother in Israel. There was no point in creating further strife and humiliation with a visit that would only be traumatic. Emily could see that I was deeply hurt and supportively said she did not care to meet her grandmother anyway. We picked ourselves up and carried on with our trip, but inside I felt my wound open and gaping. I realized with horror that if wholeness came from making peace with my mother, I would never in my lifetime be whole. During the next days I led my daughter by the hand as I introduced her to her Jewish culture. But I felt humiliated and broken down, half a person.

Passover arrived and we found ourselves in Jerusalem with our friends Roger and Sharon Dreyfus, the first couple I had married as a rabbi. On seder night the windows and balconies stood open to the full moon, the spring night air wafting through the apartment bringing with it the holiday sounds of singing voices, laughter, and interacting families from the surrounding homes of the neighborhood. As we sat around our table performing the Passover rituals, the pain of my motherlessness clutched at my heart until it was tight as a fist. I felt physically weak and joyless, my enthusiasm for life gone.

The next morning the city was quiet. Roger and I woke up early, leaving Emily and Sharon asleep, and took to the Jerusalem streets for a walk. Because it was a holiday, there was little traffic and the air was fresh. As we walked from neighborhood to neighborhood toward the Old City, the birds sang and hopped about us cheerfully and the new grass and leaves sparkled in the sun after many days of chilly rain.

My love for Jerusalem was enormous. I imagined I could feel the very soul of the city that morning, ancient and wise and beleaguered. How much blood she had seen shed over the centuries, and how much human arrogance! She had witnessed all of her children at various times trespassing the laws of the heart for the sake of their own religious dogma, and there was still no end in sight.

As Roger guided me toward the ancient city walls and through the Damascus Gate, the atmosphere began to change. We were taking a chance walking in the Old City; there was trouble fomenting here. The sun shone less brightly in these narrow streets. Arabs were everywhere—for them it was not a holiday. Men sat out in sweater vests and kaffiyeh headdresses nervously fingering their rosaries or playing games of backgammon while dark-haired children scurried about. The women were well shrouded, hauling loads on their heads, their long, brightly embroidered dresses and scarves whipping in the morning breeze.

The Moslem quarter was a world apart; its rich odors, colors, and costumes sent me back into another time. As Roger and I walked single file down the narrow streets, the smells of Turkish coffee, donkeys, goats, and freshly tanned leather mingled in my nose. All sorts of wares—brightly painted ceramics, rugs, and candies—were strung up or piled plentifully on display, grabbing my attention. Yet the Arabic voices were halting and hushed, and the uneven cobblestones under my feet made me feel off balance. Something about the sweet heaviness in the air felt disturbingly familiar. I grew increasingly uncomfortable and a dark feeling hovered over me.

As we continued to walk through the Arab marketplace and streets, I began to notice the faces and bodies of the Palestinian people we passed: despondent faces with troubled, shifting eyes and furtive body movements. They carried themselves as if they were small in stature, with the hopeless, lackluster look of one who had not been deigned to be acknowledged in the eyes of another. Suddenly I felt ashamed. What was I doing here walking through their streets, watching them as if they were different from me?

Although our situations were vastly different, and in so many ways I was far more fortunate than they, I began to feel I had something in common with these people whose streets I now walked. The helpless ineptitude I saw in their bodies was familiar to me; I had experienced something akin to it after encountering my mother. Her refusal to relate to me, to hold me in her gaze, had the same shriveling effect upon me that I thought I saw in these people. The Palestinians were clearly a demoralized people. The lack of recognition and the dishonor paid them as a people by their Israeli occupiers was a heavy mantle to wear.

Whether this perception was the truth about the people I passed in their narrow streets or merely sprang from my imagination, I do not know. But that day I felt that I knew all about their heavy silence, the furtive, dark brows, the kind yet sheepish demeanor, a facade for the wild frustration and rage that knows no recourse. I imagined that all of these people had spent years—no, decades—in a relationship with their Jewish neighbors that mirrored mine and my mother's, a relationship where there was wounding upon wounding, and walls that no longer allowed for human recognition, neither eyes to meet nor hands to touch in common experience.

The instant I realized that my own small suffering was all around me, mirrored and magnified in the dark faces of hundreds of people, something broke loose from the prison of my tight chest and bled like a river. Bigger than life, far bigger than me was this feeling which flowed out into the rank-smelling streets: my streets, my odor, my family. My eyes filled with tears and everything around me ran together in a blur. Roger was a bit ahead of me, not noticing that my pace had changed. I took a moment to pause and wipe my eyes. When I picked my head up, I saw a gray-mustached man in a kaffiyeh across the way watching me. For a split second, our eyes met and the gentleman bowed slightly in my direction. For that moment, held in his gentle gaze, I was comforted. Then I picked up my gait to catch up with Roger.

A teaching popped into my mind which a Chasidic master had taught in relation to breaking the middle *matzoh*, the unleavened ritual bread at the Passover seder: *There is no whole heart but a broken heart.* If your own suffering does not serve to unite you with the suffering of others, if your own imprisonment does not join you with others in prison, if you in your smallness remain alone, then your pain will have been for naught.

I continued to walk as I thought about this teaching, which I had known for years but which had only now sprung to life for me. I imagined the small *s* of my personal suffering floating up and away. It was no longer my small suffering, but *Suffering* that I encountered, the suffering that is born when people are not met with human dignity, the feeling that we all experience at least once in our lives when we are not recognized or listened to but are shut out. The personal pain I felt at not meeting my mother was what we humans inflict upon each other by not meeting one another with openness, by not acknowledging the existence and experience of the other.

I came back from my walk with my heart in upheaval. I had gone out to see Jerusalem, but I had touched and been touched by another, more hidden stratum of the city, one born of grief, helplessness, and the daily reality of being treated like one who does not exist. I knew that this pain would in time build and change, fomenting into rage, and I vowed to circumvent my own rage.

In facing these realizations, I also had to remember that the one who seemed to be inflicting this pain on me was herself locked in her own small prison. My mother, too, had undoubtedly felt a similar helplessness, lack of recognition, and indignity at the hand of others, including my own. In living my life and making the choices I felt to be an expression of my own truth, I had brought about a situation in which she too had felt unrecognized and disregarded.

It is a rare and beautiful sight to see people coexisting, living their respective lives and their truest beliefs side by side, without disallowing the truth of others. The Israelis and Palestinians will have to learn in time that lording over one's neighbor, disallowing freedom through law or terror, and withholding human recognition does not work. It constitutes a violence to the human soul that will forever be met with more violence.

Within our smaller families, too, and certainly outside them, we sometimes forget that we are each distinct human beings, each person living out his and her destined path or life myth. The unfolding of one person's life simply cannot be controlled by another. Coexistence (not to mention love) requires that we give one another the freedom to be, not controlling or dictating to others, but allowing, even encouraging, their "otherness" to unfold.

During the remainder of our trip, as I mulled over these ideas, it grew clearer to me that I too needed to allow my mother her freedom to be, and that included her resistance to me and her refusal to heal our relationship. She had put up a strong boundary and I had to respect it. With this realization, I felt my inner peace beginning to return.

Emily and I returned home exhausted. It was particularly difficult to encounter my friends and community members who were anxious to hear about an anticipated reconciliation with my mother that had not occurred. I had no wisdom but to say that the situation was unhealable (unless of course I was willing to perform a radical surgical bypass on my marriage, my beliefs, and my personality!).

In my desire to close the chapter so that I could move on in my life, I began to search for a ritual. I needed to mourn my hopes of having a loving mother and to let go of the stalemated relationship with the one who had cut me off. I figured that a ritual would help me make this transition through my grief to the other side.

I went out and bought seven *yahrzeit* memorial candles and prepared to do a weeklong ritual of mourning. My intention was not to sit shiva, the seven days of mourning, as if my mother had physically died, but to take a seven-day period to fully grieve our relationship and the lack of her presence in my life. By the light of the traditional candle of mourning, I would say good-bye to my mother at last and to the torment that this relationship had caused me.

I set out the first glass candle on the wooden table just opposite the meditation chair in my study and sat down. This chair was my sanctuary; I called it my launching pad. In this swirling burgundy and green paisley velvet armchair I returned to my Self whenever I needed to lift up and out of my picayune detail orientation, back into peaceful silence. Sitting opposite the lit *yahrzeit* candle, I focused on release, on letting what was dead fall away so that a new chapter of my life could arise. After an hour or so, I got up and resumed my normal activities, letting the candle burn all day and through the night.

The next morning as I passed by my study, I noticed that the flame had not yet died. The glass container was full of hot, melted parrafin and the wick still burned tall. Instead of lighting the second candle, I left the first to burn itself out. Emily had left for school, Evan was out at class, and I went downstairs to straighten up before going up to my study to meditate.

All of a sudden, I heard a loud *boom!* from overhead. Startled, I raced back up the stairs to my study. At first I saw nothing, but on second look I noticed that the *yahrzeit* candle was not on the table as it had been just minutes before. An eerie chill passed through me. I stepped into the room and gasped in disbelief. The glass container was sitting upside down, empty and unbroken, on my meditation seat. The wax, now hardening, had splattered everywhere, covering my beloved velvet chair.

"Oh, my.God!" I cried aloud. I dashed over to determine what had happened. But I found nothing to explain how the jar of hot wax had traveled from the table to the chair to discharge its contents. I fell to my knees beside the chair in awe. There was a palpable charge in the air that I had never before experienced. A grim, foreboding presence had taken over my study.

I still do not fully understand what happened in that room that morning. But I did get the message: What is dead is dead, and for this, the mystical rites are strong and purifying and appropriate. But what is alive, even if it does not make you happy, must never be treated as dead. I had no right to close the door on what was still alive. That was, in a way, trying to kill it. In using the candle of mourning to mourn a relationship that, despite being an inscrutable mess, was nevertheless a living entity, I had crossed a line that should not have been crossed.

I stood corrected and humbled. The inexplicable sight of the glass candle that had been tossed by a secret hand made me tremble. It was instantly clear to me that I did not know everything, perhaps not even a small part, of the drama at play between me and my mother. I would not so easily be rid of this unresolved tension in my life; I had to live with it.

MY PERSONAL PAIN was mitigated by the joys of my community, which continued to flourish, with new *chavurot* forming steadily and a quickly growing general membership. I was now the paid part-time rabbi of the Jewish Renewal congregation and worked closely with our governing body, composed of councils (called *va'adim*) which had representation from each of the *chavurot*. Every week brought me new lessons about the tricky balance between serving congregants as a leader and empowering them to use their own strengths. Over time, I felt less and less alone in the enterprise of building a community, as resources of all sorts emerged from our membership: artisans to design and build an ark, talented cantors and musicians, people skilled in public relations, accounting, group facilitation, and mediation.

The Kosher Hams, an uproariously funny theater group, was birthed by Betzalel, the community's artistically inclined third *chavurah*. The Hams were a zany group, of improvisational actors who were determined to balance the community with a humorous perspective (lest we get too pompous or self-satisfied). Their offerings, satirical plays and musical spoofs such as *West Side*

Megillah and *The Feminist Herstory of Hanukah*, brought the audience together in side-splitting laughter, regardless of any disparate points of view held in the community.

The Kosher Hams took care to remind our community that it was important not to take any single ethic (or ourselves) too seriously. A couple of times a year, my ego would feel utterly dismantled to see and hear myself portrayed in caricature, in skimpy burlesque attire under a tallis, or strutting about in a bouffant hairdo and overdone makeup while waxing hyperbolic about the joys of prayer or love of God. But though I cringed at jokes that cut too close, I also knew that the health of our community lay in its ability to laugh at ourselves. In fact, the Jewish holiday of Purim was expressly designed to release the pent-up "shadow side," all the closeted feelings and images that one dare not express for fear of trampling some sacred cow or another. The Kosher Hams trampled every sacred cow possible, becoming a sort of court fool for our community, saving us through satire from our would-be sanctimony.

Our community's members, not only rich in talents, also brought with them a wide array of spiritual backgrounds. Like me, many members had traveled and quested widely before their return to Judaism, and many still maintained a commitment to non-Jewish practices such as Vipassana and Tibetan meditation. I encouraged these Jews of "dual citizenship" to join in, to bring their knowledge of and expertise in other forms of spirituality into the community rather than create a wall that divided their spiritual interests into compartments. For many students of Eastern spirituality, the Hebrew chanting and silent meditations that we practiced in Jewish Renewal, as well as our fervent prayer, created a remarkably familiar atmosphere that was easy to harmonize with other disciplines.

In addition, a great many of our congregants were intermarried couples. As a rabbi who knew intimately about intermarried life, I went out of my way to let it be known that Judaism is wide enough to include all levels of participation, by Jews and their non-Jewish partners, and by anyone interested in Judaism regardless of their level of education.

I loved seeing so many formerly alienated Jews come back to their tradition with joy, excitement, and fresh energy. But I also had many concerns about the direction our new brand of Judaism was taking. Jewish Renewal did well at drawing Jews back to their Jewish identity, inspiring them with joyful prayer and sacred dance. But as time went on, I wondered whether this was enough. Were we to be satisfied with quick fixes of spiritual energy that came from dropping in at a weekly or monthly service? Could these ecstatic highs possibly sustain people through life's trials? What about the vast body of Jewish ethics and sacred literature that stood waiting to be studied? Much of this could be taught, but I knew that to truly experience the exquisite beauty and depth of the tradition, discipline and painstaking study were required, including knowledge of the Hebrew language. However inspired people got at our services, many lacked the time and determination necessary to penetrate beneath the surface of the tradition or to create their own means of connecting with divinity outside services.

Another problem that I was keenly aware of was also related to the issue of commitment. Like many other Jewish Renewal congregations around the United States, we held our services in rented spaces, churches and auditoriums, never having put our energies toward building or buying our own synagogue. From our beginnings as a group of twelve, we had been stressing spirituality, as opposed to our parents' brand of Judaism, which smacked of their generation's heavy emphasis on appearances and monetary security. None of us had wanted to deal with building funds and public appeals. Now I found myself wondering: What had we given up? By avoiding a monetary ethic that had been repugnant to us, we had subtly skirted the work of creating our own sustainability, represented by a building, a library, and grounds where we and our children could grow together. Jewish Renewal children were receiving their Jewish education in Christian houses of worship, and our arks, Torahs, and holy objects were laboriously carted hither and yon, into and out of rented spaces.

I realized that I had come a long way in my vision of what was needed for religious fulfillment. It was not at all the case that I was ready to run back to my parents' brand of Judaism, but I did wonder whether we renegades had not thrown the baby out with the bathwater. The fierce determination and commitment of our parents' generation to help Judaism survive and be passed down to their children needed to be resurrected. Perhaps our parents had been overly absorbed with appearances and money, but some of us had erred in the other direction, to the point of forgetting how to support what we believed in, by being unwilling to make the personal sacrifices that our parents took in stride as they donated vast amounts of time and money to build and sustain their Jewish institutions.

I now had the perspective to see what I had not seen at any time earlier in my life: My generation of Jews had chosen to partake of the rich smorgasbord of consciousness alternatives that the sixties and seventies had made available to us in the United States. We had filled ourselves on every manner of spiritual idea and practice. But if we truly wanted to make manifest our vision of a renewed and revitalized Judaism and bring it into the next century to be lived by our children and grandchildren, we would have to harness our resources to build spiritually vital Jewish institutions that would last.

These and other thoughts about the Judaism of our generation churned in me. I realized that I could not negotiate these issues singlehandedly; I needed the support and insight of other rabbis in my position. With Reb Zalman's blessing, I embarked upon a project to organize a retreat in the hills outside Boulder for Jewish Renewal rabbis from around the country.

In addition to my concerns, I had many questions I wanted to ask these colleagues. We were all serving the Jewish public, but what was our service based upon? Our focal point was radically different than that of centuries of rabbis before us. *Halacha*, the chain of rabbinic laws and legal interpretation passed down for generations, was no longer our exclusive polestar for living a Jewish life. Nor was tradition per se. We were all dedicated to perpetuating Judaism as a living spiritual path. But what was incontrovertibly our common ground? What template of holiness did we draw from? The Chasidic masters? Textual mysticism? Depth psychology? I was eager to see if I could establish a system of norms for our decision-making process as Renewal rabbis. On a more personal level, the retreat would be a means for me to rally around me my ideological brothers and sisters, in the absence of my biological family.

Twenty of us excitedly gathered at the mountain retreat for our first meeting. About half had received ordination from Reb Zalman, as I had, while the rest had graduated from the Conservative, Reform, and Reconstructionist seminaries and private Orthodox yeshivot. Roughly half of the group's members were women.

I was surprised to find such great diversity among us as to our beliefs and practices. For example, when it came to observance of the kosher laws, among us were rabbis who kept *halachic* kashrut strictly, those who held to a purely vegetarian diet, and still others who looked to ecological standards as their prime directive. And when it came to intermarriage, there was an extreme difference in views: Some of the group were vehemently opposed to intermarriage and would never consider officiating at an intermarriage, while others, like me, were committed to working with interfaith couples, marrying them even if the non-Jew did not wish to convert, and bringing them into our congregations from the start. Regardless of our personal positions, though, every one of us was devoted to the work of renewing and revivifying our common heritage so that it was more readily available and relevant to the lives of future generations.

And the future was already here! Over the course of our five days together, many of the strange and difficult questions being put to us by our congregations were shared, questions that startled even the most liberal among us. In the category of intermarried families, one of the rabbis shared the following question brought to him by one of his congregants: "My daughter has chosen independently of her father and me to become a Bat Mitzvah and is studying hard. Is it okay to hold her ceremony in the Hindu ashram where she lives with her father, and if so, do we need to cover up the big statue of Hanuman, the monkey god, who sits in the central hall?"

Regarding the question of who is a Jew, a female rabbi from upstate New York shared the pain of a young woman who came to her with another sort of dilemma: "I had always considered myself to be a faithful Jew, but recently at the [Lubavitch] Chabad house on campus, I was told that I'm not legally Jewish nor have I ever been! They said that my mother, who used to be a Roman Catholic, was not Jewish because her Conservative conversion was not kosher. Now my Jewish boyfriend, who has gotten involved with this Orthodox group, is telling me I need to convert if we are to stay together. I feel discriminated against. My faith in a Jewish God is gone and I'm losing my interest in being connected to the Jewish people."

Questions about kashrut abounded. "How do we live with the fact that seventy-five percent of all the kosher slaughterhouses hoist and shackle their animals? How could this cruel treatment be kosher?" And "Is it more correct to ship in frozen meat that was butchered according to laws of kashrut but is full of steroids and antibiotics than to feed our sick child fresh organic, free-range meat? Isn't the latter more kosher?"

Finally there were the sorts of dilemmas that rabbis of another age never anticipated: "I don't belong to a group of Jews; I deliberately live out in the sticks. But my father just died. Can I get a minyan together on the Internet for him? I could punch in the Kaddish and have nine of my E-mail cronies respond with *'Amen, Yehay shmay raba m'vorach l'olam ulalmay almaya.'*"

All of these questions, both bizarre and heartbreaking, were authentic ones, coming from serious seekers with their modern dilemmas. How were we to deal with these unprecedented problems being put to us by our cusp-of-the-century congregations?

The answer comes in part from the fact that in the movement of Jewish Renewal, we are not looking to restore the Judaism of our ancestors. The post-Holocaust world that we live in is forever changed. It is an unghettoized world broadened by cyberspace and instant travel, by America's freely open-flung doors—open to any school of thought or spiritual discipline imaginable. It is a world that has as yet been largely unfrequented by rabbinic Judaism, and

Jewish Renewal rabbis find themselves going into places and situations that are unparalleled in history. In order to keep Judaism growing and relevant, it must be reformated for these strange and unparalleled times, informed by our past and its vision of holiness, but in step with the wild confluence of ingredients that compose this turn of millennium.

By what means do Jewish Renewal rabbis answer the questions being put to them by their pluralistic American congregants? In the open, respectful and brilliantly opinionated circle of our gathering, there was room to see that the process itself—that of listening and sharing from the heart—was at the root of the answer. Although our politics widely diverged, our group never once became polarized in its discussions. As all of us completed sharing our stances on many difficult, often emotional issues, the others would make eye contact and answer the speaker, "*Shamati!* I hear you!" No matter how opposed one may have been to a particular opinion, each rabbi's sharing was so deeply personal and moving that it became utterly respectable, and more, it was no longer just *the other guy's shtick*, but now belonged to us all.

Jewish Renewal *halacha* is born of this sort of a responsive process. Our Jewish path into the next century needs to be based upon a dynamic relationship not only with our legacy of Torah, but also with other factors that are mentioned in the ancient texts but need accentuation for our particular era. For example, the criteria by which we answer questions or guide others must take into account each person's transformative process, our relationship with non-Jews, and with the earth itself as well as the preservation of the Jewish people.

An act (or way of thinking) that furthers Judaism but harms another person, for instance, cannot be said to be correct. I remember Evan's experience in the synagogue when he was invited and then disinvited to carry the Torah. His pain was overlooked for the sake of performing Jewish ritual in the right way. In this and many other cases, the "right way" is wrong if it brings about pain and separation in other human beings.

Likewise, maintaining the well-being of the earth figures prominently in Renewal thinking. Many of our Kabbalistic texts and the Talmud itself allude to a fact that modern science has borne out: We are all interconnected and our every action affects all of humanity as well as our shared environment.

Historically, Jews have expressed concern exclusively for their own people and land. In the early stages of our peoplehood and throughout centuries of persecution, this self-centeredness was appropriate and to some degree (given the fragility of our people nowadays) is still understandable. But this narrow approach must now be expanded to include what we know to be true about the interconnectedness of all life and the planet's plight. As Jews, we are taught never to endanger life; but to sustain it at all costs. But it is not the case that Jews are interconnected only with Jews or that Jews are responsible for the land of Israel and no other parcel of earth. If we fail to care for one another and the earth that sustains us all, regardless of our nationhood, we simply will not continue as a human species. That includes Jews.

Then, too, a person's individual growth and transformation is also an important factor in a rabbi's guidance. When a person approaches a rabbi with a question or need, care must be taken to assess the person's entire situation, developmental stage in life, spiritual maturity, and the real need behind the question. In our times it is becoming more common that people bring questions to rabbis that require not a pat answer or piece of advice, but help in puzzling out an underlying need. Gently redirecting questions with a new focus can help people to answer their own questions as well as to feel empowered by the process of self-discovery. This requires that a rabbi provide a person with the safety to speak his or her truth without shame or judgment, *regardless of how far the person has digressed from tradition.*

Finally, we must stay mindful of the fact that the Jewish people is splintering into many directions, with many Jews choosing to leave Judaism behind. It is vital to offer Jews a sense of identity and pride, to teach them to access the depths of their religion and to model Judaism as a viable spiritual path. While we should avoid approaching the issue of Jewish preservation with a sense of alarm and fear, we need to take very seriously the level of spiritual impoverishment our people are suffering from as well as the tremendous pull of our secular culture. The onus is on us to find ways to shift the current trend of Jews exiting from Judaism and offer them the deep nourishment their tradition has to offer.

Perhaps the most wrenching issue that the rabbis dealt with during our time together, one that overrode all others, was the fact that our rebbe was in transition. Reb Zalman was entering what he called the winter of his life, and wanted to focus on teaching and writing about the topic most dear to him, spiritual eldering. He had devised a program for guiding elderly people into the full empowerment of their lives—by means of life review, reconciliation and forgiveness work, and contemplation—so that the last period of their lives could be spent as sagely mentors rather than in mental decrepitude and spiritual impotence. His programs were now being taught throughout the country.

In order to carry out this calling and do the contemplative work that the eldering project demanded, it was time for Reb Zalman to pass the baton to his students, the next generation of rabbis, who would carry out the work of bringing Jewish Renewal to others, and who would help train the next generation of rabbis. This was the first time that many of us looked this fact in the face. In the course of our time together, I heard many versions of a similar sentiment: Reb Zalman has bridged Old World Judaism and the modern era. Now it's upon us to take over the vast scope that he has been holding for us. Can we do it? Or, as expressed in Reb Zalman's favored computer terminology: "He's our hard drive. It's time we rabbis start some serious downloading."

I was the youngest and most recently ordained in the group, and many times throughout the five days I felt daunted by the company, green, and in no way ready to think about picking up Reb Zalman's baton. Nevertheless, I felt comforted by the quality of respect accorded to me by my colleagues. We were a generation of colleagues preparing ourselves together to inherit the expansive legacy of a rare and wise soul. Even more impressive than any of the volatile subject matter of our discussions was the atmosphere of honor and mutual respect. This atmosphere of reverence for one another and for our holy mission gave me hope that Reb Zalman's legacy would be safe with us.

In this meeting of minds and hearts, I would say that not one rabbi was swayed from his or her position or politics, but we were all profoundly moved. We never reached a consensus about intermarriage or about kashrut, nor did we come to any definitive conclusion about motivating commitment in our congregations. What was clearly more important was our own commitment to deepen our Jewish studies and explorations and, above all, to listen respectfully to the questions brought to us before considering them in the light of our learning.

Before we took our leave, we all experienced a distinct feeling of awe at the formidable work ahead of us inherited from our rebbe: to continue the legacy of the ages by midwifing our venerable and complex heritage into the twenty-first century. The Mishna gave us sober encouragement in the words of Rabbi Tarfon:. *"The day is short and the work is great.... We are not responsible to complete the work; nevertheless, we are not free to desist from it."* This was the path of the new rabbi: to listen, ingest, and respond with great care to the voices of the situation at hand, using the maps of the past to bear upon the questions of the future.

I RETURNED TO my community from the retreat infused with a new awe and care for my role. I had always cherished the possibility that people could sit together side by side with honor despite their divergent views of life, but I'd never had good models for it. I had never experienced this sort of respect in my original family and certainly not in the state of Israel, where not only Jews and Arabs but Jews and Jews were constantly at one another's throats. Now I knew what it was like to contain the tension of opposition while remaining open and honoring. I also knew how nourishing it was to listen and be listened to with equal respect. I made myself a promise never to forget what this sort of respect feels like, to bring it back in whatever ways I could to my own community, to strive for it in all my interactions.

As I grow older, Rabbi Tarfon's words become increasingly poignant: Indeed, the day is short and the work is great. I do not believe that there is a finish line, nor even a final goal. The work of becoming whole never ends.

Looking back on my journey so far, I see how the years have sobered me. I've finally discovered that I cannot change everything I set out to change in the world, that I must learn to live with the limitations of being human, as well as with my unanswered questions and my unhealed wounds.

Yet I am still an incorrigible idealist. I believe in our ability as humans to live with one another side by side, regardless of our differences. The challenge is to honor and give an ear to all voices, even to the most unpleasant and critical, inside and out—the Yiddish tricksters and the angry ancestors, resistant spouses, political opponents, and even one's own flesh and blood, who rail at us for going against the grain—to say to each and every one of them: *Shamati!* I have heard you.

All voices require respectful tolerance. But only one voice must be followed. This is the voice of our own heart. It calls to us devotedly throughout our lives, and the greatest task we can undertake as humans is to listen for this voice and follow it with equal devotion. Although we may travel out of its range for years at a time, and although it may be submerged by other, more forceful voices, we can always endeavor to return to it. Because this voice of our heart will, in the end, keep us on our true life path, guiding us to our soul's secret destination.

EPILOGUE

THE JOURNEY THAT WE ALL MAKE THROUGH LIFE IS GUIDED BY FORCES FAR beyond our conscious knowledge. We are like travelers who innocently buy our tickets for a trip, never quite knowing where the journey will end or how. The destinations of our lives and their meanings are revealed only later on. Only after we arrive at our stop, shake off the dust, and look back at the distance may we say, "Of course! This makes perfect sense."

Like all of us, I too began my travels through life unaware of the secret destinations at which I would arrive. Like most of us, I am wiser now than when I began. Where my journey will end, I cannot say. The final destination of our lives is determined by an inscrutable interweaving of the mysterious forces that guide us and the power of the choices we make, big and small, throughout our lives.

One of the big choices for me came in the years immediately following my ordination as a rabbi, and it was in the area of relationship. The stressful incongruities of my marriage to Evan had continued to intensify. While Evan's private, scholarly work and teaching sustained him, my life had become exceedingly public and frenetic. The intense path of service that I chose as a congregational rabbi with a still flourishing private psychotherapy practice stood in sharper and sharper contrast to Evan's quiet, almost monastic lifestyle. Many nights I would arrive home late, buzzing with the energy of a large event or filled with concern over a congregational crisis. Evan, who had spent the day in relative silence and calm—studying, cooking, and parenting Emily— had less and less access to my world. And while I still honored Evan for his brand of spiritual integrity, the sturdy bridge that had once led me into Evan's world had now grown frail.

Ironically, the spiritual beliefs that had once brought us together had not changed. Rather, the forms and practices by which we each chose to live out those beliefs had grown increasingly disparate. The third, shared place we had cultivated—meditation, music, and prayer—was still present, but no longer strong enough to span our vastly differing lifestyles.

During this time, Evan and I sought counseling. We also began to pray intensively, asking for divine guidance: Should we continue together or move apart? What choice would serve the greatest good of our little daughter? Our concern for Emily crushed us both and delayed what we both knew to be inevitable.

Finally, one evening, after several months of soul searching had passed, Evan said to me, "I haven't received any earth-shaking directive to fight the current, Tirzah. Have you?" I answered sadly that I had not. Evan then turned away and said, "I think we both know that life is taking us in opposite directions." Even though I knew it had been coming, my breath failed me, as if I had been kicked hard. We had arrived at the truth. After sixteen years, the most transformative relationship of my life had completed its purpose. The dream we had fostered together, to be pioneers of reconciliation and healing religious opposites was over; not failed, but no longer ours to hold.

Evan and I had been powerful alchemical agents for each other, and our paradoxical relationship had led us to develop areas in ourselves that would never have been explored without the other's influence. For me, marrying "the stranger" and becoming an outcast were, ironically, the necessary alchemical ingredients to my coming home to my Jewish roots, to becoming a rabbi, to standing in the honorable position of one who can help heal her people.

Now we are divorced, but Evan's and my faith in the mystery we call God has remained our mutual touchstone. We still share books, speeches, poetry, and, most important, the raising of our daughter. Emily, who now lives with each of us on alternating weeks, is an athlete, a poet, and a lover of fashion. Though she is comfortable in the religious worlds of both her parents and respects the Christian faith of her father, she identifies herself as Jewish and is excitedly preparing for her Bat Mitzvah. I do not know where Emily will end up religiously, but I have faith in her choices.

WHEN THE INVITATION to attend Laya and Tom's daughter Elianna's wedding in Miami first arrived, I was thrown into conflict. Now that I was no longer married to Evan, it was certainly easier for my family to welcome me back. But how would I make peace with such conditional family affection? My sister Laya let me know that the entire family would be flying in from all parts of the United States and Israel, including all of my siblings—and my mother. Tom made clear that we were welcome. But how could I face the same people who had disowned me years ago and were now only willing to receive me because my goy husband was no longer in the picture? How was Emily to respond to these people who had rejected her beloved father?

Not until the last minute could I decide to board the plane to Miami. The determining factor was Emily. At ten years old, she would finally get to meet her grandmother, aunts, uncles, and cousins and begin to know the large extended family she had outside of Boulder. Behind her aloof little face (she was not prepared to show the disappointment she had suffered in Israel nor the excitement of going to a big family wedding), I could tell that she was ready to inherit the family that was rightfully hers.

The night before the wedding, I received a call in my Miami hotel room from my sister that my mother wanted to meet with Emily the next morning. Seeing me was still too uncomfortable for my mother; I was to wait outside for my daughter. This was virtually the same scenario I had resisted in Israel; nothing had changed. Only now, I was willing to let go of my staunch insistence that my mother acknowledge me and I allowed the events to unfold as they needed to. I no longer had a need to stand on ceremony, to wait for words of reconciliation or apology to pass between us. I was finally willing to let my mother be who she was.

The next morning, Emily and I arrived at my mother's hotel room with hearts fluttering. My mother appeared at the door looking much tinier than I had remembered her, and quite shriveled. As soon as she saw me, she averted her eyes and rested them instead on Emily's smooth face. She smiled and greeted Emily, putting forth her wrinkled hand. Emily took it, looking back at me nervously. I kissed the top of her head and told her she would be fine, that I would be back for her in thirty minutes. In the meantime, I went for a walk on the windy Miami Beach boardwalk. Despite my mother's chilliness toward me, watching her lay her loving eyes on her blond-haired, blue-eyed granddaughter was all the healing I required.

When I arrived to pick Emily up at my mother's door, my mother looked at me for a moment and smiled stiffly. Then quickly, she turned to Emily. "We had a good talk, didn't we?" My ten-year-old nodded; she somehow seemed more mature than when I had dropped her off. As we walked away, I put my arm around her and whispered to her how brave I thought she was.

Later, as we were dressing for the wedding, Emily said to me, "Mom, you know what Grandma Katie said? She told me I was a hundred percent Jewish. Also that I'm a hundred percent her granddaughter."

"She did?" I was overwhelmed, but continued cautiously. "What else did she say?"

"She said that even though you married Daddy and he's Christian, you will always be one hundred percent her daughter."

Tears welled up in my eyes. The words of reconciliation that my mother could not impart to me directly had come by way of my little girl.

The wedding of Elianna was an event that Emily and I will never forget: sumptuous, lively, and very Orthodox. Emily was asked to walk down the aisle with two Israeli cousins who spoke no English, and at the very end of the evening, I sat next to my mother briefly and exchanged a few kind words.

Making the trip to see my family was the right decision, but not a painless one. Reconnecting with my family after so many years made it clear that swift, happy endings appear only in fairy tales. In real life, broken relationships take time to repair. As for me, I must remind myself not to condemn as I have been condemned, and not to cast others out of my heart as I have been cast out, but to listen openly and say "*Shamati!* I hear you," even if I disagree.

To my joy and delight, Reb Zalman and his wife, Eve Ilsen, now reside in Boulder, where Reb Zalman holds the World Wisdom Chair at the Naropa Institute. Now working at a more relaxed pace, Reb Zalman continues to transmit his vision of spiritual eldering and a renewed Judaism from the foothills of the Rocky Mountains. His disciples, Jewish Renewal rabbis from around the country, now hold biannual retreats in Colorado and elsewhere in the United States for the sake of sharing ideas, energizing one another and refining the rabbinic ordination program, which continues, under Reb Zalman's leadership, to educate the next generation of rabbis. Other Jewish Renewal rabbis and many constituents have also moved to the Boulder area to make it a thriving center of Jewish life. And Jewish Renewal communities continue to grow and flourish across the continent.

The view is remarkable from here. As I stand in my mid-forties looking back on my life, it is plain to see that my journey has taken me in a great circle, or, more accurately, a spiral. The path that revolves again and again around the same territory brings with it greater awareness with each pass.

On this great spiral journey, every path hints of return. I have returned to my religion, not to the familiar ritual practices alone but to its very essence. And I have returned to my people, not with the old judgments I once bore, but with a heart filled with understanding, compassion, and a commitment to create change where it is needed. I still study and am intrigued with the works of many non-Jewish traditions and teachers from around the world. All are useful; all inform my Jewish life path. In the end, I have learned from many teachers, not by way of losing myself to their authority but by receiving their wisdom and then returning with it to my own inner guidance.

Standing at the crossroads between the millennia and poised in a lineage of venerable elders who came before me, I hear an urgent voice reminding me that the wisdom of the ancestors is desperately needed now—the ethics, the rituals, and the mysticism that can give us a meaning bigger than ourselves and help us out of our modern-day narcissism. As a rabbi, I feel the tremendous privilege of making the ancient wisdom more public, of proclaiming the loving soul of my own and other honorable traditions. These traditions beg to survive, to be renewed and empowered by those who sense their greatness, so that they can in turn renew and empower humanity. On this great spiraling journey, I take my place among all people who are working to forge a path across the threshold of the millennium, aiming toward that which is both ancient and new, timeless and utterly relevant. May the great mystery guide us on our way.

abba Father

avoda zara Idol worship; literally: a foreign worship.

Ba'al Shem Tov Rabbi Israel ben Eliezer (ca. 1700-1760), founder of Chasidism; literally: Master of the Good Name.

bachor Firstborn son.

beis din Jewish court or council of rabbis.

Beit Hamikdash The Holy Temple in Jerusalem.

be'shert Meant to be, synchronistic.

b'ezrat hashem With God's help

bimheyrah biyameynu Soon and in our time.

bubbe A Jewish grandmother.

charoset A ritual food served at the Passover seder, made of apples, nuts and wine.

Chasid An individual follower of a Chasidic rebbe.

Chasidic Of or pertaining to Chasidism, a religious and mystical spiritual revival movement beginning in the eighteenth century in the Ukraine and Poland.

chavurah Fellowship; group of like-minded individuals with a common task or endeavor.

chelek eloha mima'al Literally: Our divine portion from above; our higher self which is part and parcel of God. Coined by Rabbi Schneur Zalman of Liadi, who lived in the eighteenth century.

chilul A desecration.

chometz All yeasted breads and other foods prohibited on the Jewish holiday of Passover, replaced by matzoh, unleavened bread.

chutzpah Nerve, audacity.

davka Precisely, exactly so.

davven To pray the prescribed Jewish prayers.

davvenen The prescribed Jewish prayers.

Degel Machaneh Ephraim A Chasidic interpretation of Torah written by the grandson of the Ba'al Shem Tov in the nineteenth century.

devekut Literally: Clinging (to God); God consciousness.

Eheyeh Asher Eheyeh One of God's names; literally: I shall be that which I shall be; used by God in the encounter with Moses at the burning bush in Exodus.

Elohim One of God's names.

Eyn Sof Literally: Without bounds; in Kabbalah, the ultimate aspect of God from which all creation stems.

frum One who observes Jewish law; Orthodox.

gemilut chasadim Deeds of loving kindness

Gemora Aramaic commentary on the Mishnah written between 200 B.C.E. and 500 C.E. Together, the Mishnah and Gemora make up the Talmud.

Gott in Himmel God in Heaven!

goy A non-Jew; literally: nation or people.

goyim Gentile people, plural of goy.

gurnishcht Nothing at all.

Gut Yom Tov Happy holiday.

halacha Rabbinic Jewish law.

halachic Of or pertaining to Rabbinic Jewish law.

Harachamana Liba Ba'ee A phrase from the Talmudic tractate Sanhedrin, meaning: the Compassionate One seeks but the heart.

Hashem God; literally: The Name

hitlahavut Ecstasy

Kaddish A Jewish prayer declaring God's greatness, recited by those in mourning.

kallah A Jewish study convention. The term dates back to the time of the Babylonian academies.

kavvanah Intentionality; correct motivation.

kibitz Chat; joke around

kiddushin Formal Jewish wedding ritual.

Klal Yisrael The Jewish people in its entirety; Jewish unity.

kvittel A personal prayer or plea written on a small piece of paper given to one's rebbe or brought to a sacred site.

lamdan A scholar.

lehitra'ot See you later!

l'khavod For the honor or glory

Lubavitch Literally: Town in Belorussia that became the center of Chabad Chasidism in 1813; a sect of Chasidism, very prominent in the United States. (See Chasidic)

Malchut A term from Kabbalah to denote the imminent face of God, the earth plane; sometimes synonymous with Shechinah.

Mashiach Messiah.

matzoh Unleavened bread eaten on Passover.

mazel tov Congratulations

mechitzah A dividing wall or curtain used to separate men and women during Jewish prayer.

mensch A decent, honorable human being.

meshugas Foolishness, craziness.

meshugge Crazy.

mezuzah A handscribed parchment hung in a small box on the doorposts of Jewish homes, serving as a reminder of God's presence and protection.

midrash Explanatory story expanding on Torah text

Mishnah The oral Rabbinic interpretation of the Five Books of Moses, compiled in 200 B.C.E.

Mishne Torah The first systematic code of Jewish law, written by Maimonides in the twelfth century.

mitzvah A commandment from Jewish law. (Plural: mitzvot)

mochin d'gadlut Great mind; expanded consciousness.

mochin d'katnut Small mind, ego.

musar Jewish teachings on everyday ethics and morality.

neshama The human soul.

neshama Elohit Godly soul or Self.

niggun A Chasidic wordless melody used in contemplation.

pashut yiddin Simple Jewish folk.

rebbe Literally: Rabbi; title given to one's Chasidic teacher or master.

Sanhedrin The Jewish high council or supreme court of ancient Judea, disbanded under Roman persecution around 425 CE.

schnorrer A solicitor.

schvartze Black person; often used derogatorily.

seder The ritual Passover meal.

sefat emet A Chasidic interpretation on Torah written by Rabbi Yehudah Arye Leib of Gur.in the nineteenth century.

Shabbat The Jewish Sabbath.

Shabbos The Jewish Sabbath; synonymous with Shabbat.

shalom aleichem Peace be with you!

shamati I heard you.

Shechinah The in-dwelling presence of God; the feminine face of the Divine.

shefa Divine abundance which flows from the Eyn Sof.

Shema Yisrael "Hear O Israel!" A central prayer in Judaism which declares God's unity.

Shevuos A Jewish holiday, also known as the Feast of Weeks, which comes in the spring seven weeks after Passover.

shiddach A brokered match between a Jewish man and woman.

shiva The seven days of Jewish ritual mourning prescribed to the next of kin of the deceased.

shofar The ritual ram's horn blown on Jewish New Year.

shul Synagogue.

Shulchan Aruch Code of Jewish law compiled by Rabbi Joseph Karo, who lived in the sixteenth century; literally: a set table.

smicha Rabbinic ordination; literally: the laying on of hands.

tallis Jewish prayer shawl.

Talmud Compilation of the oral Torah, the Mishna and Gemora, which constitutes the basis of religious authority for traditional Judaism.

talmudic Of or pertaining to the Talmud.

Torah Literally: the Five Books of Moses; denotes the entire body of Jewish sacred literature.

tzaddik A righteous person.

tzedakah Acts of justice, charity.

tzitzit Sacred fringes on the corners of the prayer shawl.

tzuris Trouble, pain.

yahrzeit The anniversary of the death of a loved one.

yeshiva Academy of Orthodox Jewish study.

yiddin Jews.

Yiddishkeit Judaism.

zeide Jewish grandfather.

RABBI TIRZAH FIRESTONE, PHD, is an author, Jungian psychotherapist, and leader in the international Jewish Renewal Movement. Ordained by Rabbi Zalman Schachter-Shalomi in 1992, she is the founding rabbi of Congregation Nevei Kodesh in Boulder, Colorado; she has also served on the board of directors and as co-chair of T'ruah: The Rabbinic Call for Human Rights.

Raised in a large Orthodox family in St. Louis, Missouri, the younger sister of the late, groundbreaking radical feminist Shulamith Firestone, author of *The Dialectic of Sex* (William Morrow & Company, 1970), Firestone's spiritual curiosity called her to search beyond the confines of her family's strict Jewish upbringing. Leaving home, she embarked upon a life-changing spiritual odyssey that she chronicled in *With Roots in Heaven: One Woman's Passionate Journey into the Heart of Her Faith* (Dutton Books, 1998 / Monkfish Book Publishing Company, 2024). After immersing herself in a wide variety of spiritual practices and worldviews, Firestone returned with fresh vigor to a pluralistic and egalitarian Judaism, continuing in the tradition of Rabbi Schachter-Shalomi. Her studies in the feminine wisdom tradition and Jewish mysticism yielded *The Receiving: Reclaiming Jewish Women's Wisdom* (Harper San Francisco, 2003). Originally published in 2019, *Wounds into Wisdom: Healing Intergenerational Jewish Trauma* has received the 2020 Nautilus Book Award Gold in Psychology and the 2020 Jewish Women's Caucus of the Association for Women in Psychology Book Award.

Firestone earned a master's degree in counseling at Beacon College in Boston, Massachusetts in 1982, and a doctorate in depth psychology at Pacifica Graduate Institute in Santa Barbara, California in 2015. Her research on the transformation of collective trauma draws on the fields of neuroscience, psychology, Jewish literature, and mythopoesis. Through interviews, case studies, and autobiographical stories, she demonstrates how trauma residue passes from generation to generation and how it can be transformed.

Now Rabbi Emerita of her congregation, Firestone maintains a private practice in depth psychology and teaches internationally about this topic, Kabbalah, intergenerational trauma healing, and the reintegration of the feminine wisdom tradition within Judaism. Her emphasis regarding all these topics is on honing ancient wisdom practices to assist us at this critical time in world history. Rabbi Firestone lives in Colorado with her husband David.

To discover more resources on intergenerational trauma healing and share your individual or community group experiences exploring these questions, visit TirzahFirestone.com and follow @TirzahFire on Instagram and Twitter.